Nagai Kafū's Occidentalism

Nagai Kafū's Occidentalism

Defining the Japanese Self

RACHAEL HUTCHINSON

SUNY
PRESS

Published by State University of New York Press, Albany

Printed in the United States of America

For information, contact State University of New York Press, Albany, NY
www.sunypress.edu

Production by Eileen Meehan
Marketing by Michael Campochiaro

Library of Congress Cataloging-in-Publication Data

Hutchinson, Rachael.
Nagai Kafu's occidentalism : defining the Japanese self / Rachael Hutchinson.
p. cm.
Includes bibliographical references and index.
ISBN 978-1-4384-3906-8 (paperback : alk. paper)
ISBN 978-1-4384-3907-5 (hardcover : alk. paper)
1. Nagai, Kafu, 1879–1959—Criticism and interpretation. 2. Civilization, Western, in literature. 3. East and West in literature. 4. Japan—In literature. I. Title.

PL812.A4Z6565 2011
895.6'344—dc22 2011003126

10 9 8 7 6 5 4 3 2 1

Contents

Acknowledgments

The bulk of this volume was completed on a sabbatical supported by a Picker Research Fellowship, granted by the Colgate University Research Council. I owe sincere thanks to Julie Nelson Davis and Cappy Hurst of the University of Pennsylvania Center for East Asian Studies for hosting me as visiting researcher for 2006–2007. The original research project was carried out at the University of Oxford, with the generous support of the Kobe Steel Postgraduate Scholarship at St. Catherine's College, in conjunction with an Overseas Research Students' Award. The dissertation was completed with the assistance of the TEPCO Senior Studentship at Pembroke College. I would like to express my sincere thanks to my dissertation supervisor, Brian Powell, for his confidence in my approach and his continued support. I am grateful to many people for their insightful comments on various stages of the manuscript, including Roger Goodman, Arthur Stockwin, Ann Waswo, Phillip Harries, Keiko Tanaka, Stephen Dodd, Peter Kornicki, and Ivo Smits. I thank Mark Morris, Atsuko Sakaki, Susan Napier, Stephen Snyder, and Charles Shirō Inouye for their useful questions at conferences and workshops. For their encouragement I must thank Mark Williams, Michael Bourdaghs, Faye Yuan Kleeman, Hiroshi Nara, Caroline Rose, Frances Weightman, Nicky Bray, and Jacqui Langford. I must also acknowledge the support and encouragement given to me by Henry Chan and Leith Morton, who saw this project grow from its very beginnings in my Honours thesis at the University of Newcastle, Australia. Leith challenged me to find my own response to Kafū's material, and gave me the confidence to carry through with it, while Henry's teaching on national and cultural identity has shaped all my work to the present day.

For funding that enabled me to present my work at a number of conferences, I would like to thank the British Academy, the British Association of Japanese Studies Council, Gakushūin Women's University, the University of Leeds School of Modern Languages and Cultures, the Colgate University Faculty Development Council, and the University of Delaware College of Arts and Sciences. Many thanks are due to Hiroshi Nara, Amy Dooling and Fred Dickinson for inviting me to present on my research at the University of Pittsburgh, Connecticut College, and the University of Pennsylvania. I would like to thank Jeffrey Angles for his warm welcome in Kalamazoo, especially for showing me Kafū's boarding houses and introducing me to so many people interested in the local history. Many thanks go to the Soga Japan Center for supporting my talk at the University of Western Michigan, where discussion and questions were very helpful.

Some material in Chapter 1 appeared originally in a somewhat different form in *Monumenta Nipponica* 62.3 (Autumn 2007), pp. 323–345. Chapter 1 also includes some material revised from the essay 'Who Holds the Whip? Power and Critique in Nagai Kafū's *Tales of America*,' in Rachael Hutchinson and Mark Williams (eds.), *Representing the Other in Modern Japanese Literature: A Critical Approach*, Routledge, British Association of Japanese Studies Series, 2006, pp. 57–74. Some parts of Chapter 4 are revised from my article "Occidentalism and Critique of Meiji: The West in the Returnee Stories of Nagai Kafū," *Japan Forum*, 13.2 (2001) pp. 195–213.

I am grateful to the University of Delaware College of Arts and Sciences and the Department of Foreign Languages and Literatures for granting a publication subvention for this book, and to Nancy Ellegate at SUNY Press for her guidance in manuscript preparation. I thank the two anonymous readers of my text whose questions and comments helped me refine my approach and express it more clearly. Thanks go to Carrie Lorensen for her help in retyping sections of the manuscript. I am extremely grateful to Izumi Tytler and her staff at the Bodleian Japanese Library for all their help and advice, as well as the helpful people at the East Asian Library at Princeton University. I would like to thank all my students at the University of Leeds, Colgate University, and the University of Delaware for listening to my ideas on Nagai Kafū during our literature courses, regardless of whether he was included in the original syllabus.

Finally, I thank my family, who have supported all my efforts with unceasing good humor and encouragement. I am sorry that my Mum is not around to see the final product of a project that took so long in the making, but thank her and my Dad for their unfailing support through the years. My sister Ruth has long put up with my ramblings on Orientalism, while the Bohm family provided a cheerful environment in which many early drafts of chapters were first completed. Thanks especially to my wonderful husband Chris and daughter Natalie, who help me every day to do my work and be a Mum as well.

❋

Japanese names will be given in the Japanese order, with family name first. I follow general usage with writers' names, so that Tanizaki Jun'ichirō is referred to as Tanizaki while Natsume Sōseki is referred to as Sōseki. Where the pen name is more recognizable than the given name it is used throughout—Futabatei Shimei instead of Hasegawa Tatsunosuke; Nagai Kafū instead of Nagai Sōkichi.

Introduction

In the opening years of the twentieth century, Japanese intellectuals were faced with a pressing, seemingly unsolvable question. How could Japan modernize without losing its sense of identity, rooted in hundreds of years of aesthetic tradition? In the rapidly changing environment of the Meiji period (1868–1912), was modernization just another word for Westernization? How could Japan achieve an indigenous kind of modernity? By 1900, Japan already had overcome many of the initial, practical problems involved with rapid industrialization and the institution of a new government. The colonization of Taiwan, following victory over China in the Sino-Japanese War of 1894–1895, heralded a new age of territorial expansion, to be cemented with victory over Russia in 1905 and the addition of Korea as a protectorate in the same year. The Japanese were no longer on the receiving end of Western imperialist pressure, but exploring the role of imperialist themselves. But what was the role of Japan to be on the world stage? How could Japan assert itself as a nation without becoming the clone of other modern nations? The idea of entering the modern world without sacrificing the Japanese identity seemed both impossible and crucial. Politicians, journalists, and novelists alike debated the "modern dilemma" verbally and in print. Vital to the discussion were a small number of people who brought a fresh perspective to the problem. Those who had traveled abroad and experienced the culture and power of modern nations firsthand were seen to have special insight into both the processes of modernization and the importance of indigenous culture.

One group of writers in particular was significant in the discussion. Mori Ōgai (1862–1922), Natsume Sōseki (1867–1916), Nagai Kafū (1879–1959), and Shimazaki Tōson (1872–1943) all traveled in Europe and saw the countries of the West with their own eyes. Of these writers, Mori Ōgai and Natsume Sōseki in particular have been regarded as great thinkers and critics of civilization. Their works grapple with the pressing question of Japan's changing identity in the modern world, as well as the authors' own personal positions as cultural ambassadors occupying a liminal space between the East and the West. Shimazaki Tōson most recently has been examined at length in terms of Meiji nationalism (Bourdaghs, 2003), while his "pilgrimage" to France is one of the best-known journeys of that period (Rimer, 1988). Of all these authors, however, it was Nagai Kafū who created the most persuasive argument for the definition and preservation of Japanese identity. In Japan, the association of Kafū with Japanese identity is a strong one. In the growing nationalism of the 1930s, it was Kafū's work that inspired a closer focus on cultural authenticity. Although the words "authentic" and "genuine" do not point to any tangible reality, they were significant ideas in early twentieth-century discourse as intellectuals strove to articulate Japan's national cultural identity.[1] Kafū's strong argument for the importance of traditional Japanese culture in *Edo geijutsuron* (On the Arts of Edo, 1913–1914) formed the basis for Kuki Shūzō's *Iki no kōzō* (The Structure of Detachment, 1930), itself a major component of the so-called "Return to Japan" movement of the 1930s. If Mori Ōgai and Natsume Sōseki are considered the foremost critics of the "Japanese Self" at the end of the Meiji period, then what made Nagai Kafū's work so central to this later discourse on national identity?

Nagai Kafū is singular among Meiji writers in that he spent more time abroad than any other writer of his generation, writing more than thirty stories about his five years of travel in America and France alone. Kafū's elevation of Paris into a timeless cultural entity is one of the clearest examples we have of a Meiji writer constructing a particular representation of the Western Other. On his return to Japan in 1908, Kafū delivered a scathing attack on what he saw as the Meiji government's superficial approach to modernization. For the next two years his novels outspokenly criticized Meiji Japan and its façade of modernity, often encountering censorship in doing so. From 1910, Kafū focused increasingly on the past, writing mainly about remnants of the old capital Edo and the importance of preserving what was left of "authentic" Japanese culture. In a controversial decision, Kafū resigned from his position teaching French literature at Keiō University and gave up editing *Mita bungaku* in 1916, isolating himself almost completely from wider society. His novels took as their main characters the geisha who lived in the ephemeral "floating world," celebrating their role as guardians of civilization. It is this focus on traditional Japanese culture and the concentration on defining an authentic Japan that ensured Kafū's position as a forerunner to the Return to Japan movement.

The question of whether Kafū may be seen as a serious critic, however, is a subject of much debate. This book examines the development of Kafū's criticism of Meiji Japan, and seeks to resolve some of the ambiguities in conflicting representations of Kafū to date, by demonstrating that his works of 1903–1912 may be read as a reasoned and sustained critique of the Meiji approach to Japanese modernization. Kafū's works of the early twentieth century dealt primarily with the problem of defining the Japanese Self in relation to the world. By defining Japan through contrast with the West and then with an imaginary "Orient," Kafū constructed a system in which, finally, Japan could affirm its status as "Self" in contrast to these "Others." Kafū was thus acting in a very positive way in the construction of the Japanese image. Throughout this volume it will be my contention that Kafū's Meiji critique and his constructions of Self and Other form two sides of the same argument in his work, and that both critique and constructions may be best understood by reading them as Occidentalist works in their own right.

There exists an enormous amount of research on Nagai Kafū to date, mostly in Japanese, but Kafū's place in the Japanese literary canon is somewhat ambiguous. He is described variously as an "epicurean" hedonist (Takada, 1984), a nostalgic admirer of Edo literature (Takahashi, 1983), a staunch "individualist" in modern Japan (Isoda, 1989), and a reclusive, "cantankerous" figure who died alone in self-imposed isolation (Earhart, 1994). One of the most problematic issues in regard to Kafū's classification has been how to balance his great popularity and aesthetic appeal with his stature as a serious critic of civilization. An enduring image of Kafū is that of the pleasure-seeking man about town, a *flâneur* whose works often focus on the demimonde—the underworld of prostitutes, café waitresses, and geisha, and the red-light districts of New York, Paris, and Tokyo. Kafū's aesthetics are bound up in his use of the erotic element, which provides a link between many of his interests—the naturalism and decadence of French *fin-de-siècle* literature, the tradition of *eros* in Tokugawa fiction, and the ephemeral nature of the floating world. The image of Kafū as an irresponsible hedonist, however, is balanced by the view that French naturalist polemics and Modernist narrative technique gave Kafū an introduction to the serious study and depiction of the erotic.[2] This image of Kafū as a scholar and thinker holds considerable weight in Japan, where he is classed as one of the great figures of Meiji literature, presented with the Imperial Cultural

Decoration in 1952 for his contributions to Japanese literature and culture. Less often is he described as a critic, particularly in the West, and yet some academics in Japan, including Satō Shizuo (1995) and Shiozaki Fumio (1992) see Kafū as a serious critic on par with Mori Ōgai and Natsume Sōseki in his grasp of issues of national identity and modernization.

It is without a doubt that much of Kafū's writing is erotically charged, and that the women who appear in his pages are striking and powerful in their sexuality. The blonde divorcée who opens the door in New York, the gypsy snake charmer on the outskirts of Lyon, the drunken dark-skinned nude in the painting at the Worlds' Fair—even from his early travel stories, Kafū had a remarkable ability to create women with instant and lasting appeal. But Kafū's narrators also provide detailed observations and thoughtful commentary on the societies in which these women lived; on the gender dynamics operating between men and women; and on the distinctions of class, race, age, and marital status that made relations between men and women exciting, daring, or taboo. Kafū thus managed to combine erotic allure with astute critical commentary, right through to his later works featuring geisha and café waitresses in Taishō and early Shōwa. It is the critical side of Kafū's work that will be foregrounded here, to provide an English-language analysis of his *bunmei hihyō* (critique of civilization) that has been minimized in the Western literature to date.

Another factor complicating the classification of Kafū's literature has been his status as a "pioneer of naturalism."[3] Kafū certainly had a great affinity for the French naturalistic style. His works of 1901–1903 are strongly influenced by Zola's concepts of heredity and environment, and Kafū's summary-translation of Zola's *Nana*, published as *Joyū Nana* (The Actress Nana, 1903) has been hailed as one of his finest early works (Isoda, 1989, p. 34). But Kafū's European style of naturalism did not fit well with the contemporary Japanese literary establishment (or *bundan*). As Nakamura Mitsuo observes, Kafū was overseas when Japanese literature experienced its own naturalist movement, called *shizenshugi*. This style of writing tended toward self-absorbed confession, which was not a significant theme in Kafū's work at the time.[4] As he did not see literature as a medium for opening one's true self to the world, Kafū's views set him apart from the popular *shizenshugi* writers, and so Kafū was classed as an "anti-naturalist" even though his style was much closer to so-called "pure" European naturalism.[5] Of his contemporaries, Kikuchi Kan and Akutagawa Ryūnosuke held quite a low opinion of Kafū, although Mori Ōgai and Ueda Bin were impressed by his scholarship and grasp of French literature.[6] Later writers most sympathetic to Kafū were Tanizaki Jun'ichirō, Satō Haruo, and Kuki Shūzō, all of whom were influenced by Kafū to some extent in their own works. Such a mixed reception by his peers and colleagues has naturally led to a mixed reception in the academic literature.

One reason for the varied nature of these representations of Kafū is his experimentation with many different literary styles through his career, as well as the wide range of subject matter and thematic focus in his texts. He was a somewhat erratic person, who wrote when the mood struck him, according to his interests at the time. This leads to an underlying element of chaos in Kafū's work, whether in subject matter, literary style. or creative process, which does not lend itself to easy categorization. The tension in the work between East and West, the tirades of abuse against Meiji on one hand contrasted with the beautiful lyricism of his aesthetic works on the other, the relative dearth of translation of Kafū's early works compared with the prolific translations of his later period, and the many suggested reasons for his withdrawal from society in 1916, all make Kafū a complex subject. A re-examination of Kafū's work is necessary in order to clarify these ambiguities of literary classification and categorization. Many of Kafū's interests are present in his work throughout his life: the role of the intellectual in society, the joys of connoisseurship (whether literary or erotic), and artistic resistance against an oppressive state. I hope to reconcile the various aspects of Kafū's work into a comprehensible whole, and to demonstrate that it is possible to read his literary output as a coherent and homogeneous body of work with a visible line of development. Kafū's argument for the definition of the Japanese Self, developed in his early period, may be seen reverberating through his mature work and indeed explains his focus on the disappearing traditions of Edo. While this study examines Kafū's early work in detail, it also provides a way of reading Kafū's later works in terms of continuity rather than disjunction.

One of the main reasons why many academics in the West have not read Kafū as a critic involves the enduring nature of Edward Seidensticker's 1965 book *Kafū the Scribbler*, the only English-language monograph available on Kafū until Stephen Snyder's *Fictions of Desire* appeared in 2000. Seidensticker represents Kafū as a cantankerous eccentric who used a love of the West and of the Japanese past to escape from modern Japanese reality, and whose criticisms of Meiji modernization never amounted to more than complaints. Kafū's eccentricity cannot be denied, but Seidensticker does not explain Kafū's great stature as a novelist and social critic in his own country. His portrayal of Kafū primarily as a writer of fiction about the lives of the geisha played a part in the process of what Edward Fowler has called the postwar "re-Orientalization" of Japan, where academics and translators made efforts to portray a nonthreatening, exotic Japan in order to promote peaceful relations after World War II. By bringing out those critical works of Kafū that Seidensticker underplayed in order to present a nonthreatening, "Orientalized" Japan, this book seeks not only to present a fuller picture of Kafū's text, but also to balance these postwar Orientalist readings of Japanese literature.[7]

Balance will also be found by bringing forward the Japanese scholarship on Kafū in recent years, including the unprecedented "Kafū boom" of 1996–1999. Suzuki Fumitaka (1995), Kanno Akimasa (1996), and Sakagami Hiroichi (1997) turn particularly to Kafū's early life and works of 1903–1908 to comprehend the reasons for his violent reaction against Japan on his return there in 1908, and his withdrawal from society after 1916. Suenobu Yoshiharu (1997) contextualizes Kafū's American experience in terms of American–Japanese relations in the late nineteenth and early twentieth centuries, while others examine colonial structures in Kafū's early work. Komori Yōichi (1997) analyses Kafū through what he calls the geopolitical (*chiseiteki*) aspect of his works—a keen awareness of place and history underlying all of Kafū's writing. Kōno Kensuke (1997) also examines Kafū's construction of America in terms of America's colonization by Europeans, especially in the intersections of race and place so visible in New York. Minami Asuka (2007) is the latest critic to re-read Kafū in light of postcolonial theory. Komori, Kōno, and Minami apply the theoretical framework of Orientalism to Kafū's work in terms of the European colonization of America, and Kafū's comprehension of America as an Orientalized and colonized space. I build on this work by examining Kafū's complex relationship with the West and the "Orient" of European literature in terms of Occidentalism.

Because Kafū's criticism heavily depends on contrast with the West, and deals with problems raised by the Westernization of Meiji Japan, the theoretical framework of Occidentalism is very useful in examining Kafū's critique. The term *Occidentalism* has been defined in many different ways, all of which share a fundamental idea—that Occidentalism is the practice of writing or otherwise constructing and representing the West. Ning Wang points out that Occidentalism is still "indeterminate and problematic" as a discipline, in contrast to the now well-established body of work dealing with representations of the Orient. Wang situates the Occidentalist discourse in contemporary terms, to signify the construction of a particular kind of West for political reasons. This contemporary Occidentalism may be seen in Islamic anti-Western feeling and activity; as a decolonizing strategy against Western hegemony in India; and in Japan's "own unique manifestation" of Occidentalism in its recognition of cultural colonization since the American Occupation (Wang, 1997, pp. 62–63). In this view, Occidentalism has had the effect of intensifying opposition between East and West rather than encouraging cultural dialogue, and is seen as a negative reactive force against Western hegemony in the anti-colonialist discourses of the third world. Ian Buruma and Avishai Margalit also have used Occidentalism in this way to talk about "the West in the eyes of its enemies," starting with Japan's views of the West in the aftermath of Pearl Harbor and concluding with contemporary views of America among fundamental Islamist groups such as Al-Qaeda (2004). In particular reference to Japan, some have used the term *Occidentalism* to refer to Japan's wartime discourse on Western arrogance, materialism, and selfish individualism, or to the portrayal of the West as a social model to be avoided.[8] In contrast to this rather negative usage, James G. Carrier (1992, 1995) and Couze Venn (1993, 2000) use "Occidentalism" in a much wider sense, comparable to Edward Said's use of "Orientalism," to refer to an ontological and discursive system of perception and representation. Xiaomei Chen (1995) has perhaps the clearest working definition of Occidentalism, as "a discursive practice that, by constructing its Western Other, has allowed the Orient to participate actively and with indigenous creativity in the process of self-appropriation, even after being appropriated and constructed by Western Others" (pp. 4–5). This definition has three parts—construction of the Western Other, the use of that construction for a political purpose (whether for or against the prevailing political discourse), and construction of some kind of "self." It is this definition that I use as the basis for my analysis of Kafū's representations of the Western Other and definition of the Japanese Self.

In this book, I examine how Kafū constructed a particular vision of the West, and how he used this representation of the West as a contrast, by which he could criticize Japan's modernization in comparison to the genuine article overseas. "Nagai Kafū's Occidentalism" thus points to a number of ways in which Kafū used the West as a springboard for criticism of his own country, and the chapters of this book correspond to the different ways in which Kafū used his idea of the West. First, Kafū constructed a specific image of the American Other as a defining contrast to Japan, an idealized vision of liberty contrasted against a restrictive Meiji society. Second, Kafū envisioned Paris as a timeless, unchanging city of art and civilization, a construct that would inspire his later argument for an authentic civilization that could attain modernity without sacrificing its cultural heritage. Third, in the process of exploring the idea of what it meant to be a Japanese writer overseas, Kafū drew heavily on the rhetoric of Western literature to construct his own vision of the Other. In particular, Kafū's work came to reflect the ideas and thought structures of Western Orientalist discourse, as his vision of the Middle East, Colombo, and Singapore closely resembled the Orient of Pierre Loti and Rudyard Kipling. Fourth, on his return to Japan, Kafū used his construct of the Western Other for a specific purpose, to criticize the Meiji government's superficial and misguided efforts at modernization. Kafū questioned the validity of reform in Japan, and asked how to reconcile the idea of an authentic Japanese culture with modernization. Based on his understanding of the importance of cultural heritage in countries like France, Kafū's argument engendered a search for true Japanese identity and culture. Finally, Kafū found his solution in a "return to Edo" and oppositional *gesaku* stance, here re-examined in regard to his later works. Over the course of this volume, I argue that Kafū's varied uses of the West are fundamental to his critique of Meiji, ultimately providing his solution to the modern dilemma.

Before examining Kafū's texts in detail, it is useful to outline some of the problems involved with applying the frameworks of Orientalism and Occidentalism to Japanese literature of the Meiji period. In the Japanese academy, Edward Said's book *Orientalism* has been extremely influential, although the mode of application has been limited. The term *Orientalism* is most often invoked in the Japanese scholarship to describe how Japanese intellectuals represented China and Korea, rather than how Japan was represented by the West, so Japan emerges as the subject, not the object, of Orientalist discourse (Oguma, 2002, pp. 352–353; Pinnington, 2006, p. 75). While this approach would cast Kafū's description of the Middle East simply as Orientalism, I argue that such a usage would be inappropriate, ignoring the complex dynamics of power operating between Western Orientalist discourse and Japanese literature. I aim rather to draw out the complexities of Kafū's view of the Orient—not the least interesting aspect of which was Kafū's clear admiration for Pierre Loti, whose Orient provided perhaps the most influential and long-lasting template for "exotic Japan" in Western culture.[9]

In Western scholarship on Japanese literature, the paradigms of *Orientalism* have enjoyed a revival in recent works (Slaymaker, 2006; Williams, 2006), although the text itself continues to receive ample criticism. Many of the problems of *Orientalism* stem from

Said's representation of the West and its discourse of Orientalism as a homogeneous, monolithic, ageless whole, a totalizing system. Many critics have argued that the discourse of Orientalism was neither monolithic nor homogeneous, but pluralistic and complex.[10] My own reservations about using Said center on his denial of agency and the possibilities of writing from the margins of a discourse. Although Said's denial of agency within a dominant discourse depends on a closed binary system, the existence of writers from within the so-called Orient such as Nagai Kafū, who took the Orient as object for his own writing, demonstrates that such a closed system cannot be upheld. This book thus joins a number of critiques of Said that challenge his work on the issues of monolithic structures as well as the idea of the free agent writing from within a discourse.[11] For although Said is a useful starting point and one of the greatest influences on postcolonial and cultural studies, he has based his theory on Michel Foucault while ignoring one of Foucault's fundamental ideas—the possibility of counter-discourse, from the margins of even the most seemingly "monolithic" discursive structures. This criticism forms the basis for Xiaomei Chen's work *Occidentalism*, which puts the Foucauldian possibilities of counter-discourse back into the theories of Orientalism and Occidentalism. Chen (1995, pp. 8–9) argues that in his denial of the possibilities of counter-discourse and resistance, Said is missing the main point of Foucault's extensive work on the center and margin in structures of power and knowledge.

In my reading of Chen's work on post-Mao thought in China, I was struck by the ways in which her arguments on Occidentalism in China could be applied to Meiji Japan. The theories of civilization abounding in early Meiji, when the state was under pressure from the West and from economic and political theorists to modernize and attain *fukoku-kyōhei* (rich country, strong army) and *bunmei-kaika* (civilization and enlightenment), were full of images of a culturally and technologically superior West. These images were used by the state and the Meiji ideologues to exhort the nation to catch up to the West.[12] This model is very close indeed to what Chen calls "official Occidentalism," a construction of the Western Other by a government, not for the purpose of dominating the West, but for purely domestic political purposes. In the same way, Chen defines "anti-official Occidentalism" as that constructed by the opponents of the establishment, especially the disaffected intelligentsia, as a local or peripheral discourse to be used against the status quo. I argue that Kafū's appropriation and use of Western Orientalist discourse to his own ends, to protest against the façade of Western culture without substance that was dominating Meiji thought and the face of Tokyo itself, constitutes a critique and counter-discourse to the Meiji state.[13] In this way, my work follows Xiaomei Chen's, both in the terms that I have chosen to use, and in the reinsertion of Foucauldian counter-discourse into Said's methodology. It is in Kafū's depiction of the Orient that Said's work becomes most useful, as Kafū's references to Orientalist writers like Pierre Loti and Rudyard Kipling act to place him in a certain position vis-à-vis the body of Orientalist discourse. To make sense of the power dynamics operating in the text through these referential connections in particular, I employ Said's "methodology of the text," and discuss this approach in detail in Chapter 3.

The idea of the Orient in Kafū's work was certainly complex, informed by various overlapping and contradictory images of the East held by both Japanese intellectuals and European artists. At the same time that the West (*seiyō*) was occupying such an important place in Meiji intellectual discourse, Asia and the East (*tōyō*) were equally terms under discussion. Closely connected to the question of the modern dilemma was the question of where Japan stood in relation to Asia. Japan had inherited much of its culture, language, religion, and social structures from China, once the undisputed Middle Kingdom of the region. But China's primacy had slipped as a result of British imperialism in the Opium Wars of 1842 and 1860, and Japan's victory in the Sino-Japanese War of 1894–1895 seemed to prove that Japan had finally superseded the old power. As China had once been first in the region, that position now passed to Japan. But was the position of first in Asia enough? It was a small but crucial step from being first in Asia to being better than Asia—a step that would separate Japan from the rest of the region. The question of whether Japan was or was not part of Asia occupied the minds of the same people struggling with the modern dilemma, and indeed the two problems were closely related. If Japan were to act on the world stage as a modern yet authentic nation, it would need to retain its cultural heritage in some way, necessitating acceptance of cultural ties to China and the mainland. However, if Japan was too closely aligned with a backwards and old-fashioned Asia, how could it claim to be modern?

Kafū himself struggled with the Asia problem in his early work. Confronted with the British colony of Singapore in *Furansu monogatari* (Tales of France, 1909), the next year saw him pondering the problem in *Reishō* (Sneers, 1909–1910), resulting in his well-known "*Tōyō shisō*" or "Theory of the Orient." Kafū's analysis of Japan's cultural debt to China stands out as a thoughtful contribution to the debate at the close of the Meiji period. Complicating Kafū's understanding of *tōyō*, however, was his wide reading of works by French and British authors who had imagined an "East" of their own, the "Orient" of the Middle East and lands of the Bible. Kafū drew a distinction between these imaginary lands of the Orient and the real countries of Asia close by. We are fortunate that Kafū was able to travel through the Middle East and Asia on his way back to Japan from Europe in 1908. On his way through Port Said and the Red Sea he recorded his impressions of the Arab peoples and linked what he saw directly to Orientalist literature. Kafū thus acts as an important connection between Orientalist writers of the West and writers from the purported Orient, a relationship that hinges on the uncomfortable position of being in-between cultures and discursive systems. Kafū was well aware that French and other European writers saw Japan as an Orient, and he was caught in the double bind of identifying strongly with the French subject, while still remaining the object of that Orientalist gaze. Kafū was one of the first of many artists for whom Paris posed the question of personal versus national identity, as the problem of how to express oneself simultaneously as an artist and a Japanese person became central in their work—the artist Fujita Tsuguharu (1886–1968), poet Kaneko Mitsuharu (1895–1975), and writer Yokomitsu Riichi (1898–1947) being notable examples in this regard.[14] Artists coming to Paris from the Orient depicted in French art and literature occupied a position that could be seen negatively, as a sort of limbo, or positively, as a site of infinite possibility for self-reinvention and for fluid movement between multiple individual choices. As I argue, Kafū employed a fluid and flexible method of positioning, for himself and his nation, to find a solution not only for the artists' double bind, but also for Japan's *tōyō* paradox and the modern dilemma.

Throughout his early work, Kafū used images of both West and Orient as defining Others for the Japanese Self.[15] The idea of the defining Other is one of the most basic structures of phenomenology. Definition through opposition, using mutually defining diametrical opposites, has long afforded human beings simple models of understanding the universe and remarkably effective ways of defining objects and things: It is far easier to define something by what it is not, than to pin down what something actually is. By situating Japan in terms of its Others, Kafū was better able to theorize and think about what constituted Japan's own identity. Indeed, the act of situating, or positioning, was to become the underpinning logic of his early work. The link between positioning and definition was pointed out in the 1960s by Kenneth Burke (1969), who wrote that "[t]o tell what a thing is, you place it in terms of something else. This idea of locating, or placing, is implicit in our very word for definition itself" (p. 24). Throughout his works, Kafū was to use strategies of positioning both for himself as an individual person and for the nation of Japan as a whole. These strategies allowed him to come to a better understanding of his own identity as "Japanese" and what that meant in the context of Japan's place in the modern world. Kafū's use of positioning and binary structures was very fluid, depending on the point he wished to make. Thus, at any one time Kafū could be working with a simplistic and superficial Japan versus the West model in order to emphasize contrast, or he could be using a sophisticated array of interconnected spaces acknowledging subtle differences between cultures and cultural communities. For this reason I have chosen to call Kafū's literary strategy *flexible positioning*. By emphasizing the flexibility of Kafū's positioning, and showing how it developed over time, I hope to avoid casting his work as a static, totalizing system.

A focus on Kafū's positioning also serves to emphasize that Self and Other do not function as discrete and separate entities in his work, but in a relationship. Identity is always formed vis-à-vis the Other, or in relation to a number of posited Others. Two of the most prominent thinkers on this relationship have been Emmanuel Levinas and Jacques Lacan, both of whom recognized the importance of the human gaze in establishing relations between Self and Other. The face-to-face moment of Levinas leads naturally to a feeling of obligation to the Other—recognition and acknowledgment of the Other being key to the process (Levinas, 1999). Lacan similarly focuses on the relationship between Self and Other through a face-to-face meeting, yet with a crucial difference—Lacan's meeting takes place through a mirror, rendering the vision of the Other untouchable and unattainable, even while the process of recognition and acknowledgment remains the same. It is Lacan's gaze of Self upon the Other that seems to have attained dominance in literary analysis concerning Japan. Lacan's unfulfillable desire for the Other is popular in Western scholarship on modern Japanese literature, much of which draws on René Girard's concept of "triangular desire."[16] If we take desire as just one of the many emotions and feelings that act to fill the gap between Self and Other—others of which may be prejudice, hatred, love, admiration, and so on—then this approach is useful as a way into exploring the Self–Other relationship (Hutchinson & Williams, 2006, pp. 6–7). However, desire has been privileged to such an extent in recent scholarship that the Other has been almost taken for granted as a distant, unattainable object of eternally unfulfilled desire. In this paradigm, Self and Other remain completely separate, and the focus of discussion turns to the gap between them. Given the rhetorical focus on the West in Meiji discourse, the writer's desire to close the gap between Japan and the West is often seen to be a primary motivating factor in Meiji literature. I have called this model *gap theory* to draw attention to the common linkage of desire for the Other with an inferior–superior binary (Hutchinson, 2006, pp. 57–59). Such an approach may also be seen in terms of modernization theory, where "modernity implies a teleological historical movement, a single path of social development, and a relentless march toward the Western model" (Lamarre, 2005, p. 17). I wish to get away from such "West and the Rest" models and focus rather on the relationship between Self and Other, emphasizing the pluralities of Selves and Others in flexible binary systems, and the many possible positionings that a writer may take up in such systems. To this end, I do not focus on desire in Kafū's works, but on his positioning strategy vis-à-vis the Others he encounters. This is not to say that desire plays no part in Kafū's literature. Given the demimonde setting of his fiction, the panoply of prostitutes and geisha that fill his pages, such a claim would be insupportable. But I hope to make it clear that desire for an unobtainable, distant, superior Other is not the primary motivation for Kafū's work.

In focusing on Self and Other, Orient and Occident, and employing the theoretical frameworks of Orientalism and Occidentalism, it will be necessary to keep in mind one of the major problems associated with such terms: All depend on binary structures to understand systems of power. Binary oppositions have been extremely useful for critics in the twentieth century, seeking models with which to understand social structures as well as the relationships between literary texts and their historical contexts. Just as Foucault used binary oppositions to describe and analyze Western society, such as legal–criminal, normal–deviant, sane–insane and so on, Said's *Orientalism* set up East and West, or Orient and Occident, as mutually defining diametrical opposites, in order to better understand the relationship between imperialism and literature.[17] The two related theoretical approaches of Orientalism and Occidentalism are thus predicated on a binary structure, and bring with them all the associated problems of binarism—essentialization, totalization, and the naturalization of an arbitrary hierarchical structure.[18] The danger is that by speaking in terms of Orient and Occident, Japan and the West, and so on in my analysis of Kafū's work, I run the risk of perpetuating binary structures that do not really exist, and have never existed except as imaginary constructs by which people have sought to understand and configure their world. Similarly, because the word *Occidentalism* implies a whole array of discourse and discursive practice—a whole structure of thinking, writing, and representing "the West"—involving intellectuals both in and out of government as well as poets and fiction writers, it seems we cannot examine Kafū as a single "Occidentalist" as if separate from this wider context. However, a project of this size cannot hope to undertake a mapping of the Meiji intellectual discourse on the West as Occidentalism, and indeed such a study would face serious theoretical difficulties in presenting Occidentalism as a totalizing discourse and ontological system similar to Said's Orientalism. Xiaomei Chen (1995) warns against using Occidentalism as a total theory to apply to all historical periods at will: "No theory can be globally inclusive," she argues, and so "The critical discourse of Occidentalism should not become a new orthodoxy that could easily be applied to all countries and all historical periods" (p. 13). Chen suggests that concentration on the particular historical moment and particular case studies may help to avoid both the tendency toward totalization as well as the setting up of a closed binary system of Orientalism–Occidentalism.

Throughout this volume, I aim to avoid such totalizations by concentrating on the specific case of Kafū and his texts. The West and Orient presented here are the observations and constructions of the author Nagai Kafū, and are not meant to form a totalizing binary system. This kind of determinist system is indeed challenged and disrupted by Kafū's texts. The relationships between Japan and America, or between Singapore and colonialist Britain, are presented through Kafū's text by quotation as singular instances of observation of the historical moment in literature. I aim not to generalize about the relationships between nations in the early twentieth century, but to discover how Kafū saw these relationships, and what effect his observations of them had on his perception of Japanese modernization. By locating Kafū in his historical moment and discovering his specific point of view, I hope to avoid ascribing anachronistic value judgments and attitudes to Kafū and other writers of the Meiji period. Kafū and his contemporaries read avidly in French, British, and other literature of the eighteenth and ninteenth centuries, and translated many of these works for the Japanese audience. Popular literature of the time happened to be Orientalist literature, steeped in colonialist attitudes and specific ways of viewing the world. Kafū breathed the literary air of Orientalism just as the European audience had done for years. He certainly would never have thought of Flaubert or Kipling as Orientalists the way that we do today, nor would he consider his own constructions of the West as Occidentalist. Therefore, I use the terms *Orientalism* and *Occidentalism* as part of the language of current research, indicating ways in which we may read these discursive structures now, not how they would have been perceived in Kafū's time.

Focusing on the particular historical moment also necessitates some description of the historical and intellectual context, in order to understand Kafū's reactions against the modernizing policies of Meiji Japan. Throughout this volume, I do my best to explicate Kafū's references to contemporary events and issues of the day. The main issue for Kafū was undoubtedly modernization. The history of the early Meiji modernization process, and the push to modernize along Western lines, is well documented in English, as are the physical changes wrought upon the city of Tokyo.[19] By Kafū's return to Japan in 1908, the major structural reforms (legal, political, educational, and social) were already in place. What received the brunt of Kafū's attack from 1908 onward was the superficial, shoddy, confused chaos of Tokyo, with new buildings, bridges, and streetcars giving a wholly cosmetic lift to the external face of Japan with no discernible change in the underlying thought. Kafū despaired that the Japanese had no deep appreciation of the Western culture they sought to emulate, nor any real understanding of what modernity might mean for Japan. Kafū's intellectual context, or the discourse of the Meiji period, was one of great concern with issues of modernization, meanings of modernity (*kindai*), Westernization, national identity, individualism, and the authenticity of culture. These themes appear again and again in the works of Meiji writers of Kafū's generation. Tomi Suzuki (1996) and Hisaaki Yamanouchi (1978) have recognized Kafū as an integral part of this discourse. Viewing Kafū in his particular historical moment means viewing him as part of a constellation of Meiji writers, all searching for a new definition of what it meant to be Japanese. Taken in context, I hope that this study sheds light on Meiji literature as a whole in its search for the Japanese Self.

Thinking of Nagai Kafū in terms of his relation to the wider intellectual discourse of the time, it is well to keep in mind that not everyone in Meiji Japan would have thought the way Kafū did about the West, Asia, and the Orient. Indeed, hardly anyone would have thought this way—Kafū was one of the very few writers of his generation to travel overseas, and even fewer people travelled to as many different places as Kafū. He was able to compare North America with Europe, the Mediterranean with the Indian Ocean, and Egypt with Singapore. Kafū's vision of the West was informed by years of reading European literature, as well as an upbringing quite different to that of many writers of his generation. Kafū's father, Nagai Kyūichirō, was himself an interesting man caught between two worlds, well known as a writer of Chinese-style poetry and at the same time an executive for the Yokohama Specie Bank, traveling all over the world on business. Kafū would later describe his father as smoking a pipe, reclining in an armchair, and wearing a Western-style suit. The Nagai house was filled with Western furniture and art, as well as Christian iconography belonging to Kafū's grandmother. Thus, while Kafū was part of the generation brought up in the uncomfortable double school system of Confucian and Western learning that Mori Ōgai likened to the feeling of wearing two different sandals on the one pair of feet (Katō, 1979, p. 113), Kafū's home life exposed him to a far higher degree of Western culture and material goods than that experienced by most of his contemporaries.

Nagai Kafū's vision of the West was therefore his own vision, even as it was part of a wider Meiji period discourse on the West, and it is his view which interests me here: how he utilized the West to formulate his views on Meiji Japan, and how he developed his own construction of the West in order to pursue his passion for Japan's future, in the hope of reconciling that future with Japan's past. Throughout Kafū's work, those spaces called Japan, the West, and Asia are defined in a specific and limited way, in order to achieve a particular purpose. They do not map directly onto our own understandings of Japan, the West, and Asia, because these terms are just as arbitrary today as they were in the early twentieth century—always under negotiation and subject to our own imaginations. The tension between binarism and complexity in Kafū's work is precisely what makes it so interesting, because we are still struggling with the same problems of binarism and complexity today. By analyzing Kafū's use of the West and seeing what he was trying to achieve through his particular representation of the Western Other, we not only can arrive at some new understanding of what was important to people in the Meiji period, but also come to a clearer understanding of how various Others are represented in our own time. While the immediate subject of this book is Nagai Kafū's attempt to define the Japanese Self, it is in the interplay of Self and Other in his work that we see our own definitions of national identity.

CHAPTER ONE

Constructing the "West"

Binarism and Complexity in Kafū's America

Nagai Kafū sailed for America on the *Shinanomaru* on September 22, 1903. Kafū's dream was to travel to France and become a writer, as he had a keen interest in French literature. An acquaintance with the playwright Fukuchi Ōchi had introduced him to the works of Émile Zola in 1900, after which membership of Iwaya Sazanami's Thursday Society, the *Mokuyōkai*, gave Kafū the opportunity to read and discuss many foreign works in their originals and in translation. Although Kafū's father, Nagai Kyūichirō, was well known as a writer of Chinese poetry, he wanted to quash any literary leanings in Kafū in order to separate him from his delinquent literary friends, theater life, and the geisha of the Yoshiwara. Kyūichirō also suspected that his son would come to no good in Paris, and so sent him instead to America to learn banking.[1] Thinking that once he was away from Japan he might stand a better chance of traveling to France, Kafū acceded to his father's wishes, and was to stay in America for four years. This chapter aims to establish how Kafū represented the West in his collection of short stories *Amerika monogatari*, written between November 1903 and 1907.[2]

Much has already been written on *Amerika monogatari*, with each critic proposing a different interpretation of the collection. Like Kafū himself, *Amerika monogatari* has so many facets that it is difficult to pin down a central theme to the whole. As a result, the literary attributes of the collection have been analyzed from many different standpoints—the development of Kafū's naturalistic style, Western literary influences on the collection, and Kafū's experimentation with narrative being the most common.[3] The collection has also been analyzed in more biographical terms—as an expression of Kafū's individualism, as a psychological representation of Kafū's relationship with his father, or as an exercise in the aesthetics of dilettantism.[4] The numerous different approaches to *Amerika monogatari* show the complexity and variety that make the collection a fascinating work in its own right. It can be read as the thrilling adventure of a young Japanese newly arrived in a foreign country, eager to write of his experiences for the audience at home, and also as a thoughtful exploration of new ideas encountered abroad, leading to a critique of both American and Japanese values. In this chapter, I focus on how Kafū constructed America as a representation of the West, concentrating on those parts of the text where Kafū intrudes on his narrative to point out specifically how and why America is different from Japan, or where he directly comments on the nature of the West as opposed to the character of the Orient. Like much of Meiji discourse, Kafū creates representations of place through what he feels are its essential or fundamental qualities, where particular qualities come to stand in for the whole. However, unlike the simple binary of Japan versus the West used by many Meiji journalists and politicians, Kafū's comparison of Japan and the West shows a more complex layering structure, featuring many different subsets of Japanese and American communities.

Amerika monogatari features frequent comparison and contrast between Japan and America, creating a particular vision of the West for Kafū's readers. This comparison is made through various motifs of difference.[5] Through the motif of geographical difference, for example, America is constructed as the ideal country of wide-open spaces and bustling modern cities, a "new continent" in contrast to the island nation of Japan with its confusion of old streets and hemmed-in countryside. Two other major motifs of difference that run throughout *Amerika monogatari* are the contrasting moral systems of America and Japan, and the attitude toward race held by the two countries. Kafū contrasts America as the "sacred land of liberty" with the restrictive Confucian mores of Japan, while Japan's racial homogeneity is contrasted with America's mixed society, giving rise to the question of racial discrimination. Kafū's vision of America swings between the ideal of the country of freedom, symbolized by the Statue of Liberty, and the reality of a nation deeply divided by racial tension and discrimination, felt by Kafū himself as a Japanese visitor. Kafū's sense of disjunction between the ideal and reality of America provides much of the dramatic tension of the collection, played out by a host of Japanese narrators coming to grips with living in a foreign land.

At times, however, the narrator becomes American or European, and we see Kafū's perception of America's relationship with the wider West. Kafū's West departs from the homogeneous, amorphous mass of pure binary opposition, instead comprising a number of distinctly diverse countries, each with their own peculiarities, customs, climate, and landscape. Depending on the point he wishes to make, Kafū switches fluidly between invoking the wider West and its constituent parts. The clearest example in *Amerika monogatari* is the contrast drawn between America and France, as France increasingly comes to represent the epitome of beauty and civilization. This image of France derives largely from Kafū's passion for French literature, so this chapter also charts the progress of Kafū's attention through Zola, Maupassant, and Baudelaire, as reflected in the pages of *Amerika monogatari*.

My use of the word *construction* in analyzing the image of the West in Kafū's work may be taken to refer to a particular way of writing, deliberately building an image through choice of words for a particular effect. In *Amerika monogatari,* Kafū explores a number of different narrative styles, and throughout his diary entries we find Kafū agonizing over the slow development of his art and the style he should use.[6] In the experimental nature of the collection and in Kafū's own awareness of narrative stance and literary construction, we see that the act of writing was very deliberate for him. In a later essay, Kafū would describe his method of writing as largely dependent on selection and emphasis, the careful choosing of one word or phrase over another, to produce the required effect.[7] Japanese critics have noted the deliberation involved in Kafū's writing for many years, as Kafū constructed realities in certain ways for certain purposes. The most obviously constructed works of Kafū's are his diaries, described by Nakamura Shin'ichirō (1970, pp. 98, 103) as "cool" and "calculating" in their deliberate approach to recording a particular version of his life. Isoda Kōichi (1984, pp. 24–25) also maintains that Kafū had no qualms about changing reality to suit his own stories, using selection and artistic license to portray objects and settings in ways that enhanced their beauty or significance. These critics thus emphasize that Kafū, a keenly observant writer in the naturalistic style, also adjusted and constructed reality to suit himself. Contemporary receptions of *Amerika monogatari* in *Waseda bungaku* saw the collection as a casual, aimless, postcard format with no underlying intent, far from the purposeful deliberation of writing a novel. But Takemori Ten'yū (1992, pp. 20–21) argues that we cannot read it in the same way today, as we recognize the self-conscious writing technique. Takemori observes that the sometimes overly literary style even of the dialogue points to this self-conscious construction.[8] The deliberation and critical awareness behind Kafū's use of "America" is seen right from the start of *Amerika monogatari,* where a superficial binary contrast soon gives way to complexity and questions.[9]

Kyabin yawa (Night Conversation from a Ship's Cabin), written in November 1903, presents an idealized image of America given form by the expectations and ambitions of two Japanese making the crossing.[10] This idealism is apparent from the first mention of America in the collection as *Amerika no shinkaichi Shiatoru,* the "newly-opened land" around the port of Seattle (KZ 3.6). From its first appearance, America holds the promise of growth, development, and commercial enterprise. This image is reinforced by the personal stories of two men who come to the narrator's cabin for a chat late one night. The self-assured Yanagida embodies the Westernized Japanese businessman, who wears a flashy striped suit and loud necktie, smokes a cigar, speaks in affected English, and handles alcohol well. Yanagida is escaping frustrated expectations in his work, where he holds a lowly translating job even though he has spent time overseas. It is notable here that Kafū already has some idea of the disillusionment experienced by returnees from abroad, who, bursting with new ideas to share, felt unable to explain the West and its culture to the Japanese at home. Yanagida chooses to seek a new life in America rather than try to share his experiences with the narrow-minded company men of the "island nation." Kishimoto, by contrast, is the traditional Japanese scholar who wears a kimono and is afraid of the storm, the steam whistle, and of catching a cold. Recently dismissed from his Tokyo company, he has left a faithful wife and child in Japan and aims to return to them with a university diploma in hand. This story illustrates many different reasons that Japanese might have for crossing to America—a broken heart, dissatisfaction at work, the humiliation of not graduating from university, feeling out of place in Japan after having traveled abroad, and so on. This method of construction through characters who act as ciphers, or representations of types, is one that will recur throughout Kafū's work. Characters are given not individual depth but symbolic significance as they embody the different modes of thought, dress, speech, and lifestyles of Meiji Japan and Japanese abroad. The technique we see here is crude as Kishimoto and Yanagida are so obviously opposites, but the complexity of the cipher Kafū uses in later works is hinted at in the fact that their reasons for leaving Japan are not simple and clear-cut, but composite. Kafū's contrast between the two representative character types, one Westernized, one traditional, has the effect of encouraging the reader to make comparisons between the two, and to become accustomed to such contrasts, the construction of which will take up a good part of the rest of the volume.

Throughout *Amerika monogatari,* the narrator seems so similar to Kafū as to be almost equivalent to Kafū himself: a leisured gentleman, traveling first class, new to America, and keen to observe and muse upon the workings of a strange new country. The nature of semi-autobiographical travel writing is complex, but it is fair to say that Kafū is creating a persona in these works, many of whose attributes are shared by the author. For many years, research on *Amerika monogatari* and its French counterpart *Furansu monogatari* tended to conflate the author with the narrator, with Akase Masako (1976) sometimes speaking of the main character as *sakusha jishin,* or "the author himself" (p. 35). This conflation is difficult to avoid, as the characters tread the same paths as Kafū and speak with the cultured, knowledgeable voice we would expect from someone of Kafū's background and education. But the figure of the narrator in *Kyabin yawa* is shadowy and indistinct, as the focus on his two visitors deflects attention away from the narrator himself. On finishing the story, the reader realizes that the narrator's reasons for making the crossing have remained a mystery. We assume he occupies a space between the two extremes of Westernized and traditional Japanese, an assumption encouraged by the conciliatory role he takes on the issue of Western versus Japanese clothing. But Kafū's refusal to define the narrator's background makes us think more about his motivations than we otherwise would. This purposeful situating of the narrator draws a line between Kafū and the voice that speaks in the stories. While I could refer to the narrators of these tales as a thinly disguised Kafū, I continue to refer to them as "the narrator" so as not to lose sight of Kafū's constructive act.[11] *Kyabin yawa* thus serves as a good introduction to the collection, not only in the locational aspect of the sea crossing, but also in its focus on contrasting opposites and the possible positions between them.

On October 8, 1903 Kafū arrived in Tacoma, Washington. Through the offices of his father, he was to stay with a branch manager of the Furuya Shōten, Yamamoto Ichirō, for one year. The first set of stories of *Amerika monogatari* deal with the Japanese immigration experience, revolving around the Japanese communities in the western coastal towns of Seattle and Tacoma. These stories do not focus on the physical attributes of "America" as much as on the adjustments needed to live in a foreign country and on the hostility encountered from Americans who feel threatened by the flood of cheap labor from Japan and China. The immigrant stories together are often referred to as the *Jappu shōsetsu* or "Jap stories," as they deal directly with the idea of racial discrimination against Japanese immigrants. These stories give a detailed historical picture of immigrant culture in America circa 1903, but here I am interested in how Kafū perceived "the West" and what "the West" meant to him and the other Japanese who made the journey.[12]

In these stories "the West" is originally a dream or ideal of the perfect country, but expectations of meeting this ideal soon give way to harsh reality. Shunsuke Kamei writes that this process of disillusionment is characteristic of novels regarding America in Meiji literature. Kamei names Fukuzawa Yukichi as the man who did most to popularize the image of America as the foremost nation in the Western civilized world and as the "sacred land of liberty" (Kamei, 1975, p. 60). In the late nineteenth century, Kamei writes, the main image of America portrayed in Japan, "although some Japanese objected to it and others denied its reality" (p. 55), was as a land of democracy and freedom. By the 1880s, political novels were popular and many were set in the United States as a utopia for liberty and people's rights (p. 66). Kamei notes that one of the best of these was *Kajin no kigū* (Chance Meetings with Beautiful Women) by Tōkai Sanshi (meaning "exile wanderer of the eastern sea"), who visited America in 1879.[13] The one thing tarnishing this perfect world was racial discrimination, in the form of anti-Chinese attitudes. Such a shift, from an emphasis on individual liberty to concern about national rights and discrimination, was common in literature of the period (Kamei, 1975, pp. 66–67). By the end of the nineteenth century, the ideal vision of America was crumbling, and the beginning of the twentieth century saw serious problems arising between Japan and the United States, a situation intensified by increasing numbers of Japanese immigrants in California. Kamei (1975) writes:

> Criticism of contemporary America became widespread in Japan in the early years of the twentieth century. But the criticism . . . betrayed nostalgia for the past, for an image of America that had been deeply held in Japan. The nostalgia itself gives eloquent testimony to the depth and seriousness of that earlier image of the United States as the sacred land of liberty. (p. 72)

The process of disillusionment is seen in *Makiba no michi* (The Farm Road),[14] written in January 1905, where Kafū first evokes the ideal "America" through the hopes of the Japanese immigrants on board the *Shinanomaru*:

> Living only on the dream that if they worked overseas for three years, they would then be able to live comfortably for the rest of their lives when they returned home, they left behind the land where their ancestors were born and had returned to the earth; they bade farewell to the skies of the East, even more beautiful than the skies of Italy; and patiently submitted to the manifold humiliations they would be subjected to under the pretext of immigration laws and health checks, in order to come to this new continent. (pp. 20–21)

On a bicycle ride in the country near Tacoma, a friend tells the narrator the story of a mental asylum nearby where two or three Japanese immigrant laborers are among the inmates. One of them has a particularly pitiful story, from six or seven years ago:

> It's a story from the time when Japanese had begun to emigrate in numbers to Seattle and Tacoma. Back then things were not as ordered as they are now, so all sorts of crimes were more widespread. Villains who wandered up from California, sailors from unknown seas, and veteran immigrants who had already been in America for some time all preyed on the newcomers. It was to this dangerous place that the Japanese who went insane had come with his wife from Japan. This farmer had the ambition to come to America because he'd heard a Japanese recently returned from Hawaii talking about the gold-bearing trees there. He also heard that women's wages were higher than men's, so he brought his wife as well. (p. 22)

The husband takes work as a lumberer in the forests about ten miles from the town, his wife working in a laundry. Three of his senior workers tell the man that it is dangerous to leave a woman alone in Seattle, and suggest that he bring her to the logging cabin. When the wife arrives, the three men are drunk, and decide to take the wife for themselves. The howling of the wind and the rain in the forest heighten the tension as the men ask the husband to share his wife. The man turns deathly pale, powerless to stop the rape. The husband loses his mind completely as a result of the event. He would never fully recover, and is now in the insane asylum (pp. 25–27). The story ends on a note of resignation, concluding that all people must surrender themselves to fate and forces higher than themselves. The overall tone is one of disillusionment with this so-called "promised land," where danger and disaster are the reality, in contrast to the dreams of riches and status which brought many of the immigrants to America in the first place.

Akase Masako observes the similarities between this story and Maupassant's *Sur L'eau*, arguing that Maupassant's vivid depiction of the harsh life of the immigrant worker would have made a strong impact on Kafū living on the West Coast. Akase points out that Maupassant's *fou* (craziness, insanity) was generally connected to a war of some kind and notes the absence of war in Kafū's writing, but *Makiba no michi* shows a critical sensibility regarding the position of the individual vis-à-vis the state, illuminated by the idea of the insane.[15] The mental asylum in this story is first described neutrally as *tenkyōin*. But at second and third mention, the word is given a katakana gloss, "*asairamu*." The katakana emphasizes the knowledgeable status of these gentlemen immigrants, who pepper their speech with English words. But it also marks the word as foreign, highlighting the idea that the Japanese patients are inside a foreign institution, run by the Washington State government. The friend next mentions that the Japanese in question are all "immigrant laborers" (*dekasegi no rōdōsha*), in contrast to their own status as first-class passengers. In the space of just a few lines, we see Kafū's critical use of language, as well as his awareness of power dynamics operating in the new continent. The Japanese community in America is divided into subsets based on class. Although gentlemen may freely bicycle through the countryside, laborers seem to be at the mercy of the state, subject to health checks and locked in the asylum. Divisions are also apparent between urban and rural communities; lawless and law-abiding citizens; the sane and the insane. Not only has the image of America as the "sacred land of liberty" given way to disillusionment, but the simple Meiji binary of Japan and America is shown to be a mere construct in the face of a vast number of internal divisions. The power operating between the first- and third-class passengers also is re-examined through the narrative structure. At the end of the story, the narrator's friend laughs at the vagaries of fate and cycles away, while the narrator remains shocked and silent. The callous attitude of one gentleman is thus highlighted, whereas the narrator's silence shows us the complicity of those bound by the systems they inhabit. As in *Kyabin yawa*, the figure of the uninvolved yet involved narrator points to the possibilities and limitations of the external observer.

The positioning of the external observer is examined more closely in *Yoru no kiri* (Night Mist), written in November 1903. This story has a more literary style than others of this period, as Kafū experimented with different literary forms to refine his writing technique. The story is a thoughtful exploration of the attitudes felt toward the Japanese immigrant laborers in Tacoma, not only by the Americans, but by Kafū himself as a gentleman of a higher class. Kafū's narrator returns to Tacoma from Seattle one night toward the end of October. Walking home, he comes across a noisy bar full of voices and music. The narrator stands outside the bar for a while, but gradually the livid faces and rowdy behavior of the people coming out of the bar begin to frighten him. They all have threatening, glittering eyes and plod heavily in their thick-soled shoes, and the depressing sight of their retreating backs is like that of shadows disappearing into the mist. The narrator comments: "I couldn't help thinking of the fearful lives (*osoroshiki seikatsu*) of the laborers frequently portrayed by writers of the West (*Taisei*), especially in Zola's *L'Assommoir*" (p. 324). For the first time, Kafū is identifying what he sees in front of him with what he has read of Western laborers in Zola's novels. Here he is seeing his favorite author come to life. But Kafū shows that outside the novels the reality is very harsh indeed, as his narrator comes face to face with "the worker" in the form of a drunken American laborer. The narrator is terrified and looks for escape, as if he wants no part of this reality for himself:

> As he would have low wages, and would be selling his labor every day, his worst rivals for labor were the Chinese and Japanese, but most of all us, the Japs,[16] the most hated of the invaders into their territory. I knew that the people of this land universally disliked the Japanese, so I stood rooted to the spot in fear and couldn't get away. (p. 324)

The narrator's fear stems from his knowledge of the hostility felt by American workers toward the Chinese and Japanese "invaders." Akira Iriye states that the relationship between Japan and the United States in the period 1895–1917 was defined by economic competition. American fears of a flood of Japanese commodities onto American markets in the 1890s were never realized, but what did occur was a flood of immigrants, mostly to the West Coast. Since the 1860s, there had been American protest against Chinese immigration, but Japanese immigration seemed to pose a more real threat because of Japan's status as a rising world power. Japan's victory in the Russo–Japanese War in 1905 frightened many Americans, who believed the Japanese intended to inundate the United States with immigrants who would take over

Americans' jobs. Iriye argues that the immigration dispute, especially in the years from 1906 to 1908 when the issue was most fraught, was couched in an intellectual framework that heavily depended on the "image of a Japanese immigrant as a potential rival and threat."[17] Thus, when Kafū, who wore a black suit to distinguish himself as a gentleman and not a laborer, walked around Tacoma, he was aware of the Americans looking at him as something offensive. This context does much to explain the narrator's discomfort in the ensuing scene.

The narrator is hailed suddenly from behind by the drunken, staggering laborer, who by his language reveals himself as Japanese, not American as the narrator had feared. The man tries to appeal to the narrator's sense of brotherhood with a fellow countryman (*dōbō no hito*), but the narrator is taken aback and asks him his business. The man replies, "You're from the same country as me. We're fellow citizens. . . . How can you say such heartless words to a man of your own country?" (p. 325) and pulls at the narrator's coat. The narrator panics, but there is no escape. The laborer continues loudly that he knows none of the "American language," showing the closed nature of Japanese society in Seattle and Tacoma that exists entirely apart from the wider American community. The man shouts even more crazily, when suddenly two or three American people appear behind him, "standing there giving us that look of disgust (*imawashiki manazashi*) they always have when staring at Japanese people" (p. 326). The narrator is extremely embarrassed, ashamed to be associated with this so-called "fellow countryman." The laborer tells the narrator not to be afraid of the "Yankees" and reminds him that they are possessed of the Japanese spirit (*Yamato-damashii*) in their hearts. The laborer catches sight of a young woman among the Americans leaning her head on a man's chest, a hood pulled low over her eyes, her blonde hair escaping around her face. As she gives the laborer a look of abhorrence, he explodes in anger—"You bitch!" he yells, and spits on the girl's shoes. She screams, while her companion raises his fist and steps forward. Luckily, a policeman intervenes and hauls the Japanese laborer away (p. 327). We are told how the laborer ended up as a penniless beggar, finally placed in the insane asylum outside town. A Japanese immigrant who has been in America many years tells the narrator: "once you get put into a mental institution in this country, it's ten to one you'll never see the world again." The insane asylum is a strong link between this story and *Makiba no michi*, both of which illustrate the disillusionment with America as the promised land, and we are led to believe that the laborer swindled out of his money is keeping company with the laborer who lost his wife in the forest. Kafū is painting a dismal picture of immigrant life in America.[18]

Perhaps to balance out this bleakness, the next story, *Shiatorukō no ichiya* (One Night in Seattle Harbor), published in May 1904, presents a more optimistic outlook. Kafū had been told by a crew member on the *Shinanomaru* to avoid Seattle's "Japantown" because it was dangerous. Naturally this makes Kafū curious, and he sneaks off to Seattle one Saturday night in December 1903.[19] In contrast to the bright, bustling First Avenue, the narrator realizes that Japantown is a completely different area with predominantly low wooden buildings. In a second-floor window, the narrator sees Japanese characters on a restaurant signboard. All the signs around him are in Japanese, for tofu, *shiruko* soup, sushi, soba, indeed everything that one would see at home. It is just like looking at a Japanese town. "I had heard about this, but to see it for myself gave me a queer feeling, and all I could do was stare at the sign. As I did so, I could hear the sound of a samisen from the second-floor window" (pp. 315–316). This is a scene which often appears in Kafū's later works of the *shitamachi*, but here he notes that the sound of the samisen, and the voice of a woman singing, do not carry well through the Western building. America and "Japantown" are not suited to the same romantic symbols as Japan, and the sound of the samisen jars in the narrator's consciousness. Three Japanese in the street also are looking up at the window, and one comments that the samisen is wasted in America. All three wear felt hats and black suits, but their Japanese legs are too short for the suits, making them look ill-fitting to Western eyes (p. 316). The first part of the story is thus characterized by a strong sense of disjunction. The narrator next goes into a soba shop, and eavesdrops on the conversation of some workers in the next room. They speak of hard work in the homes of Americans (referred to as *ketō* and *hakujin*) and their difficulties in learning the language. One man becomes philosophical, and speaks at length:

> But we can't get depressed about it. After depression comes desperation, and then degradation. I really advise against it. There are so many examples of it happening. At first you come to America with the intention of studying hard even under adversity, but then instead you fall into degradation, and then when you're thirty or even forty, you're still a failure working in a white man's house. These are the mistakes of our predecessors. If you make haste you'll fail, so we can only study in a calm, deliberate way. (pp. 319–320)

Shiatorukō no ichiya is a quiet, realistic look at the hopes and plans of everyday Japanese workers in Seattle, whose hopes of study and advancement are hampered by their working environment. The conversation ends on a hopeful note, and Kafū shows that these workers are essentially optimistic in outlook, believing that if they concentrate and work steadily they will in the end achieve success. Once the men leave, however, the narrator follows and sees them quickly disappear into what we assume to be a brothel or gambling den. This somewhat patronizing observation once again reveals the distance between the gentlemen of leisure and laborers in the immigrant community.

Akuyū (Bad Company) was written much later than these stories, in June 1907, but it shares the same theme as *Shiatorukō no ichiya* and *Yoru no kiri*—the efforts of a Japanese intellectual to cope with the hostility of American society against the "invasion" of Japanese laborers. In its setting, based around Seattle's Japantown, *Akuyū* has much in common with *Shiatorukō no ichiya,* but the sense of disjunction in *Akuyū* is even more profound. *Akuyū* opens with a strong reminder of the political tension between Japan and America in 1906–1907, as a nameless narrator and his expatriate Japanese friends discuss the possibility of war.

> At one time, when the problem of the expulsion of Japanese schoolchildren from American schools was rife in California, various hypotheses arose in the American newspapers, beginning with those in New York, that there might be a war between Japan and America. At that time the Japanese living in New York naturally started to talk more about the situation on the Pacific coast whenever they came together. One night, at a certain place, we were talking as usual on everything from the theory of race, the "Yellow Peril," theories of internationalism, and the character of Roosevelt, to the question of justice regarding humanity, when someone suddenly said as if they'd just remembered: "There are a lot of Japanese prostitutes over there, aren't there." It was a stupid remark but it completely changed the thread of our conversation . . . (p. 118)

This opening links the current political situation to the immigration problems on the Pacific coast, and Kafū's awareness of current issues is reflected in the story's thoughtful exploration of attitudes held by both Americans and Japanese toward the racial Other.

The central tale of *Akuyū* is narrated by Shimazaki, who arrived in Seattle three years previously. The sight that greets Shimazaki from his hotel room on arrival is similar to that described by the narrator in *Shiatorukō no ichiya*: dirty wooden buildings; crowded streets filthy with horse manure; and the huge, black gas tower that marks the beginning of Japantown. The overwhelming effect is one of disgust at the filth of the Japanese quarter of Seattle, an effect heightened by Shimazaki's description of the area as a "den" or "nest" (*sōkutsu*) of the Japanese:

> These alleys, these dirty wooden houses, these were nothing but the nest of the Japanese and Chinese, a colony of Orientals, while at the same time it was also a place where out-of-work Western laborers and Negroes suffering from poverty and oppression could find a roof over their heads. (pp. 121–122)

The population of this "colony of Orientals" (*Tōyōjin no koronii*) is thus supplemented by the unwanted of American society. Flinching from the sight of coal smoke, Shimazaki packs his bags to move to a Western hotel: *seiyōjin no hoteru* (p. 122). The contrast between the "Oriental colony" and the "Occidental hotel" is emphasized by their proximity in the text and by the equivalence of the two opposing terms *tōyōjin* and *seiyōjin*: one denoting dirtiness and oppression, the other cleanliness and comfort. Shimazaki's desire to move to the Occidental hotel echoes the narrator's feelings in *Yoru no kiri*, wanting to have nothing to do with his Japanese "fellow countrymen." However, as Shimazaki wanders around the town, whenever American children see his Japanese face they shout "*Sukebei!*" The word for "lecher" has come from the Japanese prostitutes in town and is now often used by the lower classes (p. 122). Shimazaki, like Kafū, is lumped in together with the "Oriental colony."

Shimazaki also feels a sense of disjunction walking through the brightly lit streets of Japantown. The air is full of voices, band music, the noise of bars, and shooting galleries, and every now and then, from here or there, comes the sound of a samisen, a woman singing, and men clapping. Kafū's writing is expressive as Shimazaki tries to explain the effect of hearing the samisen in such surroundings:

> Well, try to imagine it. In contrast to the glory of the surrounding environment, called America, with its steamship sirens, train whistles, and phonograph music—in the middle of the boisterous noise called "the Occident" (*seiyō*), is this long, trailing, howling, groaning, sleepy country song from the Kyushu region, interspersed with the broken sound of

> the strings—can there be any other such sorrowful music which could arouse such extremely complex feelings, even while being as out of tune, unpleasant, and monotonous as this? (p. 123)

In striving to articulate Shimazaki's sense of disjunction, Kafū juxtaposes the glorious modern "Occident" with the sleepy, sorrowful "Orient," not only to express the feeling of being out of place, common to all immigrant communities, but to emphasize the great difference between America and Japan. Here the effect is to elevate America to the status of advanced, civilized nation. But *Akuyū* takes pains to point out that behind the glorious façade of modernization there lurks a racial prejudice in the perception of "Orientals and Negroes" in the town. Kafū does not take this racial prejudice as a given, however, and observes that the reverse also happens: Because the streets of "Japantown" are full of Japanese people and Japanese shops, Japanese archery places and Japanese billiard halls, it is the Westerners who look like the foreigners here (p. 123). Kafū is taking on the stereotypes of Self–Other, native–foreigner, and playing with them, giving an ambiguity to the meanings of these words. Identity is seen as something that can shift depending on one's position vis-à-vis other people and other places, and is thus revealed as fundamentally relational in nature. This relational aspect to identity opens the way for a very fluid, changeable, complex positioning in Kafū's work, whether applied to the individual self, Japan, the "West" or any other entity. I call this *flexible positioning,* and believe it to be the key to understanding Kafū's oeuvre as a coherent whole.

Kafū's use of flexible positioning sets him apart from most other writers of his generation. It is the ability to stand back from his surroundings and remind the reader that although he is "Oriental" himself, he can stand outside the boundary enclosing the meaning of "Oriental" and make comments about both "Orientals" and "Westerners," that gives his work an original quality. Kafū is writing from some "in-between" position, different from the "Japs" and drunken labourers, but also obviously different from the Americans who share his social status. It is this in-between position that allowed Kafū to construct his images of both West and Orient in a unique way, and it is here in *Amerika monogatari* that Kafū is starting to make the contrasts and comparisons between Orient and Occident that would later inform his construction of how Japan, the "Orient," Asia and the "West" were positioned relative to each other. However, Kafū not only draws contrasts between the two opposing spaces of Orient and

Occident. He also draws comparisons between the Westernized Japan and traditional Japan, seen in the two contrasting characters of *Kyabin yawa;* between the native country Japan and the Japan recreated by the immigrant population in Japantown, seen in *Akuyū* and *Shiatorukō no ichiya;* and between both kinds of "Japan" and the "West," seen in the sounds of the samisen being distorted in its new surroundings, the uneasy clash created by the Japanese men in ill-fitting suits, and the sense of disjunction felt by Kafū and his character Shimazaki. Contrasts form the foundation of *Amerika monogatari,* but Kafū does not limit himself to a simplistic configuration of two opposing poles of East and West. Rather, traditional Japan, Westernized Japan, the recreated "Japantown," the ideal America, and the reality of the American economic and political situation form a field in which Kafū is constantly positioning and repositioning himself in relation to others.

Kafū's use of the in-between position is clearest in the positioning of his external observer-narrator. Through the immigrant stories, Kafū has his gentleman narrator encounter many different kinds of people, who act as "Other" to the individual self. Kafū explores many ways of positioning this individual self, moving through liminal space in order to determine where he fits in and how he relates to others around him. Such relational positioning of the individual is the tool that would later allow Kafū to position Japan itself in relation to other nations and cultures. While the method essentially is the same, the individual subject and national identity are two distinct formulations of the concept of "self." To maintain the distinction, I will refer to the individual subject as the "self," but use the capitalized "Self" to refer to the larger national identity and position of Japan. Although Kafū is well known as a champion of national culture in Japan based on the reputation of his later work, it is interesting to see this method of positioning the "self" surface so early in *Amerika monogatari.*

Taken as a set, the "Jap stories" are realistic in tone and powerful in their visual and emotional effect. Because of their extreme realism, these stories have been criticized for being more journalistic than literary (Minami, 2007, p. 40; Suenobu, 1997, p. 47). However, it is too easy to dismiss these stories as merely "journalistic." The beautiful descriptions of the mist in *Yoru no kiri,* the long descriptive passages of landscape, urban bustle, people's clothing, and drifting music, are full of rich, varying vocabulary, far from the sparse, objective style of reportage. Kafū writes in flowing passages that are precursors to the lyrical style of *Sumidagawa* and his later works. Moreover, "Japantown," although gritty and unsightly, feels real to the reader in the same way that Zola's streets feel real, as Kafū employs all five senses in his detailed descriptions of places and people to more fully evoke the surroundings of the narrator. When recalling passages in the "Japantown" stories it is the sting of acrid smoke in the eyes and throat, the feel of leaning on a cold wall, the stench of alcohol and sweat, the sight of neon lights and bustling crowds at night, the overwhelming clamor of traffic in the streets that come most vividly to mind. This kind of writing is not so much journalistic as naturalistic, modeled after the style of Zola. Before leaving Japan, Kafū had produced numerous translations of Zola, as well as novels written in a self-consciously Zolaesque style.[20] Kafū compares the laborers in Japantown to something out of a Zola novel and is excited to find himself inside such a scene. The drunken laborers of Japantown may have stepped out of the pages of *L'Assommoir*, or out of Kafū's own *Jigoku no hana* (The Flowers of Hell, 1902).[21] In the Zola references and naturalistic style, the immigrant stories show strong continuity with Kafū's earliest works. Not only are these stories fine examples of Kafū's early writing, but they also show his leanings toward social commentary and critique in their focus on issues of racial hostility, and classifications of "Orient" and "Occident."

In 1904, Kafū left the West Coast to visit the World's Fair at St. Louis and to pursue studies at Kalamazoo College in Michigan. Kafū's reasons for choosing Kalamazoo are much debated, and it does seem strange that he would go to such an out of the way spot to study the French language. In the diary, Kafū first describes his wish to study French in New Orleans, but decides on November 16 to attend college in Kalamazoo instead. Hearing that New Orleans had a climate that would be bad for his constitution, perhaps he thought the wide-open spaces of Michigan would be more healthful. David Strauss (1985) argues that Kafū may well have had a personal connection to Kalamazoo. As his mother was Christian, Strauss suggests that Kafū may have met American missionaries back in Japan—the Reverend Scott in Tokyo and the Reverend Fisher in Yokohama later sent their children to Kalamazoo College, and may have recommended the college to Kafū or his family (p. 27). Certainly, Kafū's father was prominent in the Yokohama Specie Bank, so the idea that he may have met Reverend Fisher in Yokohama is not impossible. Timothy Light also believes that Kalamazoo's status as the preeminent Baptist college of the time would have made it known to Japanese Christians in Seattle, who could then have recommended the college to Kafū directly.[22] Kalamazoo seemed to agree with Kafū, partly because of the welcoming environment he found at the college and in the town.[23] On moving to Kalamazoo, Kafū wrote a short postcard to a Japanese friend expressing his relief at finally being in a place relatively free of discrimination: "I am very happy now in Michigan because I am treated no more as a 'Jap' as in Tacoma." The fact that this postcard was written in English has prompted Jeffrey Angles (2006) to wonder whether Kafū might have been trying to convey his feelings to the American postal workers and others who would have seen the message (p. 49). Given Kafū's evident critical awareness in regard to race and discrimination, such a theory is highly plausible. Certainly, the word "Jap" appears frequently in *Amerika monogatari,* and Kafū's relief at escaping the immigrant environment is palpable.

Kafū's next three stories were inspired by his move away from the insular world of the Japanese communities in Seattle and Tacoma. *Oka no ue* (On Top of the Hill) is set in a "remote country college," the action of *Suibijin* (The Intoxicated Beauty) is set in and around St. Louis, and *Shikago no futsuka* (Two Days in Chicago) is based on Kafū's experience of the city on a break from Kalamazoo College. Much of the tension of the first part of the collection came from the contrast between the hoped-for ideal and the disappointing reality of America. However, as Kafū moves away from Seattle, we find the ideal America resurfacing. As he leaves the predominantly Japanese communities of Seattle and Tacoma, Kafū embarks on a completely new experience, and his encounter with the American midwest prompts him to write for his Japanese audience back home, trying to convey the impression of space and rustic beauty on the one hand, and the bustling modernity of the great cities on the other. Kafū begins to construct his America in a particular way, as the ideal country of modernity, technology, sexual license, individuality and liberty. Kafū uses Japan as the foil for this idealized space, and so these middle stories depend greatly on contrast, or binary opposition, to achieve the required effect.

A major motif of difference through which Kafū constructs his "America" in contrast to Japan is that of the physical, geographical difference of the two countries. On leaving the West Coast, Kafū glories in the wide-open spaces of the countryside around the train, his idyllic portrayal of quaint farmhouses and grazing cattle stemming from the pastoral ideal of America combined with the newness of his own experience. *Suibijin,* published in June 1905, begins with the narrator undertaking a fifteen-hour train journey from Michigan, across Illinois to the Mississippi and St. Louis, passing "vast fields of corn, occasionally a stream bank where farm animals were drinking, or two or three farmhouses on top of a hill, or luxuriant trees, which looked like orchards . . ." (p. 52). Coming out of St. Louis, the factories give way to forest with the sunlight filtering through the leaves: "When I remembered the fear inspired in people by the deep, gloomy forests covering the west coast of North America from the Cascades to the Rockies, I thought that this forest of Missouri truly possessed the most gentle of charms" (p. 54). The further the narrator travels from the Japanese settlements, the brighter and more welcoming the countryside becomes. The narrator's friend S, who meets him in St. Louis, tells him that they will stay at a house in the country, "in a village in the forest like this, a place with nothing but green grass, ribbonlike streams and a constantly blue sky." The landlady also keeps cows and sheep "and could make delicious cream" (p. 54), in Kafū's vision of a country paradise. The light and airy *Natsu no umi* (The Summer Ocean), written July 1905, reinforces this charming image, with its clear summer skies and the ocean dotted with sailing boats and yachts. The narrator of *Natsu no umi* confesses that the quiet country scenery of these nameless villages, previously unknown to him, hold much more emotion and poetry than famous places like Niagara, which had been a disappointment compared with the sunsets over orchards in Michigan and the falling autumn leaves in Missouri (p. 218). Later in the same work, the narrator daydreams about the Michigan countryside and muses that in Japan, one has to travel far up into the mountains to experience such closeness with nature, but in "the new continent" of America one need only go two miles out of town to find solitude and harmony (p. 224). The repetition of "new continent" (*shin-tairiku*) in this passage strengthens the image of America as the newly opened colony, with vistas of open countryside just waiting to be explored.

The newness of the country is linked to the modern outlook of Western civilization, represented by the bustling cities of St. Louis, Chicago, and New York. The orchards and hills in *Suibijin* give way abruptly to the train station of St. Louis, where "there were so many railway lines gathered there in this Midwestern city, at the terminal point of lines from all over the North American continent, that I could not count them all" (pp. 52–53). The crowded station scene reappears in *Shikago no futsuka,* where the narrator is surprised that the train doors open and close automatically (p. 202). Kafū emphasises crowds, movement, the smoke and soot of trains, traffic, concrete bridges and buildings, to construct an image of modernity, and even the black smoke and dirty shacks on the outskirts of cities near the factories are seen as aspects of progress and industrial development. The narrator comments that it will be easy to find his friend's house in Chicago because in America the cities are so well laid-out and orderly—the numbering of city blocks and streets means that there is none of the long searching for houses that one finds in Tokyo (p. 203). As he gazes at the skyscrapers across from the grey buildings of the University of Chicago, the narrator muses that they are in harmony with the clearing sky and bright clouds (p. 204). But later, in the midst of the city, the narrator is seized by "a vague fear," overwhelmed by the sight of the central business district on Michigan Avenue, where the skyscrapers tower twenty stories above the street, creating cavernous darkness between them. The air is full of dust and smoke, and he loses sight of the people from the train who disappear "into the darkness that is Chicago" (p. 212). The narrator's friend James smiles at his reaction, saying "Great city" in English. The narrator can only reply "Ah! Monster," also in English, using the only word he can think of to describe the scene (p. 213). Afterward, however, gazing down from the top of the Marshall Field's store, he is struck by the glory of human endeavour in creating the "monster" of civilization that he had been criticizing a short moment ago (p. 214). The glory of human effort appears again in *Yoaruki* (Walking at Night) as Kafū describes "the nights in this big city of the new continent" (*shintairiku no taito*). The lights of New York are testament to the powers of human invention, and the world they illuminate is the world of magic (p. 280). In this way, America is set up as new, modern, technologically advanced nation, in contrast to a hemmed-in, tradition-bound Japan. Together with the geographical and technological binaries, Kafū constructs a further binary of individual freedom versus Confucian restriction.

This process begins in *Oka no ue* (On Top of the Hill), with the moral dilemma of a man torn between a life of pleasure and one of virtue, which leads to a commentary on the difference between Japanese and American moral society. *Oka no ue*, written in December 1904, is a quiet piece involving the narrator and one other Japanese, Watano, an intellectual who has come to America in order to make a moral decision about his life.[24] Watano had achieved success in Japan early after graduation, was popular with women, and led a carefree life of pleasure. However, he realizes that his lifestyle is hypocritical, as society regards him as a righteous man. Watano decides to marry to save himself from decadence, but feeling no love for his wife, he realizes that he is hiding his true self, trapped in conflict between pleasure and virtue. He decides to escape the situation altogether, and so goes to America to get his thoughts in order. But in America, Watano finds that both extremes are present in society—the pious and puritanical exist right alongside the decadent seekers of pleasure. Unlike Japan, where pleasure is not regarded as something that should be overtly pursued, "America" (*beikoku*) is constructed as a place where vice and virtue can exist openly, side by side. This portrayal of the West as a place where anything can happen, and where society is not as strict as in Confucian Japan, would become a major theme of *Amerika monogatari*.

This theme is clearer still in *Shikago no futsuka*, written in March 1905. The moral attitudes of the Americans are depicted here in such a way as to emphasise the concept of America as a land of freedom, a freedom that extends even to the behavior of young lovers in proper society. The narrator is visiting his friend James from Michigan, who is engaged to Stella, the daughter of his landlord.[25] The two fell in love through their shared interest in music—after dinner he would play the piano and she the violin. They realized that they were in love one night when they played Schumann's "Dreams" together,[26] and Stella shows the narrator a photograph album full of their Sunday dates at Jackson Park and Michigan Avenue. This is the stuff of almost nauseating romance, and through this exaggerated story of love Kafū emphasises that in America, people are free to choose their own partners based on shared interests. Stella herself is a pretty blonde with dimples, "with the gentle voice characteristic of an American maiden" (p. 204), yet at the same time is not afraid to speak and laugh, "a maid of this country who represses not a whit of her emotion" (p. 206). Stella has the confidence of knowing she is the happiest girl in the world, and the narrator comments: "How lucky you are, you people born in the country of freedom!" The image of *jiyū no kuni* is underscored by the sharp contrast Kafū sets up between American and Japanese social and moral tradition:

> If a scholar of Japan, with the *Analects* in his hand, were asked to comment on this, what would he say? She would probably be a hussy, or perhaps a nymphomaniac. However, in the country of freedom there exists no troublesome teaching to go against the natural emotions of human beings; only the gospel of love. (pp. 206–207)

Kafū has set up a direct opposition between American freedom or independence (*jiyū*) and the restraints of Japanese Confucianism. The Japanese scholar holds the text upon which much of the ethical and scholarly tradition of China, and therefore Japan, has been based: the *Analects*. The scholar would disapprove of the engagement between two young people to the partner of their choice, based on love and similar interests rather than on familial duty or economic concerns. To emphasize the difference between traditional Japanese Confucian ethics and the social mores of this "country of freedom," Kafū next sets up a surprising scene of passion to illustrate the strength of the "gospel of love." After dinner, James and Stella agree to play the "Dreams" piece together. Stella is overcome with deep emotion, and when they finish she can no longer restrain her feelings, but flings herself on James' breast and kisses him twice with great passion. Stella's parents applaud happily, and the couple go on to play "Dixie," the all-American favorite (p. 207).

Of course, this kind of scene is difficult to imagine for 1905, especially when Stella is the daughter of a respected judge. Ken Ito (1991) argues that the "West" as portrayed in *Amerika monogatari* is "a particularly stirring 'West,' a West reconstructed through Kafū's imagination" (pp. 34–35). Kafū's imagined West takes on such an exaggerated form that Ito comments: "the portrayal of Americans in *Amerika monogatari* occasionally seems so lacking in social observation that it raises doubts about the quality of Kafū's experience of the American environment" (p. 37). The scene in question is the passionate embrace of James and Stella. Ito argues that Kafū's observation of America is so mediated by French literature and sensibilities that *Amerika monogatari* is not true observation at all but rather a representation of an imagined ideal. However, the point is not whether Kafū was "lacking in social observation" in the melodramatic scene. What Kafū sets out to do in *Amerika monogatari* is not to paint a real-to-life portrait, but to paint an idealistic picture of the perfect American life as imagined by the Japanese who were going to read his stories at home. America thus becomes a place where passions overflow, where people speak their minds, where women throw themselves upon their loves even in front of their parents. Ito makes the same observation, that "James and Stella's behaviour has been exaggerated to illustrate a certain abstraction, the sexual freedom of Americans" (p. 38). An exaggeration used to reinforce the myth of American sexual licentiousness is less a literary failure lacking in observation than a literary technique, creating a point of contrast with the ideal "America" in order to show something about the fundamental characteristics of Japan. We can interpret this scene as an example of a constructed representation, set up in order to make a particular point.

The contrast could not be sharper than that drawn between the *Analects* and the "gospel of love." This kind of contrast may be called *essentialization*, where elements of a culture or society are typified as its core features, the essential, fundamental characteristics that define that culture. The essentializations of American sexual liberation and Christianity, and Japanese dependence on ancient Confucian texts, have a timeless quality, spanning time from the age of Confucius and the Gospel to the present. As James G. Carrier (1995) points out, such timeless essentialization is a major component of both Orientalist and Occidentalist discourse (pp. 4–5). Kafū's "America" is everything that Japan is not—a clear example of binary opposition, where America and Japan are defined as fundamentally opposed, mutually exclusive polarities. Where the first set of stories in *Amerika monogatari* displayed a complex field of positions between Japan and the West, here in the middle section of the volume that field is reduced to a simpler binary construction. The complexities of "America" in relation to Japan have retreated as Kafū concentrates on the positive ideal of America as the "land of liberty," and Japan and America become increasingly polarized in the process. Kafū uses America as a conflicting and contrasting opposite in order to throw into relief the essential characteristics of Japan. The binary opposition is not static, however, but a process of dialectic between the two, by which Kafū comes to a clearer definition of Japan. The process continues as Kafū contrasts the moral systems of America and Japan, particularly focusing on romantic love and sexual freedom.

A good example is *Haru to aki* (Spring and Autumn), written in May 1906, where Kafū contrasts the freedom of modern American courtship with traditional Japanese expectations of love. Toshiya, a student of politics in a Michigan college, becomes obsessed with Kikue, a conservative student of theology.[27] Toshiya's modern, aggressive, "American" approach to courtship, expecting the relationship to be easy and light-hearted, is completely at odds with Kikue's expectations of a serious, dignified relationship leading to marriage. Bound by the two value systems of Confucian tradition and the Christianity she studies, Toshiya's ideas of romance prove too much for the traditional Kikue, who is driven to attempt suicide when he finally leaves her. Kafū emphasizes the difference between the two attitudes by having Toshiya whisper his propositions and write his love letters to Kikue in English, suggesting that there are no Japanese words suitable for expressing "American" romantic love. The fundamental incompatibility of the two conflicting value systems stems from the fact that the restrained social values of Japan cannot yet cope with American ideas of romance and open physical affection.

The contrast based on liberty and sexual freedom takes on even greater significance when Kafū moves to the East Coast, illustrated by two stories set in New York and New Jersey. The first is *Natsu no umi,* noted earlier for its emphasis on breezy beaches and beautiful countryside. The narrator takes a steamship down the Hudson River to spend the day at Asbury Park, a beach resort in New Jersey. Gazing about at the Brooklyn Bridge and the tall buildings on either side, the narrator is dumbstruck when they pass the Statue of Liberty. Immediately overcome with awe and a sense of artistic power, the narrator wants to hurl himself at her feet to worship. "This statue was the representative of the new continent, the elucidator (*setsumeisha*) of the new thought, and at the same time, stronger than the fortress of an impregnable castle, it was the protector of the American spirit" (p. 218). In contrast to the old civilizations of Europe and China, America had something to offer the world—a fresh start, a spirit of enterprise, and a promise of equality. The Statue of Liberty was designed to be viewed from the water, welcoming ships into the harbor. Kafū was aware that the positioning of the statue was both strategic and significant: He writes that the narrator's devotion "was certainly inspired by what one might call the first principle of the statue's construction, the advantage of its location" (p. 217). The narrator muses, "Who among those travellers, gazing from their leaflike boats towards the great capital of this democratic nation and looking up at this massive statue rising from the Atlantic Ocean, would not be struck by some profound emotion?" (pp. 217–218). Kafū is well aware that the statue has been put there on purpose, for a particular effect, by the officials of the "democratic nation." However, even given this critical consciousness, Kafū's portrayal of the Statue of Liberty is positive, emphasizing the values of democracy and freedom.

The ideal of America as the country of freedom is repeated later in *Natsu no umi* through the figure of the alluring and passionate American woman. The narrator admires "the physical beauty of Western women" (*seiyō fujin*) with their expressive eyes, full chests, small shoes with high heels, and artful makeup. He especially admires the way they choose their clothes to suit their hair color, face, and figure. In comparison, however, "do not Japanese women seem to lack absolutely all of these arts?" Where American girls are free to develop naturally, the education and training of Japanese society are so full of "reproach and intervention" that Japanese girls are restrained and shrink in fear rather than making full use of their natural endowments (pp. 220–221). American and Japanese women are thus placed in direct opposition to each other, adding to the essentialized vision of America as "free" versus Japan as "restricted." The freedom of American women to give full reign to their emotions, seen in Stella's passionate outburst in *Shikago no futsuka*, is taken to extremes in *Chōhatsu* (Long Hair), where passion is shown to have a dark side.

Chōhatsu, written in May 1906, is set in New York, where

Fujigasaki Kunio, a young exotic-looking Japanese with curled, shoulder-length hair, lives openly with an American divorcée. The couple are first spotted by the narrator (*jibun*) in Central Park, and Kunio's striking appearance causes the narrator to muse upon his origins, casting him as an exotic, mysterious romantic hero. The narrator's curiosity is satisfied a few days later when a Japanese acquaintance reveals he was at Columbia University with Kunio some time ago. The narrative structure shifts, so the acquaintance becomes the second narrator (*watakushi*) who gives the central story. *Chōhatsu* is one of the most playful and erotic tales of *Amerika monogatari*, as Kafū plays with narrative structure and places sexual pleasure at the center of the story. *Watakushi* himself is attracted to the woman, made clear when she opens the door and invites him into the apartment she shares with Kunio. She possesses "the usual indefinable expression of the Western woman" (*seiyō fujin*), with bright green eyes and blonde hair. Her arms and shoulders are visible through her gown, "vulgar yet fascinating" (pp. 72–73). *Watakushi* highlights America's libertarian attitude by saying that "In this country there was nothing at all unusual in a man and a woman keeping company" like this. The woman had been married less than a year to an American millionaire when she had an affair with a Polish musician, and the American divorced her. She could no longer take place in polite society and so took a succession of lovers to divert herself. Kunio admits that their relationship will only last until she finds someone else. The relationship is thus described through the concerned, naïve eyes of *watakushi*, who observes that Kunio has not an ounce of "strong, manly love" about him: "It was just as if man and woman had swapped their social positions (*chi'i*) and he, despite being the man, was embraced in her arms, wishing to spend his days under the woman's protection as if in a dream, like a male concubine" (p. 77). The woman orders Kunio to grow his hair to satisfy her own sexual fetish, and *watakushi* tells *jibun*: "When you saw him in the carriage, you probably thought that his long hair was done to be fashionable. But actually when that woman loses her temper, he lets her tear out his long hair, and grants a kind of painful pleasure to the frenzied woman" (p. 79). This description is never answered, as *jibun* remains silent and the story ends.

Stephen Snyder (2000) argues that the negative value judgments of *watakushi* are brought into question by *jibun*'s more accommodating, positive view of Kunio as romantic hero, making Kafū one of the first Japanese writers to successfully create an unreliable narrator, problematizing narrative in the manner of Maupassant (pp. 46–47). The unreliable central narrative also allows Kafū free reign in creating a realm of almost complete sexual license in *watakushi*'s imagination. The gender roles in this story are completely reversed, ending in the man's complete submission to the powerful, yet dangerously unbalanced, Western woman. Her sexuality is such a threat that *watakushi* ascribes it to derangement. Kunio also forsakes the most binding of all Japanese traditional ties, with his family and country, in order to satisfy this woman and his own masochistic tendencies. In the central fantasy of *Chōhatsu*, America represents an inversion of Japan's gender roles and family expectations, reinforcing the image of America as everything Japan is not, where anything is possible.

The major point of contrast that emerges in the middle section of *Amerika monogatari* thus revolves around Kafū's idea of *jiyū*—freedom, liberty, and independence. America regains its ideal quality most clearly in its construction as a democratic nation. Masayuki Akiyama (1981) objects that Kafū's aestheticism is at odds with American puritanism, so that his "understanding of American democracy may be said to be external, sensuous, subjective and self-centred" (p. 97). However, a lack of deep understanding or an aesthetic literary approach did not stop Kafū from using the image of America as a land of freedom to great effect, portraying a value system far removed from Japanese Confucianism. Kafū by no means accepted America uncritically as a true country of freedom, as evidenced by his shock in *Saiyū-nisshishō* and also his indignation in a later essay at the banning of Strauss' *Salome* and the treatment of Gorky in New York.[28] Kafū's attitude toward American democracy could be read as quite critical and even cynical, especially considering the attention given to racial discrimination in the immigrant stories and later in the collection. At times, Kafū makes wry comments revealing his skepticism, as when he notes that modern electricity only makes it easier for prostitutes to work the streets at night, and that many of these prostitutes were originally wholesome Michigan farm girls, tricked into coming to the city by unscrupulous pimps. It is possible that Kafū deliberately injected such cynicism in order to challenge the reigning Meiji image of America as the sacred land of liberty.[29] But freedom and independence, which Kafū calls *jiyū*, is still an extremely important concept in *Amerika monogatari*, used to introduce a severe criticism of a Japan that could not experience such freedom itself.

Kafū had thus constructed the ideal "America" by contrasting it with Japan through motifs of geography, technological advancement, value systems, and sexual liberty. But after three years in the country he was tiring of America, and the ideal became increasingly difficult to maintain. From this point in the collection the tone becomes darker, and Kafū's critical side reasserts itself. At the same time, he was longing for France, and the diary is filled with dreams of Paris and references to French literature. In July 1905, Kafū's cousin secured him an undemanding office job in the Japanese Legation in Washington as extra help during the Russo–Japanese War, which left Kafū with "plenty of spare time" for reading at night.[30] As he planned to go to France as soon as possible, he devoted himself to reading things like Maupassant's *Sur L'eau*, the translation and analysis of which would later form the bulk of an essay entitled *Mōpassan no henshū kikō* (An Account of Maupassant's Boating Travels).[31] But in late August and September, Kafū received letters from his father forbidding him from going to France. On September 23 Kafū despaired of ever seeing Paris, declaring: "I want to destroy myself in dissipation."[32] Dissipation was certainly close at hand—on a night out in Washington on September 13 Kafū met Edyth, a prostitute who would become a major figure in the diary as their relationship deepened.[33] However, Kafū's job at the Legation ended with the Japanese victory over Russia, and he returned for the fall semester at Kalamazoo College to complete his third term of elementary French.[34] At the end of November, Kafū's father wrote with news of a job at the New York office of his bank. A telegram from the bank itself followed, urging Kafū to come for an interview. Although banking was far from Kafū's ideal profession, he realized that he could earn the money to go to France, or could at least follow the path of literature and become a writer in the big city. The decision may have been hard for Kafū, who describes looking out at the beautiful snows of Kalamazoo with a heavy heart pondering his future. The possibility of traveling to France finally proved impossible to resist, and Kafū left Kalamazoo on December 3, 1905.

The stories written on the East Coast are in some ways reminiscent of the immigrant stories set on the West Coast, as Kafū comes into contact with more diverse groups of people and revisits the issue of racial discrimination in America, directed against African Americans in Washington and Japanese in New York. *Rinkan* (In the Forest), written in November 1906, examines the problematic relations between black and white in Washington and how the history of slavery is still alive in the modern consciousness. The opening of *Rinkan* has Kafū's narrator commenting on the two things that travelers most notice about Washington, DC—first, that the city is open and parklike in design, and second, the surprisingly "large numbers of black people (*kokujin*) wherever you go" (p. 108). Crossing the Potomac into Virginia, the narrator looks back at Washington for the view of Capitol Hill:

> It was a clear, wide panorama. I was suddenly aware that this was the capital city which presided over this great continent of the Western hemisphere, and gazing at the setting sun reflected in the water, my abstract impressions of race, nation, political power, ambition, reputation, history—all these things, began to pile on top of each other in my breast, coming and going, like the clouds on a summer's day. (p. 110)

Kafū draws attention to Washington as the capital, with all the images of power that go with it, and the narrator cannot help but feel a strong sense of respect. Washington is thus set up as the center of American democracy, a construction that intensifies the following scene illustrating the racial problems lurking beneath the façade. Strolling through the forest, the narrator comes across a white soldier with a young black girl kneeling at his feet, begging him in tears not to leave her. The girl is of mixed blood, but Kafū refers to her through the American soldier's point of view as he arrogantly breaks off the relationship: "He was a fine American, and she was a daughter of the black race, who were previously slaves" (p. 112). The narrator fears being discovered, and leaves the forest pondering the racial question:

> Why on earth, I wondered, was the black race so despised and looked down upon by the white race? Could it be because their appearance is ugly, perhaps, or because it is black? Or perhaps it is simply because fifty years earlier they were slaves. As long as it is one race which forms a political group, perhaps oppression can never be avoided. (p. 113)

By setting the story in Washington, and by contrasting the scene in the forest with the heart of democracy, Kafū points out that even great political ideals are beset by problems, and even American democracy is not perfect. The story ends with the narrator "mulling it over yet coming to no conclusion, this extremely large problem, so difficult to put into words" (p. 116). Sakagami Hiroichi (1997) argues that Kafū is not interested in the deeper racial problem and has no conclusions about it himself because it is so far outside his own experience (p. 96). But even though he can come to no conclusions about the problem himself, Kafū, as representative of the "Oriental Other" to the West, is here deconstructing American society in observing how it views the Others within itself. *Rinkan* demonstrates that "America" cannot be taken as a monolithic entity, but needs to be understood as a diverse community with its own social divisions of class and race.

The issue of racial discrimination resurfaces in *Nezame* (Awakening), written in April 1907, in the treatment experienced by a Japanese businessman in New York. Sawazaki Saburō persuades his company to send him to America to head the New York office, happily leaving his wife and child behind in Japan. But after just three months Sawazaki is numbed by tedium and loneliness. He cannot go out with his young Japanese co-workers, nor can he afford to frequent the clubs Western businessmen attend, and even whisky offers him no solace. Sawazaki feels the effects of racial discrimination—he is "looked upon as a Jap" (*Jappu to mikubirarete*) and experiences unbearably long waits for bank services. He feels there is not one person who will look on him with kindness. Sawazaki finds it hard to trust Americans' motives, fearing that they will be racially prejudiced. When Mrs. Denning, a secretary new to his office, begins calling in sick, Sawazaki fears that she might feel uncomfortable working in a Japanese firm, and when he runs into her on the street one night he asks if this is the case. They walk and sit in the park by the river, and she speaks of her inner struggle to return to work after her husband died. Sawazaki realizes that Mrs. Denning is the first Western person ever to speak candidly to him, and is deeply moved. But when she calls in sick again, he immediately reverts to his fear of prejudice: "Sawazaki immediately showed the strange, patriotic, biased disposition that is usual for Japanese people staying in America, and became extremely angry . . ." (p. 161). Afterward Sawazaki finds out that the woman has taken to prostitution, the result of a gradual downfall after her husband's death. Sawazaki feels a deep remorse, especially because she was the only American who had talked to him openly. Sawazaki's fears of racial prejudice turned out to be unfounded in this case, but Kafū surprises the reader by making Sawazaki himself the prejudiced one in the end. Even though the secretary fell victim to circumstance, Sawazaki forgets his former feelings of remorse and gratitude and enjoys telling other Japanese about the corrupt nature of American women on his return to Japan. This story transcends its mundane tale of the office and Sawazaki's fears of racial prejudice in its criticism of the hypocritical attitudes held by Japanese themselves.

While *Rinkan* and *Nezame* show a complex critical awareness toward American democracy, Kafū continued to employ binary structures at this time, notably invoking the ideal of American freedom whenever it suited his purpose. Although Kafū was not blindly in love with American democracy—far from it—he still was able to use the imagined "country of freedom" as a springboard from which to criticize Japanese "feudal" attitudes. We see this criticism emerge clearly through the image of the overbearing Japanese father in two stories written in May 1907, *Ichigatsu ichijitsu* (New Year's Day) and *Akatsuki* (Daybreak). The hero of *Ichigatsu ichijitsu* is Kaneda, a Japanese working in New York, who cannot stand the sight or smell of traditional Japanese cuisine. This stems from his childhood, as his long-suffering mother was subjected to constant criticism on everything from the quality of her cooking to her choice of tableware from her husband, a High Court judge with a pre-Restoration education. Kaneda first comes into contact with Western values in middle school and is astounded:

> When I began to read English textbooks and contemporary magazines and so on, the Western ideas that were so full of words like "love" and "home" made a truly violent impact on my heart. And I felt at the same time that the teachings of Confucius and words like *bushidō* that came from my father's lips were the enemies of human happiness. (p. 173)

Although his fellow Japanese expatriates find fault with the independence of American wives, Kaneda thinks it is marvelous:

> I don't care if it is just a superficial hypocrisy, a formality—if the husband carves the meat at table and places it on dishes for the wife, she in return will make the tea and cut the cake for him. Just seeing this gives me great pleasure. . . . When I see a girl laying out sandwiches and apples and so on for a picnic, or when I see someone's wife sharing champagne and conversation with her husband and other men in a restaurant on the way home from the opera or the theater, these in particular make me even more happy. Is this not a great consolation to my eyes, which had never before seen the happiness of a wife or a mother? (p. 175)

Kafū is well aware of the "superficial hypocrisy" of American gender relations, which were fundamentally no more "free" than those back home. But by contrasting the apparent gender dynamics of America and Japan, *Ichigatsu ichijitsu* can still present a harsh critique against Confucian morals and traditional samurai values. Throughout the story, Kaneda's father is made to stand in as a representative of all that is outdated, autocratic and unfeeling in the older generation of Meiji.[35]

This kind of father figure reappears in *Akatsuki*, where we are introduced to a student who has been in America for five years, sent there originally to study. He is a cultured, well-educated individual who nonetheless has embraced the uncertain beach life on Coney Island in order to escape the pressure from his father to be a success in life.[36] Having lost contact with his father and family some time ago, his allowance has stopped coming from Japan. Although this young man feels a great deal of guilt toward his family, he also feels an overwhelming sense of relief and freedom because all his responsibilities have now disappeared. It is no coincidence that *Akatsuki* and *Ichigatsu ichijitsu* both feature young men seeking an escape from an overbearing traditional father in a new life in America. This is, on the one hand, a direct reflection of Kafū's own relationship with his father and their argument over Kafū's wish to go to France. However, it also represents a deeper underlying protest at the Meiji value system that produces such fathers, and a critique of that system through contrast with a freer "America." Here then in May 1907 are the beginnings of Kafū's harsh critique of Meiji values through the construction of an opposing system of values in the West. It is this construction of contrast that Kafū would use to great effect in his critique of Meiji society on his return to Japan in 1908.

Despite its severe criticism of Japanese values and tradition, *Amerika monogatari* has not usually been taken as a critical work. Many argue that Kafū cannot be regarded as a serious critic at all in the years between 1903 and 1908 because he was not interested in the political situation in Japan while he was away in America. As evidence for Kafū's apolitical attitudes, critics give examples ranging from the lack of comment about the Russo–Japanese War in *Saiyū-nisshishō* to Kafū's later silence on the outbreak of World War I, or his callous comments on the assassination of the Prime Minister Hara Kei in 1921.[37] Admittedly, Kafū's interest in the Russo–Japanese War was limited to how long he could hold his job in the Japanese Legation in Washington, but we must remember that Kafū had left Japan in September 1903—in a year one can feel very cut off from the political happenings of one's own country. Nakamura Mitsuo (1978) also argues that Kafū felt alienated from what was going on at home, and missed the intellectual impact of the Russo–Japanese War felt by his contemporaries (pp. 291–292). We know that Kafū did read the Japanese newspapers and was moved to comment on them in his diary,[38] but to a certain extent the critics are correct in saying that Kafū makes little mention of Japanese political events. However, pointing out Kafū's scanty awareness of Japanese events does not logically lead to the conclusion that Kafū was apolitical or had no political awareness whatsoever. To argue in this way is to ignore two fundamental characteristics of Kafū's writing at the time.

The first is Kafū's evident interest in the social and political situation of Japanese in America, shown in his detailed and patient depiction of the life of Japanese immigrants in that country, in his use of the "Yellow Peril" discourse and the worsening situation between Japan and the United States as the background to *Akuyū*, and in his depiction of racial discrimination against "Orientals" because of job scarcity in the region. Kafū's writing about the experiences of the Japanese immigrants may be read further as social commentary, as he portrays the details of their hopes and aspirations, the ignominy of the routine health checks on arrival, as well as the difficulties of learning the language, finding work and surviving in the harsh environment of Seattle and Tacoma. Kafū easily could have ignored all these aspects of life in America, but he made a point of writing about these issues. The second characteristic is Kafū's interest in wider questions—the ways in which Japan differs from the modern, technologically advanced America; the issue of modernization itself and its value to Japan; the issue of the traditional Confucian moral system and its restrictive nature in a modernizing world. Kafū also shows interest in ideas of "Orient" and "Occident" and how Americans and Japanese perceive each other. It hinges on the definition of "critic" as to whether we see Kafū as a critic or not. Kafū's thoughtful explorations of Japan through contrast with America show the beginnings of a critique of Meiji values and the Confucian moral system, while the first part of *Amerika monogatari* shows solid social observation and political awareness. The middle section of *Amerika monogatari* branches out into further questions of race and sexual power in America, as Kafū muses on the nature of a democracy, in the so-called "country of freedom." The last part of the collection is different again, as Kafū's love of the demimonde comes to the fore and he turns to the darkness and decay of the Decadent School.

In New York, Kafū was doing his best to immerse himself in French literature and culture, moving in with a French couple in January 1906 and spending much of the next three months attending plays, operas, and concerts. March and April 1906 find Kafū frequenting French rental libraries and secondhand bookshops, learning French at night school, and reading the works of Zola, Maupassant, Flaubert, and Daudet. The diary entry for April 23 sees Kafū gazing forlornly at the Statue of Liberty, reflecting that he still has not been to France, where the statue originated. In 1908, Kafū would publish an essay entitled *Mōpassan no sekizō wo haisu* (Worshipping the Stone Monument to Maupassant), in which he explains his reasons for studying French while he was in New York (KZ 18.271–6). Kafū writes that he began to study French in order to appreciate Maupassant's style in the original French and not to have to depend on English translations, and he wanted to be able to pronounce from his own lips each word and phrase penned by the great writer. Although after two years in America he admitted that he could not understand the conversations of Americans in English, he was almost able to read Maupassant's novels in the original (18.272). Kafū says he rented the room from French immigrants so that he could "listen to French day and night." More than anything, Kafū confessed to his "sensei" Maupassant, he wanted to travel to France and experience "the inside of the world of your novels" (18.273). The essay reveals Kafū's feelings about the reality of Maupassant's work to him: To travel to France would be the equivalent of entering the inner workings of Maupassant's novels, even of becoming a character in them himself. Kafū was to spend four years in America and nine months in France, but even though the time spent there was shorter, France looms larger in Kafū's works of this time.

Kafū was not the only Meiji writer to feel indebted to Maupassant, whose narrative technique, humor, and critical eye influenced a whole generation of young writers. Tayama Katai, for example, was greatly influenced by reading *Sur L'eau* in English translation, particularly impressed by Maupassant's depiction of the pain and psychological turmoil of the artist. Shimazaki Tōson also gained from the portrayal of loneliness in this work. As Minami Asuka (2007) argues, Kafū, Katai, and Tōson are good representatives of Maupassant's impact on Meiji naturalism, as all three writers were moved by the pain and solitude resonant in Maupassant's works, but the ways in which they connected bodily sense perception to the depiction of the natural world were very different in terms of method and resulting effects (pp. 72–73). However, Kafū was arguably the writer most influenced by Maupassant's "narrative within a narrative," which he took as the structural basis for many of the American stories,[39] and Akase Masako (1976) notes that Kafū never spoke of any writer with as much love as he did Maupassant (p. 77).

As he immersed himself in French culture as much as possible in New York, Kafū's writing changed accordingly, taking on the theme and tone of late nineteenth-century French literature of the demimonde. From mid-1906 Kafū wrote increasingly of the seedier side of New York, its prostitutes and entertainers, its streets, bars, and brothels.

Yuki no yadori (Shelter in the Snow), written in June 1906, is set in the world of the prostitutes who worked on Broadway. The story of a novice prostitute, Annie, is told to the narrator by his acquaintance Betsy, a streetwalker of some experience. Annie only arrived in the city a few days ago, fooled into coming from the country to make money for a man. This often happens, says Betsy, and the narrator realizes that even the strong, independent American woman can be duped into a life of prostitution. Once the girl is stranded in the city, she has no choice but to turn to prostitution to make a living. Betsy herself remembers the experience: "You could probably get by and have enough to eat, but how can you live in New York like that? . . . If people get dressed up ready for a big trip you want to wear those clothes too; if people go to the theatre you want to go too. I wanted that luxury" (p. 105). After this night the narrator often goes to see Betsy, and is surprised to see Annie's transformation into a sophisticated coquette. As he tells his friends: "She's really fine now. With her hand behind her back she holds her skirt up neatly, and trips down Broadway in her French high heels. How about it? If you like I"ll introduce you sometime" (p. 105). This is a cynical yet beautifully written piece, as much influenced by Kafū's reading matter as by his own experience.

Kafū's attraction to the demimonde was not limited to his writing. The tone in both the diary and *Amerika monogatari* darkens during this period. Kafū spends more time in Chinatown, drinking late into the night and vowing to "wield the brush of realism" in depicting its bars, brothels, and dancehalls. By June 1906, Kafū can no longer bear working at the bank, and writes increasingly of his visits to Chinatown to drown himself in drink and to meet the prostitutes who give him "a cold kind of consolation, while at the same time making me shudder at their ugly, wretched lives." Kafū's diary entry is moving as he contemplates the lives of these prostitutes, as "they too are fundamentally human" (*karera mo moto wa hito-nariki*). Themselves mothers, daughters, and lovers to other real people, the women of Chinatown are written with real sympathy, although this is subject to a heavy dose of romanticism. Not wanting to disturb the picture of tragic degradation by offering his hand in help, Kafū admits, "I am only waiting for the chance to yield to a grain of opium with them."[40] July is a particularly trying time for Kafū—harsh letters from his father refusing to acknowledge his chosen career in literature and forbidding him to go to France drive him to despair, while at the same time he is pressured by letters from Edyth in Washington, who wants to come to New York to live with him. Kafū is unable to decide on a course of action, and wishes that he could "disappear into a life wandering foreign lands, and work as a boy in a hotel or a waiter in a restaurant."[41] When Edyth suddenly appears in New York, Kafū feels trapped, "like a character in some French novel." Torn between Edyth and his love for literature, Kafū dramatically compares himself to Tannhäuser.[42] Struggling with his father's expectations of him and his own abhorrence of the banking life, Kafū drafts *Yowa no sakaba* (The Midnight Bar) on July 22.

The dismal opening of *Yowa no sakaba* reflects Kafū's growing despondency. Kafū describes the rundown area of the city comprising Little Italy, Chinatown, and what he calls *Jū-machi,* or "Jew-town," an area where all the laborers and immigrants gather. If the West Side, representative of this "great city of the new world" (*shinsekai no dai tokai*), is the resting place of the successful, Kafū observes, then the East Side is the hiding place of the failure. Kafū describes the filth of the sidewalks and their inhabitants in almost repulsive detail, and the narrator finds to his surprise that there are tattoo artists "in the West as well" (p. 229). The narrator is walking back from the theater one night through this area and comes across a noisy, smoky basement bar, reeking of alcohol and filled with sailors, laborers, and prostitutes. He sits and takes in the crowd, until two Italian musicians visit the bar. The narrator cannot understand the words of their song "from Southern Europe," but is deeply moved by the melody, almost Oriental (*tōyōfū*) in its gentle sorrow. The song has the power to silence the drunken crowd, and the narrator is filled with "a poetic sentiment." Matsumoto Hajime (1998) uses *Yowa no sakaba* as a typical example of Kafū's naturalistic depiction of dirt, poverty, and decay (pp. 20–21). Together with *Yuki no yadori,* this story shows Kafū's predilection for the decay of the demimonde in French literature, which he could recreate in his own works.

At the height of Kafū's literary forays into the demimonde, the diary entries of August 1906 see the writer facing a crisis. Due in no small part to his reckless behavior out of office hours, Kafū is in danger of losing his job. The possible loss of funding has Kafū overcome with anxiety, even to the point of contemplating suicide, over having to return to Japan without ever seeing his beloved Paris. Kafū buries himself in Maupassant[43] and moves in with his cousin Sogawa, but is struck down with typhoid and hospitalized in September. Kafū writes that he would rather die right now than waste his money on the hospital, make a complete recovery and have to return to hateful Japan without ever seeing Europe. October sees Kafū recovering, buying a copy of Maupassant's *Les Soeurs Rondoli,* visiting an old French lady for conversation, and visiting a French café run by a Frenchman, where he orders in French and reads a Parisian newspaper.[44] The stories of *Amerika monogatari* after this time refer increasingly frequently to France and French literature, and as the collection progresses, France assumes almost mythic proportions, acquiring a timeless air of mystique, age, and deep cultural heritage.

Kafū had hinted at the superiority of French culture throughout *Amerika monogatari*, beginning with *Shikago no futsuka*, where American newness and mercantilism were contrasted with the fullness of an older European culture, and the narrator found American literature dull because "in this new continent he could not find any authors of the calibre of Daudet or Turgenev" (p. 210). The painter S in *Suibijin* is a Francophile who has not yet been to France but has French ancestry, maintaining that men must spend their lifetimes studying women, and the best at it are the French (pp. 58–59). The main protagonist, meanwhile, is a French journalist who cannot even bear to be in such a vulgar country (*sappūkei na kuni*) as America (p. 59). In *Saiyū-nisshishō* we find Kafū attending an exhibition in oils at the New York Academy of Art and finding nothing to admire, since "America seems to be no good" at such things.[45] The cumulative effect of such comments is to set up France and Europe in general as superior to America in culture and taste. *Kyūkon* (Old Regrets), completed in January 1907, is most notable for the way it constructs Europe as the epitome of beauty, art, and civilization. The narrator, an American, identifies closely with *Tannhäuser*, regretting that he left his own Venus, a New York prostitute, for the sake of ambition and a place in society. The narrator and his wife travel to Austria for their honeymoon and stay in an extremely old hotel. "For us Americans, in the middle of the night in the capital of this silent, old world, it seemed that we could hear the voices of people long gone, from many centuries ago" (p. 144). For Americans, Europe is a place of mystery and intrigue. Kafū is keen to remind readers that America does not represent the whole "West," but has developed from European civilization. Kōno Kensuke (1997) takes this point further and argues that Kafū comprehended America primarily as a former colony of Europe, with no independent culture or tradition of its own, a thesis borne out by Kafū's repeated classification of America as the "new continent," "newly-opened land," and "new world" (p. 172).

The distinction between "America" and "Europe" is further explored in *Ochiba* (Falling Leaves), written in October 1906. *Ochiba* is a quiet lyrical piece describing Kafū's love affair with Western art in New York. Conflation between author and narrator is hard to avoid in this story, as the impact of Western art on Kafū during his time in

New York is undeniable. However, the narrator is constructed clearly as a character, a romantic hero called *jibun* who perfectly reflects the persona of the published diary.[46] Sitting in the park one autumn Sunday evening, the narrator meditates on his good fortune in experiencing life in the enormous city. The main attraction of New York, however, is its theaters and concerts, where he has seen Shakespeare, Racine, and Ibsen, and has heard the soaring ideals of Wagner and the technical artistry of Verdi (p. 240). He frequently attends classical music concerts and art galleries, collecting a mountain of catalogues and ticket stubs. To fit in with the fashions of the day he buys a new wardrobe for spring, but Kafū's bias against American commercial values shows through:

> However, American fashions are vulgar in form, as might be expected from a mercantile country. As a result of my many efforts to show that I had not been influenced by America's commercialism, every morning I would curl my hair and tie a wide cravat deliberately casually, in order to look like the young Daudet, who wrote *Les Amoureuses*, or even better, like Byron. (p. 241)

Kafū seeks to imitate the artists of Europe whose taste is not sullied by commercialism, and thus sets up "Europe" as a higher kind of civilization than this new nation of America. The narrator reads in a Boston newspaper that Ibsen would deliberately mess his white hair so it looked untouched by a comb, and "joyfully survey himself in the mirror." The narrator does not know whether this is true or not, but in any case he longs to be like these artists:

> For good or bad, when you speak of a great Western poet, I am overcome with tears of adoration, and cannot but copy them. For the same reason I wear my hat on an angle deliberately and with a volume of poetry under my arm and a cherrywood cane in the other hand, I"ll look at my reflection in the mirror for awhile and then set out. . . . I"ll go to the tree-lined walk with the statues of Shakespeare, Scott and Burns, sit on a bench, and smoke a cigarette, facing them. The warm spring sun makes me dreamy, and I feel that I should be added to that line of poets, and I laugh softly to myself. (pp. 241–242)

Ito (1991) notes the tone of irony in the passage, the self-conscious artificiality of a Japanese in European disguise (p. 41). But this scene, depicting the narrator studying his image in the mirror, entails a double irony. Kafū writes in his diary that he spends June 9, 1906 in the park reading Maupassant's poetry—to lift his spirits, Kafū explains, he sometimes messes up his hair, puts on "a poetic appearance" as if tired of life, lies down on the grass between the trees and invites public censure: "let others laugh if they will." The passage in *Ochiba* thus presents an exact reflection of Kafū's own activities as described and constructed in *Saiyū-nisshishō*, right down to the details of the hair, the volume of poetry, and expecting the laughter of others. Kafū is recreating himself in the image of his literary heroes, an image carefully presented in both the journal and *Amerika monogatari*. The narrator of *Ochiba* next indulges in daydreams of a romantic future, writing in elegant English that attracts female American readers and buying a cottage on Long Island or New Jersey. But he finally succumbs to pessimism, the story ending with a long quotation from Baudelaire on the necessity of dreams and illusions for carrying on with a difficult human life. This quotation anticipates Kafū's search for an escape from reality in daydreams, alcohol, and the intoxication he finds in the slums and back alleys of New York.

Yoru no onna (Women of the Night), written April 1907, is a detailed account of the events of one night in a brothel in the back streets of the theater district near New York's Sixth Avenue. The madame, Mrs. Stanton, and her five regular girls are portrayed with all their flaws and quarrels as well as their good points, emerging as real people to the reader. The madame's room is an interesting mix of antique Western furniture and "bright Oriental colour" in a Japanese parasol, red lantern, and folding screen, perhaps imitating the rooms of Flaubert's heroines, but Kafū restrains the piece and limits it to a detailed description of the women and their work, allowing no room for authorial comment. The piece is entertaining in its transportation of the reader to a different world, and its realism and detail show Kafū's firsthand experience with brothels like Mrs. Stanton's, but perhaps the most we can say about this story is that it shows Kafū's interest in the darker side of New York with which most of the later stories are concerned. In particular, *Chainataun no ki* (A Record of Chinatown) and *Yoaruki* (Walking at Night) stand out in their bleak approach to the degradation and corruption of human life. Because of its singular treatment of the "Orient," *Yoaruki* is analyzed at length in Chapter 3, and so is not discussed here, but the two pieces are similar in tone and in Kafū's evident attraction to the New York demimonde. Keene, Seidensticker, and Ito agree that these stories show the influence of Baudelaire in their fascination with darkness and decay.[47] Until this point, Baudelaire has not been mentioned in the journal, but Kafū now refers to the author directly, and uses quotations from Baudelaire's poetry to enhance the depth of his own work.

Chainataun no ki begins with the narrator mulling over his own changeable moods and especially the ease in which he can sink into depression, gloom, loneliness, and thoughts of suicide or self-destruction. When he is in this state, the narrator seeks out the darkest side of the city, and "seized by an uncontrollable craving I wander through the night streets, the places where there might be corpses, beggars, people lying dead in the street—anything, as long as it is something ugly, pathetic or frightening like this" (p. 269). The narrator has been all over the city, "but it seems that there is no other place except the back streets of Chinatown, which people so fear and despise, where I can satisfy this dreadful desire. Here in the back street tenements is a virtual exhibition of immorality and shame, sickness and death, as if to show that human beings cannot sink any lower than this extreme point of corruption" (p. 269). The narrator describes how to get to the back alleys, where all the shops, restaurants, grocers, and houses display red paper lanterns, paper doors, and signs in Chinese characters, a different world, "as if the very light itself has been Sinified there" (*Shina-ka sashite iru*). Kafū takes us into the tenement building of a brothel, its yard with an outdoor toilet and pools of stinking water—and finds the sublime even there in drifting incense. From inside the building come the smells of cooking, incense, and opium, and also voices speaking the Chinese language "like monkeys screeching." Kafū is betraying his superiority complex here, but we are reminded that Japanese, too, are looked down on as "an inferior race, like animals" by American society, and only the American prostitutes who work here in Chinatown will take the Orientals as customers (p. 273). Kafū describes the awful scenes of the brothel as the women take opium, quarrel with the homeless, and abuse the hangers-on who also inhabit this other world. The narrator romanticizes the opium abuse, the *Paradis artificiels* of French poetry, and envies the prostitutes their courage and freedom in abandoning themselves to vice so completely, yet he leaves quickly when suddenly frightened by a violent argument. The scene reminds him of Baudelaire's cry on the ruin and dissipation of a life: "*Ruines! Ma famille! O cerveaux congeneres!*," and he concludes, "I love Chinatown. Chinatown is a treasure house of material for the poetry of *Les Fleurs du Mal*" (p. 277).

With these direct references to "the father of the Decadent School," and a stark, black outlook on the corruption and vice of the back streets of New York, it seems that Kafū has indeed been influenced by Baudelaire in the final stages of *Amerika monogatari*. Sakagami

Hiroichi (1997) likens the depictions of the derelict West Side in *Yuki no yadori, Yowa no sakaba, Yoru no onna, Chainataun no ki,* and *Yoaruki* to the realistic style and technique of Zola's naturalism, while taking after Baudelaire in the poetic sentiment of darkness and evil, recreating the atmosphere of the Decadent School's works (pp. 96–97). The collection *Amerika monogatari* may be interpreted as a journey through Kafū's own literary predilections, the influence of Zola strongest in the beginning, Maupassant through the middle sections and Baudelaire in the final few stories. Although this is oversimplifying the concept of literary influence, it does correlate with the record in *Saiyū-nisshishō* of the works that Kafū was reading at the time that the stories were written.[48] Many scholars have performed detailed comparative studies of the relevant texts, linking *Yoru no onna* to Maupassant's *La Maison Tellier, Chōhatsu* to *La Moustache,* and so on to show similarities in plot, structure, and stylistic techniques.[49] Akase (1976) and Iriye (1969) are persuasive in arguing that Kafū learned specific techniques from each of the French writers, while struggling to articulate new ideas in the Japanese language.

Kafū's pursuits in the field of the critical essay also reflect the progression in his interests during this time from Zola to Maupassant, while his references to and quotations from Baudelaire in 1907 reflect the influence of the Decadent School in the final stories of the collection. When *Amerika monogatari* was published as one volume in 1908, Kafū added another quotation from Baudelaire's *Le Voyage* to the finished whole. One of the main reasons that Kafū referred to Baudelaire so frequently at this time is because he obviously loved Baudelaire's work, and French literature in general—demonstrated by the many quotations from Musset and Maupassant, and the references to Zola and Loti, as well as Verlaine, Huysmans, and Daudet. Kafū was deeply moved by their writing and he idealized France as the country that produced such literature, music, and art. Iriye (1969) describes Kafū's relationship with French literature in terms of "resonance," suggesting that he found something in the French literature that perfectly matched his own feeling, allowing him to respond so strongly to the works and experience them so intimately (pp. 85–86). Meeting the artistic Other is always an aesthetic and personal experience, as one inevitably has an emotional reaction of some kind to the original work. Although Kafū does indulge in posturing and exaggeration, both in the diary and the travel stories, it is hard to overstate the depth of his emotional investment in the French literature.

Moreover, the works of these French writers enjoyed international popularity in the early twentieth century, admired for their bold experimentation with narrative structures and style, as well as their romantic, exotic, or thrilling subject matter. Kafū wanted to learn from these literary models in training to become a successful writer himself. Critics are divided on how deeply Kafū understood the French originals, with Iriye (1969) emphasizing his struggles with the language to argue that he remained fundamentally cut off from the source of his inspiration.[50] Without detracting from Kafū's passion, Akase (1976, p. 56) demonstrates his subjectivity in selecting Maupassant as his teacher, neither doubting Maupassant's method nor questioning how well he understood the material. More recently, however, Minami Asuka (2007) argued that Kafū gained great insight into the French poetry and literature through his translation work, maintaining that he not only understood what was written, in terms of content, but also how they were written, in terms of style (p. 60). Minami uses the word *tori-ireru* to describe what Kafū was doing with the French texts—literally taking the French words out of the original texts and putting them into his own works in Japanese. Translating poetry and literature word for word, the expressions, phrasing, and rhythms permeated Kafū's consciousness, and were then repeated in the structures and wording of his own Japanese sentences (pp. 74–75). Minami's assessment explains not only the close similarities between Kafū's texts and his models, but also gives us a practical vocabulary with which to articulate Kafū's relationship with French literature. Overall, it can be seen as an organic process of absorbing the structure, rhythm, and sound of French, as well as internalizing French ideas, imagery, ways of thinking, and ways of expressing. This view of Kafū's texts is useful when considering French literature in terms of Orientalism. If most nineteenth-century French literature and poetry was informed by Orientalist modes of thought, it would follow that this way of thinking would also have been expressed in both Kafū's translation practice and his own writing through this period. The Orientalist thinking of the Decadent School in particular makes its presence felt in *Rokugatsu no yoru no yume* (Dream on a June Night), written in July 1907.

Rokugatsu no yoru no yume is set on Staten Island, where Kafū spent the last month of his stay in America before sailing for France. Kafū's narrator is moved by the natural beauty of the island and the dreamlike summer nights. Even if he had the chance to see the Swiss summer, or the Italian spring, he would never forget the summer nights here:

> Now, with the sleeping ocean before me, the forest in repose behind me, half-buried in the tall wild grass, I look up at

> the countless stars in the vast, infinite sky, eavesdropping on the whispers of the myriad things of nature, and especially following with my eyes the sombre, tremendous rain of light from the fireflies, somehow I don't feel in my body that I am in the great continent of North America to which winter will surely come, because I am struck by a kind of strong sense of mystery and rapture—the kind which might wander under the skies of "the Orient,"[51] which poets of the so-called Decadent School sing of as the land of dreams. (pp. 295–296)

The sense of summer, wild nature, the infinite stars and rain of light present to the narrator an outlandish scene that he finds irreconcilable with the idea of "North America," which will soon experience winter—it seems as though summer here should be endless, and the strength of this feeling transports him to the "Orient," full of mystery and rapture (*shinpi, kōkotsu*). One result of the appearance of the Orient here is to reinforce the idea of America as the exotic representation of an idealized "West." Exactly one week after this the narrator is walking home and comes across a young woman in white holding a Japanese fan. The petite, blonde, blue-eyed Rosalyn represents the ideal American woman, and through the narrator's conversations with her, Kafū creates a perfect, idyllic West: "More than anything, I like to discuss the arts of the Occident since Greek times, with a Western woman—in English or in French, as long as it is a Western language—under a Western sky, on the banks of Western waters" (p. 298). The five repetitions of the word *seiyō* in this passage make the West an enduring, timeless place, and coming right after the lyrical evocation of the Orient, the contrast is a strong one.

On the surface, this story reads as a simple romance featuring Kafū's ideal woman, but we can note three significant points about it: First, it represents the culmination of Kafū's love for the Decadent School, French literature, and France itself, as Kafū finally leaves America to fulfill his dream. Second, we see the appearance of a particular kind of "Orient," originating in French art and acting as a place of boundless mystery on the one hand, and an alternative reality to the "West" on the other. Third, we have the reinforcement of "America" as representative of the wider "West," seemingly reverting to the simpler binary structures of mainstream Meiji discourse. The first two points lead directly to the next two chapters of this book, examining Kafū's France and Kafū's Orient, respectively. But the last point serves as a fitting conclusion to this chapter, as Kafū's "West" returns to the binary field. With the repeated emphasis on *seiyō* here,

Amerika monogatari has come full circle—dismantling the "sacred land of liberty," glorifying the wide open spaces and advanced technology, criticizing the superficial American democracy, and back to the endless summer of North America, rooted in classical tradition. Binarism and complexity are both present in *Amerika monogatari,* arguably in equal measures, each used at specific points to create the greatest possible effect. At the end of the collection, *Rokugatsu no yoru no yume* reminds us that the "West" is above all a construct, whether it be the homogeneous contrast to Japan or the complex nation beset by internal divisions. The story is a very romantic, poetic one, intensified by the knowledge that the narrator must soon leave. The ending sees the narrator boarding his ship for Le Havre, finally realizing his dream of traveling to France. This is a direct reflection of reality, as Kafū was transferred to the Lyon branch of the Yokohama Specie Bank, and sailed on July 18, 1907.

CHAPTER TWO

Imagining Authenticity

Literature and Civilization in Kafū's France

It is clear from the final stages of *Amerika monogatari* and Kafū's diary of 1906–1908 that it was the literature and lifestyle of France that captivated Kafū in New York. Given his view of America as merely a stepping-stone on the way to France, it is not surprising that the wish to complete his travels weighed heavily on his mind. As time dragged by without his father's permission to travel to France, Kafū had done what he could to bring "France" closer to himself. Immersed in French literature, Kafū wrote in the naturalistic style; referring constantly to French authors, he reminded his audience of his true aim in life. Neglecting American writers and the English language in favor of all things French, Kafū formed an exaggerated, romanticized ideal of France as the epitome of beauty and civilization. As France became the principal referent for culture and civilization in *Amerika monogatari*, the next collection of Kafū's travel stories, *Furansu monogatari*, saw France and Paris elevated even further to a timeless, perfect ideal. Where the "France" of *Amerika monogatari* may be understood as a crystallization of Kafū's longing to travel to the inside of Maupassant's novels, Paris had remained distant enough from New York for Kafū to be able to wield the brush of naturalism while still remaining grounded in reality. In contrast, the "France" of *Furansu monogatari* would come to efface reality almost completely. Whereas the stories set in Lyon show bold experimentation with naturalistic depiction and lyrical feeling, those set in Paris are almost overwhelmed by the artistic legacy of the capital city. This chapter examines how Kafū's expectations of France colored his observation and representation of that country, a process evident from the beginnings of *Furansu monogatari.*

The collection *Furansu monogatari* comprises the novel *Kumo* (Clouds), the play *Ikyō no koi* (Love in a Foreign Land), a selection of stories set in Lyon and Paris called *Furansu nikki* (Diary of France), a set of artistic vignettes called *Tochi no ochiba* (Fallen Horsechestnut Leaves), and four stories set on board the ship home to Japan entitled *Kaerimichi* (The Way Home). A further set of essays on Western music and drama make up the appendix. The collection as a whole was due to be published from Hakubunkan on March 25, 1909, but was banned on the day of its submission to the censors. The police worked so quickly in confiscating copies that none made it to the booksellers (Rubin, 1984, p. 117). The banning of the work certainly contributed to Kafū's persona and reputation as an oppositional writer, and elicited much discussion as to the authorities' reasons. The sexual content of *Furansu monogatari* is no more explicit than that of *Amerika monogatari,* and the critique against Meiji Japan may be seen as a continuation of that in stories such as *Ichigatsu ichijitsu.* Because most of the stories and essays had been published previously in other venues, some assumed that it was the novel and play that caused the most opposition. However, as Rubin points out, many of the other pieces include sections and passages that may have been equally objectionable (pp. 117–118). Kafū's portrayal of Japanese abroad as loose-moraled diplomats and whiny expatriates is certainly not limited to the novel *Kumo,* as parts of *Furansu nikki* show similar characters. Looking at the collection as a whole, however, Meiji authorities may have been most uncomfortable with Kafū's general attitude toward war, patriotism, and the nation-state (*kokka*).

Kafū commented on the banning of *Furansu monogatari* in a *Yomiuri Shimbun* article, stating that although he could not see how his work counted as "harm to public morals," neither was he surprised at its suppression. As a weak poet facing a strong government, in a nation where no artist ever arose to fight for the rights of literature in court like Flaubert and Baudelaire had in France, his own thoughts on the ban were "irrelevant," especially because the greater part of Japanese society was more concerned with winning wars than with artistic freedom.[1] Commenting on the banning of an Oguri Fūyō story later that year, Kafū concluded that writers and the authorities occupied two completely separate worlds. The state regarded fiction as merely "printed matter" rather than literature or art, holding no respect for either art or the artist. Rubin (1984) traces Kafū's famous anti-authoritarian stance of later years to these 1909 experiences with censorship (pp. 120–121). However, even before *Furansu monogatari* was banned in March, Kafū had already established an anti-authoritarian stance, seen in the critique of Meiji found in *Amerika monogatari* the previous year and developed further in the stories of *Furansu nikki, Kumo* and *Kaerimichi.* In France, Kafū reflected more on the role of the artist and his own writerly responsibility to address issues of individual freedom of expression. His artistic persona would become more political over time, culminating in his famous *gesakusha* stance of later years. This chapter focuses on the works of *Furansu monogatari* to analyze Kafū's critical stance toward the Meiji state, which intensified as he realized he must eventually return to Japan.

In terms of critical constructions of Self and Other, the dialectical element that we saw in *Amerika monogatari* is still present in *Furansu monogatari,* as Kafū continues to construct particular images of European and French Others for contrastive purposes. But as the French collection progresses, Kafū's own identity formation is also called into question, as he explores the problem of origins and the action of time upon civilizations and their people. The national character of "the Japanese" comes under scrutiny to a far greater extent than in *Amerika monogatari.* Where the earlier collection dealt in criticism and censure, it seems that a more mature Kafū is trying to pinpoint not just the differences between Japan and Europe, but what Japan itself is all about, where Japan came from, and how modern people should conceptualize their country. In this way, the abstraction of a national Self is given more attention in this work. The individual self also comes under greater scrutiny—the gentleman persona of *Furansu monogatari* is not just wondering where he fits in the society of Lyon and Paris, but starts asking "why am I Japanese, how did that come about, can I ever be anything else, and what does it mean to me to be Japanese?" The idea of authenticity—being true to one's origins, whether real or imagined—becomes increasingly significant in the collection as Kafū contrasts modern France with a modernizing Japan.

The foreword of *Furansu monogatari* states that the stories within represent Kafū's impressions of France as they struck him, written under trees, in parks, in cafés, and on board the ship home to Japan (KZ 3.347). This suggests that Kafū's observations of France would be fresh and natural. Before Kafū even arrives in France, however, his description of the shore betrays the extent to which his high expectations and reading of French literature would influence his perception of France. In the first story, *Fune to kuruma* (Ships and Trains),[2] the narrator is gazing at the approaching lights of Le Havre from the deck when a bright light suddenly shines out from the hills. The sight brings to mind scenes of the harbor depicted by Maupassant in *La Passion, Mon oncle Jules* and *Pierre et Jean,* and he looks around eagerly to compare the real harbor with the literary one (p. 351). Entering the harbor proper, the streets and houses of the town "glimmer in the light, like a stage set seen from far away." Compared with the tall, four-square buildings of New York, the narrator comments that these houses look particularly natural, beautiful, and small in scale, "looking remarkably like a picture" (p. 351). The French houses look unreal to the narrator, created for picturesque effect as in stage scenery or a painting. Next, he momentarily mistakes a casino for a house, ready to believe how huge and glorious French houses must be (p. 351). In the morning, the chill surprises him, as "it was strange to think that France would be such a cold place" (p. 353). The narrator shows disappointment as the France in front of him does not meet up exactly with the France of his imagination—the countryside is wet from rain, the sky overcast, far from the sunny and cheerful scenes of the Seine he had envisioned. At the train station, however, he is comforted by gazing at posters of Switzerland and southern Europe, which impart a strong feeling that "I was now standing with my own feet on the European continent" (p. 353). The narrator thus reconnects with his sense of place and reality through the medium of travel advertisements.

On the train to Paris, the narrator continues his artistic comparisons, commenting that everyone who reads Zola will know that the stretch of line running between Le Havre and Paris is the setting for the murderous events of *La Bête Humaine*. Craning his neck from the train window, however, he is disappointed that the scenery not only is not murderous, but fails to leave any particular impression at all (p. 354). Even so, he is delighted to find that the countryside is beautiful, especially when compared with the vast loneliness of the American plains. Indeed, the countryside hardly seems natural—the fields, the cows on the banks of rivers, the groves of trees and so on "were exactly like those I had seen in oil paintings for so many years" (pp. 354–355). The red-tile roofs of the country houses also have the narrator sighing in envy: "Ah, how the people who live here are the citizens of paradise!" The beginning of the story thus swings wildly between ecstatic raptures on the French countryside as a "paradise," and crashing disappointment when expectations are not realized. Both extremes have in common the notion of France as somehow unreal, only achieving a sense of reality when experienced through the representative medium of advertising, painting, or literature. The comparison of French scenes to paintings and plays in *Fune to kuruma* recurs often through *Furansu monogatari.* The technique has a distancing effect, separating Kafū the observer from the observed scene. Framing the scene in terms of an oil painting or a stage set also implies ownership and commodification, as one may purchase a painting or tickets to a play for one's own viewing pleasure. Similarly, travel advertisements imply leisured tourism, the commodification of seeing places. While these interpretations of his surroundings are primarily visual in nature, once Kafū arrives in Paris it is literary references that come to the fore.

Kafū's Paris is so informed by literary constructs that they sometimes threaten to overwhelm reality. In an essay entitled *Mōpassan no sekizō wo haisu* (Worshipping the Stone Monument to Maupassant, 1909), Kafū wrote that his first act in Paris was to visit the monument to Maupassant in the Parc Monceau.[3] Some critics take this statement at face value, but the visit is not mentioned in *Fune to kuruma* or the diary for July 1907.[4] However, whether this was in fact Kafū's first act in Paris is irrelevant. In the essay, Kafū is presenting Maupassant's monument as the first thing that he associates with being in Paris, as Paris is first and foremost the representation of the world of Maupassant's novels. That Kafū's "France" exists as an extension of its literary representation is evidenced time and again in the narrator's reactions to his surroundings. Pulling into the station in Paris, the narrator of *Fune to kuruma* sees the houses, flower gardens, and balconies of the city, but is struck most by the French women, who remind him of "the many heroines who had appeared in the French novels and plays that I had read up till now" (p. 356). It is a woman who makes the strongest impression on the narrator—the landlady of his hotel is large, aging and barrel-chested, a woman "just like those you often see in magazines or newspapers—a real matron of the city of Paris" (p. 357). Taking her suggestion to hire a cab so as to see as much as possible in his two days in Paris, the narrator takes in the famous Place de la Concorde, the Champs Élysées and the Arc de Triomphe, comparing the sights with their faithful representations in naturalistic novels:

> At all the places I saw and visited I was struck by how faithfully, how accurately the life of this city had been reproduced in the novels of French realism and the poetry collections of the Parnasse school I had read. . . . We realists of Meiji, had we studied Tokyo so accurately? I wondered if Meiji realism had matured enough to reach the level of the Naturalist and Symbolist schools that were already upon us. (p. 358)

In this passage, Kafū demonstrates that he is thinking about realism in terms of critical issues of representation, reproduction, accuracy, and observation. Moving on from merely seeing the content of French novels in his surrounding environment, he now recognizes the method of depiction itself, realizing the importance of accuracy for the realistic novel. The numerous references to paintings, literature, and advertisements before this passage have readied us for such a critical assessment, and act as a self-reflexive link between the narrator's behavior and Kafū's thoughts. The passage may also be read as Kafū reflecting on his own tendency to compare real scenes of France with images taken from French art, analyzing the process from the standpoint of a Japanese realist (*wareware Meiji no shajitsuha*). The question that plagues Kafū as an artist is whether he will be able to reproduce the France he sees in front of him in an accurate manner, and more to the point, whether he will be able to do so when his vision is compromised by expectation.

Isoda Kōichi (1989) once observed that for Kafū the reality of France existed as an imitation of its art (pp. 64–65). The subtext to Kafū's observations of America had been his vision of what France must be like, from reading French literature and trying to immerse himself in as much French culture as possible. This "France" functioned as the ideal of civilization to which America (and Japan) should aspire. When Kafū arrives in the real France, the subtext of *Amerika monogatari* is fulfilled. Kafū's whole perception of the country is colored by expectation and the thrill of finally arriving "inside the world of Maupassant's novels." It could be argued that the observations of Paris and the French people that fill *Furansu monogatari* are more like a recognition of parts of French texts or an affirmation of his own expectations than direct observation, as Kafū finds that "this is the place that Maupassant meant in this passage" or "these are the streets where Thérèse Racquin must have lived." Because of this recognition effect, the "France" in *Furansu monogatari* seems very similar to the "France" in *Amerika monogatari*. In this sense, there is some substance to the common criticism that *Furansu monogatari* is not as fresh in observation as the earlier collection (Keene, 1984, p. 405). There is quite some debate over the nature of observation in the two collections, however, so it is worth a brief comparison here.

Amerika monogatari is seen by many critics to be a fresh and unsullied observation of America by a writer new to the country, while others argue that French literature mediated *Amerika monogatari* to such an extent that we cannot speak of it in terms of pure observation. Both views take "pure observation" as some kind of gilt standard for successful travel literature. However, if we take observation as a theme rather than a method, *Amerika monogatari* may be seen as a prolonged meditation on observation itself. Vision is significant in many of the stories, and the subjectivity of the narrator often depends on whether he is seeing others or being seen by them. Two striking examples are *Akuyū,* where Americans become the "foreigners" in Seattle's Japantown, and *Rinkan,* with the narrator viewing the central action from his hiding place and commenting on the essential invisibility of African Americans in the nation's capital.[5] As suggested by the title of Suenobu Yoshiharu's 1997 book *Nagai Kafū no mita Amerika,* Kafū was in one sense a tourist, intent on observing the country for himself. But on the other hand, he was also a critically astute writer interested in the power dynamics operating between observer and observed. The final stories of *Amerika monogatari* combine the pure observation of naturalism with romantic and erotic scenes clearly derived from the Decadent School of literature. Pure observation was thus not idealized as a goal in itself for Kafū, who employed fantasy, dreams, and imagination to heighten the dramatic tension and reader interest. Taking a practical approach to the issue, we may view the combination of observation and romance as the culmination of Kafū's efforts to find a comfortable and effective literary style in this period.

Once in Lyon, Kafū would experiment with this combination further, mixing naturalistic observations with lyrical feeling and evocative modes of expression. Clues to his experiments are given in quotations that point to his literary models, notably Stendhal and Verlaine. Where the function of "seeing" in *Fune to kuruma* is limited to a recognition effect, once settled in Lyon Kafū was more able to "see" his surroundings and work on translating what he saw into the written word. This ambition is heralded in *Fune to kuruma,* in the passage cited earlier where Kafū recognized the importance of realism and accurate depiction. Kafū realized that the method of French novels was equally, if not more important than their content, and that this method could serve as his model as he continued to refine his personal writing technique. Interpreting the passage this way bears out Minami's (2007) argument that Kafū understood both the content and style of what he was reading in the French language (p. 60). Thus, although one could argue that *Fune to kuruma* is a prime example of the "recognition effect" in Kafū's writing, this particular passage is significant for demonstrating Kafū's ambition as a "Meiji realist."

Fune to kuruma ends on a sentimental note, as the landlady chats with the narrator about his upcoming trip to Lyon and presents him with one white rose to take on his journey. The rural scenes from the train window remind him of a poem by the pastoralist painter Jules Adolphe Breton, and fifteen lines of verse are quoted, first in French and then in Japanese translation.[6] Gazing at the passing fields the narrator slips into a dreamlike state, unable to distinguish between real scenery and his dreams, an effect heightened by moonlight and fog. Arriving in Lyon at 3:30 a.m., the narrator hurries off the train and takes lodging, waking in the morning to find he has left the white rose behind on the train: "It was probably in Marseilles by now. Or maybe it had been trampled on the way by other passengers coming and going" (p. 364). The narrator's first thought on waking is thus sorrow that his last tangible remnant of Paris has been left behind, rather than excitement at starting a new life in Lyon. *Fune to kuruma* was apparently written in July 1907 while Kafū was in Lyon, so he may have been even more disposed to look back fondly on his exciting arrival in the capital, in contrast to the gentler pace of life in the country.

The next six stories of *Furansu monogatari* are set in Lyon and the surrounding countryside, drawing on Kafū's experiences of working in the Japanese bank and exploring his new environment.[7] *Rōngawa no hotori* (The Banks of the Rhône), written in August 1907 in Lyon, is a romantic meditation on the nature of dreams and reality. Short and melodramatic, it follows the narrator's thoughts as he sits against a stone embankment on the Rhône, taking in the beautiful twilight after work. The narrator has been in France for two weeks, and feels mentally and physically exhausted. Allowing his mind to wander freely, he describes his emotions as his thoughts pass from one subject to another. Nostalgia for America is followed by a focus on what he can see before his eyes in the present moment, creating tension between reality and illusion. The hills, orchards, and houses on the opposite bank look hazy in the setting sun, yet also are surprisingly distinct in their detail, almost tangible yet out of reach (p. 367). The motifs of dream and illusion are linked to the fleeting experiences of travel, love, and happiness, all of which are destroyed by reality—one must return home, lovers forget one another, and perhaps it is better to die right now, he sighs melodramatically (p. 368). Opening his eyes, he believes he can hear songs, voices, and whispers in the rush of water flowing by. As the narrator strains to hear the voice of his loved one in his heart, reality intrudes again with actual voices of a young couple above the embankment. Eavesdropping on the couple, the narrator is plunged again into rapturous memories of his lover in America. However, as the girl above him mentions Italy, the narrator immediately starts wondering whether he will ever see Italy or Spain.

Weeping at the fickleness of his own heart, the narrator notices that night has fallen, ending the story.

Rōngawa no hotori could be taken as a very shallow, self-indulgent piece of work, but it is notable for the underpinning theme of dream and reality. The detailed attention given to the narrator's fleeting emotions and thoughts highlights the ephemeral nature of human feelings. Meditating on what he can and can't see, what he does or doesn't feel, what is real and what isn't, the narrator is able to distinguish between what he would like to be the case and what his actual situation is. Just as the time spent on the banks of the Rhône is an escape from work, a hiatus before returning to his lodgings, time spent in France is an escape from "real life" in Japan, where he will eventually have to return. Travel in Italy or Spain beckons as a way to prolong the dream, but in the end night will inevitably fall and reality will rule again. Following on from *Fune to kuruma,* which posited a "real" or "seen" France against a literary representation of France, we can see Kafū's deepening interest in the notion of reality, perhaps another indication that he wished to explore the method of a Meiji realist.

Moving from summer into autumn, *Aki no chimata* (Autumn Scenes) charts the changes in the evening light in different scenes across the town. Written in November 1907, this story may be seen as an experiment with formalism, as Kafū shifts skillfully between narrative modes to bring the town to life. A narrator, *jibun,* begins by noting how sensual is the climate of France, the melancholy of autumn clinging to the skin in the same way that the summer sun had burned into the flesh. As the evening closes in with the ringing of the Angelus, the next four paragraphs each begin *"kakaru toki . . ."* (at this time, and now . . .) as an omniscient observer looks here and there in the town, describing different scenes in detail. Coming after the reference to the Angelus, it is almost as if our gaze shifts with each ringing of the bell. Each paragraph focuses on the way that different kinds of light play on the town—first, the struggle between starlight and streetlights to make some impact on the fading light of day; then the reflection of houselights and streetlights in the eddying surface of the river, contrasted with the electric lights that line the bridges; next we have the bright lights of busy commercial streets, thronged with café-goers and the odd streetwalker; lastly the quiet gas lights of the parks, shining softly on lakes and flowerbeds as night closes in. Each kind of light gives a different feeling, mirrored in the movements and clothing of the people in the scene. The formal repetition and strong focus on light make this story powerful and evocative, a beautiful experiment in lyrical depiction.

In the first part of the story, Kafū seems to have left his affiliation for Zola far behind as he quotes from Lamartine, concerned more with the feelings called forth from the landscape in the shift from twilight to darkness. After a break in the text, the next section is bleaker, as Kafū describes the rainy autumn months and what it feels like to live in such wet conditions. There is no *jibun* here, but Kafū makes us feel the damp with words that evoke the senses: *mieru, kiku, kikoeru, hibiku,* and the reader is drawn into the gloomy and menacing back streets, where "windows are motionless and unpeopled, like the eyes of the blind" (p. 378). This section reverts to a stark Zolaesque depiction, with dogs fighting in the street and a blind musician appearing from nowhere. *Jibun* materializes to give the musician some change, and we follow the narrator home as he tries to cheer his spirits with wine and dinner. Quoting Verlaine's poetry, the narrator stands at his window and tries out some words in French himself—autumn, rain, night, lamp, travel, chill—as "at that moment the words felt like a profoundly meaningful poem" (p. 380). The power of stringing words together reflects the power of stringing images together, as the story coalesces into an image-poem. But Kafū is also invoking Verlaine as a famous symbolist poet, who believed that one could produce powerful moods in writing through the magic of words, with suggestion taking precedence over direct statement. Akase (1976) argues strongly that Kafū never really understood symbolist poetry and ideas, stressing the disjunction between the meanings of French and Japanese words in this passage (pp. 29–31), but Minami (2007) believes Kafū's translation of works by Verlaine and other symbolist poets gave him a strong sense of French rhythm, sound, thought, and expression, which then allowed him to articulate his own thoughts effectively (pp. 74–75). Kafū's use of Verlaine here seems both astute and contextually appropriate, as he is not only experimenting with technique but also signaling to the reader the theory behind the application. The subsequent referential shifts to Lamartine and Zola and back to Verlaine signal different narrative modes and descriptive techniques, which Kafū successfully blends together into one story.

Aki no chimata is remarkable because it is so clearly a literary experiment, but also reads smoothly and beautifully, suffused with a gentle air of calm. Throughout the work, the scenes are extremely vivid, real, and lifelike, as Kafū makes Lyon live on the page for the reader. Kabuto Hirokuni (2005) maintains that "*Furansu monogatari* has generally been criticized as a record of impressions of France that is sentimental, believing in the supremacy of art . . . but in actuality it is very exact (*seikaku*), a 'tale' that overlays the power of concrete depiction with narrative descriptions that are full of information" (p.

12). At the same time, Kabuto argues, the collection is marked by a "surprising power of evocation" (p. 12). It is this deft combination of lyrical feeling with detailed accuracy that makes the Lyon stories so compelling. This is Kafū at his best, not self-indulgent but working toward a literary accomplishment. With *Aki no chimata* Kafū has achieved the blend of observation and lyricism that he aimed for in *Amerika monogatari*. As if to underscore this achievement, the next work *Hebi-tsukai* (The Snake Charmer) opens with a quote from Stendhal, famous for blending realism and romanticism in the nineteenth century.[8] *"Je ne prétends pas peindre les choses en elles-même, mais seulement leur effet sur moi"* (I do not claim to paint things as they are, but only their effect on me) (p. 384).[9] The story certainly attempts to put this philosophy into practice, phrasing each description in such a way that we see the scene through the narrator's senses and the emotions aroused within him.

In terms of setting, *Hebi-tsukai* explores the countryside surrounding Lyon, the narrator making the most of the long daylight hours of midsummer. He explains his habit of taking either a train or a boat up the Saône River after work, to spend the evenings strolling in the outlying areas. In the first chapter Kafū describes the charming scenery along the banks, favoring old convent ruins and picturesque villages over the "ghastly herald of modern architecture" that is the nineteenth-century basilica of Notre-Dame de Fourvière (p. 385). The second chapter describes the cobbled streets of Couzon in a similar fashion, dwelling on the conservative, almost medieval nature of the country village, where political posters on street walls have no significance but for their beautifully faded blend of color (p. 388). Entering a restaurant, the narrator discovers from the waitress that the "volk" have come to town—gypsies who travel up from the south every summer to perform for a few days in each village.[10] The narrator is seized by romantic visions: "Wanderer. Nomad. Drifter. Ah, how melancholy and nostalgic is the sound of these words that echo so deep in my heart!" (p. 390). He imagines that such wanderers are free to die without a sense of duty to any family, while their companions can abandon the body on the roadside as they travel onward. Both men and women are depicted as "ignorant and cruel, deeply jealous, living their dirty, disorderly lives in their circus carts" and easily falling into swordfights over matters of love (p. 390). The reader's expectations thus aroused by his romantic fantasy, the narrator sets off in the direction of the gypsy fair.

The third chapter brings us to the gypsy encampment itself as the narrator describes the carts, stalls, and various entertainments on offer. Two dancing sisters come to life through vivid color and movement, and our interest is piqued along with that of the crowd as we read their advertising flags for a three-act play beginning behind the curtain. As a touter calls out some other attractions—"giant snakes from the South Seas, great crocodiles from Africa, Indian giant bats!"—a woman by the side of the stage stands dramatically, "takes a purple cloak from about her shoulders, and with a flip! to show the flaming colour of its underside, drops it from her body" (p. 395). This is the snake charmer of the title, a strong and mysterious presence on the stage, enchanting the audience with her performance as the snakes entwine around her figure. Her lips are "poisonously red," her expression fearsome. Just as the narrator is thinking in a detached manner that she must be over thirty, he hears a whisper go through the crowd as to what an attractive woman she is. At this moment, the dynamic between the author, narrator, and reader is revealed. Although the narrator claims that he is in no way attracted to the cold-blooded woman, it is clear from the audience's reaction that the woman has a powerful erotic presence. The narrator gives himself away when the woman leaves the stage and orders a cigarette from the touter: "Those expressionless, cold eyes didn't even reflect the presence of the onlookers, and the wisp of smoke escaping her lips drifted into the night sky" (p. 396). The narrator cannot take his eyes off her, even though the performance has finished, and he feels a sense of sexual rejection—she does not acknowledge his presence, and while her lips touch the cigarette, the resultant smoke drifts away, emphasizing the lack of human contact.

The fourth chapter heralds a change of season, as the narrator tries to make the most of the remaining sunny days before the rains, floods, and fogs of autumn set in. Hating to waste his days working inside at the bank, the narrator plays truant one day to climb the hills of Croix-Rousse, where he sees an advertisement for the "volk" who will visit the Croix-Rousse festival. The narrator casts his mind back to that midsummer evening among the gypsies, and yearns for something new in his own life. Lost in thought, he encounters the gypsies again in the square facing an old church. He wonders whether the dancing girls and snake charmer are among them. Sitting in the fading October sunlight, surrounded by small children, a woman concentrates on her sewing. Her figure is soft, with bare shoulders and no corset, but covered by a shawl. It is the snake charmer, appearing completely different in her domestic role. As she picks up her crying baby to soothe it, the narrator is overcome with melancholy. The prosaic reality of the snake charmer's life leaves him feeling empty, as the illusion of her powerful performance is shattered. However, it is a credit to Kafū's skill here that the romance of the gypsy life remains intact. The fact that the terrible, awe-inspiring snake charmer is also "a mother holding her baby" highlights the impermanence of the stage life and the fundamental unreality of the narrator's imagined gypsy existence. Stendhal's quotation is revealed as particularly apt in the depiction of the snake charmer, as Kafū portrays both the woman and the narrator through the emotions she arouses in him. In her first appearance on stage, she is awe-inspiring, powerful, silent, masklike, inhuman, bestial, statuesque, magical, seductive, and oblivious to the narrator's existence. The vision of the woman as mother elicits a completely different feeling—she is sexually attractive in her dishevelment, but also motherly, human, real, ignorant, pathetic, with a dim air of melancholy that clings to the narrator's skin. The figure of the snake charmer is one of Kafū's finest characters. Seeing her through the narrator's eyes, feeling the depth of his emotion, her image remains in the reader's mind long after finishing *Furansu monogatari*.

It is a common claim that Kafū hated his time in Lyon, critics using this story and the next as evidence. It is certain that as the weather closed in, Kafū would have felt more restricted, unable to explore the countryside and resentful of time spent indoors at the bank. The narrator of *Hebi-tsukai* links this feeling to jealousy of the gypsies' freedom:

> My position, shut up in the same small room year round, spreading out the same account books in the same way, grew more and more distasteful. Despite being overseas, living in the tight confines of the Japanese community is the same as being cooped up in Tokyo. I'm sick of Lyon already. I want to see some new, different sky. New things always look beautiful—they bring fresh air to the weary heart. They give subtle stimulus to dulled nerves. I thought again of the homeless wanderers of the circus people, their circumstances seeming even more poetic. . . . (p. 398)

Although this passage expresses negative feelings toward his job at the bank, the story as a whole captures the life that Kafū would like to lead in his dreams, as a traveler and wandering exile. Kafū's own exile has become prosaic, utterly unlike the romance of his imagination. *Hebi-tsukai* celebrates the narrator's love of travel, his longing to see new things, experiencing the scenery of southern France and enjoying the woods and air of this new country.

The next story, *Bansan* (The Dinner), addresses the expatriate experience more directly.[11] The narrator fulfils Kafū's ideal of a traveler, having come to Europe five or six years ago. At a dinner in Lyon he meets one of his old school friends, Mr. Takejima, who now works at a bank. It is Takejima who comes under scrutiny in this story as Kafū shows how years working abroad can change a person, often for the worse. It is undoubtedly this story that critics have in mind when they say Kafū hated Lyon and the Japanese community there. Takejima is everything that Kafū does not want to become: a loud, flashy boor, while the other bankers and manufacturers at the table are not much better. Dinner conversation is circular and predictable, the men urging each other to drink and comparing Japanese geisha to French women. The company concludes that the West (*seiyō*) is boring, too cash-oriented and calculating, while not slow-paced enough. The president drones on about the main bank versus its branch offices, while his wife complains about living expenses. The bankers discuss their salary, rent, and bills, and talk turns to the sneaky tricks of gossip columnists in the Japanese newspapers. Although the narrator expects that this criticism of Japan will lead to praise for the West in comparison, the talk just turns in on itself and never gets beyond complaints (pp. 406–409). Certainly, Kafū is painting the expatriate community as insular and narrow-minded in this scene. Leaving the party, the narrator ends up in a bar with Takejima and a new bank employee named Takata, who has only been in France for ix months. Takejima shows off, ordering champagne and toasting his companions in French—*votre santé*—with no translation given. He offers the narrator expensive Egyptian cigarettes and rebukes Takata for absent-mindedly playing with his precious silver cigarette case. Takejima coldly relates how his wife has been waiting for him at home these five years, while he lives the single life in Lyon. On cue, three women appear and flirt with the group. The narrator and Takata are increasingly ill at ease, until two other Japanese acquaintances of Takejima's appear and they seize their chance to escape. The narrator wishes he could have talked quietly with Takejima about their school days, and ends up sadly walking the banks of the Rhône by himself in the night air.

The narrator and Takejima in *Bansan* are almost complete opposites: The narrator is educated without showing off, can drink without getting drunk, is generally polite and considerate, and truly wishes to communicate with others. He desperately misses the companionship of old times, especially as he has been away from Tokyo for so long, but being away for five years has not affected Takejima in the same way. Takejima is insulated within the Japanese community, not trying to experience French life by making a home there with his wife, but frittering away his time with bar girls. Ironically, it is not even a French bar he chooses, but an Anglophile pub called London House. The expatriates in *Bansan* may be compared with those in *Ichigatsu ichijitsu* from *Amerika monogatari*—very negative when taken as a group, but having the effect of singling out the narrator as a different kind of expat Japanese. He is not a long-term worker overseas, but a traveler passing through, a cultured gentleman sensitive to the feelings of others. Both stories serve to enhance Kafū's chosen persona, and act to separate his daytime role as a bank worker from his "real" life as a writer once six o'clock strikes and he can sit on the banks of the Rhône or write in his diary. Kafū's attempt to argue that one must make the most of one's time overseas and try to experience local culture is ironic, given his determination to avoid speaking English and to live a French life while in New York. On the other hand, the pain of seeing others waste such a tremendous opportunity to experience life in his beloved France must have been very real.

In short, Kafū's time in Lyon was by no means as bad as some critics would have us believe. Both versions of his diary at the time,[12] as well as the Lyon stories of *Furansu monogatari*, show someone enjoying the new atmosphere of the countryside, taking long walks in and around town, making train and riverboat trips, in all seasons, faithfully recording the vastly different moods of the town according to whether it was sunny, raining, or wrapped in thick fog, night or day, after a storm, early morning, the streets empty of people due to bitter cold or crowded on a festival night. The reader can see Lyon in all its moods, and it is clear that Kafū got to know the city well in his eight months there. Following Kabuto Hirokuni's map of the city, showing key places from *Furansu monogatari* (including London House), one can easily see that Kafū's directions were all accurate and based on reality.[13] Kafū took a painterly interest in his surroundings and used his time in Lyon well, trying out different literary techniques after models like Stendhal and Verlaine as well as pastoralist painter Jules Breton. Although the stories so far have all been set in Lyon, the next story takes us to the very south of France.

Matsuri no yoru gatari (Tale of a Festival Night) features two narrators, a real "tale" recalling the narrative structures of *Amerika monogatari*. *Jibun* and his friend go way back, and now they are both in France, although both are such poor correspondents that neither knows where the other is at any one time. *Jibun,* therefore, is stunned to run into his friend in the middle of a crowded Lyon street on a festival night in December. The friend has run out of money on a recent ill-fated trip to the Côte d'Azur. The friend takes over the tale as *boku,* describing his profligate ways when he arrived in France.

Realizing that his money could not last forever, he had vowed to stop spending it on women and planned to take a trip to the south—starting in Marseilles and possibly going on to Italy if the money held out. Told by a man on the train of the glorious ruins of Avignon and Arles, however, he leapt out at Avignon on the spur of the moment. The atmosphere conjured up by the castle walls made *boku* feel "completely separated from modernity (*kinsei*)" and transported to a strange era, like something out of Boccaccio (pp. 425–426). The character of the "south of France" emerges as distinct and unlike any other place: "It was already November. To the north, Lyon would be in fog, Paris in rain, but this ancient city of Provence felt warmer even than Spring of the soft evening breezes, and the leaves of the plane trees were still luxuriantly green. The color of the sky and the sparkle of the stars were so bright—common in the south of France, but unthinkable in any other country" (pp. 426–427). The "south of France" may thus be seen as the third construction of a French Other in the collection, drawn in contrast to Lyon and Paris.

As he explores the Roman section of the city, *boku*'s footsteps echo off the close stone walls of the cobbled streets. Suddenly he hears a guitar, but with a different timbre than usual—it is "a sound that wells from the captivating, warm, fragrant and languid emotions of the South" (p. 427). The narrator imagines the soft, full breast of a woman, throbbing under thin nightwear as she sleeps . . . but interrupting his vision, the guitar music stops and he sees a light in a window. A quotation and reference to Baudelaire enhance the romantic fantasy of the moment and heighten the dramatic tension (p. 428). When a woman appears at the balcony, the narrator impulsively blows her a kiss. She disappears, and the narrator is filled with regret at having blown his chance at a beautiful rendezvous, never experienced "by us Northern people" (*wareware kita no ningen*). This identification with the North is significant. We know from the first narrator that the two friends come from Japan, but this comment draws a dividing line between prosaic North and passionate South, with Japan clearly located on the North side of the divide. This small aside shows us the versatility of Kafū's worldview, forgoing the usual East–West dialectic to create a particular North–South contrast. The comparison underlying the story is no longer about just the north of France and the south of France, but about "North" and "South" as distinct hemispheres with their own conventions and rules of discourse. The woman reappears at street level to open the door to the narrator, proving that what one might expect in the North is not what happens in the South.

After a break in the text, the narrator claims that for people with no imagination, living in Lyon, Paris, London, or indeed anywhere, nothing could be stranger than this woman waiting in the night for someone she has never seen or met. But for the narrator, nothing seems strange. Rather, it is just as when Caesar caught sight of Cleopatra's sleeping form at the foot of the Sphinx, under the stars in the midst of the Egyptian desert (p. 429). The close juxtaposition of Northern place names like Paris and London with words like "Caesar," "Cleopatra," "Sphinx," and "Egypt" here is startling. Standing at the doorway, the narrator is in a transitional state, passing from Northern to Southern sensibility. He has fallen under the woman's spell just as Caesar did in ages past. This timeless construction of the Orient serves to exoticize the south of France to a high degree, taking the tale out of the realm of the mundane and into the realm of fantasy and legend. The ensuing scene throbs with sexual tension, as the woman invites the man in and he follows her vague form up the stairs and into her bedroom, wondering if she is wearing anything in the dark. The woman throws herself on the bed and the narrator is left to gaze about the room himself. Regarding the bed, "the disarray was stunning . . . petticoat, pantaloons, underwear, brassiere, stockings—all the things I would never see in the light of day were piled and coiled, lying and hitched up on the chair in all their colors and shapes, in varying degrees of soil" (pp. 430–431). High-buttoned boots and ribboned garters are abandoned on the floor, while the woman lies with sheets peeled back and pillows thrown aside. The narrator rises from his couch, unable to resist the pull of such a scene any longer. Kafū's narrator lives out the fantasies of his young male readers in Japan, but the end of the story brings us back to reality.

The next night, the narrator is taken in by a staged scene between the woman (whose name we find out is Paulette) and an athletic young man in a café, and he misses his train to Marseilles in order to stay with the woman as her protector. Finally catching his train on the fourth day, he feels he has "arrived in the absolute south of France" (*mattaku no minami Furansu e kita*) when the train stops at Tarascon. Soldiers from the African colonies are on the platform, while the women remind the narrator of Daudet's works. Cheered by the bright sky and noisy surroundings, the narrator continues to Marseilles, where he discovers all his money has gone, the result of paying for five days' and nights' worth of expensive food and drink for Paulette. Suddenly downcast, all the cheerful things "that can only be seen in a bright southern port" have lost their power to console him. Feeling thoroughly deceived, the narrator leaves Marseilles without even tasting its bouillabaisse. Although the fantasy of the "south of France" painted a bright picture of passion and romance, the seductive image is revealed to be dangerous and above all, deceptive. Kafū seems to be drawing the reader's attention to the disjunction between image and reality, as if to warn us that his constructions of the Other are just as untrustworthy as Daudet's.

The last of the Lyon stories, *Kiri no yoru* (A Foggy Night) is set in winter, at the turn of the New Year.[14] Driven out to the foggy streets by the monotonous boarding-house dinner, the narrator comes upon a New Year's market across the Lafayette Bridge. Looking at the faces of the hardworking stall owners, he reminisces about a similar night years ago. He had attended a cheap cabaret with an aging dancer on stage, well past her prime but doing her best to put on a good show. In the details of her appearance, from the loose dry skin at her neck to the small eyes peering from thick makeup, the pathos of the woman's performance is perfectly conveyed, and the narrator finds himself gripped by sympathy for her situation. His thoughtful frame of mind carries over to the conductor, who surely must long to play Mozart or Beethoven, and even the old flower-seller, who must have had a different life once. Outside on the foggy streets, he finds no solace—the thought of entering a bright café makes him think of the harsh lives of the poor waiters, while he can't catch a train home without pitying the driver on such a cold night. Plodding along the streets, the confusion of back alleys reminds him of the poetry of Baudelaire. Lost in a reverie of corpses and murderers, the narrator is surprised by the footsteps of two women. Blasting him with alcohol breath, the taller woman tries to solicit his favor, but she is of such a low class and bedraggled appearance that the narrator is put off. Irritated, she offers her sister instead, whom she promises is a virgin of fourteen. Just as the narrator is wondering how to get out of the tricky situation, a new set of footsteps comes along, breaking up the conversation and rescuing him. A break in the text brings us back to the present, where the narrator concludes that walking on a cold foggy night will always remind him of that experience. In the midst of the New Year celebrations, he is mindful of the factory children working through the night, the café waiters and train drivers, and is gripped with the old sense of pathos as he crosses back over the bridge.

The plight of the worker and the harshness of existence for the poor are clearly expressed in this story, even though the narrator's melodramatic expression makes it overly sentimental. Akase (1976) criticizes the story for its shallow treatment of Baudelaire, describing

Kafū as a mere fan who did not fully comprehend the pain that inspired *Les Fleurs du Mal* (p. 36). The story is somewhat self-indulgent, whereas the narrator's bourgeois guilt is overstated and therefore unbelievable. What stands out in *Kiri no yoru,* however, is the desperation of the dancer on stage and the rough, bold attitude of the older streetwalker. Taken together with the sexual power of the snake charmer and the seductive Paulette all dishevelled in her twisted sheets, the women of these stories possess great depictive force. As with *Amerika monogatari,* the figure of the foreign seductress was popular with Japanese audiences and would have boosted sales at home (see Snyder, 2000, p. 47). The figure of the narrator is also similar in both collections, a cultured gentleman who observes others from a distance while inwardly negotiating his social position in relation to them. Although the characters are similar, the literary techniques have developed. There is more play on the idea of fantasy versus reality as a theme, with many of the stories incorporating deception, performance, dreams, and the contrast between travel and "real life." In terms of the narrative method, there is a more determined effort to follow French models in order to combine lyrical expression and feeling with accurate observation. Overall, Kafū's attempts to bring theme and method together in the Lyon stories show his renewed interest in developing his writing skills and exploring the meaning of being a Meiji realist.

Kiri no yoru ends with the clock striking the New Year for 1908, as the narrator passes back over the Lafayette Bridge. This bridge played a large role in Kafū's own life at this time, marking a turning point between his experiences in Lyon and Paris. In his original draft diary, kept in a notebook marked "Agenda pour 1908," Kafū begins the New Year with the question of whether to return to Japan or commit suicide. He is in low spirits overall—feeling ill, disappointed not to have heard from Edyth, and wanting to quit work at the bank. In both the original and published versions of his diary, Kafū writes to his father and mentor about quitting his job, and goes to visit the bank manager to discuss his desire to leave. But the diaries diverge on the circumstances of Kafū actually leaving his position. In the Agenda, Kafū himself "finally puts in his formal resignation at the bank" on March 5, while the published edition of *Saiyū-nisshishō* has Kafū "finally receiving his discharge from the bank."[15] On March 21, in the Agenda, Kafū is wondering whether to go back to Japan and struggle to make a living as a writer, or return to New York for a life of dissipation (KZ 19.63). The published version does not consider the option of returning to Japan, as he does not want to see his father, but he is in equal torment over whether to go to New York (KZ 19.52-3). Later that week, on March 27, the Agenda shows Kafū's colleagues giving him a farewell dinner, after which he stops for a moment on the Lafayette Bridge (19.63). In the published version, the vice-manager of the bank comes to Kafū's boarding house to offer him a farewell party to make up for having treated him badly, but Kafū feels he has nothing to say to them now, and goes for a solitary walk along the river instead (19.53). Both versions show the writer weeping as he watches the water flow under the bridge, and the next day he buys a ticket to Paris. The minor differences between the diaries point to the persona that Kafū was creating for himself. The mild-mannered Kafū of the Agenda tenders his own resignation, considers returning to Japan and attends the bank dinner, whereas the more defiant Kafū of *Saiyū-nisshishō* gets the sack, proclaims his hatred of his father and refuses to see his colleagues again. The published version is certainly more dramatic, painting Kafū's life in Lyon as unbearable and making his "escape" to the capital more effective.

Kafū arrived in Paris on March 28, 1908 and left on May 28. As he was only able to stay for two months before his money ran out, the problem of dwindling time and resources would have been constantly on his mind. These limitations undoubtedly would have made Kafū's time in Paris seem more precious. Many studies of Japanese literature of the Meiji period have taken Lacanian desire for the unobtainable Other as a base. In this vein, Paris could be read as the distant exotic Other far superior to Japan and constantly out of reach.[16] But there is a wide and diverse range of material to be considered. Many Japanese writers and artists took France as their primary cultural referent, and France may be seen as providing a major point of contrast for Meiji-Taishō literature (Akase, 1995) as well as postwar Japanese thought as a whole (Slaymaker, 2002). French culture and literature had an enormous impact on Japanese literature and intellectual discourse, much of which saw Paris as the "city of flowers," a beautiful model to be emulated, with varying degrees of angst over whether the goal was reachable. Not all artists responded to France in the same way, whether or not they traveled there themselves. Of those who did travel to Paris, all had different attitudes about both France itself and what it meant to travel there. Mitsuko Iriye (1969) describes the experience of Shimazaki Tōson as essentially insular, as he was content to read French literature in translation and associate mostly with fellow Japanese (pp. 97–100). Yokomitsu Riichi, by contrast, experienced Paris as a truly global city in the 1920s, on par with Shanghai and Tokyo in its bustle and international outlook (Slaymaker, 2006). France provided a wide range of literary stylistic models, while different writers could take a single text in very different ways, as was the case with Kafū, Katai, and Tōson reading Maupassant's *Sur L'eau.* It is impossible to generalize about the meaning of Paris or French literature for all Japanese writers, or to say that Paris represented an "unobtainable Other" for everyone. In Kafū's case, he had the good fortune to be able to travel to France and Paris himself, satisfying his desire for travel, as well as the desire to consume French foods, entertainment, literature and the arts, and women. Although getting to Paris had been problematic, Kafū had been able to surmount such obstacles as his father's opposition and lack of funds to actually reach his destination. Once in Paris, however, Kafū experienced a deep sense of dissatisfaction. Having reached his lifelong goal, what was he to do next? And could he live the true bohemian life without actually being French? Now he had arrived in Paris, Kafū's object in life was not to get there but to stay there, to find some way of being French himself. This goal, to actually change his essence and origins, is what we may see as "unobtainable" in Kafū's French experience.

Most Japanese writers and artists who lived in Paris over the years experienced an existential double bind—at once wanting to fully join the community of artists in Paris, and yet remaining Japanese in identity, appearance, and native language. This double bind has produced the deepest emotional frustration as well as the subject matter for searching works exploring identity, hybridity, and the possibility of living in two different worlds at the same time. We see it in Fujita Tsuguharu's fashionable costume and flamboyant "Parisian artiste" lifestyle as well as Endō Shūsaku's struggle with Catholicism and religious pluralism.[17] Kafū has much in common with both artists, displaying the outward hybridity of Fujita while inwardly struggling with the keenly felt pain of his outsider status in the country. Iriye (1969) describes Kafū's encounter with the French language and literature as one of despair, rejection, and self-hatred, as the linguistic barrier between himself and his artistic idols proved insurmountable (pp. 54–55, 96). But Kafū's frustration may be seen as running even deeper than this, as he realized that his goal—becoming French—was an impossible one. The inability to change his origins made a deep impact on his work at this time. Kafū's Paris stories, with their investigations into origins and their role in identity formation, provide another way of analyzing his thoughts about France. What we might call Kafū's mindset or *shisō* in regard to France—this thinking about origins, one's own culture, one's own authentic heritage, is also what would set him on the path to understanding the problems of Meiji Japan.

The first story set in Paris, *Omokage* (Traces) begins: "For how many years now had I been dreaming of the life of the Quartier Latin, the student area of Paris?" (p. 458). The narrator's dreams had been fuelled by Ibsen's play *Gengangere* and Puccini's *La Bohème*, along with a host of other works by Maupassant, Bourget, Zola and others that acted as his "guides" (*annaiki*) to the area.[18] Moving in to the Quartier Latin himself, the narrator realizes his dreams and Paris emerges as the ideal city of beauty, gaiety, and civilization. A list of famous buildings in and around the quarter is enlivened by Kafū's vision of the student life, the bustling halls of the many colleges in the city, and the overwhelming image of Paris as the center of European learning, as students travel here from as far away as Egypt and Turkey (p. 459). Kafū describes the student quarter in terms of its theaters and bookshops, the music that spills out into the street from windows where youths practice their violin and piano, and the cafés that come alive with music and dancing after dark. The description of the area ends by noting a certain type of woman on the street, distinguished by their makeup and points of dress—"these are the harlots of the Quartier Latin, often found in poems and novels" (p. 460). The beginning and end of the narrative introduction thus point to literary sources for the narrator's image of the quarter. Once this image is set, *jibun* makes his appearance in person, stopping at a café on the way home from dinner. As *jibun* gazes around the café, we are treated to a detailed portrayal of the scene, including all five senses and heightened by words appearing in French text, representing the voices of customers and waiters shouting above the din. The words carry no gloss to show the meanings or pronunciation, so as not to lose the rhythm and effect of the sound that envelops the narrator. Minami (2007) suggests that this long descriptive prelude shows Kafū's sheer joy at being able to recreate the atmosphere of a Parisian café in words, and to convey that joy to his readers (p. 128). Kafū is so successful that by the time the female character appears, the reader feels as if they were eavesdropping on a conversation happening at the next table.

The central story unfolds as a woman sits in a nearby empty seat, catches the narrator's eye, and says, "You're from Japan, aren't you." The narrator has no way of knowing how old the woman is, thinking that Parisian women are truly ageless (p. 464). It turns out that the woman was intimate with the famous Japanese painter Tsukuhara when he was in Paris ten years previously, and had often modeled for him. The woman shows the narrator a ring Tsukuhara had given her, and he recognizes it from a famous nude painting that had caused a great stir in Japanese art circles.[19] The narrator had once written an essay on the painting for a magazine, and is stunned to find that the "Naked Beauty" herself is sitting right across from him.[20] Tsukuhara was the first of many Japanese lovers she had taken, and she tells the story gazing deeply into the narrator's face, as if nostalgic for the Japanese visage. When the woman reveals the names of some of her lovers, now old men or dead, the narrator realizes that while he will go back to Japan to join their ranks of "sullen, bitter faces," the woman will remain youthful in Paris, enjoying the nightlife and music forever (p. 470). Although he asks her name, he is unable to bring himself to ask her age. The band strikes up Jules Massenet's *Thaïs* (1894), a piece of music about a young Egyptian prostitute who asks the goddess Venus for eternal youth and beauty. Oblivious to the significance of the music, the woman merely taps on the table with the fingertips of her ring hand (p. 471).

The famous nude model of *Omokage* thus remains ageless, removed from the processes of time, standing for the greater myth of the ageless Parisian woman from the poems and stories of French literature. The title word *omokage* appears in hiragana, but can mean a memory, a person's face, or the traces of something left behind. The woman sees the traces of her own memory within the narrator's Japanese face, but the narrator is unable to see anything within her face except a mixture of sorrow and experience under the careful veneer of cosmetics. The made-up face acts as a mask of timelessness, linked to Egypt and the Orient (as it was in *Matsuri no yoru gatari*). Through the figure of the "certain type of woman," Paris itself becomes associated with timeless beauty, sexuality, and Oriental mystique. In this instance, the association is effected primarily through literary and artistic references: The courtesan is first and foremost a character from French literature, while her setting, the Quartier Latin, is the background of opera and the theater. Kafū's construction of a timeless "Orient" through literary and artistic reference is a recurring motif treated at length in the next chapter. But this aspect of timelessness is certainly significant for *Omokage* as a whole. In normal circumstances, the passage of time causes marks of change on the face, as well as old age and death. However, a contrast is drawn between Japan as a place where time clearly changes a man, and Paris as a place where women remain unchanged. For the narrator, Paris and France become part of an illusory world that cannot last, as he must bow to his inescapable fate and return to Japan.

The tantalizing world of Parisian cafés reappears in the next story *Saikai* (Reunion), which opens on an elegant boulevard by night. Men in silk hats stroll past jewelry shop windows with beautiful women on their arms, whereas others alight from carriages in the bright lights of the cafés (p. 478). Happy to be jostled by the crowd and drunk on the dizzy movement of the traffic, *jibun* is concerned for his friend Shōu, who seems quiet and somewhat depressed. The two men used to live in New York and often shared dinner together, and they reminisce at length about the city over the course of the evening. The narrator attempts to cheer Shōu by pointing out how much better Paris is than New York (pp. 479–480), but it seems to have little effect. When Shōu comments that he seems happy in Paris, the narrator replies:

> You could say I am beyond happiness. It is not enough to merely say "happiness." When I think that I may be breathing the same air, living on the same ground upon which so many of the French artists suffered and agonized for their art, from Classicism to Romanticism, from Romanticism to the Symbolism of the present day, a feeling arises which is much more than simple happiness—a much deeper, more passionate feeling. (pp. 480–481)

It is not just the brightness of the scenery that captivates the narrator, but the resonance of French art and literature throughout the city. France is not only the raw material for literature and oil paintings, but is the atmosphere that produced the artists themselves, and "Paris" for Kafū was not so much the city itself as the place where his favourite authors lived and wrote their masterpieces. Komori Yōichi (1997) writes that because the symbols that make up the represented "Paris" are of history and art, we may say that Kafū perceives Paris through a literary-historical framework (p. 127). However, it is also clear that Kafū sees this artistic Paris carrying through to the present day. In the passage above, the present and past are collapsed into a timeless whole, so that the narrator not only feels close to artists of the past but can also breathe the same air and walk upon the same ground as them. By collapsing time in this manner, Kafū changes the nature of his relationship with the artists, so they can occupy the same space. This positioning of the narrator in time and space leads naturally to the question of identity in the Paris stories—why can the narrator not live in Paris his whole life and become a Parisian person? It is in this sense that Paris becomes an "unobtainable Other" in Kafū's work.

As *jibun* and Shōu reminisce about America, Kafū uses direct binary contrast in order to represent Paris as an ideal Other to New

York, a place where art and civilization are prized and the whole city acts as a monument to artistic endeavor. In *jibun*'s glowing testament, Paris is better than New York in all respects—whereas the overhead trains in New York were enough to drive one insane with headaches, here in Paris the air is filled with the gentle sounds of women's laughter and violin music (pp. 479–480). In Paris, Gorky would be treated with respect and *Salome* would never have been banned. America falls far short of the ideal civilization represented by Europe and Paris in particular. Where American newspapers ignore the arts, French papers celebrate the election of even the most minor artist to the Academy. Americans erect statues to their presidents, whereas Paris is filled with statues to poets, artists, and scholars (p. 480). Saitō Ichirō (1992) uses this passage to demonstrate that Kafū idealized Paris as a perfect example of what "civilization" should be like. Saitō's article examines the passion for Paris shared by Kafū and the Goncourt brothers in such a way that it becomes clear that all three writers are creating a "mythical" Paris rather than the real city of Paris, a distillation of elegance and beauty, in contrast to other places.[21]

While Kafū certainly is using contrast in order to represent the French Other in a particular way, however, the "New York versus Paris" comparison should not be taken at face value. The contrast is established in a particular context, the narrator deliberately painting Paris as better than New York in order to cheer up his depressed friend. Immediately preceding this passage, the narrator recounted some fond memories of New York and both men recalled the city with affection. The comments about American public opinion holding sway over art, resulting in the banning of *Salome* and the harsh treatment of Gorky, are repeated in Kafū's diary, and we can certainly imagine that the din of elevated railways and so on caused legitimate complaint. But Kafū is careful to show that Paris, too, can lose its lustre after the initial love affair with the city has worn off. The original title of *Saikai* was *Seikō no nayami* (The Burden of Success),[22] referring to Shōu's depression. He explains that for two or three months, he too had been "wrapped in passion" for the city (p. 481), but was eventually overcome by loneliness and melancholy. Although he achieved success in his artwork, receiving recognition for his sketches, once his dream was fulfilled he found himself empty: "I who had not been able to even touch my brushes once a week in New York had no sooner come to France than my dream of becoming an artist was realized. When every single thing turns out as your heart desires, I tell you, it's strange. I felt all the spirit knocked out of me, as if I'd been poleaxed" (p. 484). The opening of *Omokage* referred to the narrator's dreams of the Quartier

Latin, and one feels that the narrator of *Saikai* is also looking forward to living out his dream in Paris. But once the dream is realized and success has been attained, there may be nothing to look forward to. Shōu confides that travel is the last refuge of his own dreams now. Although he would like to travel to Italy, he never will: "At least I want to keep the blue skies and seas of Italy for the eternal dreams of my heart, without actually seeing them" (p. 486).

As the attainment of desire is problematized in the different perspectives of *jibun* and Shōu, Kafū demonstrates his awareness that Paris often functioned as a seemingly "unobtainable" goal for the Japanese artist. The contrast between the experiences of the two characters also allowed Kafū to analyze his own reactions to the city. *Jibun*'s happiness at attaining his goal of arriving in France and living in Paris may be seen as Kafū's own, even as the author realized that part of his reaction was due to the novelty of being in a new place. Kafū was only in Paris for two months, so his image of the city would not tarnish. Moreover, he had been working in New York and Lyon but was merely staying in Paris for his own pleasure, all of which made Paris seem more satisfying and carefree in comparison. At the same time, through the perspective of Shōu, Kafū realizes the function of the "unobtainable Other" as something to be cherished, as once lost, it would be lost forever. It seems that Kafū is examining the idea of the unobtainable Other from every angle, including the initial yearning, the satisfaction of desire, and the various emotions associated with fulfillment. Under this scrutiny, the status of the Other as eminently and eternally "unobtainable" disappears, instead being opened up to negotiation and change depending on personal experience.

Before leaving Paris, Kafū completed two other pieces set in the city—the novel *Kumo*, and a short piece entitled *Hitoritabi* (Solitary Journey). The latter is radically different in narrative mode, one of the very few Kafū works to begin in the third person. Count X and his wife are gazing out their hotel window onto the Champs Élysées when a letter arrives from one Miyasaka, an art student whom they have asked to act as a tour guide on their upcoming trip to Italy. The letter is written in a formal *sōro* style, befitting a student addressing a prospective patron, but Miyasaka soon reveals that he is unable to accompany the count and countess to Italy, as such an undertaking would spoil his love of solitary artistic reflection. Miyasaka is carried away with his own feelings on the matter: "Aah, there is nothing in the world so beauteous as the solitude of travel! Solitude is my matchless muse; all my dreams and poetry issue forth from its springs" (p. 492). Miyasaka's phrasing takes on exaggerated characteristics as he beseeches the count and countess to listen to the music of Berlioz to understand his feelings (p. 493). The wording is so overblown as to appear absurd, especially as he is passing up a perfect opportunity to gain patronage and advance his position in the art world by refusing these influential people. Miyasaka values art above all worldly affairs, living out his romantic ideals rather than inhabiting the mundane world of reality. He prefers his back-alley apartment in Paris, sparsely furnished and open to all noises of the streets, to any splendid hotel in greater Europe. Even at the theater he stands at the back, against the railings, so as not to betray his emotions in front of strangers. He is adamant that music, poetry, novels, sculpture, paintings, even architecture, should be appreciated in solitude: "I believe that the true meaning of art is something to be tasted alone, discovered alone" (p. 496).

Hitoritabi may verge on the parodic in its extreme romanticism (Seidensticker, 1965, p. 28), but the story as a whole centers on art: living for art, and being so absorbed in one's art that nothing else matters. From the outside, Miyasaka seems ridiculous, but Kafū seems to be saying it is worth being seen as ridiculous if, in return, one gets to experience life completely free from convention, living for one's art and knowing the glories of losing oneself in music, poetry, and contemplation. Japanese readers of the Meiji period would surely have envied Miyasaka this freedom, in a society so bound up in *risshin-shusse* (worldly success and advancement) that such self-absorbed idealism was frowned on. Mori Ōgai had drawn a similar opposition between self and state eighteen years earlier in *Maihime* (The Dancing Girl, 1890), where a young man of artistic sensibility is forced to give up his German romance in favor of duty to his benefactor—also a count in the Meiji government. In both stories, the choice of whether to follow one's heart or one's duty is up to the protagonist, but where Ōgai's hero of 1890 is too weak to defy social expectation, Kafū's poet of 1908 is able to dismiss the count's offer by invoking the glory of art itself. Kafū admired Ōgai, whom he saw as a friend and mentor, and the similarities between *Hitoritabi* and *Maihime* are clear.[23] By having his poet reject the count and live out his dream of artistic poverty, Kafū gives new force to the ideal of the romantic hero in Europe, and shows the loosening hold of *risshin-shusse* on Meiji youth. Where Ōgai's criticism of duty and state must remain oblique, Kafū is able to end his story with a pointed jab at Meiji values.

Kafū's use of the epistolary style in *Hitoritabi* allows the letter to speak directly to us, provoking our reaction at the same time that it provokes a reaction from the count. The reader's conflicting feelings of envy and contempt for the poet may make that reader question their own reactions, particularly given the count's intriguing conclusion, that Miyasaka represents a "new Japanese man." The count cites Germany as a complex modern state whose very complexity is the hallmark of progress and civilization. Comparing Germany with Japan, he then says: "The fact that crazy people like Miyasaka can appear, people with a sickness of ideas (*shisō no byōjin*), is proof that Japanese society has become complex through progress. I think it's to be celebrated" (p. 497). Miyasaka's ode to the glory of art is completely lost on the count, who merely sees it as a sickness or symptom of modernity. Kafū's picture of the insensible nobility thus laments the dismissal of art in modern society. A member of the Meiji aristocracy and political establishment, the count is hidebound by tradition and unable to open his mind to new ideas, even when physically transported to Europe. It is clear that for Kafū, art and the Japanese state are completely at odds with each other, in stark contrast to France where statues are erected to artists and poets. Positing the private life of an artist against the public realm of the state, *Hitoritabi* is one of the most politically oppositional works of *Furansu monogatari*.

This critique of the modern Japanese state continues in *Kumo* (Clouds), written in December 1908. Critics largely blame this novel for the banning of *Furansu monogatari* in March 1909. Its original title *Hōtō* (Dissipation) was changed to *Kumo* for a 1923 collection entitled *Futarizuma* (Two Wives), but more than five hundred characters had been replaced by *fuseji*, a format repeated in a 1926 edition. Quite a few passages were also deleted from the original for the *Two Wives* edition. What was it that made *Kumo* so objectionable? It could not have been the sexual content, no more intense than that found in *Amerika monogatari* the year before. Rather, the fact that *Kumo*'s hero is a diplomat clearly disaffected with the political and military aims of Meiji Japan must have struck the authorities as "harmful to public morals." At a time when patriotism and national fervor were at their height, *Kumo* gave entirely the wrong impression of the young Japanese diplomat abroad. Koyama Teikichi's lack of patriotism is clear from the start, as he notes that he is free to return to Japan now that he has passed the age when draft exemption takes effect (p. 501). However, having spent eight years abroad he feels out of touch with Japan and his family, and if he returned home he would have to think seriously about his future—better far to stay in Paris and live a meaningless life. One rainy evening in November, Teikichi meets the waitress Rosanette at a café near the Moulin Rouge—as he leaves, she slips in underneath his umbrella, and in this way he falls into a relationship.[24] Back at her place, he gazes dispassionately at her naked body in the firelight, only moved to action once he looks at her face carefully for the first time. The original edition included three lines here about the heat from the fire on their bodies, making the room like a steam bath as she touches him with her fingertips. Their intimacy reminds him of another relationship seven or eight years ago in Washington, when he experienced "the passionate love of a Western woman" (*seiyō fujin no hageshii koi*) with the prostitute Irma, his guide to the "new world" (p. 510). Teikichi passively allowed Irma to put him up in expensive hotels, and feed and clothe him according to her taste. He was at once madly in love and deeply ashamed of the relationship; elated at his success in love yet melancholy at the realization of his fantasies (p. 511). This ambivalence also affected his job at the Japanese legation in Washington, and it is here that *Kumo* takes a decidedly critical turn.

When the Russo–Japanese War started, Teikichi felt far removed from the security concerns of his country no matter how he tried to inspire himself with Chinese-style fighting slogans (p. 511). His translating job struck him as meaningless, and he wished for peace to come if only because he would no longer have to stay up all night with the telegrams (p. 512). In short, Teikichi just wants to resign, or be a person with no nationality, like the Jews or gypsies (p. 512). This is not the kind of attitude that the Meiji state would have wanted in one of its diplomats, but the original version is even more damning. In a passage deleted from the *Two Wives* edition, Teikichi states that he is not at all worried about the outcome of the Russo–Japanese War—even if Japan lost, it wouldn't be the end of their nation. Japan would just lose money, and the burden on the citizenry would become heavier. Even so, it was not as if people would starve in poverty—his own father was well off, for example, and the government couldn't very well requisition those who had nothing. But Teikichi concludes that thinking along these lines is useless, as the outcome of the war will undoubtedly be victory for Japan, and he will translate the resultant telegram as part of his job, feeling neither passion nor interest in the work (KZ 3.647). It is little wonder that this passage was cut from later versions, openly surmising the possibility of Japanese failure in the war. Teikichi is mercenary in his thinking about government levies on the poor, selfish regarding his own fate and completely uninterested in the idea of victory. His role is "only a diplomat," a lowly translator, who does his job because he is told. For a government official to be so entirely lacking in patriotism would be a great embarrassment to the Meiji authorities.

Taking this passage in context of the story as a whole, we see that Teikichi is always vacillating, leaving his actions up to fate—following random people in a crowd rather than choosing his own direction, falling into relationships at the insistence of others, making no decisions and showing no backbone whatsoever. Teikichi is hardly a poster boy for the Meiji government. Chapter 2 ends with his split from Irma (after which he cries, falling to his knees in resignation), while his vacillating nature is illustrated further by his relationship with Rosanette. As they quarrel over the rent money, he wavers between leaving this troublesome woman and having to go and find another; he swears never to keep a mistress again yet cannot bear the confines of marriage. By the opening of Chapter 5, Teikichi has finally broken with Rosanette and slept with most of the prostitutes who walk his familiar streets, and he feels tainted and unable to regain his old innocent life. Entering a park, he romanticizes his shameful situation: "what an elegant fate it was to wander the lamplit scenes of flowers, silks, embroidery and perfume, unconcerned about one's homeland, unconscious of the body, abandoning one's parents, homeless, wifeless, waking one morning to regret one's extremes of indulgence" (pp. 530–531). Just as he is musing on the satisfactions of suicide, he is distracted by two beautiful women in a carriage, one of whom throws a bouquet to an admirer on the street. Teikichi is transported to rapturous imaginings of dating an actress himself—how can he say he's really enjoyed Paris to the full without such an experience? All shame forgotten, Teikichi hears the strains of *Carmen* coming from a restaurant, bringing to mind the violent passions of the south of Europe (*nankoku*), likened to "a languid Oriental dream" (p. 532) as it was in *Matsuri no yoru gatari* and *Omokage*. Teikichi imagines a clear blue ocean, the fierce light of the sun, a treeless dry plain, and a naked barbarian woman, sleeping in a house with walls as thick as a prison. "There would be no coming back from that kind of land, a paradise of laziness, indolence and nothingness" (p. 533). The chapter ends with Teikichi rising from his bench, "feeling as though he would like to go there tonight if he could" (p. 533).

In Chapter 6, Teikichi is just as easily distracted from a serious matter. A letter from Irma says that she traveled to Panama but was stricken with disease after only three months, deciding to write to her old lover as she was now on the verge of death. Teikichi's mind goes blank—he had nearly forgotten her, poor thing. Moving on to his other correspondence, he finds a letter from a Westerner inviting him to the theater in Montmartre. Told that an actress will be accompanying them, Teikichi takes particular care getting ready, and Kafū describes his beautifying paraphernalia in detail. "These cosmetics—embellishments—are what distinguish us from natives, wild animals, vegetation and clods of earth" (p. 535). On his way out, the dark staircase makes Teikichi think of Irma's body, now corrupting in the earth, and he is struck with fear. A minute later in the street, however, the scent of makeup and perfume sends him into a reverie at the actress he is about to meet. Teikichi now feels neither pity nor fear in association with Irma, just the realization that his heart is so fickle he cannot even mourn her properly, not even for one night (p. 536). The chapter ends with Teikichi's bleak assessment of his own character.

The last chapter is very drowsy, set on the riverbank outside the city one late May afternoon. People are napping and relaxing, when suddenly all eyes are caught by the appearance of a splendid gentleman in fine clothes, arousing everyone's curiosity. "A foreigner—a Japanese—it's Koyama Teikichi." He settles himself on the riverbank as well, musing on his future. Having been in Paris for three years, he is sure to get his relocation orders, but does not want to return to Japan. Perhaps South America or Spain would be suitable. Two or three days earlier he had thought of spending all the money he possessed for a night of pleasure with the actress from Montmartre, then to throw himself into the Seine and have his death reported in the beautiful French language of the Paris newspapers. But of course, dying is too much trouble, and the last we see of Teikichi he is gazing dispiritedly at the diamond ring on his finger, his hands in his lap (p. 540).

Seidensticker's (1965) criticism of this story as overly wordy and exasperating (pp. 26–27) is certainly understandable, as Teikichi's vacillating nature makes for tiring reading. The real character in the story seems to be Paris itself, emerging as a place ripe with promise and too many choices for a young man. Whether one succeeds or fails in the city depends on one's character, and it is clear that Teikichi, who has no character, is failing to make much of his time in the capital. Taken as a whole, *Kumo* may be seen as a character study after the style of Balzac or Flaubert, with far more in common with *Illusions Perdues* or *L'Education Sentimentale* than with *Nana* or *L'Assommoir*. It seems there is no concrete substance to Teikichi, as he is pushed around by the wind like the clouds of the title. Incapable of change from within, holding no substance of his own, Teikichi will no doubt continue to float through life. It is a critical portrait and unsympathetic, but certainly successful in its depiction of a flawed human being.

The last of the Paris stories appears not in *Furansu nikki* but in a new section of *Furansu monogatari* entitled *Kaerimichi* (The Way Home), supposedly written on the boat taking Kafū home to Japan in June 1908. The theme of origins is clear in *Pari no wakare* (Farewell to Paris), as the narrator wonders why he could not have been born in France and lived in Paris all his life. He cannot feel pity for the hard lives of Turgenev and Chopin because they at least lived in the "capital city of art" (p. 543). The narrator muses that "the France I saw in reality was even more beautiful, even more tender, than the France I had imagined" (p. 545). His last day in Paris is spent in the Jardin du Luxembourg, with the statue of Leconte de Lisle at the entrance and the tulips in bloom. Ladies read novels on the benches, nursemaids push sleeping babies in strollers, and young lovers are lost in each others' company on another bench: "All of it was a living poem" (p. 547). Kafū has finally arrived inside the world of Maupassant's novels just at the point when he must leave it. Thinking that Baudelaire and Maupassant must have been absorbed in similar thoughts under the same trees in this park, the narrator decides that even if he is unable to become a famous man of letters on his return to Japan, the fact that he has experienced life in this city is already the highest good fortune and glory as an artist (p. 547).

Masamune Hakuchō recognized Kafū's debt to France, calling him a "*Pari no Nihonjin*."[25] French literature, and the essentialization of France, made Kafū's work of this period what it is: strong, yearning, full of gritty depiction, and yet beautiful as well. French literature was the main motivator behind Kafū's work between 1903 and 1908, borne out by his obsession with French writers even before he left Japan. In *Pari no wakare*, the park may be a beautiful sight with its trees in full leaf and the women with their parasols, but for Kafū the park exists as a link between the present and the past—this is the ground where Maupassant, Chopin, and Baudelaire once stood, and the piece is more an elegy to these artists than an observation of the park itself. The France of Kafū's work is the France of Maupassant, Baudelaire, Musset, Molière, and Flaubert, all at once, even though the Paris appearing in the works of these authors was actually a disparate set of entities separated by time and change. Kafū's Paris and France show no evidence of change over time, but remain as a homogeneous vision of civilization and beauty. This technique of collapsing time may be seen as continuous with *Amerika monogatari*, where *Shikago no futsuka* references Confucius and the Gospels to describe a modern love affair and *Rokugatsu no yoru no yume* lumps together the Greek myths with Shakespeare and Ibsen. The result is a sweeping vision of "Western civilization" that encompasses all ages without problematizing change or mentioning the passage of time.

Although Kafū spent only two months in Paris, nearly all his works between 1908 and 1910 refer back to the city, giving the impression that he had spent far longer than two months there. Kafū's repeated references to Paris, against which he was to contrast everything from Meiji Japan to Singapore (to their detriment), make Paris stand somewhere out of time, forever suspended in a perfect definition of "civilization." On his return to Japan, Kafū had the luxury of being able to reflect and compare the essentialized Other of French civilization with Japanese *bunmei*. The idea of time became crucial to Kafū's conceptualization of both "modernity" and "authenticity," both of which seemed necessary for Meiji Japan. For Kafū, "modernity" seems to have meant a number of things—technological and scientific advancement, liberty of the individual, the latest fashions in clothing, hairstyle, and architecture, a way of writing that expressed one's feeling passionately yet reflected one's surroundings accurately, the overbearing nature of the nation-state, the necessity of war and imperial conquest, city planning, and 24-hour urban life, with mass-produced entertainment like printed novels, magazines, and newspapers all readily available. "Authenticity," on the other hand, encapsulated ideas of being true to oneself both as an individual and a nation—eschewing hypocrisy, superficiality, and imitation in favor of true expression of the self, knowing one's place of origin, cherishing the cultural heritage built up over hundreds, if not thousands of years, and having confidence that one's own culture is worthy and valuable in its own right. In Kafū's eyes, France was a country in possession of both "modernity" and "authenticity" at the same time, so the two things were not fundamentally incompatible. Kafū's task was to find a way for Japan to achieve one without losing the other.

Kafū noted that civilization, progress, and development were all teleological processes taking place over time—in the West, over a span of three hundred years or more, but in Japan over a much shorter period. Where the process of modernization seemed natural and organic in France, it seemed rushed, forced and somehow false in Meiji Japan. The idea of modernity in Kafū's work thus becomes associated with the goal of authenticity—achieving some kind of modernity best suited to the nation at hand, which could therefore be seen as organic and genuine rather than a superficial imitation. The trope seems to be one of natural growth over time in one's own soil rather than a grafting from somewhere else or a forced hothouse environment. The problem with this goal, of course, is one of time: Japan could not possibly acquire "modern civilization" in fifty years and expect it to fit well with the existing aspects of Japanese culture. But Kafū's use of timelessness in *Furansu monogatari* takes the teleological aspect out of the idea of civilization. Once "authentic culture" is defined as timeless, it becomes applicable to all periods and places, including Meiji Japan. Furthermore, Kafū defines "civilization" in a particular way: French civilization is constructed as a perfect balance between technical progress and cultural preservation, so the blending of these two elements should allow Japan to achieve a similar kind of authentic modernity. The timeless balance of material and spiritual civilization that Kafū depicted in the Paris of *Furansu monogatari* would later provide him with a model for Tokyo. This particular vision of Paris would reappear countless times in Kafū's work from late 1908 to 1910 as he proposed his own solution to Japan's modern dilemma.

Pari no wakare provides a fitting end to the Paris stories, as it combines the timelessness found in *Omokage* with the critique of Meiji modernity found in *Kumo* and *Hitoritabi*. At the height of his raptures, the narrator proclaims that he was born for the sole purpose of seeing France (p. 545). In the original version of the story, titled simply *Adieu*,[26] the passage runs as follows, although everything but the first sentence was deleted from later editions:

> Aah! My France! I feel as though I was born into this world for the sole purpose of viewing you. Even though I observe the Japanese nation-state (*Nihon no kokka*) mistreating art and judging love as immoral, I no longer feel unnecessary resentment. I'd as soon let Japan act according to Japanese tradition and be its own downfall. The world is large. In that world is a country called France. How powerful a comfort and strength this gives to my tyrannized heart! France, prosper for all eternity! If in the future the citizens (*kokumin*) of Asia demonstrate such power as to unify the world, then Frenchmen! Use all your power to protect the palace of the Louvre! Polish your swords, so the statue of Venus will not have her hips girdled with cloth! For the sake of sacred art and the muses, I grieve at the advancement of a people who banned Molière. I fear it. (KZ 3.648)

Kafū is referring to the banning of a Molière collection in 1908, which also elicited protest from Uchida Roan at the time.[27] The image of a Japanese state strong enough to overpower the world and force its prudish "morality" on others is presented as something to be feared and lamented. The unification of the world under an Asian power was not likely in 1908, but Japan was certainly making inroads into the Asian mainland at the time, appropriating Taiwan in 1895 and formally annexing Korea in 1910. Just when the Meiji state was at its expansionist height, here was one of its famous authors fearing that expansion and opposing it from the realm of art. This passage is not the first instance in *Furansu monogatari* where art and the state have been set against one another, but it is perhaps the most vivid. What is most notable in this passage is the repeated reference to birth and origins—in the narrator's birth into the world, the citizens (*kokumin)* of Asia, and the advancement of a "people" (*kokumin*) who would ban Molière. In *Pari no wakare,* the question of Kafū's origins comes to the fore as he faces the reality of returning to his homeland. Why that homeland should be Japan and not France was a source of deep frustration for Kafū at this time. Having to leave a country where art was sacred for one where art was despised undoubtedly concerned the writer, who was only now coming into his own in terms of literary development. Additionally, Kafū was questioning the idea of where Japan stood in relation to the rest of the world, particularly in relation to Asia. This question had been building through the stories of *Furansu nikki*—is Japan part of the prosaic North or the passionate South? Or is it merely representative of the East, in contrast to Europe's West? If Japan should be classified as part of the East, then which "East" would it be—the head of an advancing Asian civilization, or part of the mysterious "Orient" that has appeared at intervals through *Furansu monogatari*?

The Orient appears regularly in the stories of *Furansu monogatari,* often in association with great works of European art such as opera or literature. The Orient functions as a counterpoint to France, as well as a locus of imagination and mystery. In the next chapter, I examine Kafū's Orient in detail, particularly in terms of literary reference and Kafū's positioning of that Orient vis-à-vis Japan. In *Furansu monogatari,* as in *Amerika monogatari,* Kafū's use of contrasting opposites in order to make a point does not stop him from moving flexibly between these contrasts. It is Kafū's flexible positioning that would allow him to address questions of Japan's identity in relation to the West and to the "Orient" and Asia in his work throughout the next few years. The next chapter examines Kafū's construction of the "Orient" in relation to his position as a Japanese writer, and analyzes in detail the intertextual dynamic operating between Kafū's texts and the European works that shaped them.

CHAPTER THREE

Positioning the Observer

Kafū's "Orient" and Orientalism

Where *Amerika monogatari* constructed an image of America through contrast with Japan, and the beginnings of *Furansu monogatari* saw Kafū reveling in an idealized world of art and aesthetics, the latter part of *Furansu monogatari* turns to an examination of the wider world as Kafū leaves Paris and begins the long journey home to Japan. Kafū's route from Paris took him through the Straits of Gibraltar, across the Mediterranean to Port Said, then on through the Persian Gulf and the Indian Ocean to Colombo and Singapore, arriving in Japan in July 1908. Kafū was an observant traveler, writing vivid depictions of the peoples and places he encountered on his journey through the Middle East and Asia. Through the middle sections of *Furansu monogatari,* these places emerge in terms of a sensual, nonrational, mysterious space, whose people are described as animals or inanimate objects. A significant factor in shaping Kafū's constructions of these places was his idea of the "Orient," which had transported him into raptures in *Rokugatsu no yoru no yume.* Just as Kafū's imagined "France" functioned as a subtext to *Amerika monogatari* and overpowered his observations of the actual city of Paris, once again, Kafū's association of the "Orient" with the French poets proved to be stronger than his powers of observation when he arrived in Port Said. This chapter examines Kafū's vision of the "Orient," first formulated by his reading of French and other Western authors while he was in America and France, and what happened to that vision when he arrived in the Middle East himself.

In discussing Kafū's construction of the "Orient" through *Amerika* and *Furansu monogatari,* it is necessary to address his relationship to the

Orientalist discourse of the French and British writers he so admired. As shown in Chapter 1, Kafū made frequent references to French writers throughout *Amerika monogatari*, especially in the final stories that increasingly focused on the Decadent School and Baudelaire. In *Rokugatsu no yoru no yume*, Kafū associated these writers not only with decay and corruption, but also with their portrayal of the "Orient" as a land of mystery and rapture, the place "which the poets of the so-called Decadent School sing of as the land of dreams."[1] While Kafū was in America, he used images of the Orient in his works in order to convey this same sense of mystery and color. The Orient appears most often in *Amerika monogatari* in references to Turkey, Persia, and Arabia, when Kafū is describing outlandish beauty, unnatural quiet, or the sorrowful qualities of music. The most striking appearances of the "Orient" in *Amerika monogatari* occur in *Suibijin, Rinkan,* and *Yoaruki,* where it is employed to heighten a sense of mystery and eroticism in the observed scene, or to invert usual power structures of gender and race.

Suibijin (The Intoxicated Beauty) describes a visit to St. Louis to meet with S, a painter whose work is included in the art exhibition at the World's Fair. The work depicts a nude woman with dark skin reclining on a couch, a wine glass half full in her hand. On seeing the painting Kafū's narrator muses: "She was probably a model from Egypt or somewhere in Arabia, as her hair and eyes were black" (p. 56). The woman had been involved with the painter's friend Mantellaut, a French journalist who was charmed by her dark skin and fleshy, almost corpulent figure. The painter describes the difficulty of capturing the intoxicated look in the woman's eyes, but then adds:

> . . . even more difficult is getting the color of the skin right for a person of a colored race. As the warmth from the alcohol flushes through her whole body, in every blood vessel there comes welling forth the passion of what they call the tropics—in my heart I wanted to express that significance in the color of the skin. (p. 56)

We find out later that the woman is actually half black, a dancer in an American vaudeville theater. But the passion of "what they call the tropics" (*iwayuru dankoku*), the fact that she smokes a Turkish pipe, and the assumption that she is an Egyptian or Arabian model give us the impression she is from the exotic "Orient" of Kafū's imagination. This impression is reinforced by the description of her eyes: "Those eyes were not the eyes of we civilized peoples. They were the eyes of an animal—the eyes of a domesticated animal when its master feeds it." Emphasizing the contrast between civilization and barbarism, S says "this woman of mixed blood was not at all like women of civilized countries," because her pleasure in men was concerned not with the externals of appearance or flirtation but with the physical pleasure of the body (pp. 60–61). The woman's first appearance in the story is nude in S's painting, objectified in art for the viewer's gaze. The erotic quality of the painting pales in contrast to the erotic power of the woman herself, however, as S recounts how she ensnared his friend Mantellaut some time ago. Taking Mantellaut back to her lodgings, reclining on a couch, she stretches and twists her body in the firelight to absorb all its heat. Her movements seem at once intended to arouse the young man and also completely natural, so she embodies the essence of seduction and temptation. The fleshy curves of the woman are emphasized throughout the tale, but her sexuality is so powerful as to be almost unearthly, proving her seduction to be not only irresistible but also fatal.

After three months of their physical relationship, Mantellaut tires of it and tells her he can no longer visit her. Suddenly, standing on the street corner, he is seized by a strange power and is compelled beyond his control toward her house. Once inside, the man loses all willpower and strength. As she stares into his eyes he is mesmerized and realizes there is no escape:

> As a shudder passed through his whole body, he realized it was no use trying anything now—he was her victim, like a mouse before a cat, or a lamb before a wolf: a sacrifice. How pitiful. In the beginning Mantellaut had confidently believed that he was the man, the master, sporting with her in love as if with a tamed, docile, domesticated animal, but at some moment, unknowing, unrealizing, he had been dominated by a strange invisible force pervading her body, and since that moment he could neither resist nor fight against it. (pp. 63–64)

The tale is compared with "the ancient legends of Persia and Turkey, where an animal exercises a horrible fascination upon a young, beautiful empress, and in the end she is caught and killed. In this sense the French gentleman too was completely taken in by a black woman who had more animal blood in her than human" (p. 64). The man eventually dies from weakness one year later in Europe.

Suibijin is a complex entanglement of gender roles as well as race, and examines the concept of power through sexual domination and racial difference. As in *Chōhatsu,* the man is ultimately sacrificed to the woman's power, but in this case, the sacrifice is complete in the man's death. *Suibijin* may be read not only as an inversion of gender roles, but also as an exploration of the many power structures involved in the ideas of Orient–Occident, domination–docility, human–animal, civilized–uncivilized. The woman's possible racial origins in Africa recall the North African "Orient" of Chateaubriand, Lamartine, Daudet, and Loti, while she is repeatedly associated with Persia, Turkey, Egypt, and Arabia. The "Orient" brings color and mystery to the events of the story, and transforms an American dancer into a barbaric goddess of sexual power. In short, here we see operating an essentialized, symbolic function of the Orient.

It is tempting here to push the idea of poetic surplus to an extreme and read in all sorts of statements Kafū may have been making about power structures operating between the sexes, between races, and between Orient and Occident in this story. Minami Asuka reads *Suibijin* in "geopolitical" (*chiseiteki*) terms, emphasizing Kafū's knowledge about power structures at work in the early 20th-century world. The American painter S, in imitating the Orientalist nude, acknowledges the cultural power of French civilization, and the story can be read as a contrast between new, commercialist America and old, imperialist Europe. The mere fact of the "Louisiana Purchase International Exposition" in 1904, celebrating America's purchase of Louisiana from France, reveals the colonial subtext of the World's Fair.[2] The Japanese narrator admiring the painting also reminds the reader that Japan looked to both America and Europe for art and culture, but Minami observes that all three places possessed more financial, cultural, and military power than North Africa and the Middle East at this time. The subject of the nude is supposedly Arabian, objectifying the Middle East for the American and Japanese gaze. Kafū did not explore the ramifications of this objectification here, and Minami (2007) says that he shows no anti-imperialist or anti-colonialist sentiment at this stage of his work (p. 56). Certainly *Suibijin* is not an overt exploration of these ideas, reading more like a parable or "ancient legend." But Minami raises an excellent point: *Suibijin* may also be read as an early example of Kafū's oppositional stance against the Meiji government.

Suibijin depicts the World's Fair almost exclusively in artistic terms, ignoring the broader Japanese exhibits of technology and manufacturing. In 1904, Japan was at war with Russia, and used the Fair to show its military progress and strength. Minami argues that Kafū's choice to ignore the wider exhibit is an early indication of his oppositional stance (p. 56). This view is given some support by the contrast drawn between war and sex in the nature of Mantellaut's death:

"Just as a soldier falls in war, he fell on the path of his own passions" (p. 65). *Suibijin* was published in 1905, only two months after the end of the Russo–Japanese War. Likening a soldier's death to an excess of sexual decadence would have been shocking for the time.[3] Minami finds the story's publication in *Taiyō* surprising, given the nationalistic tenor of the magazine, but perhaps the editors appreciated Kafū's emphasis on modern U.S. technology and the presence of a Japanese writer at such an important international event. The geopolitical reading of *Suibijin* points to many elements of Kafū's work that are still emerging at this stage of *Amerika monogatari*, suggesting ways in which we can read the later works of *Furansu monogatari* with their more direct references to colonialism and Kafū's opposition to the Meiji state. What we can say without fear of anachronism is that the role of the Orient in *Suibijin* is to open the door onto a world of sexual power, exotic color, and the "uncivilized" in human nature.

Another passage featuring the Orient in *Amerika monogatari* appears in *Rinkan* (In the Forest). In Chapter 1, we saw how Kafū used the issue of racial discrimination in *Rinkan* to show that America was not a homogeneous whole. There is another facet to *Rinkan*, however, and that is Kafū's use of the Orient when describing the panorama of Washington D.C. from his vantage point on the Potomac. Kafū leans against the railings of the bridge and looks back toward the city, aflame in the colors of the sunset:

> Imitating the soldiers, I leant against the railings of the bridge and gazed at our surroundings. The setting sun, just at the point of sinking below the horizon, at that moment blazed over the entire surface of the sky as if to burn it, and as its sharp light was reflected over Washington, the autumn-colored belt of treetops in the park facing the Potomac looked just like a voluptuous hanging curtain of Turkish weave. And above it, the side of the astounding Washington Monument, which they say stands 555 feet tall, looked to my eyes like a pillar of fire. Even further on in the distance, the dome of the Capitol and the white buildings of the various government departments here and there were all dyed an even crimson, and the windows of the tall hotels in the city were without exception sparkling like colored lights. (p. 110)

The blazing sun dyes the Capitol crimson and turns the Washington Monument into a "pillar of fire." But Kafū adds an extra dimension by bringing in the striking visual imagery of the Turkish weave to describe the brilliant interweaving of color in the trees across the river. The introduction of the "Orient" emphasizes the radiance of the color, but the fact that this is Washington, heart of American democracy, could tempt the modern reader to ponder the power structures underlying both the city and the democracy it represents. The issue of race and power is a major theme in *Rinkan,* and it is clear that Kafū had a high degree of critical awareness with regard to racial dynamics in America. It could be argued that Kafū introduces the Orient in *Rinkan* in order to draw an analogy between the power structures operating between white and black in Washington and those of the Occident and Orient. But Kafū does not directly draw such an analogy, and the Orient does not appear again in the story. At this stage of *Amerika monogatari,* the appearances of Orient are limited to brief metaphors and similes—a curtain of Turkish weave, a Persian beauty, a Turkish or Persian legend, an Arabian appearance in the skin. The Orient lends itself to the surrounding text in a limited and particular way, in order to enhance the exotic quality of the observed scene. This function of the Orient is also seen in *Nezame*: Mrs. Denning, Sawazaki's secretary, is easily fatigued, and takes to lying around the house rather than working. Her husband jokes: "You weren't meant to go to work like other American women. You're a woman like a Turkish or Persian beauty, made to lie around in a big house all day, vacantly listening to the sounds of water" (p. 161). The Orient is thus presented as the antithesis of modern society and productive work, and languor becomes an element of Oriental beauty. Just as the dancer in *Suibijin* and Mrs. Denning in *Nezame* are compared to Egyptian or Persian beauties in order to emphasize their mystique and sensuality, Kafū does the same thing in *Rinkan* with the Washington landscape, so that the city becomes a place of otherworldly color and excitement.

Kafū's use of the Orient in these stories has much in common with Western writers' use of the Orient in the eighteenth and nineteenth centuries, as the representation of an exotic ideal. The Orient of French and British literature of this period may be defined in terms of geography, and in terms of character, although both kinds of definition changed over time. In terms of geography, Said (1995) writes that the Orient in French and British literature of this period, although not homogeneous, primarily occupied the Middle East, Persia, India, and the lands of the Bible (pp. 4, 17). Although Said has been criticized for this geographical limitation on Orientalism (Wang, 1997, p. 61), Lisa Lowe (1991) has charted how the geographical limits changed over time. She demonstrates how French writers emphasized the Middle

East in the early colonial period and North Africa in the nineteenth century, while China and Japan were not as significant in the discourse on the Orient until the twentieth century.

The character of this so-called Orient also changed over time. In the seventeenth century, the Egyptian, Arabian, and Semitic civilizations were regarded as models of knowledge and as the source of contemporary European civilization. However, a shift to emphasizing racial difference was seen in the eighteenth century with works such as Montesquieu's *Persian Letters*. By the nineteenth century, racial theories from Hanover had cemented the idea of a racially and culturally inferior "East" (Bernal, 1987). The literary and artistic Orient of the nineteenth century was essentialized as different, foreign, backward, childlike, and innocent, a Utopia of the nonmodern and nonrational. At the same time it was characterized as lawless, barbarian, sensual, colorful, and dramatic, a place of boundless possibility and adventure. The Orient envisioned by Kafū in *Amerika monogatari* reflects the sexual, uncivilized, non-modern aspects of the Orient used by Flaubert and the Decadent School. Indeed, Kafū takes pains to connect himself to this literary tradition by speaking of "the skies of "the Orient," which poets of the so-called Decadent School sing of as the land of dreams" (p. 296). The link with France is emphasized by Kafū's choice of script in which to present the word "Orient," written in quotation marks as *"Higashi no kuni,"* "Land of the East," but with katakana superscript pronouncing the word *"orian,"* marking it as a French word.

This Middle Eastern Orient of French literature was a very different kind of Orient to the one being described at home in Japan at the time. Stefan Tanaka charted the development of the word *tōyō* (Orient) in Meiji Japan, drawing on Tsuda Sōkichi's genealogy. As Meiji historicists theorized about an Oriental history distinct from world or Western history, *tōyō* came to define an essentialized space representing "that which was not the Occident (*seiyō*)," in response to a perceived Western threat against Japan.[4] Kafū's "Orient," on the other hand, also represents an essentialized space opposite to "the Occident," but it seems to come directly from the French and British Orientalist writers of the nineteenth century. Kafū's Orient in these works emerges not as the Far Eastern *tōyō* of Asia that engaged the Meiji historicists, but as the same Orient that was constructed by the Western writers he admired—the Orient of Turkey, the Middle East, India, and Arabia, which appears in Kipling, Loti, Lamartine, and Musset.

That Kafū associated this idea of the Orient with French literature, the Decadent School and Baudelaire in particular, is seen clearly in *Yoaruki* (Walking at Night), written in April 1907. *Yoaruki*, like *Chainataun no ki,* is another foray into the dark side of the streets of New York. The narrator begins by extolling the virtues of the night scenes of the city, especially its bright lights, which transform the streets into an otherworldly space. The women of ill repute under these lights look more virtuous than the most chaste wife or maiden, and "the fallen poet who sang of the indestructible soul to the glory of God first saw the beauty of sin and darkness in these lights" (p. 281). Kafū quotes Baudelaire's verse on "beloved night," the silent accomplice to crime and sin, which calls forth in the narrator a sense of mystery and intrigue. People on the street or in passing carriages become possible thieves, accomplices to sin and illicit love. Those in the red-light district become "butterflies dancing in a flower-garden of dissipation," where the women are angels called forth by Mephisto. Walking through a park he comes across "a woman of the night" and goes back with her to her apartment. The narrator trembles unconsciously and lets himself "fall headlong into blackness" in the adventure of sin and the lure of evil. In the room, the woman lets her coat fall to reveal a long white chemise, and she sits down to smoke. "I folded my arms, and gazed at her figure in silence, just like an archaeologist gazing up at the Sphinx standing in the Egyptian desert" (p. 285). The woman and her sexuality are thus directly associated with the exotic Orient, and she becomes an Oriental object to be examined. The striking incongruity of the phrase "Sphinx in the Egyptian desert" leaps out from the page, followed immediately by a quote from Baudelaire describing the woman's eyes. They appear as a swamp emitting noxious vapor, an oasis at which the poet's desire may slake its thirst, and as two jewels that burn through the narrator in their intensity (p. 286). He will never again be satisfied with ordinary women, intrigued by this woman's power. Where ordinary women are simple blossoms, this "queen of evil" is rather a poisonous flower spreading forth tendrils of evil and leaves of sin (pp. 286–287).

The epistolary *sōrō* style of *Yoaruki* elevates the narrator's experience and gives it solemnity and grandeur. Kafū has turned an ordinary meeting with a prostitute into a lyric poem of epic mystery in this dreamlike tale of a night's seduction. It is hard to overstate the allure of the woman, felt not only by the narrator but also by the reader, and her erotic power is equal to that of the "Arabian" model in *Suibijin* or the gypsy snake charmer in *Hebitsukai*. Here, moreover, the feeling is heightened by the references to the exotic Sphinx and the poetry of Baudelaire. With the introduction of the Sphinx in such close association with "the father of the Decadent School," Kafū is pointing to French Orientalism as his source. The archaeologist here reminds us that many of the French authors on whom Kafū draws are those who had seen the Orient and its Sphinx for themselves. Kafū at this stage had not yet visited Egypt himself. He knew Egypt only from French Orientalist writings, and it is through them that he comprehends and constructs his own Orient. The Turkish weave in *Rinkan* and the Sphinx in *Yoaruki* are thus clues to how Kafū saw the world—a vision developed from years of reading popular French literature, expressed in the structures, motifs, and rhetoric of his own works. Ken Ito was the first to examine the links between the respective Orients of Kafū and Flaubert, and thus went some way toward interpreting Kafū in the light of Orientalist discourse. Ito's main concern in his chapter comparing the Orients of Nagai Kafū and Tanizaki Jun'ichirō is how these writers constructed the West as their "Orient," signifying a distant place of mystery, color, and beauty. Ito argues that the objects and people of the West portrayed in *Amerika monogatari* were transformed into colorful, enigmatic, exciting things by being mediated through a haze of French Orientalism. It is worth going through Ito's argument in some detail because he investigates some complex ideas of representation and intertextuality.

Ito (1991) observes that Kafū's use of the Orient in *Suibijin* and *Rinkan* is very similar to Flaubert's use of the Orient in the previous century, a symbolic usage that imparts color, mystery, and drama onto the object described: "Flaubert once described his experience of Egypt as gulping down a 'bellyful of colors,' and this is what Kafū's narrator does in a landscape where the Potomac substitutes for the Nile and where the Washington Monument takes the place of the pyramids" (p. 42). Arguing that the dynamic operating in Kafū's text is the same as that behind Flaubert's Orientalism, Ito quotes Harry Levin to explain how the Orient's "order, beauty, luxury, calmness, and its pleasure were happy antitheses of the confusion, ugliness, poverty, agitation, and discomfort that both Flaubert and Baudelaire discerned in their environing world . . . Orientalism, whatever else it could mean, meant gorgeous color, in contrast to the greyish tonality of the French provincial landscape" (p. 42). In this reading, the West became for Kafū the ideal place of sexuality, light, and mystery, which the Orient had been for Flaubert and Baudelaire. Ito argues that in *Amerika monogatari*, "The 'gorgeous colour' and the 'exciting spectacle' of the French view of the Orient would be superimposed on the West, creating a world where an American whore can remind a Japanese of 'the Sphinx in the Egyptian desert.' . . . The 'Occident' could become the 'Orient'" (pp. 42–43). In other words, Kafū uses the symbols and signs of the Orient in his description of America in order to construct America as an "Orient" itself, an exciting contrast to the dullness and repression of Japan. Ito thus argues that Kafū's use of French Orientalism in depicting the West took the form of a dynamic that worked in exactly the same way on the West as the way in which French Orientalism worked upon the Orient. As we have seen, Kafū did treat America as an idealized country of sexual and individual liberty, a place where anything could happen and gender roles could be inverted. In this sense, America for Kafū was indeed a kind of Orient as the French writers envisioned it, a distant land of inversions and mystery. Ito takes this idea further, however, arguing that the intertextual dynamic between Kafū and the French writers is best explained by René Girard's concept of "triangular desire."

Ito first mentions French Orientalism in regard to Kafū's use of the femme fatale in *Suibijin*. In response to Seidensticker's suggestion that *Suibijin* was influenced by Poe,[5] Ito (1991) agrees that the story is "Poe-like," but has more in common with French literature:

> . . . the description of the deadly seductress, part Negro and radiating sexual heat, suggests that she is not as much a direct descendant of Poe's translucently white enchantresses as a femme fatale by way of the French fascination with the tropics. In the later stories of the collection, where the influence of Baudelaire is strongest, the American whore is clearly viewed through French eyes. (p. 38)

Ito thus introduces the way in which Kafū interprets the American prostitute, sexuality, and America itself, as an interpretation through French eyes, that is, mediated through Kafū's knowledge of French literature (here, Baudelaire). In the same way, Ito argues, Kafū's vision of the West is "conditioned by French exoticism," which gives the American landscape bright color and light, so that the treetops near the Potomac "looked just like a voluptuous hanging curtain of Turkish weave," and the Washington Monument becomes "a pillar of fire." Ito (1991) interprets the Turkish weave as "the mediating presence of French nineteenth-century Orientalism," which sets the Washington scene alight (p. 42). The key to Ito's analysis lies in the words "mediating presence." Ito argues that the America of the collection is so exaggerated and strange because "It has been transfigured by a dynamic that René Girard calls "triangular desire," where the intrusion of a mediating presence shapes a subject's longing for a given object" (p. 41). Ito gives an example of the dynamic at work in *Yoaruki*, where the hero's desire is "mediated by his worship of Baudelaire," which "transforms an American whore into a 'queen of evil'" (p. 41). As Ito maintains,

Kafū's worship of Baudelaire and his desire to become a Western artist cause him to imitate the Western writers in dress, mannerisms, and writing style—that Kafū himself is well aware of his imitation is seen clearly in *Ochiba* and *Pari no Wakare*.[6] We may thus read Kafū as an example of the subject of Girard's "triangular desire," a Stendahlian *vaniteux* who takes on not only the external appearance but also the desires of his chosen model.[7] In Girard's (1965) structural analysis, triangular desire transfigures its object, so that an American prostitute becomes for Kafū the same as Baudelaire's queen of evil, as "Desire projects a dream universe around the hero" (p. 18).

While this application of Girard to *Amerika monogatari* is useful and thought provoking, however, "desire" here is narrowly defined as reaching for the unobtainable, which raises some problems. The idea of illimitable desire certainly is prominent in much of nineteenth- and twentieth-century thought. But as Eugene Goodheart has shown, the object of desire does not always have to be understood as essentially unobtainable. Goodheart (1991) traces this view of desire from Proust through Barthes and Lacan to Girard, whose approach to literature depends on the "insatiability of mimetic or triangular desire" (p. 20). Illimitable desire, Goodheart argues, certainly is a powerful conception in modern literature and expresses some authorial experience, but desire itself does not need to be defined as illimitable by its very nature (p. 22). Depending on Girard thus can limit the reading of desire in Kafū's text, and indeed introduces a binary structure of superior–inferior feeling toward the object of that desire.

Ito argues that Kafū related so well to the French Orientalist discourse and could use it to describe the West because the mediated desire in Orientalism (objectifying the Orient) corresponds to Kafū's desire to be Western (objectifying the West). Ito (1991) describes the authorial persona of *Amerika monogatari* as consumed by "yearning to become an artist of another race" (p. 41), a yearning that was also clear in *Pari no wakare*. But Ito argues that this yearning combined with a "sense of deprivation" to produce Kafū's desire for the "given object," or all things Western:

> A writer from a developing nation, he had learned to base his definition of what it meant to be cultured and civilized upon his understanding of the West. He viewed his own country's distance from Western modernity as the essential feature of its identity. (p. 42)

Ito sees Kafū as subscribing to a certain mode of thinking about Western modernity in the Meiji period, which defined Japan's progress in terms of distance from the Western goal (see Matsuzawa, 1984). Although the Meirokusha ideologues certainly wrote in this way, however, Kafū and many other writers of the Meiji period questioned this view of the relationship between Japan and the West. Writers like Natsume Sōseki, Mori Ōgai, and Futabatei Shimei focused rather on whether Japan needed to Westernize in the pursuit of "modernization," and whether modernization was even necessary. In Ito's argument, Kafū was made to feel deprived and inferior by a sense of distance from Western culture and civilization, which is why he took so readily to the French Orientalist texts: "When his sense of deprivation encountered the yearnings expressed by the French authors he favored, the stage was set for an almost natural amalgamation" (p. 42). But emphasizing the sense of distance in Kafū's writing (and in Meiji literature as a whole) does these writers an injustice, as the questioning, challenging nature of their works points to a more complex critical awareness of what "civilization" and "modernity" might mean for Japan.[8]

It is also difficult to maintain that Kafū's sense of yearning for the West directly corresponded with the French writers' yearning for the Orient. Where the French Orientalists knew their own superiority to the colonized Orient, Kafū in Ito's argument felt inferior to his exotic "Orient" of the West. The positioning of the writers vis-à-vis their respective subjects was therefore very different. Ito's model does not answer the basic question of who wields the power in such discourses of "Orient" and "Occident," treating "Orientalism" as primarily a literary device. The questions of how Kafū positioned himself as subject, and how that position related to the Orientalist body of literature, are therefore significant. The relationship between Kafū and French literature has produced a number of critical works that all describe it in a different way: influence (Akase), a quest for literary resonance (Iriye), appropriation (Minami), and mediation (Ito). In this chapter, I explore this relationship further, to see what Kafū may have been doing with his references to Turkish weave and Arabian beauties, and look at some of the theoretical implications of the relationship in terms of situating Japan vis-à-vis the imagined Orient. In dealing with concepts of appropriation, representation, and referential authority, we need a model with a strong theoretical basis in order to examine the relationship between Kafū and French Orientalism in detail. For all his shortcomings on the points of marginal discourse, reductionism, closure, and monolithic binary structures, Edward Said developed a concrete and practical way of analyzing the relationships between texts. It is therefore useful to reconsider the methodologies of *Orientalism*, which can address the dynamics of reference operating between a text and a surrounding body of literature.

In discussing Kafū's relationship with the texts of the Orientalist writers, we should remember that Kafū would not have seen these writers as "Orientalist" in the same sense that I use it here. This point is an obvious one but cannot be overemphasized—to say that Kafū would have read their work as "Orientalist" is a gross error of anachronism. Kafū realized that these writers took the "Orient" as the object of their work. He admired their artistry and was often moved to relive scenes from their novels and writings in his own work and travels. He would have seen these writers as "Orientalist" perhaps in the original meaning of the word, referring to someone (academic, scholarly, or writer of fiction) who had traveled to the Middle East and written about it extensively. Although the word "Orientalist" could refer to scholars, academics, explorers, diarists, anthropologists, colonizers—a whole array of people engaged in the study and representation of the Orient, Kafū would have encountered the Orient primarily through the vast amount of Western travel literature, poetry, and fiction that he read.[9] It is plain from Kafū's references that he was aware that these travel writers wrote about the Orient in a particular way—as a mysterious locus of color, barbarism, and adventure, and also, as we shall see here, as the physical, geographic colonies of the British Straits with coolies working under Western supervision. The geopolitical reading of Kafū's work becomes useful in this regard, as we may say that Kafū was aware of the connection between the literary representations of the Orient and the power structures of colonialism that made such representation possible.[10]

Said (1995) acknowledges the importance of travel literature in the Orientalist tradition, and takes some time in listing the major Orientalist writers of the nineteenth and early twentieth centuries. While the "official intellectual genealogy of Orientalism," Said argues, would include such writers as "Gobineau, Renan, Humboldt, Steinthal, Burnouf, Remusat, Palmer, Weil, Dozy, Muir" and others, such a genealogy would "neglect the great contribution of imaginative and travel literature, which strengthened the divisions established by Orientalists between the various geographical, temporal, and racial departments of the Orient" (p. 99). Said argues that "Such neglect would be incorrect, since for the Islamic Orient this literature is especially rich and makes a significant contribution to building the Orientalist discourse" (p. 99). This body of literature "includes work by Goethe, Hugo, Lamartine, Chateaubriand, Kinglake, Nerval, Flaubert, Lane, Burton, Scott, Byron, Vigny, Disraeli, George Eliot, Gautier. Later, . . . we could add Doughty, Barres, Loti, T.E. Lawrence, Forster" (p. 99). Said also mentions Baudelaire and Huysmans, who wrote the type of Orientalist literature that focuses on the cult of the

"Fatal Woman," sadomasochism, secrecy, and occultism, and discusses Rudyard Kipling at length in analyzing British colonialist literature (pp. 180, 226–228).

One way to examine Kafū's references to Orientalist writings is to look at which specific writers are named in his works, as well as the contexts in which they appear. From *Saiyū-nisshishō* and the travel collections we know that he was familiar with the works of George Eliot, Hawthorne, Goethe, Hugo, Lamartine, Kipling, Flaubert, Baudelaire, Huysmans, Byron, Disraeli, and Loti, as well as other authors who are associated with their descriptions of the Orient as place or religion, such as Musset, or of the Orient as woman, such as Poe. Kafū's first attempts at reading "foreign literature in the original languages" were directed toward Eliot and Hawthorne. Kafū writes that the new works of Zola had the effect that "people like myself were so excited by these authors that we quite lost interest in Goethe, Shakespeare, and the other classics," implying a certain amount of familiarity with Goethe to begin with.[11] Yoshida Seiichi's (1971a) chronology of literary publications tells us that in the first half of the Meiji period there were many translations and adaptations of Shakespeare and Goethe being published. There were also many translations of Hugo and critical volumes about him, for example *Shikeimae no rokujikan* (The Last Day of a Condemned Man) appeared in August 1896, and June 1898 saw the publication of *Yūgō shōhin* (Literary Sketches of Hugo). Kafū was familiar with Hugo and he would later comment that to find a great politician, one must look to Western leaders such as Hugo.[12] There was a fair amount of interest in Byron in Meiji Japan, as shown by critical volumes such as Kometa's *Bairon*, published in October 1900, and *Bairon bunkai no Dai-maō* (The Devil in the Literary World of Byron), by Kimura Takatarō, published July 1902. From *Ochiba* and *Pari no wakare* it is clear that Kafū knew of Byron's image and had probably read his poetry (KZ 3.241, 543). *Saiyū-nisshishō* has Kafū reading a volume of Lamartine's poetry on December 31, 1906, while he also read the novels *L'éducation Sentimentale* by Flaubert and *Là Bas* by Huysmans.[13] Kafū was therefore acquainted with a range of Orientalists' works, and we may assume that he read many more that go unmentioned in the diary.

Kafū thus read widely in Western literature, in both English and French, including the works of Zola, Turgenev, Tolstoy, and others who are not generally associated with the Orientalist tradition. But it is difficult to divide writers of this period into "Orientalists" and "non-Orientalists," simply because Orientalism indicates a particular way of viewing the world shared by European society as a whole, rather than a systemic model of observation only utilized by some writers and not others. Orientalism as a worldview depended on empire-building and colonialism, and how colonial sites had been depicted in the art and literature of the colonizer. Wide reading in nineteenth-century European literature necessarily meant wide reading in imperialist artistic output, so the Orientalist mode of thought would have been transmitted almost naturally to Kafū as he read the popular European works of the period. Kafū's literary models taught him not only the details of style and technique, but also the tendency to view the world in terms of colonizer and colonized, subject and object, the traveler who observes and the natives that are observed. This worldview is clearest in *Kaerimichi,* the section of *Furansu monogatari* where Kafū is returning home.[14] His travels take him through the Mediterranean to Port Said, the Red Sea, the Indian Ocean, and Colombo, with Singapore as the final stop on the way back to Japan. It is in this section that the idea of the Orient comes to the fore, as well as the invocation of two writers in particular: Pierre Loti and Rudyard Kipling.

Two stories in *Kaerimichi* stand out for their representation of the "Orient": *Pōto Setto* (Port Said) and *Shingapōru no sūjikan* (A Few Hours in Singapore).[15] *Pōto Setto* is indebted to Pierre Loti, whose Orient is suffused with a gentle air of mystery and charm while retaining its exotic, distant, even barbarous characteristics. Kafū was familiar with Loti's work and had discussed his novel *Le Roman d'un Spahi* at some length in *Saiyū-nisshishō.*[16] It left a much deeper impression on Kafū than Loti's other work—on his first reading of the book, Kafū was struck with terror at "the awful hand of fate." At the time, Kafū was involved in his affair with the prostitute Edyth, and was finding it difficult to end the relationship. No doubt Loti's story struck a chord with Kafū's troubles, as the hero Jan, a soldier "miles away from home in a foreign country," was entangled in a love affair with a Negress prostitute, from which it was almost impossible to break free. But Kafū's discussion of the work also dwells on the motif of distance, as the hero is a soldier far away from home in a barbarian land. The theme of distance, the exotic, and the mysterious in Loti is what constitutes his "Orient" as a romantic contrast to everyday life in France. The same "Orient" that Kafū found in Loti is rebuilt in *Pōto Setto,* and Kafū directly acknowledges the role of Loti in his own work on the second page:

> Port Said is the place where Egypt comes to an end. It is part of the Eastern Mohammedan countries that I have imagined for many years. It is the Paradise of those who love color,

> who yearn for pleasure, who dream of indolence—so thinking I could not help but recall the many times when, under the skies of distant America, I had often dreamt about this place. And when I lived in Japan, too, when I was reading the beautiful love stories of Turkey by Pierre Loti long ago, I was then unable to feel any particular impression of Egypt, or Turkey or Persia—that is to say, in short, that the stories were only so much beautiful fiction. But, having once been to America, and having experienced unspeakable anguish and a sense of rebellion at the constantly overcast sky and the strict puritan lifestyle, I then thought of the beauty of the Oriental school (*tōhōha no bi*) which appears in part of the fine art of France, and I dispatched my disconsolate imagination away to the distant shores of North Africa and to the skies of the Balkan peninsula. (p. 571)

It is significant that, in Japan, Loti held no special meaning for Kafū, and he considered it only as "so much beautiful fiction." But once he travels to the West, the Orient of Loti and in the arts of France assumes significance in color, pleasure, and beauty: It is the contrast with the American skies and puritan lifestyle that allows Kafū's Orient to come forth. Suzuki Fumitaka takes the "*tōhōha*" here to mean "Orientalism" (*Orientarizumu*), but even without this translation, this passage certainly shows Kafū's awareness that a group of French artists constructed a particular idea of the "Orient" in their works.[17] It is the work of this group of artists that allows Kafū's imagination to travel to North Africa. Loti's Orientalist vision becomes fuel for Kafū's vivid imagination and dreams, which center on the distant Orient as the "Eastern Mohammedan countries" and "Paradise."

Although Loti is the principal referent in this story, Kafū has drawn on the Orientalist tradition as a whole in describing the Middle East: the burning sun, the line of camels on the horizon, and the old men smoking opium can all be found in the works of Flaubert, while Kafū's ennui, the sense of space, the secret terrors of the silent desert and the mysteries of nature may all be seen in Chateaubriand.[18] On his arrival in Port Said, the narrator's imagination is caught by the languid beauty of Arabian dance, music, and song, which "not only makes us forget all our modern anguish, it also releases the carnal desire of human beings from all knowledge, thought and imagination, and brings forth independence, freedom and purity—and in that actualization, so strong, heavy, and even painful, it also makes us discard the consciousness of ego" (pp. 571–572). The Orient here becomes the complete antithesis to the modern, so that the very consciousness of "self" that so perplexes Kafū through his work is made to disappear: Modern consciousness has no place in the Orient, and man returns to his "natural state." It can be no coincidence that this story was written not long after Kafū had been reading Rousseau.[19] Port Said, for Kafū, is a place completely distanced from everything Western. What first strikes the narrator as he enters the breakwater is "a profusion of different colors, all freshly painted on countless sailing boats, floating there like flowers in a garden" (p. 570). The significance of these colors, and those of the bright Turkish fezzes and the boatmen's clothes and sashes, is one of distance and difference: "set against the dazzling water and the clear bright blue sky, they held a strong sense of pleasure for me that could not be experienced in the cities of the West" (pp. 570–571). The nature of the light in Port Said contrasts markedly with that in the preceding story, *Tasogare no Chichūkai* (Twilight on the Mediterranean). On the waters of the Mediterranean:

> The shimmer of the pale twilight, much the same as one sees in France, cast a gentle shadow of mystery over all manner of things on deck—the gangway, the railings, the cabin walls and all kinds of ropes, and in particular it seemed that some kind of mysterious life had been breathed into the white, newly-painted lifeboats as well. (p. 563)

But the newly painted boats in the strong light of Port Said present an entirely different image:

> In the light of the strong tropical sun, the outlines of all manner of things—the masts, flagstaffs, and even the various kinds of ropes on the ships at anchor—were surprisingly distinct, and because the prospect of the whole harbor was so bright as I looked out over it, I felt just as if I was looking at something far distant, reflected in a huge mirror, without one spot of dullness. (p. 571)

The similarity of phrasing in these two consecutive stories emphasize the change not only in the quality of the light but in the narrator's feelings toward it: The pale shimmer of the French twilight with its gentle air of shadowy mystery has given way to the strong tropical sun and the surprising brightness of a huge reflection. The Orient has been made into a mirror of the West. The Orient here is the very antithesis of France, Other to the civilization and culture of France and the "cities of the West." By reconstructing the French Orientalists' binary system of Self and Other in this way Kafū is associating himself even more clearly with France and the French writers, and reproducing the rhetorical strategies of Orientalist discourse.

Where *Pōto Setto* is dominated by the imagination stirred up by Loti's romances, *Shingapōru no sūjikan* is filled with more direct references to colonialism. We are introduced to this theme immediately by the appearance of Kipling on the first page:

> Five days ago when we called at the port of Colombo, which they say is the island where the Buddha was born, I recalled the scenes of the opera *Lakmé*, then I also thought of the poets Kipling and Leconte de Lisle, and for the first time I encountered coconut tree forests, naked savages, fearsome water buffalo, and the fierce light of the sun. Gazing at the astoundingly luxuriant vegetation before me, I was intoxicated with the beauty of the tropics, which I had dreamed about for a long time. (p. 580)

The images conjured up by the references in this passage are of British colonial rule and the romance of the exotic. The opera *Lakmé*, composed by Léo Delibes, is about the love between the daughter of a Brahmin priest and an English officer, set against the Indian resistance to English oppression. Kipling is perhaps the greatest representative of colonialist English literature, treated at length in Said (1995, pp. 226–228). Leconte de Lisle (1818–1894), the French poet, had his most famous work in the *Poèmes Barbares* of 1862, a collection that follows the history of the races and nations after the fall of Ancient Greece and the world's descent into barbarism resulting from the decay of civilization and art.[20] This opening immediately sets the tone as one of contrast, with the savage, barbarous Orient set up against the "civilizing" influence of British imperialism. Again, Kafū's Orient is set to be a panorama of light, color, strangeness, and violence, a scene that he has "dreamed about for a long time"—even before seeing the scene he has already seen it in his imagination. What Kafū sees from the deck of the ship serves only to confirm his imagined Orient and thus to assert his authority and knowledge about it, a knowledge he has gained from French and English literature on the Orient.

The colonial theme is never far away in this story. At anchor in Singapore, "whichever ship I looked at, they were all cargo ships on route to the colonies" (p. 581), and "The freighters on course for the colonies all but tell us that, both when going out and when coming in, exile is the normal condition of life . . ." (p. 582). The ships thus introduce the subject of the colonies themselves, and so Singapore is presented as the focal point of the colonial empire in the East: "Aah, Singapore. Singapore, the harbor of the Straits Colonies under British dominion. Freighters, savages, immigrants . . . I was suddenly astounded by how fashion, elegance, delicacy and so on were so irrelevant to this world" (p. 582). This observation is followed by a lengthy and passionate discourse on the enormous contrast between Europe (Paris) and these colonies, another example of Kafū's exaggerated essentialized images of East and West:

> In front of the chair I was sitting in, natives with bare feet showing their hairy legs changed places with one another, taking it in turns to come and sell postcards or gemstones or fruit. Black fingers with long nails, unbrushed teeth appearing between thick lips, grimy chests, napes of necks, the flesh of hairy legs—the fact is that I myself even showed a kind of fear that I had never experienced until now. I unwittingly turned my face away time and again, and I thought that what we call cosmetics is actually a beautiful art. I could not help feeling, more strongly than ever before, that to have breathed the air of Europe for even one day, even half a day, is a lifelong glory. In Paris not even one tree is left in an uncultivated state. Branches are pruned. Their heights are aligned. People shave every morning. They polish their nails. At meals, wine and music are indispensable necessities. (p. 582)

Kafū is using the motif of the colonies to set up a contrast between opposites, reflecting the binary system of Orientalist literature: the West against the Orient, Western civilization against Eastern barbarism. However, there are two things to note about this passage. The first is that even though Kafū uses binary structures throughout *Furansu monogatari*, these structures do not form a totalizing, immutable system, nor do the constructs on each side of the dialectic form homogeneous wholes. Kafū's "West" is made up of a number of different and distinct cultural spaces. It is not a homogeneous "West" that Kafū chooses to contrast against the colonies, but Paris, the center of art, culture, and civilization. It is clear both from the number of references and from their context that French culture is esteemed most highly in *Furansu monogatari*, followed most closely by other European cultures including

Britain. The "West" emerges not as a homogeneous mass but as a collection of very different cultures, arranged in a hierarchical order. Kafū chooses his "West" depending on the use he wishes to make of it. Since Paris and Europe embody art and civilization, when arguing for the barbarism of the colonies it is Paris that is used as the point of contrast. Britain appears in the text as the locus of colonial power, whereas America appears as the site of both mercantile and military strength. When taken together, these disparate spaces are constructed as the "West," or *seiyō*, acting not only as the fount of art and civilization but also economic, military, and colonial might in the modern world.

The second point is that the binary system is extended in this story to include the actualities of Western colonial power against the colonized, as Kafū observes that the Malay and Chinese coolies unloading the cargo from the ship are working under Western supervision: "In front of the warehouses, two or three official-looking Westerners with sinister features, wearing hats shaped like helmets, are walking about with great strides" (p. 581). Kafū ascribes powerful actions and military physical attributes to the Western men in positions of authority, in marked contrast to the coolies given nonhuman qualities with no volition in their actions, "pitching about like potatoes being washed." From the context, we assume that the "Westerners" (*seiyōjin*) in this scene are British. However, Kafū uses the word *seiyō* rather than *Eikoku* or a similar word signifying Britain. *Seiyō* in Meiji Japan was a word loaded with images of power and military might in the context of the unequal treaties. When it comes to projecting images of power, therefore, Kafū chooses to use the word *seiyō* and invoke the idea of a wider "West." Kafū never launches into a critical discussion on the idea of colonialism per se, and could be criticized on the same basis as James A. Fujii (1993) has criticized Natsume Sōseki's travel writings in *Man-kan tokorodokoro* (Here and There in Manchuria and Korea), which "displayed significant lapses in what might have been a more critical perspective on Japan's presence in colonial Asia" (p. 198). However, Kafū's "critical perspective" may be seen in his dualistic depiction of the Orient, functioning as symbolic shorthand for the cultural Other and also for Western imperialism. Kafū acknowledged the power structures operating in Asia, connecting what he saw to the body of Orientalist literature produced by the colonizing powers. Where the geopolitical reading of *Suibijin* and *Rinkan* may have been stretching the point, it seems more applicable to *Kaerimichi*.

After Loti and Kipling, the most prominent figure in the stories is Louis-Charles Alfred de Musset, who had become Kafū's inspiration while he was in France.[21] When describing the Orient of Port Said,

Kafū comprehends the scene through the body of texts he already knows, using Musset's verse in particular to ponder the differences between Islam and Christianity when *Pōto Setto* ends with a quote:

> I suddenly recalled three lines of verse that Musset sings in his collection of poetry:
>
> > C'est le point capital du mahométanisme.
> > De mettre le bonheur dans la stupidité.
> > Que n'en est-il ainsi dans le christianisme?
>
> (The fundamental idea of Islam is finding happiness in ignorance. Why is this not so for Christianity?)[22]

Here Kafū recalls another generalization of the Orientalist discourse, simplifying Islam at the same time as defusing its danger. Islam becomes something that Kafū can look down on as inferior, childlike, and simple. Kafū's Orient has taken on the idea underlying much of later Orientalist discourse, that of the Orient's innocent, backward, nonrational character, and with this idea, its condescending attitude. Kafū refers to Musset again in *Shingapōru no sūjikan* when he is so disheartened by the disparity between Paris and the British colonies. The narrator reads out a line: "Oh poet, take up your harp, and give it to me!" We could interpret this line as a reflection of Kafū's appropriation of the Orientalists' textual tradition, as Kafū is taking the harp offered to him by the French poets and carrying on in their stead. In *Pōto Setto*, Kafū refers not only to specific authors but also to the French Orientalist tradition as a whole, as he finds that "the French poets" express his feelings in a generalization about the Orient:

> I could feel a kind of sorrow inexpressible in words, like something spouting forth from the whole harbor, the whole village, that is called Port Said. What the French poets often call "The quiet sorrow of the East (*tōhō*)" is in other words probably alluding to this feeling. (p. 573)

Kafū feels what the French feel, he understands what they are referring to, and so in referring to it he must refer to them. What he feels is inexpressible in his own words, so he must use someone else's—by taking these words he associates himself with the French poets and sees the Orient through their eyes.

We can see in these stories that Kafū is taking on the conventions of French and British Orientalist discourse for his own works. Certain images, motifs, language, and binary structures in Kafū's work directly echo those of Orientalist literature. On a brief reading of *Furansu monogatari,* it may seem obvious that Kafū could speak about "the Orient" because he was just a person traveling in a certain part of the world and writing down his observations on what he saw around him. But on the other hand, Kafū took such pains to refer to Western writers at particular points in his description of the Orient, that it projects a certain amount of deliberation or construction in the writing process. The association of Loti with the fanciful, romantic, and exotic, and the association of Kipling and Delibes with British imperial rule in India, make it clear that Kafū chose to refer to specific writers at particular points to create a specific resonance in the text. It is possible, of course, that Kafū's constant reference to other works was a natural response: When trying to describe his surroundings and the feelings they evoked in him, Kafū related to the work of people who had been there already. But the question is whether his surroundings, for example the desert, evoked feelings of awe and mystery because this was a natural reaction, or because Kafū had read the works of Flaubert and others who depicted the Orient in that way, creating an expectation of mystery for Kafū before he even arrived there. In the case of Loti, it seems to be the latter case: Kafū talks of how he has dreamed for years of the sights he is about to see, and the seeing merely confirms his ideal vision. Reality is seen to conform to the representation, so it is the representation that is perpetuated in Kafū's work. Kafū uses Loti and Kipling especially to draw attention to what he is doing in these texts—by mentioning each author at the time of describing a place, he is doing something specific.

One effect of a liberal sprinkling of names in *katakana* script, coupled with references to classical Western art, literature, and opera throughout *Furansu monogatari,* would be a boost in sales of the collection back home in Japan. Kafū was projecting a persona of himself as a cosmopolitan, well-traveled young gentleman, at home with the artistic life of Europe and willing to interpret this life to Japanese readers. For his audience to trust him, Kafū needed to project an aura of authority and knowledge about Europe and the other lands he was describing. To accomplish this, Kafū associated himself with European writers, by referring to them often, recreating the structures of their literature in his works, and by imitating their writerly personae. The narrator of both *Amerika* and *Furansu monogatari* is invariably a young, highly educated Japanese man with a well-developed sense of fashion and taste. References to famous works of Western art, music, and literature are made at every opportunity to remind the reader that the narrator, and Kafū himself, occupy a privileged cultural space. Kafū grew up in a gentleman's household surrounded by Western furniture, and on his travels continued to see himself as a gentleman scholar and aesthete with an appreciation of great art. Part of the dynamic of reference in *Furansu monogatari* may thus be explained by Kafū's own class affiliation with the European writers and his wish to project a gentlemanly persona in his travel stories. But simple models of class affiliation do not sufficiently explain the dynamics of appropriation and referential authority in the collection, nor the replication of Orientalist rhetorical strategy in Kafū's representation of the Middle East.

There is a long tradition in Japanese literary criticism of examining texts in terms of their reference to older literary traditions. Keene (1993) explains the use of China as referential Other in Japanese literature as a dynamic of allusion. The use of Chinese poetry, places, and historical events in Japanese literature is compared with the use of Latin in English poetry: "This practice was intended to give greater resonance and importance to the events in the Japanese works by demonstrating their affinity with Chinese events and thereby suggesting that they possessed universal significance" (p. 306). The use of China in this way is predominantly premodern, but may be seen right through to the eighteenth century, as David Pollack's (1986) work has shown. Keene (1993) writes that:

> A Japanese who wrote *kanshi* (poems in classical Chinese) felt that he was rising above the uninteresting, trivial matters of his daily life and associating himself with a grand tradition that stretched back for millenia. He was also being cosmopolitan, placing the writings of Japanese within the world of Chinese civilization and thereby implicitly rejecting the insularism of other Japanese who insisted on maintaining the purity of the Japanese language and the integrity of Japanese religion. (p. 307)

Allusion and reference are thus employed in the text to give resonance, importance, and universality to the event described, in the process associating the author with a great tradition, a vast corpus of Chinese works, and the civilization behind it. This process of allusion may be described as an example of "referential authority," where the reference implies the writer's connections with or familiarity with a larger, stronger cultural force. Where *kanshi* literature speaks to the power of China as a strong civilization, invoking Western literature would similarly speak to the power of the West in the Meiji era.[23] The political structures of the early twentieth century are therefore significant in considering Kafū's use of reference—by invoking French and British literature, Kafū was at once acknowledging the colonizing power of the "West" and also reinforcing the image of France as the creator and producer of civilization. Because Kafū referenced the West as the embodiment of cultural capital and symbolic power, it is useful to consider Said's theoretical models of reference, based on a critical awareness of political dynamics at work in the literary text.

Said's (1995) methodology of studying the dynamics of authority between a text and a surrounding body of literature explains the intertextual aspect of Orientalism in terms of intellectual authority. Said's concepts of strategic location and strategic formation provide a clear way of looking at the dynamics that operate both within a single text, and between a text and the Orientalist textual tradition. The first concept in Said's methodology is "strategic location," which "is a way of describing the author's position in a text with regard to the Oriental material he writes about" (p. 20). Said regards this as important because:

> Everyone who writes about the Orient must locate himself vis-à-vis the Orient; translated into his text, this location includes the kind of narrative voice he adopts, the type of structure he builds, the kinds of images, themes, motifs that circulate in his texts—all of which add up to deliberate ways of addressing the reader, containing the Orient, and finally, representing it or speaking on its behalf. (p. 20)

In this concept of location, then, Said presents a way of looking at both internal workings of structure and the idea of power held by the writer over the "Orient" in writing about it. The second concept in Said's methodology is "strategic formation," which is "a way of analyzing the relationship between texts and the way in which groups of texts, types of texts, even textual genres, acquire mass, density, and referential power among themselves and thereafter in the culture at large" (p. 20). In using such concepts it is necessary to bear in mind that Kafū approached French and British Orientalism from outside, rather than from within. However, Kafū's immersion in the Orientalist mode of thinking, and his constant reference to the Orientalist body of work in his travel stories, make this approach particularly suited to a study of Kafū's work. Reference to the Orientalist tradition, particularly

Loti and Kipling, is an integral part of the structure created by Kafū in his vision of the Orient, and so the concept of referential power is important in a consideration of Kafū's text. Strategic formation is in effect the textual context within which the writer finds his own location vis-à-vis the Orient, because:

> Every writer on the Orient . . . assumes some Oriental precedent, some previous knowledge of the Orient, to which he refers and on which he relies. Additionally, each work on the Orient *affiliates* itself with other works, with audiences, with institutions, with the Orient itself. (p. 20, emphasis in original)

It is this affiliation that provides the basis for Kafū's constructions of his "Orient." Kafū affiliates himself with French and British Orientalist works, setting himself up as an authority on the "Orient" for his Japanese audience. Kafū derives his authority from two sources—the fact of his having traveled to America, Europe, and Asia in a physical sense, and also from his knowledge and familiarity with the tradition of texts written by others who also traveled there.

Said argues that the body of Orientalist travel literature comprises its own analyzable "formation" or structure of interrelated texts, where:

> The ensemble of relationships between works, audiences, and some particular aspects of the Orient therefore constitutes an analyzable formation—for example, that of philological studies, of anthologies of extracts from Oriental literature, of travel books, of Oriental fantasies—whose presence in time, in discourse, in institutions . . . gives it strength and authority. (p. 20)

By referring back to the Orientalists' vision of the Orient when describing places like Port Said, Kafū was, in Said's terminology, joining the "formation" of relationships between travel works by such authors as Flaubert, Loti, Kipling, and Musset, writers who had been there before. The formation of travel journals written by French and British colonizers in the Orient had its own authority in the nineteenth and early twentieth centuries, and Kafū uses this to bolster his own work. The formation of texts is explained by Said: "The unity of the large ensemble of texts I analyze is due in part to the fact that they frequently refer to each other: Orientalism is after all a system for citing works and authors" (p. 23). The dynamic at work when Kafū cites Musset, Flaubert, and others is thus one of referential authority, where the quote is what gives the author's own description its validity.

Said describes this literary formation in terms of a "dialectic between individual text or writer and the complex collective formation to which his work is a contribution."[24] Kafū's work cannot be analyzed in terms of this kind of dialectic, as Kafū was an outsider to the Orientalist formation. Although he could make use of the discourse, take authority from it, and show his mastery of the tradition by referring to all the right sources, the relationship between Kafū and the Orientalist collective could only ever operate in one direction: from France to Kafū, never the other way. Kafū was writing in Japanese for Japanese audiences, and his work would not itself become part of the discursive formation, having no determining imprint on the Orientalist discourse in the West. While Kafū may have in one sense "appropriated" the rhetoric of Orientalist discourse for himself in his replication of its themes and structures, we cannot say outright that Kafū's writing represents an appropriation of the Orientalist discourse, for he ultimately had no effect on that discourse or the structures underpinning it. As Masao Miyoshi (1991) argues, the relationship between the West and Japan was permanently "off center," and we cannot forget that the West held the power in the relationship.

Mitsuko Iriye (1969) considers the problem of the dialectic between Kafū's text and the Orientalist literary formation from another angle. Why did Kafū not have his works translated into French or English? Iriye notes that Kafū had wondered when Japanese literature would be translated and available for the American audience, but suggests that perhaps he "did not consider the matter in his own case." Iriye offers one possible reason, that he may have been "too style-conscious to endure the inevitable loss in that direction caused by translation," a guess that can be justified by Kafū's attention to detail in quoting Musset and Baudelaire in the original along with his own translations into Japanese (p. 97). Certainly, if Kafū's command of French had been greater, he could have attempted to write in French or translate his own works into that language, but most critics agree he was not linguistically up to the task. Kafū's intricate style in Japanese, with long, convoluted sentences, word play dependent on kanji and kana combinations, and beautiful, fleeting imagery captured through juxtaposition and disjunction, would have been too difficult to translate without full command of the target language. Perhaps he could have asked a colleague to undertake the translation, but his great ego may not have permitted him to entrust such a precious task to another person. Some authors in the Meiji period did in fact write in foreign languages—Natsume Sōseki is well known for publishing poetry in English, which admittedly made little impact on the English-speaking world at the time.[25] In the Meiji-Taishō era, those who wrote in English did so mainly for their own pleasure or to impress the Japanese audience with their cosmopolitanism, rather than to break into the English-speaking literary world.[26] In *Ochiba,* Kafū's narrator had laughed to himself when imagining that he would one day join the ranks of great poets like Scott, Burns, and Shakespeare. That narrator had also dreamed of writing something in elegant English (*uruwashii Eibun*) that would attract female readers eager to meet the author (p. 242). In real life, however, Kafū had to content himself with writing in Japanese, situating himself within the Orientalist tradition as much as possible through literary reference, while remaining uncomfortably aware of his own lack of impact upon it.

This sense of discomfort was common among Japanese artists abroad, struggling with the double bind of trying to join the European artistic formation yet having to express their thoughts, ideas, and emotions in the Japanese language. Kafū experienced another layer of this double bind, as a writer steeped in Orientalist language yet "Oriental" himself. Kafū's personal artistic experience thus raises wider questions of power and authority. On the surface, Kafū projects a writerly persona who is perfectly at home with the Orientalist mode of thought and expression. In writing on "the Orient," Kafū seems blind to the fact that Japan was one of the mysterious and exotic favourites of Loti, Huysmans, Kipling, and others, and that these people would have labeled Kafū himself as an "Oriental." However, it is impossible that Kafū would not have been aware of the image of Japan created by these writers. Given the breadth of Kafū's reading, the many passing references to Japan could not be overlooked: The fans and artwork adorning the walls of boudoirs in Flaubert and Maupassant, the influence of *ukiyo-e* on Impressionism, the travels of Loti and Kipling to Japan, all would have made an impression. Kafū demonstrated his knowledge in *Amerika monogatari* that "*tōhōha no bi*" was a specific style of art representing a beautiful Orient, while the Decadent School created a poetic Orient of dreamlike mystery. In short, Kafū would have known that Japan played a role as Oriental object to the European gaze. This knowledge placed him in a difficult position, having to convincingly construct himself as subject in observing the Oriental Other.

To some extent, Kafū got around the problem by having his narrator take on a European persona, so close to Kafū's own writerly persona as to be almost indistinguishable. In the binary system of

Furansu monogatari, with the civilization of France set up as contrasting Other to the exotic, barbarian "Orient," Kafū places his narrator completely on the side of Loti, Musset, Byron, Daudet, and Kipling in his position with regard to the Oriental object. As an author, Kafū takes up this position in his daydreams, where he actually becomes these people. He dresses like them and writes in their styles, and refers to the same classical myths and Western culture in his work. Gazing into the water from the ship's deck in *Tasogare no Chichūkai*, the narrator muses that all the classical legends make perfect sense in such an atmosphere, even "the myths which say that the beautiful goddess Venus was born out of the purple waves" (p. 562). Everything about the Mediterranean brings to mind Western history, literature, opera, and art: "The stars began to twinkle. Their light was sharp, their forms huge, and it seemed that they must have exactly five points, like those one sees in Symbolist paintings" (p. 562). Or again, he exclaims: "Oh, the beauteous night of the Mediterranean! By chance I recalled a nude portrait of antiquity, with exceeding clarity of outline. I recalled the beauty of classical art. I recalled the rows of shrubs trimmed neatly in the gardens of Versailles. That my own works could be like this!" (pp. 562–563). The association with Western classical culture is portrayed as completely natural—even when gazing at the Suez Canal and the Turkish flag it is Musset who springs to mind. Unlike in *Ochiba*, the narrator is not permitted to feel any self-consciousness or sense of irony in his performance.

Kafū's own writerly persona is also placed completely on the side of the Orientalists. He sees the Orient, observes it, writes it, and constructs it as an Orientalist would. While he remains in Europe, this façade is successful, but cracks begin to appear on the homeward journey, as Kafū is forced to realize his identity as fundamentally Japanese and not French. The moment of realization is dramatically expressed in *Tasogare no Chichūkai*, as the narrator is moved to song by the beauty of the Mediterranean night, but is confused as to what sort of song could possibly express his feelings:

> I was exceedingly dismayed, and I tried in earnest to dredge up from my memory some kind of tune I had learned . . . I finally hit upon a verse of "Siciliana," which is sung to the accompaniment of a solitary harp in the opening of *Cavelleria Rusticana*.[27] . . . I was cheered up enormously and attempted the first line of it to begin with, but with the very first phrase, "O, Lola, bianca come"—I completely forgot all that followed. It is not unreasonable to suppose that I

> could not recall it because it was Italian, which I do not know very well. Perhaps the opening of *Tristan*,[28] the song sung by the mariner atop the mast, was much better suited to the circumstances. But this time I could only remember the words of the song, and was unsure of the melody to which it had to be sung. No matter how I longed to sing, European songs were too difficult. Did being born in Japan mean that I could only ever sing the songs of my own country? My feelings at this juncture—leaving behind the love and art of France—were that I was journeying toward the edge of the Orient, where only death awaited at the end of a monotonous life. I wondered whether there was a song in Japanese which could fully express such emotions. (pp. 564–565)

In many ways, this passage shows us an artist struggling to articulate the "self" in some authentic manner. The urge to sing, to express, is there, but foreign words and music are simply too far distant from the narrator's own experience to be able to express his true feeling. The narrator's failure to remember words and melodies brings home the essential foreignness of the European medium. Caught between European culture and his Japanese origins, he turns to his own language and musical heritage in the search for a suitable mode of expression, but again comes up short:

> All the recitation plays,[29] beginning with Takemoto[30] and Tokiwazu[31] manifest complex, deep emotion splendidly, but looking at it from the musical point of view, it is better to call them poetic recitals which employ musical instruments rather than true songs, and they are too cool to appeal to spontaneous emotion. The Utazawa songs[32] are only weak lamentations from the red-light districts of a bygone age, and Noh chants only imply Buddhist pathos, are merely classically elegant, and have something about them which is in no way compatible with a twentieth-century steamship. They have to be set in a scene looking at distant shores of pine trees like an India-ink drawing, while listening to the sound of oars in a rush-roofed boat . . . I gave up all hope. No matter how I agonized over my overflowing feeling and my chaotic emotions, I came from a nation of people possessing no music with which I could express myself. Could such a nation, such a race, exist anywhere

> else in the world? . . . Meiji civilization! It has only given us a limitless anguish, providing nothing to which we can entrust that anguish or complain of it. Our emotions are far too distantly removed from the music of the feudal period to be able to cling to what long ago became a second-hand relic, but if we run headlong toward the music of Europe, no matter how deep our biased love for the West, we will still feel an irreconcilable distance from its customs and sentiment. (pp. 566–567)

Kafū's narrator is driven to despair, for he can neither express himself through Western song, whose lyrics and melodies escape his memory, nor through traditional Japanese music, which remains utterly out of place aboard a twentieth-century steamship in the Mediterranean. Kafū depicts the essence of the Meiji intellectual's dilemma after having once experienced the West: His experiences are so alien to Japan that its outmoded forms of expression are no longer useful. But neither can Western forms of expression or systems of thought ever provide a true alternative. Kafū could never be French. Japan was not the West, and no matter how Kafū and other writers tried, they could not change their origins. Although this is a heart-wrenching realization, Kafū manages to carve out a solution, returning to the fluid, flexible positioning of the self that he used to such great effect in *Amerika monogatari*. If the narrator's position vis-à-vis Europe was fixed and immutable, then he could still manipulate his position in relation to the Oriental object. In the two stories following *Tasogare no Chichūkai*, Kafū takes the European position vis-à-vis the Orient for himself, and so we see an emerging feeling of superiority over the Oriental people.

This sense of superiority begins to show itself as soon as Kafū arrives in Port Said. As he embarks on a smaller boat to go sightseeing in the town, the narrator has "hardly enough time to wonder at the Egyptian pronunciation of 'K,' unaccustomed to the Egyptian spoken by the boatman in a loud voice" (p. 572). The narrator next sees a group of girls playing and feels sorrow "in sympathy for these girls, with no carnivals, festivals or dance on the edge of this lost desert at the end of the world" (p. 574). The clearest sense of Kafū's feeling of superiority comes from his descriptions of "the natives" of the countries he visits. Most often they are likened to animals. The Arabian dance, for instance, is described as "the dance which makes the muscles of both arms and shoulders, chest, stomach, and waist, with the ample, slightly oily skin of the colored races, undulate sinuously like the gliding movements of a snake" (p. 571). This simile is repeated later in the same story:

> In among these people sound asleep, silent and unmoving, women wearing long, black veils on their heads just showing the eyes, and wearing wooden ornaments on the bridge of the nose, glide by like snakes, with no sound of footsteps from the clogs on their bare feet, even though they bear the strong, fleshy curves peculiar to the Arabs under the same thin, black clothing. (p. 575)

When not likened to animals, people become inanimate objects: "Under the eaves of the houses, many old men with white cloths wrapped about their heads were also sitting cross-legged, like things made of wood, not moving at all" (p. 575). Kafū sees the people of the Orient as things that are frightening, ugly, or savage, but never as human beings. Kinya Tsuruta (1998), in his review of Westerners in Japanese literature, argues that Japanese depictions of Westerners as ugly/evil or beautiful/sexual, as well as the obvious animal metaphors, "dehumanize" the Western subject by refusing to acknowledge their psychological existence. The dehumanization of the Arabians in Kafū's text is also a refusal to acknowledge the subject in the Oriental Other. But the very "inhumanity" with which these people are treated makes a deep impression on the narrator. In *Shingapōru no sūjikan*, it is this inhumanity that frightens him into realizing that the Orient is indeed a very different place from either the West or Japan:

> Countless numbers of hideous Malay natives and filthy Chinese coolies jostle one another. . . . They all wear only one torn piece of cloth wrapped about their hips, and so in the light of the hot day and the coal dust, and in the swirls of dingy smoke, the movements of these laborers going back and forth at first could only be considered, not as human beings, but only as black dirty lumps of flesh pitching about like potatoes being washed. At length, as the muscles of their moving arms and legs were repeatedly burdened with heavy objects, they jutted out like knots on a pine tree, and when I realized that the sweat was pouring down them like a waterfall, I, who had for a long time been stunned only by the power of machinery and electricity, was hit with a sadness and fear which threatened to pluck out my heart. The place called the Orient was truly an awful place. I felt that it was a country of terrible physical labor. (p. 581)

The narrator's sympathy for the "natives" recalls the British professions of sympathy toward Indian people, as in Kipling's "Lo!

the poor Indian," which simultaneously celebrates the native's pure and innocent understanding of the natural world. The depiction is also consistent with tropes of travel writing in general, and the appearance of "natives" in other Japanese travelogues of the time. Like Kafū, Natsume Sōseki (2000) found his feelings change as he watched coolies in Dairen, Manchuria. At first he observed: "They were tractable, had strong physiques, and put energy into their tasks. Watching them at their work was thus a source of pleasure." But "In their silence, fixed gestures, perseverance, and energy, they resembled shadows guided by Fate. As an erect flesh-and-blood observer, I found that after a time spent watching them, strange thoughts came to my mind" (p. 65). Similarly, Arishima Takeo is moved at the sight of parentless children in Colombo: "I saw in their lives most neglected humanity . . . I watched them and almost wept."[33] All three observers thus comment on the "inhumanity" of the natives in some way, but Kafū associates his narrator with technology in a way that Sōseki and Arishima do not.[34] In the face of "terrible physical labor," Kafū's narrator is made to feel not only his own humanity, but also his modernity. While the Malay and Chinese natives in *Furansu monogatari* are likened to natural occurrences such as pine trees and waterfalls, the narrator remains squarely in the realm of machinery and electricity. Positioning himself in relation to the natives, then, Kafū's superiority is assured.

Coming so soon after the despair experienced on the Mediterranean, this scene draws our attention to Kafū's positioning as an act of will. Both scenes take place on the deck of a ship; both have the narrator confronting his own position, somewhere in between the civilizations of Europe and the Orient. Both scenes also express strong emotion: The first evidences Kafū's despair at not originating in the Occident, whereas the second shows his relief at not belonging to the Orient. If he belongs to neither tradition, then where exactly is he positioning himself? The location of the self here is hard to pin down, occupying a fluid "in-between" position, exterior to both Europe and the Orient. There is no doubt that Kafū felt deep frustration at not being able to change his essential origins and fully join the Orientalist formation of European writers and artists. Kafū felt himself as having more in common with the French and British writers than with their Oriental objects of discussion, sharing the same social class, education, and a similar knowledge of literary texts. His ego and background gave him a feeling of equality with European artists, where only the linguistic barrier and mistake of his birth kept him from joining their cultural formation. On the other hand, Kafū clearly did not feel himself to be part of the "Orient" set in Egypt, Suez, the Middle East, India, and

Singapore, as he felt nothing in common with the natives of these countries. In the lands of this Orient, Kafū was as far away from Japan as he was from Europe, and the dance, music, and heat of this Orient were equally as far removed from the Japanese experience. In short, Kafū did not see Japan to be part of the Orient constructed in French and British literature. In *Furansu monogatari*, the "Orient," "Japan," and the "West" are separated into three distinct spaces, each defined in contrast to the other two. Kafū's separation of "Japan" from the idea of "Orient" would not have been uncommon in Meiji Japan. Japan in 1908 was not regarded as an integral part of Asia, but as a rapidly developing country throwing off the shackles of a backward Asian (mainly Chinese) tradition. After winning the Sino-Japanese War of 1895, Japan felt itself to be in a position of superiority, from which it could assume the role of teacher and leader to the rest of Asia. As Mark Peattie points out, these developments were also given ideological foundations by beliefs in the unique, divine nature of the Japanese race and current theories of Social Darwinism, to bring out a strong sense of superiority over Asia (Myers & Peattie, 1984, p. 13).

By separating Japan out from the wider idea of the Orient, Kafū disrupts the simplistic binary structure of civilized, colonizing West against barbaric, colonized Orient that has so far dominated *Pōto Setto* and *Shingapōru no sūjikan*. In *Amerika monogatari*, although the main contrast was drawn between the two opposing spaces of "America" and "Japan," Kafū was able to position himself at many different points within these two spaces, constructing an array of contrasts between the traditional Japan, Westernized Japan, the immigrant Japantown, the ideal America of liberty, and the real America of racial discrimination. In the same way, although the main contrast in *Pōto Setto* and *Shingapōru no sūjikan* is that drawn between the West and the Orient, Kafū does not limit himself to a simplistic configuration of these two poles, introducing the possibility of a position outside the binary system of West–Orient by his own presence as narrator and observer. Kafū's disruption of the binary system in both *Amerika* and *Furansu monogatari* is thus made possible by the flexible positioning of the external observer.

This flexible positioning is clear in *Shingapōru no sūjikan* where Kafū is standing on the deck of the ship at anchor, watching the Malay and Chinese coolies unloading the ship, while Western supervisors "are walking about with great strides" (p. 581). We earlier recognized Kafū's awareness of colonialism in Asia in this scene, as well as his feeling of superiority in regard to the Asian "natives," but it also shows Kafū's position as an outsider in the binary system of West–Orient. From his vantage point on deck, Kafū constructs himself as an uninvolved observer to the scene being played out in front of him. The tableau presents Kafū as observer of both colonized object, the "black dirty lumps of flesh," and the colonizing subject, the "official-looking Westerners with sinister features." Kafū is stunned by the appearance of both groups, one animalistic and inhuman, the other official and sinister. By rewriting the Orientalist relationship from his own point of view Kafū in effect reconstructs it and destroys the closed nature of the binary system. The narrator's exterior position introduces a noncolonized Asian/Oriental as the speaking observer, that is, as subject/agent rather than object. That Kafū is able to write in this way comes from his choice of position outside the binary system of West–Orient. Kafū's use of binary opposition in *Amerika* and *Furansu monogatari* is flexible and dynamic, not static or restrictive. Kafū is able to reposition himself almost at will between a wide array of the West, America, France, the Orient, and Japan in order to make different points with different sets of contrasts. This is the point at which Said's model of the binary structure of Occident and Orient fails, for there was obviously more than one "Orient." The "Orient" of Said's *Orientalism* was observed and represented not only by writers from the dominating West but by others as well.

Kafū's flexible positioning also allowed him to articulate his feelings on the double bind of the Japanese artist abroad. While the European tradition was not his own, and Japanese art was too restrictive, Kafū used the liminal space of the travel story to express his thoughts, work through his dilemma, and articulate his complex emotion. That this expression took the form of Orientalist rhetoric is perhaps not surprising, given Kafū's love for French literature and the fact that he was traveling through places typically constructed as "Orient" in that literature. What is remarkable is the freedom with which Kafū wields the brush of Orientalist literature. Orientalism may be described as the practice of "writing the Orient," where the Orient is object to the writer. Kafū is "writing the Orient" when he constructs his Port Said, his Turkey, his India. And this act of "writing the Orient" is an act of writing in the language of the writers whom Kafū so admired. The result, however, is significant because it is a writing of the Orient in the language of Western Orientalist discourse by a writer from within the "Orient," that is, from the position of being the object of that discourse. In taking the discourse for himself, and the Orient as the object of his writing, Kafū in effect claims for himself the position of writer/subject/agent. Kafū was no passive intellectual falling in love with the beauty of French Orientalism and then merely echoing it. Nor was he an inferior "subaltern" desperately trying to reclaim a voice for that Orient—Kafū never opposed the French discourse.[35] Instead he took it as his own, appropriating it rather than opposing it, working with the discourse for his own structures of contrast and using its authority to bolster his work.

Kafū's use of the language and authority of Orientalist discourse raises questions about the nature of discursive practice itself, however, in the issue of "closure": Is it ever possible for a writer from the Orient to write in the language of the discourse that objectifies that Orient? How can the writer ever position him or herself outside the total, closed system of the discourse in order to do this? This question has formed the basis of many critiques against Said's *Orientalism,* as Said theoretically can never be totally outside the discursive structure of Orientalism in order to write a criticism of it himself.[36] The philosophical question of closure is far beyond the scope of this book, but it is a significant question in regard to Kafū's positioning vis-à-vis French Orientalist discourse. To take the pragmatic view, I suggest that the strict binary structure of Orient–Occident in this case cannot be upheld, because as demonstrated above, there was more than one "Orient." Other critics, notably Xiaomei Chen (1995), also argue that binary essentialization is more of a hindrance than a help when considering writings from places such as China and Japan, which had a different relationship with the Occident than, for instance, Egypt had (pp. 13, 21). Said's argument centers on the idea that it was the dominant culture of the West that surrounded, represented, and created the "Orient" in literature and imperialism. But it was not just the Western writer who wrote about the Orient. It was Western Orientalism that inspired Kafū's dreams of exotic foreign places. But Kafū went to the Middle East himself, and wrote his own sketches that recreated the Orient from his point of view. While Kafū's writing may have had no effect on the discourse and discursive practices of Orientalism, it is no longer possible to ignore the idea that people from outside the Western Orientalist tradition also wrote about the "Orient," even while using that tradition as their authority.

Kafū's flexible ability to reposition himself vis-à-vis the places he is describing, and his stance as a narrator outside the binary system of West and Orient, may thus be seen as a concrete example of the possibility of writing from outside Said's "closed" system. It is clear that binary opposition may be used as a literary device in drawing contrasts and defining Self in relation to Other without having to rely on the kind of closure Said envisioned. Even so, Said's notion of "strategic location" can still be of use in this case, because

Kafū's flexible positioning is so central to his construction of place. Kafū's location of self vis-à-vis the Orient was what allowed him to write about the Orient at all—Kafū felt himself to be superior to the naked savages, coolies, and Arabians even while longing to be like the elegant citizens of Paris. Kafū's positioning of himself outside the Orient lasts for the entire time he is traveling through it. The position wavers only when he nears Japan, and finds that soon he will no longer be in a position of superior exteriority. After surveying the colonies "under British dominion" in Singapore, Kafū contrasts the tropical scene before him with the exaggerated refinements of Paris, and feels an unbearable loneliness: "It was a feeling exactly as if I were the last individual of a perishing species" (p. 583). This rather melodramatic statement comes as Kafū realizes that he belongs neither to the cultured elite of Paris nor to the hordes of immigrants and laborers thronging the docks. We see Kafū's self-assured stance as one of the cultured intellectuals of Europe slipping as the question begins to irritate him: "how, how near, had the civilized nation called Meiji, that had triumphed over Russia, now approached me?" (p. 580). Kafū's flexible positioning of self in relation to his surroundings no longer applies, as he is not rejoining the (Asian) "Orient" of his own free will. It is not he who is traveling toward home but Meiji Japan that is growing ever closer to him.

Kafū's distaste at having to rejoin Meiji society crystallizes in *Shingapōru no sūjikan* in a vivid portrayal of a Japanese family who are also traveling home to Japan after spending two years in Kwantung Province. The narrator is shocked at their rusticated appearance: "Perhaps this was because for a long time I had seen only Westernized Japanese people, and the appearance of this purely Japanese couple looked extremely unusual to me, while at the same time my revulsion against modern Japan was growing more and more agitated" (p. 584). The husband, caricatured as "Mr. Educator," expounds noisily at length on the Russo–Japanese War in an excruciating rural accent. In the meantime, the wife is seasick before the boat even sets sail and the baby wets itself, bawling incessantly. The narrator takes advantage of a sudden downpour to escape below deck, afraid to venture out in case he meets them again:

> I could only consider the wife's thinning hair, dirty teeth and pale face as evidence aimed at myself, to teach me that in the place called "the East" (*tōyō*), people despise the art of cosmetics, do not permit comments on their personal appearance, and deny all the pleasures of love, women

> being only machines to produce soldiers of the future who must conquer enemy countries. At the same time, Mr. Educator's powerful, big face and his loud, overwhelming voice were telling me that the civilized nation of Meiji was the Confucian gentleman's country of benevolence, justice, loyalty, and filial piety. Ten days from now I would have to tread upon the soil of that country. They seemed to be warning me arrogantly that I would have to submit to the customs of my heritage, whether I liked it or not. (p. 587)

The caricature of the Japanese family here serves as symbolic representation of everything Kafū had grown to hate about Meiji Japan: its hypocrisy, authoritarianism, and Confucian value system. Kafū's discomfort comes largely from the feeling of being forced back into a society he had come to despise. But, as Komori Yōichi points out, it also came from an "inability to reconcile himself to the idea that his own country may be included in the category of "*Tōyō*."[37] Kafū and his contemporaries would struggle with this issue at the end of the Meiji period. What exactly was Japan's relationship to "Asia"? Should it be defined in terms of shared culture, or Japanese colonial expansion? Separating Japan from the imagined spaces of "Orient" and "Asia" was easily accomplished while still abroad, but once Kafū arrived in Japan he would have to work through these ideas properly.

What is increasingly clear at the end of *Kaerimichi* is Kafū's negativity toward the Meiji state, as the critique of *Ichigatsu ichijitsu* and the nascent oppositional stance of *Suibijin* come together powerfully in *Shingapōru no sūjikan*. Kafū's horror at the prospect of returning to the "Confucian gentleman's country" may be seen in the unequivocal original title of the work, *Akkan* (Revulsion). For the publication of *Furansu monogatari* a long passage describing the horrible prospect of modern Tokyo was actually cut out of this work, in which Kafū no longer bothered to disguise his critical attitude toward the Meiji state. Keene (1984) cites the original version of *Akkan* as an example of "Kafū's bitterness toward Japan" (p. 414). Kafū's feelings are clear in the following passage:

> Police officers, teachers, soldiers, officials, the brick buildings of Hibiya, the bronze statues of Saigō and Kusunoki, newspapers that exploit human beings for their own financial gain, signs which strictly prohibit this or that, notices, regulations, ward offices, family registers, heads of families, official seals, unattractive female students, university students from

> the country, hysterical middle-aged women with *marumage* coiffures, slum children like monkeys, outdoor toilets filled with the evening sun, sinks full of crawling slugs—all the unpleasant feelings I had harbored about the Japanese Empire, which I had almost managed to forget in Europe and America, suddenly floated up into my memory, like the traces of long-ago nightmares. (pp. 648–649)

In the original version of *Akkan,* we see Kafū using his writing as an outlet for his frustration and anger toward the Meiji government, an expression for his critical attitude concerning the trappings of the modern state. Although the feelings in *Akkan* are expressed at length, this frustration also made a brief appearance in *Pōtto Setto*. Sailing through the Suez Canal, the narrator spies a Turkish flag in the distance and becomes agitated, admiring Turkey for its despotic individualism in contrast to the hypocritical, sycophantic façade of Meiji Japan:

> I was filled with a fervent warmth and saluted to this national flag. I respect Turkey. Turkey at least is not a hypocritical country. It is not a hypocritical country carried away with the insincere vanity of wanting to get into company with Western nations and putting up a front of fake civilization to save appearances. (p. 578)

Kafū finally returned to Japan in July 1908. Shortly after his return, the stories that would be collected as *Furansu monogatari* were being published in various magazines. When all the stories and essays were collected into one volume for publication in 1909, however, the book was banned from sale.[38] Kafū's frustration and indignation at this treatment were considerable, and the strict censorship laws of the Meiji state did nothing to improve Kafū's opinion of the government. From this time onward, Kafū's view of Meiji Japan was to grow increasingly negative. As a returnee, he found himself trapped in a new double bind, despising Japan's superficial attempts at modernization yet longing for an authentic kind of modernity that would suit his own country. Kafū was hopeful that he could introduce to his readers the idea of Japan as a cultural equal to France, yet at the same time despaired of the impossibility of such an attempt. The Returnee Stories of 1909–1910 show Kafū wrestling with these problems and coming to his own solution, finding a way to articulate his Japanese identity as well as a way for Japan to be both "modern" and "authentic."

CHAPTER FOUR

Occidentalism

Contrast and Critique in the Returnee Stories

Through *Amerika monogatari* and *Furansu monogatari,* Kafū showed an increasing disillusionment with his home country, first in comparison to America and France, and then as the realization hit him that he must return to Japan. Where the young narrators of *Furansu monogatari* often wanted to remain in Europe, fiercely wishing they were not Japanese at all, Kafū's works of 1909–1910 show the author struggling to come to grips with the fact of his return to Japan and with the state of Meiji Tokyo after his absence of five years. The "Returnee Stories" refer to all of Kafū's works published between 1909 and 1910, including *Fukagawa no uta* (A Song of Fukagawa), *Botan no kyaku* (The Peony Garden), *Kanraku* (Pleasure), *Donten* (Cloudy Weather), *Kitsune* (The Fox), *Kangokusho no ura* (Behind the Prison), *Sumidagawa* (The River Sumida), *Shinkichōsha nikki* (Diary of a Recent Returnee), and *Reishō* (Sneers).[1] These works demonstrate Kafū's state of mind at the time of his return, clearly showing his reactions to the changed state of Tokyo. The Returnee Stories also show Kafū's critical stance against Meiji modernization and hypocrisy, and against what he saw as the destruction of traditional Japanese culture in this period. Critics disagree as to whether the works may be seen as true "criticism," but I argue that Kafū intended the stories to be read as a critique against the Meiji government's superficial approach to the modernization of Japan, especially in the rapid Westernization of Tokyo. In this chapter, I will provide a contextual synthesis of Kafū's critical viewpoint, showing how it developed from mere dissatisfaction at Meiji civilization (*bunmei*) to a deeper, more reasoned critique based on contrast with the Western Other, in a challenge to Japan to discover its own genuine cultural heritage.

The Returnee Stories may be seen as a series because they have so many common elements, and a progression may be seen in the set of works—from indirect criticism using metaphor, to direct, outspoken criticism, to suggested solutions in the final novels. All written in the space of only two years, the stories form a homogeneous series, sharing many common elements: The main character or narrator has usually just returned from abroad; the Westernization of Tokyo is seen as a superficial and absurd attempt when compared with the genuine article overseas; the characters find solace only in old areas of the city such as Fukagawa, Yanagibashi, or the banks of the Sumida, while new areas are depicted as little more than building sites; and the dual nature of the city as Edo/Tokyo is linked to a binary of "genuine" versus "superficial." Simply stated, Kafū comes to the conclusion that "Tokyo" is no good because it is superficial and destroying what beauty there is in the city, whereas "Edo" is good because it is genuine—old, corrupt, decaying, like the France portrayed by the Decadent School, but still representing what is truly "Japanese." In this value judgment, we see Kafū's intent in writing these pieces, articulated in the stories themselves: Writing must be an act of opposition (*hankō*) to the status quo. Through his writing, Kafū aimed to awaken his audience to the beauty of Edo culture, affirming a genuine "Japan" in the face of rapid and confusing modernization.

The narrative stance of the Returnee Stories is often so close to Kafū that we may speak of it in terms of an authorial persona, in which the narrators of *Fukagawa no uta, Botan no kyaku*, and *Shinkichōsha nikki*, as well as the various characters of *Sumidagawa* and *Reishō*, are assumed to give voice to Kafū's own opinions and attitudes toward Meiji modernization. The main characters have much in common with Kafū himself—the same experiences overseas, an overbearing yet ailing father, a house designed half in Japanese and half in Western style, literary works censored by the government, and so on. *Kitsune* purports to recount scenes from Kafū's own youth, further complicating the narratorial stance. Yet a stance it is, and it seems more calculated in the Returnee Stories than in the travel collections. Hibi Yoshitaka (1998) has analyzed Kafū's "returnee" figure, cultivated simultaneously in his works of the period and in his personal appearance, as one carefully designed to appeal to the Meiji audience. In a very short time after his return to Japan, Kafū rose to prominence in the literary world. He published in the same venues as Shimazaki Tōson, Tayama

Katai, and Natsume Sōseki, achieved public recognition from *Waseda bungaku,* and was appointed professor in French literature at Keiō Gijuku, later to become Keiō University. This appointment, made on the recommendation of Mori Ōgai and Ueda Bin, cemented Kafū's reputation as a serious man of letters in 1910—an artist returned from the West with new knowledge and a new fashionable air. Kafū's cravats, long hair, and bohemian attitude enhanced his returnee persona, which Hibi argues was designed to mesh seamlessly with the narrator of the Returnee Stories in the audience's mind. Hibi maintains that years of confessional *shizenshugi* fiction from the *bundan,* as well as Kafū's tendency to publish his travel works as "miscellanies" from abroad rather than as fictional works, had primed the reading public to see Kafū's narrators as the author himself. As a result, Kafū and his series of returnee narrators were taken at face value as experts on the European arts, and Kafū's critique was broadcast effectively through his literary works.

As well as sharing a common main character, the Returnee Stories also share their use of cipher characterization for secondary characters. Cipher characters are representatives of types rather than full characters in their own right. These types are sometimes made to represent different aspects of Kafū's psyche, most famously in *Reishō.* Edward Seidensticker (1965) sees this as a literary failure, arguing that in *Reishō,* "names and identifications do not really matter, the work being one long soliloquy" (p. 38). He later adds, "the narrative falls short of coalescing into a novel. The characters are such ready spokesmen for the novelist that in the end they are nothing" (p. 41). It does seem that the Returnee Stories as a whole never attempt characterization in any depth apart from the authorial "I." Even Ragetsu and Chōkichi remain shadowy in *Sumidagawa,* taking second place to the Sumida River itself. *Reishō* is no different in this respect, as none of its five main characters are drawn with depth of characterization as an aim. But Kafū is not aiming to create real people. Instead, as we saw earlier in *Kyabin yawa,* he purposefully uses cipher characters in order to give voice to certain points of view, each typifying some aspect of living in Meiji. As Masao Miyoshi (1991) has argued, it is misguided to apply the standards of the Western novel in judging the Japanese *shōsetsu,* and a lack of deep characterization does not automatically mean failure in the Japanese literary tradition (pp. 46–50). The Returnee Stories may be likened to the semi-autobiographical travel sketches *Amerika* and *Furansu monogatari,* and on a wider scale to the traditional Japanese genres of *zuihitsu,* diary and the I-novel. Karatani Kōjin has argued that to assume that a sharp distinction exists between "the self that expresses and the content of expression" is to assume a basic premise of binarism upon which works either "fail" or "succeed."[2] To criticize the Returnee Stories as failing on the point of characterization is to draw unnecessary lines between the "self that narrates" and the "self as content" of these works.

Before analyzing the Returnee Stories, a note on the translation of the texts is in order. All translations are my own unless otherwise stated. Where well-known English translations are available I will use them—*Sumidagawa,* in particular, is well known in the West precisely because of Seidensticker's English translation. Seidensticker also translated *Botan no kyaku* to great effect. But examining the choices he made in what to translate, it is evident that Seidensticker only translated those stories that show Kafū in a quiet, subtle mode, praising Edo for its beauty and historical value. Edward Fowler (1992) has demonstrated that the postwar publishing climate favored this kind of translation, the "aestheticized realms" of which "provided exactly the right image of Japan at a time when that country was being transformed, almost overnight in historical terms, from a mortal enemy during the Pacific War to an indispensable ally during the Cold War era" (p. 6). The result of this carefully chosen and sponsored translation was a "re-Orientalized Japan that had retreated from its role of aggressor in the 1940s to its prewar role of quaint and exotic object" (p. 42). As part of this process, Seidensticker focused on translating Kafū's works that described beautiful scenes of geisha and samisen in flowing, lyrical prose. But by not translating the most vitriolic of Kafū's criticism, Seidensticker was able to construct a false picture of the Returnee Stories as a whole, arguing that Kafū was not a serious critic, that he wrote nothing which could be called social or political criticism, and that the stories were merely cantankerous whining or unsuccessful, unliterary pieces. Seidensticker's treatment of the Returnee Stories should be seen as an argument *for* Kafū as a critic for the simple reason that, to argue to the contrary, he had to leave *Fukagawa no uta, Reishō* and *Shinkichōsha nikki* untranslated.

Fukagawa no uta (A Song of Fukagawa), written in December 1908 and published in *Shumi* in February 1909, marks the change in Kafū's approach to his subject that would define his work for the next two years. From the first page, a contrast is drawn between old and new in the streets of Tokyo: traditional pine and bamboo New Year's decorations, paper lanterns, flags, and banners hang above the crowded streets while old, dirty tiled roofs "contrasted with the fresh wooden planks of newly-built houses." Meanwhile the afternoon sun lights up a "confusion without one bit of harmony" (KZ 4.122).[3] The narrator catches a streetcar from Yotsuya and notices that the traditional carts and carriages, a moat and a high embankment with pines, and a stone wall outside the window have a peaceful beauty totally at odds with the crowded mayhem inside the streetcar. The striking contrast reminds us that Kafū would have been surprised by the extent to which the introduction of the electric streetcar had influenced Tokyo in his absence. Tayama Katai (1987) tells us that the streetcar transformed the entire transport system, leading to the decline of the waterways, the rebuilding of stone bridges into steel, and the relocation of department stores to the busy streetcar intersections (p. 229). In Natsume Sōseki's work *Sanshirō* (Sanshiro, 1908), too, it is the noisy clanging and crowds of the streetcars that startle the hero on his arrival in Tokyo, while the streetcar in *Sorekara* (And Then, 1909) conveys the main character Daisuke into a world of madness.[4] Kafū's choice of subject for the first half of *Fukagawa no uta* thus reflects one of the major upheavals in Tokyo life of the time.[5] It is impossible to overstate the horrible confusion and discord created by the collection of loud, repulsive people in the streetcar. The noise jars the ears not only of the narrator but of the reader as well, as we are forced to experience the sound of an old woman sucking on her rotting tooth, quarrels between passengers, a crying baby, the clanging of the streetcar, and brusque orders from the conductor.

The narrator turns his gaze outward at Miyakezaka to find some relief in the calming view of the old Edo castle. The picturesque description of the castle gate and pine trees provides contrast with the streetcar interior, but also gives an oblique criticism of the Meiji government, as Katsuya Sugawara points out. Kafū describes only the scenery on the left-hand side of the streetcar, ignoring the view on the right, which would have been "the administrative core of the Meiji government, from the Italianate Ministry of War and the General Staff Office (now the site of the Diet) to the stately brick pile of the Ministry of Justice" (Sugawara, 2001, p. 117). Kafū's omission would have signaled to Tokyo-based readers the strength of his disdain for the Meiji administration responsible for the current upheaval. Heading into the Ginza, the Western-style buildings look austere and utilitarian, and only the private homes of Tsukiji retain some of the elegance of Edo tastes. At Sakamoto Park the streetcar suddenly loses power and stops, jammed in between other cars in front and behind, all abandoned by their drivers and conductors. The narrator has no particular place to go, but the conductor gives him a ticket for a change to Fukagawa (pp. 131–132).

The second half of the story is directed inward to the narrator's own emotions. As he looks around at the confusion in the street—the traffic jam, train lines and badly painted houses that look more like storage huts, he is filled with indignation, and longs to "leap in one bound from the center of this wretched city to Fukagawa," the place that had always satisfied "all my tastes and longings, and all my sorrows and joys." Fukagawa was the place where the narrator found peace and beauty "in the midst of the destruction" of all that had been beautiful in the city of Edo (p. 133). Back then, he muses, the way to Fukagawa was not by train but by rickshaw, and the Fudō Shrine had been thronged with visitors. The narrator reflects on how the scene has changed, and is moved by the "beauty and sorrow" of his memories as he looks back on his younger self of ten years ago:

> I hadn't known anguish. Fully satisfied with the pleasure of my Edo interests, my heart had been at peace. . . . The oscillation of sound waves, the light and shade of color, the weight of the air—such things hadn't irritated my nerves at all. I hadn't the slightest anticipation that such things could intrude into the sphere of art. I had believed without a doubt that Japan was where I would live forever, and that the Japanese language would always express my emotions freely.
>
> Now, I sport a moustache and wear Western clothes. I'm riding in an electric streetcar and crossing the Eitai Bridge, made of steel. How could I have been oblivious to the upheavals of the age? (pp. 134–135)

Kafū would have seen the new Eitai Bridge before he left Japan, since it was rebuilt in 1897, but here its steel structure is made into a symbol of the modernization of Tokyo. As the narrator arrives in Fukagawa, however, he finds that there he can overlook the changes of the last ten years, "returning completely" to the past (p. 136). This Fukagawa is a timeless, unchanging entity, a construct that resurfaces many times in the Returnee Stories.

In the grounds of the Fudō shrine, the narrator finds fortune tellers, a satirist parodying the Buddhist scriptures, and a blind man squatting in the dust holding a samisen. As the blind man takes out an oak plectrum from his breast and plays a few notes, the narrator is stunned by the quality of the man's playing, which was "such as one would never be able to hear from the geisha of Yamanote" (p. 137). The narrator has the feeling that this man had not been born blind—he had probably learned geography and mathematics in primary school, and maybe some English in high school. But the narrator reflects that such a man, obviously a true "child of Edo" or *Edokko,* could never be reconciled with modern Tokyo and its Westernization. In the narrator's imagination, the man turns blind having never seen modern Tokyo. To do so would have been to ruin the purity of his Edo nature. Kafū's criticism of Meiji modernization operates on two levels as he claims that the player "did not know the misfortune brought on by the wretched streetcars and power lines and all the superficial things of Westernization," pointing out yet again the surface horrors of "the vulgar and unpolished 'Meiji' administered by footsoldiers from Kyushu" (pp. 137–138). But Kafū would also have been aware that such people, supported by the Guild of the Blind in the Tokugawa period, were cast adrift when the Guild was overcome by the social and economic changes of the Meiji era (Groemer, 2001). By ascribing such glorious qualities to the man's blindness in this passage, Kafū is able to criticize Meiji for both its surface appearance and its failure to support the arts.

The purity of Edo embodied by the blind player is presented as completely separate from the narrator's realm of experience, as he suffers over the problem of living a modern life. The strong emotions in this passage nevertheless remain vague and undefined—he feels a yearning, but for what? The end of the story tries to provide an answer:

> I thought that I wanted always, always to linger beneath the stone wall of the main temple, a sacred ground in superstition, and to be bathed in the fading light of the evening sun in Fukagawa, listening to the Utazawa ballads. The thought of crossing the Eitai Bridge and returning home was so bitter as to be unbearable. I felt that I wanted to cease to exist instead, like the poet Saitō Ryokū, who had been born in Meiji but who had cherished the memory of Edo.
>
> Ah, but instead I must go home. That is my destiny. To go far away, over the river, across the canals, up the hill to the shade of the grove in Ōkubo where on the desk of my study, beneath the portrait of Wagner, a volume of Nietzsche's poem *Zarathustra* is still open and waiting for me. . . . (p. 139)

While in Fukagawa, the narrator stands on sacred ground, safe from the intrusions of modernity. To cross the Eitai Bridge is to leave the protection of the past and lay himself bare before modernity again, with its "oscillation of sound waves." Kafū wants to be able to use his own literature to cherish the memory of Edo and make it live again on the page. Yet he realizes that he cannot ever escape entirely to the past, and his narrator cannot stay in Fukagawa. Kafū is here realizing that anything he does must come from the present. He is not blind. He has seen Tokyo and does suffer pangs of yearning and resentment.

The impact of *Fukagawa no uta* on the Japanese literary world was significant—Kubota Mantarō likened his reading of the work to feeling that miracles had suddenly been revealed before his eyes. Finally, here was a new kind of literature to challenge the dominant literary form of *shizenshugi*, which by 1909 was growing stale (Akase, 1995, pp. 49–50). Akase believes that the impact of *Fukagawa no uta* came from the "consciousness" expressed in the narrative voice, the thoughts and emotions of one seeing the city change before his eyes and trying to cope with the rapid transformation of his "*kokyō*" or "home" (pp. 50–51) Kafū did not speak of Tokyo or Edo as his "*furusato*" or directly address the idea of "home" as many of his contemporaries did, but he called upon the idea of "Edokko" to invoke a similar idea of belonging to the old city.[6] The blind music player in *Fukagawa no uta* possessed a heritage that Kafū did not: Growing up in the Yamanote, Kafū could never call himself a "true child of Edo." Having experienced the pain of realizing he could never be French, on his return to Japan Kafū was to struggle with yet another dilemma of not being Japanese enough—the "Edo" of the Returnee Stories was as much an imagined space as the "Paris" of *Furansu monogatari*.

One thing that stands out in *Fukagawa no uta* is the visceral sense of movement through space, as the narrator is first conveyed by electric streetcar across the Eitai Bridge and then resists having to cross it again to return to his Ōkubo home. Maeda Ai's 1982 theory of cityspace (*toshi kūkan*) applies perfectly to the spatial dynamics of this story, particularly as the narrator seems to possess no agency or will of his own. It is the conveyances of the new city that transport him from place to place, and by participating in the movement, even unwillingly, he contributes to the everyday chaos of transitional Tokyo. The narrator of *Fukugawa no uta* not only produces social meaning in his movement, but in the very appearance of his body upon which he has inscribed the trappings of a Western brand of contemporary fashion, "sporting a moustache and wearing Western clothes." Once he realizes the import of his appearance, however, he is no longer "oblivious" to the upheaval around him. Perhaps part of his anguish at the end of the tale comes from realizing that the private space he has created for himself at home has been equally invaded by the superficial trappings of Westernization, but this time by his own hand. As long as he continues to live out the life of a bourgeois intellectual in the

Yamanote, he contributes to and creates the spectre of the modern city he so laments.

The spectre of modernity in Yamanote is clearest in *Kitsune* (The Fox), published in January 1909, where Kafū recounts a "memory" of his childhood growing up in Koishikawa.[7] Although Kafū was born in 1879, Maeda Ai (2004) points out that the events of this story date from as early as 1877 to as late as 1882, a time when the old, well-ordered mansions of samurai were being bought up by bureaucrats and often left to run to seed (p. 94). Maeda's analysis of *Kitsune* recounts how the previously controlled gardens of Yamanote had come to symbolize a wild and untamed Nature, in opposition to the brick order of Ginza and Nihonbashi (p. 99). The grotesque and haunting grove at the bottom of the Nagai's property represents the literal remains of old Edo as well as its darkness and mystery, the sense of superstition heightened when a fox is sighted there. The males of the household are roused to action when the fox kills a chicken on the property, hunting and killing the animal despite the females' protests linking it to the god Inari. In Maeda's analysis, "the opposition between domestic and wild animals can be inserted into an array of binarisms that include civilization and nature, Tokyo space and Edo space, masculine sphere and feminine sphere."[8] It is no surprise that Kafū employs an "array of binarisms" in this story, a technique he perfected in the crafting of *Amerika monogatari*. When read together with *Fukagawa no uta*, the area of Yamanote emerges as a complex site of negotiation between the remains of old Edo and the new lifestyles of the intellectual class. The father in *Kitsune* may well represent the forward-looking emissary of civilization and enlightenment, inspired by the works of Fukuzawa Yukichi and Katō Hiroyuki,[9] but the child as yet inhabits a liminal space, as terrified of Nature as he is sorry for the death of its avatar.

Where *Kitsune* is lyrical and thoughtful, Kafū displayed his more cranky and chaotic side in two pieces published in March 1909, *Donten* and *Kangokusho no ura*. The first opens with a long list of things that the narrator either loves or despises, creating a disjunctive yet intriguing atmosphere with its arbitrary declarations and egotistical posturings. The narrator declares, "I respect Russia because it is gloomy and tragic. I hate the English. I am attracted by the Egyptians," and goes on to disparage typical Meiji values such as military victories, social success, and academic reputation, while reveling in scandal and stories of tragic romance. As Keene puts it, "the cranky, irritable man who takes perverse delight in what normal people hate would appear in many of Kafū's works, either as the speaker or as an important character."[10] The perverse and playful side of Kafū's returnee persona is balanced somewhat by the more serious undertones of *Kangokusho no ura*, which caused Uchida Roan to call Kafū Japan's "first authentic artist in the European sense" (Rubin, 1984, p. 124). This short story portrays the change of seasons experienced by a thirty-something narrator, an aimless intellectual despairing of finding a place for himself in hypocrisy-ridden Meiji society. Rubin cites a well-known passage:

> I thought of becoming an artist. But no, Japan is Japan, not the West. Japanese society does not need artists; indeed, it finds them a nuisance. The state has established education-by-intimidation and forces us to learn grotesque languages made up of sounds that no member of the Yamato race ever pronounced—T, V, D, F. And if you can't say them, you have no right to exist in Meiji society.[11]

On the one hand, these two works exaggerate the narrative stance to create an image of the disgruntled returnee, an aesthete who finds the vulgarity of Meiji Japan unbearable. But the complaints of these works contain the kernels of Kafū's oppositional stance against the Meiji state, much as the exaggerated artistic pose of *Hitoritabi* revealed a deep distrust of Meiji bureaucracy and a fear of the government's anti-art policy. These works may be understood as precursors to *Shinkichōsha nikki* and *Reishō*, which appeared later in the year. Here in the early months of 1909, Kafū seems to switch back and forth between contemplative works and persona-enhancing poses, but as the year wore on the two strands of work would come together to form a more mature critical position.

A major step toward this maturation is seen in *Botan no kyaku* (The Peony Garden), which, like *Fukagawa no uta*, juxtaposes Edo and Tokyo in the movement of the narrator through the city. Published in July 1909, the story opens with a scene typical of old Japan:

> At the mouth of the canal where little boats were collecting, the waters of the Sumida spread before us, the more radiant for the depth of the scene. Along the measured lines of the stone embankments, straggly willows waved in the breeze, quiet and languorous beyond description. Samisen practice in the geisha houses near the river had died away. (p. 47)[12]

The opening is full of movement, which may be "quiet and languorous," but the movement of the water and willows gives the scene life. This passage contains all the elements to be found in the

Returnee Stories when describing old Edo: the canals and their boats and embankments, willow trees, an air of languor and quiet, geisha and samisen, and of course the Sumida River. Into these elements, Kafū has suffused a radiance, a metaphor for the brightness of the Edo period compared with Meiji. Kafū is once again using essentialist binary opposition to focus on the process of modernization that is transforming the city.

Where old and new are mixed together in the city, it seems that the old is not to be displaced: "Near at hand there was a clanging of streetcars, while in the distance the horns of boats would give forth long blasts and fade away, to be followed by samisens in unison from the second floor of the Kamesei" (p. 48). But the narrator's reflection on the meaning of this scene surprises the reader, suggesting that not all is well with the city and its inhabitants:

> It suddenly seemed to me that, coming from an inn with this woman, I had nothing to do with a world that had gone on moving without me. The world and I were controlled by separate destinies, taking us in separate directions. A sort of quiet always came over me at evening, but this time there was a complete loss of strength, and it brought with it a vague, indefinable sadness. (p. 48)

This is the same "indefinable sadness" felt by the narrator of *Fukagawa no uta*, and the same sense of dislocation from the surrounding world. This tone of vague yearning, loneliness, and sadness is a recurring theme in all the Returnee Stories. Yamazaki Masakazu argues that what stands out most in the novels of 1909–1910 is a melancholy tendency and an uneasiness hard to define. Yamazaki (1986) argues that these works are novels of criticism (*hyōronfū no shōsetsu*), and in them the author's self-conscious anger at the customs and culture of Meiji can be clearly seen. They show confusion and despair at the chaotic process of modernization, and also criticize the boorish conventionality of the Japanese, but Yamazaki argues that this anger is part of a much deeper melancholy that pervaded Meiji literature as a whole (pp. 36–38). It is this self-conscious melancholy and sense of dislocation that provide much of the tension in the Returnee Stories.

The narrator of *Botan no kyaku* goes with the geisha Koren across the city to view the peonies in Honjo. This entails a journey from the old parts of Tokyo to the newer suburbs filled with factories, symbols of Meiji progress. As the journey progresses, the sky clouds over, and "the smoke from the factories spiraled upward" at Shimbashi (p. 49).

At the First Bridge their boat is rocked by the wake of a passing steamer, and the narrator notices "a line of new two-story houses, or perhaps little restaurants" which the boatman informs him are actually brothels, set up in the new area of town. Past the first bridge, the coal cooking fires from houseboats on the canal "sent up very smelly fumes," and "Here and there a red cloud of smoke reflected from the canal" (p. 50). The factory smoke and coal fumes symbolize the pall that industrialization has cast over the city. The sky clouds over as well, as if the gloom of modernization is mirrored in nature, providing a dismal contrast to the radiance suffused through the tranquil opening scene. The peony garden itself gives a bleak ending to the story. There are no other visitors to the garden, no wind, and nothing moving except the petals of the peonies as they fall, symbolizing the disappearance of an age and the narrator's own sense of uneasiness:

> The peonies were already falling. Even the blossoms that had not lost all of their petals were faded badly, their hearts black and gaping. Had they been exposed to bright sunlight and fresh breezes, they would have fallen by now. The weariness and boredom of having been made to bloom too long seemed to flow from each blossom. These peonies had something in common with us, I thought. (p. 53)

Botan no kyaku is a short piece that deals with the fading of Edo and the rise of the factories in the suburbs of Tokyo through the metaphors of brightness and gloom, radiance and smoke, and finally the falling of the peonies themselves. Shiozaki Fumio (1994) sees *Fukagawa no uta* and *Botan no kyaku* as symbolic journeys through Tokyo's competing transport systems, with the bone-jarring cacophony of modern streetcars set against the quiet waterways of Edo. Both works are carefully constructed, "scrupulous in the calculation of detail and a vigilant attention to the whole" (p. 101) Shiozaki argues that what is "epoch-making" about these works is that, even while lost in idealistic dreams of the past, Kafū's posture is always conscious of its subject, and every detail points to Kafū's "criticism of civilization" (*bunmei hihyō*) (p. 101). *Botan no kyaku* is a quieter piece than *Fukagawa no uta,* yet the tone of deep nostalgia and the initial wish to escape modernity have given way to a more perceptive view of the city. It also seems that Kafū is becoming more cynical: The hearts of the peonies, like those of intellectuals in Meiji Japan, may be "black and gaping," but the narrator and Koren turn their backs on the flowers, saying "Famous places are always disappointments" (p. 53). The couple can leave the scene and return to the heart of the old city. The reader is left with the impression that Kafū, much as he would like to follow them, is left behind to deal with the decay as best he can.

Botan no kyaku, Kitsune and *Fukagawa no uta* all explore the dual city of Edo/Tokyo in terms of both spatial positioning and the idea of time, where "Edo" simultaneously belongs to the past yet overlaps with the modern city in terms of the space it occupies. The question facing Kafū and his narrators was how to bring the idea of "Edo" into the present moment, ensuring its survival and promising a future for the city of Tokyo that did not entirely depend on a Westernized surface appearance. Older critical readings of these works focused on their French roots, particularly the influence of Henri du Régnier,[13] but newer readings take more account of Kafū's innovative use of space and time, as well as his critical stance toward Meiji modernization. Kafū is well known as an author who uses landscape, space, and time as loci of meaning, and Isoda Kōichi (1989) has analyzed *Kitsune* and *Kangokusho no ura* in terms of spatial metaphor, landscape, and folklore imagery (pp. 25–32). Minami Asuka (2007) takes this further to connect Kafū's spatial positioning with his political stance, reading the works as geopolitical (*chiseiteki*) critique. Kafū's use of the two spaces "Edo" and "Tokyo" to criticize Meiji modernization is certainly effective in these works, but the early stories of 1909 depend largely on juxtaposition and metaphor, without directly condemning the Meiji government. One reason for this may lie in the harshness of contemporary censorship. As a result of the Press Laws of 1909, there was a marked increase in censorship in the year 1909–1910 which affected even major writers like Mori Ōgai and Nagai Kafū.[14] Kafū was writing *Botan no kyaku* after seeing *Furansu monogatari* banned on publication in March 1909, so perhaps he was exercising discretion, using metaphor rather than direct statements of disillusionment and revulsion against Meiji Japan.

Another story from July 1909, however, not only enhanced Kafū's notoriety through its censorship but also cemented his reputation as an artist writing against the state. *Kanraku* (Pleasure) takes the form of bracketed narration, with Sensei, a man of letters in his forties, recounting his love affairs to a younger writer, who then narrates the tale. The story operates on a number of different levels, one of which is to contrast the truth of observed reality with the subjective experience of the senses. Prefiguring the Shinkankaku-ha debates,[15] the young narrator claims "I will not permit others outrageously to challenge any view derived from my own experience. In this confused age, the twentieth century, nothing can be accepted as truth unless it is substantiated by the senses."[16] This noble claim is proved false by the central narrative of Sensei, who reveals the strength of subjectivity when the eye is clouded by romance:

> Entirely forgetting that the woman beside [myself] was the source that stirred such beautiful sentiments in me, I indulged in a much deeper, wider and freer reverie concerning her—such an enchantment as any poet will earnestly seek. The woman then was no longer a woman, and her flesh was no longer something physical. . . . My sense of time vanished. I spent an eternity in a glorious inspiration.
>
> Suddenly, from this dream-like City of Heaven, I was brought back to earth, not by the noise of cart-wheels, a whistle blowing, footsteps, the barking of a dog or a breath of air, but by the very woman who had before enraptured me. (Nagai, 1961, p. 55)

Perfectly capturing the moment of a lover's disillusionment, *Kanraku* is remarkably self-reflexive in its critique on the observation of nature and the writer's trust in the senses. Perhaps because of this thoughtful treatment of naturalism, when the work was published in book form in September 1909 it was pronounced by *Waseda bungaku* to be an "outstanding work of fiction for 1909" (Rubin, 1984, p. 125). In contrast to the Japanese *shizenshugi* forms of naturalism that emphasized flat observation and truthful self-confession, Kafū's work up to that time had popularly been received as decadent "anti-naturalist" literature. For the supposedly naturalist journal *Waseda bungaku* to honor Kafū in this way sparked a theoretical debate on the categorization of his literature that continues today. But if we read *Kanraku* as an argument between objectivity and subjectivity, Kafū can be understood as contributing to a wider contemporary debate on what naturalism was, and what it could achieve.

Kanraku is remarkable in that it suffered from censorship twice—the July 1909 issue of *Shinshōsetsu* in which it had appeared as a short story was banned for a different piece by Takasaki Shungetsu (Rubin, 1984, p. 296n26), and when it was published as the titular work of a book-length collection (including the previously published *Botan no kyaku* and *Fukagawa no uta*), the book as a whole was banned on September 24, 1909, just four days after its publication. Unlike *Furansu monogatari*, which disappeared almost entirely from public view, the four days between *Kanraku*'s publication and its censorship were enough to ensure wide distribution and review. Rubin (1984) notes that the "theoretical war" over whether Kafū's work could be seen as naturalism, "which raged on for months during 1910, had as its object a book that could not legally be sold but which everyone seemed to have read. The fact that it had been banned was never made an issue, even by the *Waseda Bungaku* editors" (p. 125). Indeed, the censorship of *Kanraku* enhanced Kafū's reputation as an anti-state writer, helped by passages such as this:

> Now, I am utterly indifferent to what my family thinks of me. I am a poet; they are ordinary human beings. We belong to different lands, different races. Neither do I feel anger toward the state for its treatment of art. It was my choice and mine alone to rebel against parents and teachers and become a poet, a man unneeded—indeed, violently suppressed—by the state. (trans. Rubin, 1984, pp. 121–122)

Even in Matsumoto Ryōzō's dreamy translation of the same passage, the marginal position of Sensei vis-à-vis the state is clear, expressed vividly in the next statement:

> Poets are something like the weeds which spring up after a fall of rain. The state simply cannot exterminate them . . . They are fated to accept without complaint the "honorable title" of disloyal citizen or hopeless vagabond. (Nagai, 1961, pp. 62–63)

Rubin points out that this passage originally ended with a statement of indifference as to whether the "country might perish" (*kuni no sōbō*), suppressed with *fuseji* by the editor with Kafū's own permission, but even without this phrase, Sensei's position is strongly worded. The non-citizen poet of *Kanraku* is a more mature version of the oppositional artist put forward in *Kangokusho no ura*. The praise given these works by Uchida Roan and *Waseda bungaku* ensured Kafū's anti-establishment image, at the same time as shoring up his artistic prestige. While the censorship of *Kanraku* did not affect the critics, however, Kafū took it to heart. In his novel *Reishō, Kanraku* was fictionalized as *Kōkotsu* (Rapture), a novella written by the character Yoshino Kōu that was also banned. "Yoshino Kōu" would become one of Kafū's pen names in the journal *Mita bungaku*, used on occasions when his ire against the Meiji state was particularly stirred. In this way, *Kanraku* became a sort of shorthand for Meiji censorship and Kafū's artistic opposition to it, indicating the story's importance to Kafū despite the light and airy tone of the work itself.

Perhaps to escape the furore of censorship in late 1909, Kafū's next work was the quieter novel *Sumidagawa* (The River Sumida), included in the December issue of *Shinshōsetsu*. Famous for its elegiac beauty and sense of nostalgia, *Sumidagawa* explores the Meiji transition and the effect it has on the people of Tokyo through characters who, rather than being sketched in depth, each act as ciphers, representing some typical aspect of Meiji attitudes in the closing years of the era. In Kafū's own words in the preface to the fifth edition of *Sumidagawa*: "The characters in the novel . . . are nothing more than clinging shadows of people of the distant past, revived in my own memory by scenes on the Sumida River, which I am certainly trying to keep from disappearing" (KZ 5.62). None of the characters attain real depth because Kafū's aim was to present them as "clinging shadows," who remain indistinct to allow them to retain their association with the past. The irony of *Sumidagawa*, which Kafū recognized in this preface, was that the shadows would disappear in spite of his efforts. Shiozaki Fumio (1991) calls *Sumidagawa* a commentary on Tokyo as it entered the twentieth century, a fate that not one of the characters in the novel can escape (p. 180). The characterization of *Sumidagawa* is perhaps most notable for the fact that the river itself becomes the main character of the work, reflecting the changes in the city and affecting the lives of those who live on its banks.

The first chapter sees the contrast between Meiji and Edo firmly established, through the three main characters and their attitudes to the changes since the Restoration. The story opens with Shōfūan Ragetsu, teacher of poetry, the representative of old Edo life, procrastinating about leaving his narrow backstreets and making the journey across the river to Imado to see his sister. Although a teacher of traditional Tokiwazu music, his sister O-toyo represents Meiji ambition in her wishes for her son Chōkichi's future:

> . . . the single pleasure the unfortunate woman had was contemplating her Chōkichi's prospects. She knew how precarious were the affairs of merchants, not sure from one day to the next that they would not face bankruptcy; and she was determined, even if she had to go without her three meals a day, to see him through the university and established as an office worker. (p. 13)[17]

Ragetsu realizes that Meiji ideals of ambition and advancement do not suit everyone—while his sister despairs of Chōkichi's future, he is more sympathetic: "Chōkichi said that he did not want to be a stiff, bewhiskered office worker, he wanted rather to live with the theater he so loved. The one was a career, and the other was too" (p. 42). Two sets of contrasting motifs are set up here, with Meiji ambition and the bureaucracy on one side, and Edo and the theater on the other. The dilemma of Chōkichi, seventeen years old and caught between the two careers of bureaucrat and actor, is demonstrated through Kafū's comparison of new and old forms of theater. Chōkichi's friend Kichi is an actor in the troupe of Ii Yōhō, in the *shimpa* theater, an updated form of kabuki that included women as well as *onnagata* in the cast—at the time, this form of theater was very modern and new.[18] To Chōkichi's envy, Kichi wears a silk scarf, puffs on cigarettes, and smells of cologne (pp. 35, 36). But Chapter 6 is set in a far more traditional theater, the Miyatoza of Asakusa. Chōkichi is completely carried away by the theater and its music, the sets, the shouts from the audience, the stuffy atmosphere (p. 31). Chōkichi returns to see the same play the next day, "drawn with a strength he could not deny," and finds it eases his loneliness and sorrow (p. 34). In the contrast of new and old theater, it is undoubtedly the old forms that hold the greater attraction.

Once Chōkichi steps outside, however, the Sumida mirrors his introspective, mournful mood. The joys of the Edo theater are contrasted with the River Sumida of the present:

> The surface of the river was ashen, and the mists rising from it clouded the far embankment, hurrying the winter sun on its way. . . . The flowing waters seemed lonely to Chōkichi. One or two lights were already showing on the far shore. The wintry trees, the dry stones, the shabby tiled roofs—everything he saw seemed faded and chilly. The lively faces of Izayoi and Seishin, still with him from the moment of leaving the theater, floated up all the more vividly, like faces on a New Year's battledore. He found himself so drawn to them as to be almost resentful. He could not be one of them however much he wished to. It would be better to die than to go on as he was . . .
>
> He shivered, and suddenly from the depths of his throat came a fragment of a Jōruri ballad. (p. 33)

Steve Rabson (1982) observes that in *Sumidagawa*, perhaps more so than elsewhere, Kafū often uses place imagery to reflect the moods and emotions of the characters. The river is lonely, ashen, clouded, faded, and chilly because Chōkichi himself is depressed upon realizing that soon he must take his examinations and face the future (p. 228). The Sumida itself shows Kafū's characterization through the use of place and imagery. But more significant is the way Chōkichi chooses to rouse himself from his depression. Faced with the gloom and chill of the Meiji era, wishing to join the theater and bury himself in Edo pastimes, Chōkichi unconsciously reacts to the cold wind by singing a fragment of traditional song, thus returning to Edo in his mind at least. "The phrase came from his throat and was lost in his mouth; but it brought a lessening of the scarcely tolerable pain" (p. 34).

The world of Edo, however, holds a precarious position in Tokyo. Much of *Sumidagawa* portrays the changing face of the city, reflected in the waters of the river. O-toyo tells us that: "they're widening the streets, and the cemetery in Komagome is to be cleared away" (p. 13). On the banks of the river "the bathhouses had been torn down" (p. 24) in response to suggestions that Westerners find the idea of mixed public bathing offensive, while "smoke from the factory chimneys" can be seen from the banks (p. 24). It is also noticeable that the sweets sellers, vendors of sake, and so on clapping their sticks to raise customers are all old men, suggesting that their trades will die out with them. Another effect of the Meiji Restoration was that the Yoshiwara had been liberated, which meant that Chōkichi's aunt, a courtesan of "one of the great Yoshiwara houses," had become dependent on Ragetsu (p. 26). The changes of Meiji are shown to affect the lives of everyday people, and not just the streets and bathhouses. In a scene reminiscent of *Botan no kyaku*, Ragetsu and Chōkichi walk along the Oshiage Canal near Honjo: "In the low noonday tide, the muddy bottom of the canal lay bare to the April sun, and gave off a considerable odor. Industrial soot floated down from somewhere, and from somewhere came the noise of industrial machinery." Housewives busy at piecework can be seen from the road but they are completely indifferent to the spring day, while the fences bear "notices that factory girls were needed" (p. 40). The effect is depressing, but Kafū shows that even in this atmosphere the beauty of old Edo still lingers on, in the shape of a small tea stall where they decide to rest. Even so, Kafū knows that the old ways, the old buildings, are falling apart while only the new factories are maintained:

> Mossy shingled roofs, rotting foundations, leaning pillars, dirty planks, drying rags and diapers, pots and cheap sweets for sale—the dreary little houses went on in endless

> disorder, and when on occasion he would be surprised by an imposing gate, it would always be a factory. A soaring tiled roof would be a temple, more than likely in bad repair, the cemetery plainly visible through gaps in the earthen walls. Clusters of wooden grave-markers and moss-flecked tombstones lay falling over into marshes that had once been garden lakes but had so decayed that it was difficult to know where bank gave way to water. (pp. 42–43)

As Rabson points out, the dilapidation of the area is used as a literary device to express Chōkichi's feelings of despair (p. 228), but Kafū is doing more than mirroring Chōkichi's emotions in his choice of areas and buildings. It is the traditional temples that are in disrepair, the new factories that have the imposing gates. The whole scene is a reminder of the inevitability of encroaching modernity. The scene is made more poignant when Chōkichi realizes that the neighborhood is the one that had been immortalized in Tamenaga Shunsui's *Shunshoku umegoyomi* (The Spring Plum Calendar), a masterpiece of Tokugawa literature.[19] Lost in visions, Chōkichi is momentarily able to forget "the anguish of reality" (p. 43). Soon enough, however, reality assaults him again as he realizes he is caught between two worlds:

> He had therefore decided to be either an actor or a musician, but these wishes, too, had been denied him, and now, helplessly envying the good fortune of Kichi the barber's son, he passed useless, aimless hours. He did not have the courage to kill himself. His one hope was to fall ill and die.
>
> It came to Ragetsu with a sudden, intolerable conviction that Chōkichi had purposefully walked through the flood that night hoping to fall ill, and that there was no chance of his recovering. (p. 45)

Kafū's purpose in writing is symbolized by the end of the story. Ragetsu swears that he will help Chōkichi, that he is not to die, that he will help him become an actor and reunite him with his childhood sweetheart O-ito, now in training to become a geisha. If Ragetsu does not do this he will have been shamed. We can also read this ending, if we take the idea of representative characterization to its logical conclusion, that here we have Japan (Chōkichi) in danger from the Meiji modernization program (his mother O-toyo) being saved by Kafū and his literature (Ragetsu) and brought back together with its true

Edo nature (O-ito). The hopeful note at the end of the tale promises optimism for Japan's future, if only Ragetsu's words are heeded.

After the subtlety of *Botan no kyaku* and *Sumidagawa,* the final works of 1909 strike the reader as vitriolic in the intensity of their critique. *Shinkichōsha nikki* (Diary of a Recent Returnee) and *Reishō* (Sneers) are both inflexible in their abuse of Meiji, showing Kafū at his most outspoken. More negative than the other works, they are also in many ways more thoughtful, as Kafū struggles to define what it means to be modern, how Japan is to be genuine, and how the individual should conceptualize oneself in a time of such rapid change. While the Edo/Tokyo dialectic is extremely strong in both works, they are also informed by an equally strong commitment to comprehending Japan in terms of its Western Other. Kafū builds on his earlier constructions of the West, particularly France, in order to formulate his critique of Japanese civilization. It is in these works that Kafū's ideas on "genuine" civilization reach their full fruition, laying a firm foundation on which he could then turn to focus on the nature of the Japanese "Self." Kafū further develops themes that had appeared briefly in the travel collections, such as a hatred of hypocrisy and superficiality, and employs a similar structure of spatial dynamics that was found in *Kitsune, Botan no kyaku* and *Fukagawa no uta.* Exploring the discursive possibilities of the margins of the city as opposed to the official center, Kafū opens up a space for reflection and critique for both his characters and himself.[20]

Shinkichōsha nikki (Diary of a Recent Returnee) was written in December 1908, and originally published in *Chūō kōron* in October 1909 as *Kichōsha no nikki.* Nakajima Kunihiko (1992) is unequivocal in his classification of Kafū as a harsh social critic in this work (p. 31). Kafū begins by questioning the validity of reform *(kairyō)* in Japan, with the narrator (*jibun*) asking whether the "modern lifestyle" of Europe could really take root in the "soil of the Orient" (p. 178). This Orient is no longer the "Orient" of the Middle East, the imaginary *orian* that Kafū appropriated from French literature, but the civilization of China and continental Asia. Now that Kafū was back in Japan, the historical, cultural, and geographical connections between Japan and "*tōyō*" needed to be addressed. Here, *tōyō* functions as the locus of Japan's cultural past. The question of reform in *Shinkichōsha nikki* turns on whether Japan's relationship to the Orient of its heritage will prevent it from achieving true modernity.

The other stumbling block to "true" modernity is the fact that the Meiji government is rushing ahead with modernization policies without devoting sufficient time to planning, or understanding the philosophical basis of "modernity" in the West. Where the West "experienced political change over a period of many passing centuries" (p. 178), Meiji Japan is trying to cram a similar amount of change into only fifty years. The problem is compounded by the fundamental nature of the Japanese to place more emphasis on material, outward forms rather than inner substance when considering reform:

> Because of this, as long as the people do not individually become more aware and do not reform the fundamental ideas of society, then a hundred Diets, a hundred theaters, auditoriums, schools, in short, won't be anything more than the newest-style imported Western knick-knacks. It's the same as imitation goods which quickly lose their color. (pp. 183–184)

Where wars in the West were historically fought over philosophy or religion, the narrator continues, the Japanese have only ever fought tangible, visible enemies to expand their physical territory—"the Japanese have never once been tormented by their imagination" (p. 185). The philosophical substance of the modernization process in the West is characterized by an underlying spirit of opposition or resistance (*hankō*), something yet lacking in Meiji Japan. When the narrator's friend Uda Ryūsui complains that the idea of "opposition" is ruining his life, he answers passionately that opposition is the very source of progress: "The good tidings of the modern world, which we call independence (*jiyū*), were born from opposition" (pp. 201-202). The oppositional stance may be uncomfortable and demanding, but it is necessary for the achievement of independence and true modernity.

In the contrast of Western and Japanese attitudes to modernization and change, Kafū essentializes both spaces. Western society is characterized by attention to "inner substance" and "the fundamental ideas flowing through the innermost heart of the individual" (p. 194), whereas the Japanese devote their energies to acquiring the "material civilization" (*busshitsu bunmei*) of factories, bustling cities, and other tangible gains of modernity (p. 194). Kafū despairs of his countrymen ever being able to think in terms of the inner substance, or meaning, of "civilization," which stems from a country's unique culture and history. This leads Kafū to ponder the meaning and origins of Japan's own civilization, engendering a lengthy comparison between superficial Meiji *bunmei* and the culture of the Edo period. Where Edo culture grew organically and naturally out of the processes of Japan's own history, Kafū sees Meiji as forcing the matter, trying to graft on foreign "material civilization" rather than nurturing the inner substance of indigenous civilization. The superficiality of Meiji *bunmei* is interpreted as hypocrisy (*gizen*), a subject that takes up a sizeable proportion of the diary.

Not only is the narrator angry at specific people whose behavior he perceives to be hypocritical, but the situation is so bad that he now believes honesty and sincerity have no place in the Meiji period (p. 212). The most painful thing about Meiji hypocrisy is that the narrator also feels himself to be a hypocrite. He shrinks from being called a Viscount by Westerners, because Japanese officials would not even be able to afford a carriage without their government allowance. He wants to let the secret out, but is pained by the "mask" worn by his country (p. 215). Japan makes a big show to the West with its façade of modern civilization, but in the Russo–Japanese War, he argues, the fact that there were many Christians in the Japanese army was promoted and publicized "in order to attract the sympathy of the world," while behind the scenes the conservatism of the old school persisted. The narrator ends up wishing that Japan would just settle on either barbarism or civilization with good grace (pp. 230–231). Having vented his spleen in this manner, Kafū turns to more practical suggestions, using the second half of the diary to put forward ideas that could be implemented to solve the mess of Meiji modernization. Kafū suggests that the preservation of Edo culture, rather than wholesale destruction for the sake of imitated "*bunmei*," is the obvious answer.

It is here that the dual nature of the city as Edo/Tokyo comes into effect, with the city in such sharp focus that it seems like a character in its own right.[21] Other Meiji writers usually used the city to provide a backdrop to the action of their novels, where the city's confusion acted as a metaphor for the author's confusion (as in Mori Ōgai's *Under Reconstruction*) or its changes became the object of observation by a hero whose movements in the literary world were the focus of the narrative (seen in Tayama Katai's *Thirty Years in Tokyo*), but in Kafū's work it is the city itself which comes to the fore at major turning points in order to emphasize the need to preserve what elements of traditional culture still remain. Where *Fukagawa no uta* focuses on the Edo that is disappearing, in *Shinkichōsha nikki* we are made to feel that it has already vanished. Visiting Maruzen bookshop on January 20, the diarist is shocked by the appearance of the streets: "On the way back, along the Nihonbashi road, I was left in stunned amazement by the strange, unsightly scenes of lines of telegraph poles and road repairs and the crude buildings on both sides of the road" (p. 222). He comes upon his friend Ryūsui and they stumble along together through puddles and tangles of wire. Where the narrator expounds upon the beautiful cities of Europe and North America, Ryūsui focuses rather on the beauty of Edo, which had never been subject to this so-called "civilization" (p. 223). The two viewpoints illustrate Kafū's solution for modern Japan: The genuine nature of civilization in the West stems from respect for its cultural heritage. Therefore, if Japan is to achieve genuine civilization, it must also respect and preserve its own cultural heritage, here encapsulated in the idea of "Edo." As the narrator explains:

> Paris is not all about newly-made subways and aeroplanes. It is also about building great churches, like the Sacré-Coeur. If on the one hand they build a factory, then at the same time on the other hand they also undertake an achievement for posterity, not for utility, which will last a thousand years. . . . The Japanese use as their one defence that they haven't any money, but even if they did have the money, the Japanese are so very absurd that such an idea, unconnected to utility, would not even occur to them. (p. 226)

Parisian citizens had all the advantages of modern civilization but at the same time preserved the civilization of antiquity. Even new buildings like the Sacré-Coeur, still under construction at the time of Kafū's visit, were full of beauty and reflected the glory of French cultural tradition.[22] In Kafū's thinking, Japan should show a similar reverence for its past, and draw on that past for new endeavors.

The narrator parts from Ryūsui here and does not see him again until ten days later, when Ryūsui takes him out to go drinking in Yanagibashi. All the trains are full, so they walk again, and as they walk Ryūsui explains his thoughts on Japanese culture and modernity. Just like the cities of Europe, Tokyo also has places that retain the feel of the past, like Fukagawa and Yanagibashi. The geisha of the Yanagibashi quarter in particular, he says, bring to mind the history of the place. Linking this history directly to the idea of "Edo," Ryūsui argues that the geisha and their "flower and willow world" deserve respect, as "Today they have become the guardians of Edo civilization (*Edo bunmei no hogosha*)" (p. 233). This argument of Ryūsui's has been called the *Geisha-ron* of *Shinkichōsha nikki* (Nakajima, 1994, pp. 60–61). Ryūsui observes: "If there had been no flower and willow world in the period when Europeanization was popular, the music and drama of Edo would probably have been totally eradicated" (p. 233). The areas of the city associated with the geisha and their arts thus represent Edo itself, and its rich history and culture. To preserve these places is to preserve the Japanese heritage.[23] Kafū's choice of words is telling as he makes the geisha guardians of *Edo bunmei*, pointing to "civilization" as rooted in the past. Many Meiji ideologues saw *bunmei* in terms of progress toward a future goal, usually technological in nature. But Kafū reminds the reader of a broader definition that includes culture and the traditional arts. By defining *bunmei* in this way, a genuine modernity could be found without sacrificing the nation's culture or dignity.

Much has been written on the idea of urban space as discursive structure in literature, particularly by Maeda Ai (1982, 2004) and Isoda Kōichi (1990) in relation to Tokyo. Koizumi Kōichirō has argued for the significance of spatial dynamics regarding the two conversations between *jibun* and Ryūsui in *Shinkichōsha nikki*. The first conversation on January 20 takes place in the central parts of the city, as the two men contrast Tokyo against Paris on one hand and Edo on the other. Limited to an enclosed space defined by Nihonbashi road, the Ginza, Kyōbashi, Hibiya, and Hanzōmon, the men see the reality of Japanese modernization before their eyes and discover that they too must find a way to live in the changing city. The second conversation on January 30, by contrast, has Ryūsui taking the narrator outside the central cityspace to Yanagibashi, and it is on the way there that he is able to question, to search for solutions, and find those solutions in the Edo past (Koizumi, 1984, p. 48). That Ryūsui is able to find solutions in the margins of the city speaks to the counter-discourse inherent in his *Geisha-ron*. When Ryūsui argues that the Japanese should be grateful to the geisha for protecting and sustaining Japanese civilization, he is talking about women near the bottom of the Meiji social structure, looked down on by polite society. Kafū's elevation of the geisha to the role of guardians of Japanese culture suggests that hope for an "authentic" Japanese modernization lies only in the margins of the despised, the non-new, in the space that is non-central to the city of Tokyo. In the binary opposition of Edo and Tokyo we find a counter-discourse to the Meiji state.[24] The oppositional nature of Kafū's choice of guardian may also be seen in the fact that *bunmei* was historically seen as a male domain, an energetic masculine activity linked to the public sphere of the state. By placing *bunmei* in the hands of women, Kafū is arguing for a softer or at least more balanced view of "civilization."[25]

Another way to interpret the conversations between *jibun* and Ryūsui is in terms of the construction of a modern Japanese "self." The counter-space to Meiji found on the margins of the city brings to mind Roland Barthes' ideas of self and other, expressed in terms of center and periphery:

> Paris as a center was always experienced semantically by the periphery as the privileged place where the other is and where we ourselves are other, as the place where we play the other. In contrast, all that is not the center is precisely that which is not ludic space, everything which is not otherness: family, residence, identity. (Barthes, 1997, p. 171)

If the city center is where one interacts with strangers, in other words, one retreats to an inner world of the self on going home. As Maeda Ai points out, exchanges in the center also involve power relationships, work and shopping being two examples that depend on commodification and the transfer of labor and wealth.[26] The suburbs or *kōgai* are set apart from the self–other power exchanges of the center, being rather a place of emotional exchanges with family and friends. When Ryūsui takes *jibun* out to Yanagibashi, his real feelings can emerge in the more subjective space, and it is in the movement toward the geisha district that Ryūsui can develop his solution for Japanese identity in the modern world.

The importance of movement in the story, from the center to the periphery and back again, becomes clear when we consider the context of Meiji modernization and the idea of "modernity" that Kafū was exploring through his characters' conversations and thought processes. If, as Maeda Ai (1982) theorizes, modernity is inscribed on and produced by the cityspace, and the movement of bodies through that space creates and reproduces the everyday "modern," then it is no surprise that Ryūsui and *jibun* find possible solutions for modern identity in the course of moving through the city. Such movement features strongly in all Kafū's early works, from the bicycling gentlemen of *Amerika monogatari* to the strolling narrators in New York, Chicago, Paris, and Lyon. Many have linked the strolling narrator to the idea of the *flâneur*, the essentially modern urban figure who at once observes the city playfully and becomes part of it through that play and observation.[27] But the movement in *Shinkichōsha nikki* seems not playful but purposeful, perhaps signaling a more serious outlook on modernity and what it might mean for Japan.

The act of walking in *Shinkichōsha nikki* is a way for Kafū's characters to see the changing city firsthand and verbalize their reactions to it, confronting reality at every step and progressing toward a solution to the dilemma of "authentic modernity." The dual nature of Edo/Tokyo is seen as a problem to be unraveled and solved, something that could only be addressed through active engagement in the cityscape. Kafū would continue to walk the streets of Tokyo for many years, depicting them with great care and detail. Kafū's attention to the surface and space of Tokyo reached its highest point with *Hiyorigeta* (Fair-weather clogs) in 1915, a collection of observations about places significant for the local people—not just shrines and temples, but also woods, waters, lanes, cliffs, and slopes.[28] Kafū became a familiar sight on the streets of Tokyo, with his umbrella, *geta* clogs, glasses, and tobacco pouch, and the reader cannot help but be swept up in his excavations of old places among the new. One chapter entitled "Maps" gives real insight into how Kafū comprehended the dual nature of the city. When walking through the city, he says, he always carries a small Edo-period map with him:

> It's not that I hate the lithographic maps of Tokyo published nowadays and particularly love the woodblock charts of ages past. It's because, if I compare as I walk the map of long ago with the contemporary city streets—the ones I walk down in the shuffling gait of my *geta*—I can compare and contrast the ancient times of Edo with the now of Tokyo, spontaneously and effortlessly, with my very own eyes. (KZ 13.316)

Kafū distinguishes between the ancient times of Edo (*Edo no mukashi*) and the present day of Tokyo (*Tōkyō no ima*), thus temporally disconnecting the two cityscapes from each other. Yet it is his movement along the contemporary streets (*gendai no gairo*) that naturally connects the two spaces, aided by the Edo-period footwear and the peculiar clip-clopping gait it bestows on the body of the wearer. His own eyes take in both the *Edo no mukashi* from the map and the *Tōkyō no ima* in front of him, achieving a natural amalgamation of the two into a seamless whole. It is worth noting that Kafū wrote this passage some seven years after *Shinkichōsha nikki*, and the calm tone shows his enjoyment of the act of contrast that vexed him so greatly on his immediate return to Japan. The two opposing spaces of Edo and Tokyo mesh through his own active experience of walking. I believe that this is what Maeda Ai meant by the materiality of agency, the physicality of constructing identity and social meaning through movement in the cityspace (Fujii, 2004, p. 6). Kafū's sense of identity, solidified in *Hiyorigeta*, may be seen as still emergent in the movement of Ryūsui and *jibun*.

The modern Japanese "self" that moves through the space of the dual city is a complex, yet distinct idea of *Shinkichōsha nikki*. Having returned to Japan, Kafū was now in a position to work through in detail the many problems of self-expression that had surfaced at the end of *Furansu monogatari*. The conversations between Ryūsui and *jibun* are used to discuss ways for the individual to acclimatize to the modern world, and to explore how the self should relate to and cope with "*bunmei*." Kafū's attempt to comprehend the role of the individual in society may be contrasted with the broader contemporary discourse of *kindai jiga*, a term that arose in the Meiji period to describe the idea of a "modern self," an "I" that could embody the new modernity of Japanese experience. Central to the idea of *kindai jiga* was the notion that the "self" was always posited vis-à-vis the state—that a modern subject should somehow contribute to, as well as form an integral part of, the modern state or *kokka*. Looking at the bodies of Ryūsui and *jibun* as they walk through transitional Tokyo, however, we can see an alternative conceptualization of the self, where their bodies (*shintai*) are constructed in direct opposition to the nation-state (*kokka*). The characters are agents of their own identity-building process, discussing the problem of genuine Japanese identity going forward. Progressing from the center to the periphery and finding answers on the margins, the characters provide an alternative to the *kindai jiga* in both their actions and their words.

As James Fujii (2004) points out, the ideology of *kindai jiga* gave Meiji intellectuals a vocabulary to discuss the problem of a "modern Japanese subject," but based as it was on Western conceptualizations of the self in society, this mode of thinking also consigned the Japanese subject "to an inferior status relative to its manifestation in the West" (p. 5). As such, there were two main problems with the *kindai jiga* that were not lost on contemporary intellectuals: the external nature of the thinking that originated and sustained it, and the suddenness of its manifestation in Japan. *Shinkichōsha nikki* may be understood as a search for a Japanese "self" that did not come from outside Japan but originated within it, and a "self" that drew on ancient values and traditions instead of relying solely on new developments from the West. The problems of the self, and the sudden appearance of *kindai jiga* in Japanese thinking, are addressed more directly and forcefully in *Reishō*, the last of the Returnee Stories.

By far the longest work of the series, *Reishō* was serialized in the *Asahi* newspaper on the recommendation of Natsume Sōseki, running from December 13, 1909 to February 28, 1910. *Reishō* is notable for its extreme use of cipher characters, with Koyama Kiyoshi as the disaffected working intellectual; Yoshino Kōu as the novelist recently returned from abroad; and Nakatani Teizō as the Edo *wakadanna* attempting to escape modernity by hiding in the past. Switching frequently between monologue, retrospection, letters, and diary entries, the work is very disjointed, divided between the reflections and assertions of the characters, and authorial explanations of their circumstances and surroundings. Despite this somewhat disjunctive format, the work is widely recognized as a "novel of criticism of civilization" (*bunmei hihan shōsetsu*).[29] One of its most well-known passages takes the form of a conversation between Koyama Kiyoshi and Yoshino Kōu, where Kōu expresses his amazement at the importance ascribed to the idea of the "self" in the Meiji period:

> I guess it's the result of that fever we call "modernity" after all. Why have we come to respect the self (*jiko*) so much anyway? Why do we make the sense of self (*jiga no ishiki*) necessary to every word and deed? Speaking figuratively, the self is merely like a single candle. Because it isn't the light of the sun, a candle can only illuminate a single room—or just the area surrounding the desk in that room. It doesn't illuminate the corners, or the recesses of the alcove, or outside the window. It's obvious that one doesn't need a lamp in the light of the sun. While I know that the existence of the self disappears completely in the face of absolute truth, I wonder who on earth first began to preach to us about this thing "the self" (*jiko naru mono*). It's a fever, after all, a fever. (p. 296)

The idea of the self is exposed as not truth, but a fever of modernity, an idea that has somehow taken root without basis in fact. The problem of the self (*jiko, jiga*) is not central to *Reishō*, and indeed Minami Asuka (1992) warns against chopping up the text to focus on terms like "self," "the past," and so on, to the detriment of comprehending the work as an artistic whole (p. 158). But taking the work as a whole structure, it is possible to view *Reishō* in terms of an extended meditation on the idea of self because the narrative so heavily depends on cipher characters, each representing one aspect of the author's psyche, as well as one stereotypical viewpoint on the Meiji transition. Kamei Hideo's work on the transformation of narrative voice in the Meiji period applies well to *Reishō*, which seamlessly blends narrative observation and dialogic interaction with the inner thoughts of characters, producing the kind of "polyphonic, orally based realism" that Kamei argued was a marker of the new age (Bourdaghs, 2002, p. x). As Bourdaghs explains, the new method "respected the individuality of diverse speaking voices yet refracted them through the unifying consciousness of a single narrator" (p. xxiii). The structure and narrative modes of *Reishō* show Kafū producing the very "self-reflexive modern subject" that Yokomitsu Riichi would call for twenty-five years later.[30] Kafū's cipher characters may be seen as an argument for the complexity of the modern self, not reducible to a simple *"kindai jiga"* but multilayered, confusing, and pulling in many different directions at once.

The majority of the story revolves around the three main characters, each beset with different problems in the transitional age of Meiji reforms. Koyama Kiyoshi is the young head of Koyama Bank in Tokyo, whose reflections on the monotony of his life and career provide the opening of the novel. The Meiji ideal of *risshin shusse,* prizing social success and advancement in the workplace, is proven meaningless by the emptiness of Koyama's life (pp. 251–253). Koyama's firsthand experience of Paris make him dissatisfied with life at home, unable to distract himself with modern Japanese novels because they lack the artistry of the *Tale of Genji* and other classics he remembers from his education. Koyama thinks of things like geisha and *ukiyo-e* prints as relics of a bygone age, with little relevance for present. By beginning with this character Kafū sets the scene for his argument that Edo does hold meaning for the present, and that cultural heritage is the key to living in modernity. Koyama meets the writer Yoshino Kōu at Zushi beach, and is intrigued by his Western clothes, long hair, and intense manner. Kōu talks about life as a writer in Meiji Japan—he, like Kafū, has had his work censored on publication. Kōu finds the censorship hard to understand, as the work, a novel called *Kōkotsu* (Rapture) was about love and had nothing to do with politics or national problems (p. 264). As we know (and as Kafū's audience would have known), this work mirrors Kafū's own *Kanraku.* Kōu's life reflects Kafū's almost exactly—Kōu was also sent to America and France by an overbearing father, and he fulfilled Kafū's dreams expressed in *Saiyū-nisshishō,* working as a hotel bellboy and a waiter in a restaurant. Like Kafū, he worked in a bank overseas, and on his return to Japan was bitterly disappointed at the superficial nature of Meiji modernization (pp. 307–308).

The third chapter introduces Kōu's friend Nakatani Teizō, a playwright well versed in the arts of *kiyomoto* singing and Utazawa balladry. Nakatani is the typical Edo *"iro-otoko,"* and so much resembles the hero of a *sharebon* novel that Kōu often uses him as a character in his own works. Now married to an ex-geisha of Fukagawa called O-kimi, Nakatani lives almost completely in the past, believing that true music and drama come only from the Edo period, with no advancement in the Meiji era (pp. 271–272). A long passage in Chapter 5 depicts Nakatani as practically cut off from contemporary society, gazing at the onrush of modernity as if from an island in the middle of a powerful current:

> . . . he gazed at all the things which he did not understand and which were more newly-made than himself—streetcars, low pompadour hairstyles, department stores, rickshaws with rubber wheels, and also the new words he saw in the newspapers from day to day, just randomly created like the strange names of medicines and cosmetics and so on, which meant nothing to the outsider, and even if they had meaning it was of no importance—in this way he gazed on, with a malice, a rebellion, and a growing coldness which even he noticed in himself. (pp. 303–304)

Taking into account the different stances on modernity symbolized by these three characters, *Reishō* may be read as a working out in practice of the idea that an alternative must be found to the "*kindai jiga*" preached by Meiji intellectuals. When the disjointed structure is taken as a whole, the novel may be seen as an attempt to reconcile all the different aspects of the Japanese "self," seeking how best to formulate an identity to carry one through the transitional period.

It is through Yoshino Kōu that Kafū most thoroughly explores this problem, swept up as he is in the "fever" of the modern and assaulted by anguish at the fear he may somehow fall behind the present moment (pp. 295–296). In naming the rush of modernization as a "fever," Kafū may have been commenting on the tendency for the Meiji government to diagnose particular social ills after the Russo–Japanese War. Carol Gluck (1985) lists "city fever" (*tokai netsu*), where rural youth moved in great numbers to the cities, "business fever" (*kigyō netsu*), "success fever" (*seikō netsu*), and so on, all discussed at length in newspapers and magazines (pp. 157–163). Many ideologues sought a cure for these "ills of civilization" (*bunmei byō*) in the past (pp. 177–178). The exploration of "modernity" and "modernization" in *Reishō* places Kafū squarely within a wider Meiji discourse, trying to assess the relevance of modernity for Japan and searching for solutions in Japanese past. Kōu himself comes to a gradual awakening of admiration and respect for his own culture over the course of the novel, much as the narrator *jibun* did in *Shinkichōsha nikki*. The moment of epiphany comes in Shiba Park, when gazing at the mortuary shrines of the Tokugawa shōguns. The beauty and grandeur of the place leave him spellbound, and Edo culture is presented as a magnificent treasure of the Japanese people, something to be cherished as expressing the heritage of the Orient (*tōyō*) and equal in stature to the cultural achievements of France (pp. 310–311).

Although Kōu may have awakened to the admirable qualities of the Edo period, however, the preservation of these qualities in real-world Tokyo raised many practical problems—especially for Japanese youth who, like Kafū and Kōu, had already been overseas and experienced Western culture themselves. One problem was that the behavior of other Japanese was painful to watch—when in a Western-style restaurant, Japanese would order mountains of beef, cooked to a tough frazzle, and drink white wine with every kind of meal, with no thought or understanding involved for the niceties of Western custom (p. 314). Another problem was that once these intellectuals had experienced the "freedom" of Western culture, they saw Japanese tradition as restrictive and obsolete. Koyama, who compares the Western ideals of individuality to the constraints of living in Japanese society, with its filial piety and arranged marriages, repeats that these constraints are especially painful to Japanese youth who have been abroad (p. 320). The idea of preserving the culture of Edo would be useless unless Kafū could find some way to reconcile "genuine Japan" with the realities of the present. This would be accomplished through the character of Kōu, balanced precariously between love of the West, hatred of Meiji modernity, and nostalgic yearning for the past. The novel shows the mental state of Kōu at two critical moments in his search for a solution to this dilemma. In the central Chapter 7, Kōu is still unbalanced. But in Chapter 12, near the end of the novel, we are presented with Kōu's solution in a long exposition on *Tōyō shisō*, Kafū's "Theory of the Orient."

In Chapter 7, Kōu walks around the streets of Tokyo after a pleasant evening with Nakatani, entertained by O-kimi and their young daughter who perform traditional music and dance of the Edo period. Struck by the contrast between the performance and the reality of transitional Tokyo, Kōu feels a sense of dislocation, almost as if he is somebody else (*onore jishin wo mo tanin de aru yō*) (p. 336). This is interesting phrasing, as it seems for a moment Kōu has become the "Other" and lost his own sense of self all together. He must recapture his sense of self (*jishin*) in order to move forward. Gazing at the city sprawl from the top of a bridge, he thinks:

> So this is what they call "Tokyo." This is the representative of the time called "today" and its way of life. Once again

> Kōu was filled with an infinite fear, enmity and sorrow toward this horrible apparition. This was because Kōu believed that this apparition, as appropriate for the word he had chosen himself to describe it, would presently have to disappear. (p. 337)

As a mere transitional stage between the glories of Kamakura and Edo and the vague, unforeseeable future, Meiji appears as an "apparition," something insubstantial and meaningless. Kōu must find a way to reconcile the genuine with modernity, his sense of self with his changed surroundings. In Chapter 12, Kafū's favorite chapter in the novel,[31] Kōu realizes that the key to accomplishing this goal lies in accepting the Orient (*tōyō*) for what it is, in contradistinction to the West (*seiyō*). The binary opposition is constructed in terms of aesthetic values inherent in musical forms. Kōu focuses on the idea of an "Oriental character" expressed in traditional Japanese music, distinguished by the element of *hiai* or sorrow:

> This dark Oriental sorrow is something incomprehensible unless it is seen as something which has come down through the culture of ideas inherited from countless generations. It is enough for us, who were born in that air and who are now living in it, merely to keep silent and accept the existence of such a sorrow. There is no need to discuss its rights and wrongs, or its value. Even if we were able to discuss it, our minds and bodies, which developed on this land of the Orient, would not be able to avoid breathing the air exhaled from the depths of this Oriental soil. Kōu was surprised that not only in the music, but in all the things that his ancestors had left behind, as if they were all somehow in agreement, there appeared this particular kind of sorrow, which could not be seen in the West. (pp. 396–397)

Chapter 12 explores the idea of the Orient as opposed to the Occident at great length. The resilience of traditional music in the face of Westernization is likened to the sound of cicadas hidden in the grass near railway tracks, continuing their song in the face of the terrible roar of "civilization," while the quiet sorrow of Oriental music is contrasted against the "powerful cry" of the music of the West. Interestingly, this Oriental sorrow is expressed as "*hiai,*" not as "*aware,*" the aesthetics of pathos underlying premodern Japanese poetry and drama.[32] Kafū may have chosen the less loaded term to make the sorrow less uniquely Japanese and more universally "Oriental" in nature, further establishing Japan as part of *tōyō*. The passage in which Kafū explores these ideas is generally referred to as his *Tōyō shisō,* or "Theory of the Orient." This chapter of *Reishō* provides the solution to the dilemma underlying all the Returnee Stories, as through contrast with the Western Other, Kafū has come closer to developing his idea of what is "genuinely" Japanese. Kafū's "Theory of the Orient" may be seen as an extension of his argument urging Japan to find its own genuine civilization. Kafū seems to have accepted the idea that Japan not only had strong historical and cultural ties to Asia but could also be seen as part of the *tōyō* set up in opposition to the West. The disgust directed at this *tōyō* in *Shingapōru no sūjikan* has been modified to a deep respect for shared cultural heritage. This is not to say that Kafū was entirely comfortable with this positioning, but that the idea of "civilization" and "genuine culture" were so crucial to his argument that they overrode the necessity of keeping Japan and *tōyō* separate.

Kafū's position here seems at first to be a self-Orientalizing one, a simple reiteration of nationalistic essentializations. Reading his argument as a whole, however, his emphasis on finding aspects of the culture that were uniquely Japanese may be seen as a heartfelt appeal to his audience, an attempt to change the Japanese way of thinking about what true modernization might mean. Kafū tried to make his countrymen open their eyes and see the beauty and rich heritage of their own country, which Kafū saw as equal to the culture of France. Kafū's argument for an authentic Japan was not employed to impress or charm Western audiences with images of beautiful geisha or quaint teahouses (although this has certainly been a result of selective translation and publishing of his later work), but to seek a workable solution for the dilemma of modernity. Looking at the current state of Tokyo from a European perspective, Kafū saw Japan as not exotic or quaint, but as a failure in the quest for organic modernization and reform. This seems to be more a practical or realist view of Japan than a purely "self-Orientalizing" one.

Kafū's "Orient" here represents a search for some essential quality of Japan's authentic cultural heritage, located in the past, a heritage which does not feature the West. In the process of his search, Kafū certainly emphasized particular characteristics of the Orient, Japan, and the West. This essentialization, however, is part of Kafū's method of definition by contrast, perfected in the early collections on America and France. The "Edo" of the Returnee Stories acts as an imaginary counter-discursive space, an artistic Other to the Meiji formulations of *kindai-jiga* and reconstruction. "Edo" thus takes its place among the array of Kafū's constructed spaces, used for effect and contrast rather than standing as an absolute and reified repository of the entire "Japanese Self." To define the Japanese Self, Kafū needed the whole array of contrastive Others, shifting between and among them to craft a persuasive argument. For this reason, I oppose recent readings of Kafū's work as simple examples of "self-Orientalism" or even "reverse Orientalism."[33] Rather, the frameworks of Occidentalism prove more useful in making sense of Kafū's argument, based as it was on a method of dialectical opposition. As Makoto Ueda (1976) has argued, "Kafū arrived at his ideal of beauty largely by means of East–West comparison. Ultimately, he preferred the passive, resigned Oriental ideal to the agonistic, Faustean Western one. Nevertheless, he owed much to Western culture because it gave him a clearer view of his own" (p. 41). Kafū's construction of the West in *Reishō* and *Shinkichōsha nikki* was instrumental in highlighting which aspects of Japanese culture belonged to Japan alone. The contrast between these two essentialized spaces provided the medium for his critique, depending on the Western Other to define the Japanese Self.

Of all the Returnee Stories, the West is most at the forefront of *Shinkichōsha nikki,* where the narrator tells of his childhood beliefs about the West and his idealism with regard to its culture. Believing for a long time in the superiority of imported Western goods and the English language, his misbehavior in school is attributed to a vague, undefined rebellion (*hankō*) "against the whole thought and customs of the Orient" (p. 201). However, the narrator's journey to Europe places him in an uncomfortable position, with the realization that he can no longer relate to his home country as he did in his childhood. Describing a trip back to Tokyo from Hakone, he compares the mountain ranges of Hakone to the North American plains that stretch out forever, unbroken by trees or rocks—but on seeing the sacred Mount Fuji his first thought is that it appears no taller than the triangular spire of the Madeleine church in Paris. Saddened by his reaction, the narrator expresses the double bind of the Japanese returnee:

> Because I had been born Japanese, I wanted to gaze once more in awe upon Mount Fuji with the same feeling as I had when I was a child, but as I thought this I wondered whether that had not already become impossible, and couldn't help feeling miserable. (pp. 205–206)

This kind of conflict is also symbolized by the narrator's own piano, a constant source of both joy and frustration. Although he has chairs, a desk and a chaise longue in his house, it is when he sees the heavy bulk of the piano that he realizes how utterly out of keeping it appears, surrounded by traditional Japanese sliding doors and architecture (p. 182). Whenever he sees the reflection of himself in long-sleeved Japanese dress in its shiny black surface, he "feels like crying," but it is also "a joke, enough to make me burst out laughing. These clothes, this room, and the fact that I'm trying to play this mournful music of Northern Europe which has come all the way here to this far edge of the Orient—Ah, what a reckless attempt it all must be!" (p. 182). The incompatibility of the piano with the Japanese room, and the disjunction in playing Western music at the "far edge of the Orient," are combined with a keen appreciation for the lure of the word "Occident" (*seiyō*) itself, particularly for the young audiences who flock to concerts of Western music (p. 186). While the construction of the West in these works allowed Kafū to come to a clearer definition of what it meant to be Japanese, he also perceptively explored the dynamics of yearning for the Other upon which the Meiji process of Westernization may have been based.

When describing the attraction of Western music and language for the Japanese people, the diarist repeatedly exclaims that there can be "no other people in the world" who despise their own music so much, have such a difference between the generations, or love foreign things more than the things of their own country. The girl Haruko, living with an American family, cannot understand why they collect Japanese antiques. Although Japanese yearn for the West, it seems that Westerners in turn consider Japan to be a "country of beautiful dreams." The narrator writes to Haruko, arguing: "it was probably something in the natural behaviour of human beings to love that which is distant from themselves..." (p. 221). In this statement, Kafū hits on the dynamics of Self and Other in the relationship between Japan and the West. As noted in the Introduction, desire for the Other is certainly an important element of Kafū's work, never so explicitly expressed as in this statement. But Kafū also realizes that yearning for what is different works both ways. In the epilogue to the diary, the narrator is walking along a beach near his father's house, pondering the modern dilemma in terms of the Japanese "self." He concludes in despair that people do not understand what "the West" is, but then neither do they bother to find out what *"Nihon to iu Originalité"* is. Japan must define itself, people have to think. The diary ends with a purpose: The narrator will from now on look for the *minzokuteki*—the purely Japanese—in music, architecture, painting, literature, everything (pp. 247–248). To read Kafū's comprehension of desire for the Other merely at face value is to do his critical argument an injustice. Rather,

Kafū's exploration of Self and Other through the contrast of Japan and the West has led him to focus on defining what is truly Japanese.

The contrasting constructions of the "West" and "Japan" in the Returnee Stories may be understood as constructs of Occidentalism, defined by Xiaomei Chen (1995) as "a discursive practice that, by constructing its Western Other, has allowed the Orient to participate actively and with indigenous creativity in the process of self-appropriation, even after being appropriated and constructed by Western Others" (pp. 4–5). Kafū may be seen as an "Occidentalist" writer in two ways. The first is as an active participant in affirmation of the Japanese Self, which is evident in Kafū's development of *Tōyō shisō* and in his later fiction, which is discussed in the next chapter. Kafū was not only engaged in a counter-discourse of critique against Meiji, but was also engaged in a process of self-appropriation in using constructions of the Western Other. Rather than arguing for a rapid "catching up" to the West, Kafū turned the tables on the argument by focusing on the Japanese Self and arguing for a genuine Japanese modernity. The second way has to do with the fact that Kafū's argument depends on "constructing its Western Other." Kafū's argument for seeking out the authentic in Japan's cultural heritage is based on a construct of binary opposition, in which the Western Other functions as defining contrast to the Japanese Self. The "genuine" civilization of France inspired Kafū to seek the genuine in Japan, and to locate it in the Edo past. It was thus through a process of contrast that Kafū was able to build his critical argument against the Meiji Westernization of Japan, and to construct Edo as a counter-space to Meiji. In this way we may say that Kafū used his construction of the Western Other in building a counter-discourse of critique against the modernization policies of the Meiji government. This use of the Western Other for opposition to the political status quo may be read as an example of what Chen (1995) has called "anti-official Occidentalism," where constructions of the West are utilized for critique of the prevailing government (p. 8).

In September 1910 Kafū wrote what may be regarded as a conclusion to the Returnee Stories. Entitled *Reishō ni tsukite* (On *Sneers*), it explains Kafū's intentions when he wrote *Reishō*:

> My main intention in writing the novel *Reishō* was to attempt a serious critique of the confused, tasteless externals of life in Tokyo in Meiji 42 [1909]; to lament the difficulty of living peacefully within the atmosphere of this period; and finally, to try to study and seek out whether there were

> still places where genuine Japanese characteristics could be found. (KZ 13.41-2)[34]

The basic elements of the Returnee Stories are thus identified as having a threefold purpose: critique; lament; and a search for genuine (*junryō naru*) Japan. Judged against Kafū's own purposes, then, the Returnee Stories may be described as a success. Kafū also uses the words "serious critique" (*shinchō naru hihyō*) in stating his intention to convey his convictions through writing. He continues:

> I did not say so in as many words, but I intended to somehow imply throughout the work the fact that the present-day importation of Western civilization is limited to the superficial, and that with regard to its deeper content, the Japanese people do not in any sense take delight in Western thought. Rather, in Japan there is lying dormant a far stronger theory of exclusion (*haita shisō*) even than the theories of the Yellow Peril advocated by Westerners. Within the atmosphere enveloping Japan, even now with the constitutional government, there exists a kind of Oriental, despotic something, hard to put a name to, which has not changed even slightly from the distant past of the feudal period—and no matter how much we may alter the forms of external appearances, there is a point where we must recognize that the natural features, the climate, and all the things that cannot be seen with the eye seem to harbor malice against the freedom of human will and the liberation of thought. (KZ 13.42)

Kafū did not spell this out for his readers within *Reishō* itself because he was after all writing a novel without direct authorial intrusion—it was Kafū's intention to use the characters Kōu, Nakatani, and Koyama to "hint at" or "imply" these ideas throughout the work.[35] But *Reishō ni tsukite* acts as a summary of Kafū's argument against the superficial imitation of external form without understanding of the underlying systems of thought. Kafū also points out that Japan is held back from such deep understanding, and therefore from "true" or "genuine" reform into a culturally authentic civilization, by its own thought systems based on exclusion, also translated as "xenophobia" (Keene, 1984, p. 417). Kafū's argument thus strikes at the heart of Meiji Japan—the thought systems underlying the nation, constitutional government notwithstanding.

Kafū's attempt to pin down *"junryō naru"* Japanese characteristics or *"Nihon to iu Originalité"* would be followed in the interwar years by similar attempts by a wide range of critics. Tessa Morris-Suzuki (1998) notes the main approaches as defining Japan as opposite but complementary to the West (as in the work of the philosopher Miyake Setsurei); equivalent to the West in terms of "national character" (as in Nitobe Inazō's *Bushido: Soul of Japan*); finding Japanese "roots" that were not Chinese in order to define Japan as opposed to a wider *tōyō* (an approach also examined in Tanaka, 1993); and redefining Japanese culture or *bunka* as both dynamic and adaptive (as seen in the work of Yanagita Kunio) (pp. 68–69). Examining Kafū's *Tōyō shisō* we find a different approach. Japan is defined as both opposite to the West and also equivalent to it in terms of holding its own great traditions, architecture and music; as part of a great cultural heritage both inherited from and shared with *tōyō*; as dynamic in its spirit of change yet too readily adaptive to the externals of Western modernity. If modernity developed naturally in the West over hundreds of years, then what should a modern Japan look like? Steel bridges, streetcars, and factories are necessary for a modern nation, but are imported from abroad. Kafū did not argue for an end to importation, nor did he ponder a native Japanese science as Tanizaki did twenty-four years later with *In'ei raisan* (In Praise of Shadows).[36] Rather, he argued for a balance. The "genuine" modernity he found in France was merely a willingness to cherish old culture and tradition even while pressing ahead with subways and factories; a desire for the beautiful and spiritual as well as the useful. If "civilization" is understood as a balance of material and spiritual elements, the nation can become authentic and modern at the same time.

Unfortunately, Kafū has not often been seen as a serious critic in the West, perhaps because *Shinkichōsha nikki* and *Reishō* have been virtually ignored in Western criticism of modern Japanese literature. In the final Returnee Stories Kafū used the West as a contrast with Japan in order to achieve a political agenda, in the critique of the Meiji government and the creation of a new purposeful "civilization" program which would cherish Edo heritage for posterity. Kafū was engaged in the dilemma of modern authenticity that so plagued the Japanese intellectual, seeking to define the Japanese Self in terms of the world. To understand the nature of Japanese culture, Kafū placed it not only in terms of the Western Other, but also in terms of its own past. After 1910, Kafū's focus turned to Edo, his fiction largely based in the world of the geisha, traditional arts, and the theater. Although this leaning has been described as a "withdrawal" or an "escape," when viewed in the light of the Returnee Stories the Edo thematic may be explained as part of Kafū's opposition (*hankō*) against the modernization policies of the Meiji government, an affirmation of the Japanese Self in opposition to the Westernized Meiji Self. While this chapter has focused on how Kafū used constructions of the Western Other as a contrast by which to define Japan and criticize the Meiji government, the next chapter examines Kafū's focus on the Japanese Self in his writing after 1910.

CHAPTER FIVE

Resistance

Defining and Preserving the Japanese Self

Nagai Kafū's Returnee Stories laid out a challenge to the Japanese people, to discover the meaning of "*Nihon to iu Originalité.*" Where Kafū's work of 1909–1910 puts forward an argument for preserving Japanese culture in the face of superficial Westernization, his writing after this period shows the working out of this argument in practice. Kafū's later work preserves the culture and traditions of Edo in literature, by describing and bringing to life those customs that he feared were soon to die out. Kafū's later work may thus be read as a continuation of his argument for finding and preserving "*Nihon to iu Originalité,*" although critics disagree over whether Kafū's so-called "return to Edo" (*Edo kaiki*) represents an escapist withdrawal or a critical stance. I believe that Kafū's Edo works may be read as a continuation of his critique of Meiji, and that this critique led Kafū to find a definition of the Japanese Self that was ultimately an affirmation of the "genuine" in Japanese culture.

After *Reishō*, Kafū took the position of professor in French literature at Keiō Gijuku as well as the editorship of *Mita bungaku*, contributing a series of twelve *zuihitsu* entitled *Kōcha no ato* (After Tea, 1910–1911) as well as many essays on French literature. Other contributors included Mori Ōgai, whose story *Fushinchū* (Under Reconstruction) appeared in the second issue, Ueda Bin, Satō Haruo, Tanizaki Jun'ichirō, and "Yoshino Kōu," Kafū's artistic nom-de-plume. The journal focused on introducing European art and examining the present state of the Japanese arts in comparison, the European feel of the journal heightened by numerous translations of foreign literature and contributions in English.[1] Taking Kafū's "Theory of the Orient" in context, it seems he played a significant role in the self-reflexive critical discourse of *Mita bungaku,* taking apart terms like "Orient" and "art" to examine their relevance in the new age.

Much of *Kōcha no ato* reads like the observations of *Reishō,* comparing the shallow Meiji attitude to culture and modernization with the more genuine approach of the West or Edo-period Japan. Kafū discusses particular authors and works as well as genres of art in Japan, from *nagauta* to *shimpa* theater, in terms of their effect on him and what art should be. A more rounded picture of the author emerges at the end of the series. Discussing the importation of Western goods in relation to the thriving Ginza café culture, Kafū reveals that it is not change per se that he opposes, but only thoughtless imitation. Realizing that the Ginza will go on changing rapidly every single day, Kafū declares: "Just like a child watching moving pictures, I want to watch this incessantly changing picture-scroll of the times until my eyes hurt."[2] The last installment in November 1911 is a gentle reminiscence of his longing to play the *shakuhachi* in middle school, a simple personal experience with no intrusive critical commentary. By this time the stories later collected as *Shinkyō yawa* (Night Tales from Shimbashi) were appearing in the journal, followed by the collection of essays *Edo geijutsuron* (On the Arts of Edo) in 1913–1914.[3]

In 1916, Kafū abruptly quit his position at Keiō University and resigned as editor of *Mita bungaku,* leaving no word of explanation or farewell in the pages of the journal. Turning to works of fiction, Kafū wrote the novels *Udekurabe* (Rivalry, 1916–1917) and *Okamezasa* (Dwarf Bamboo, 1918), followed by *Ameshōshō* (Quiet Rain, 1921). These novels portrayed the "floating world" of the geisha, the aesthetics of Edo art and music forms, and the storytelling halls and the theaters of Shimbashi and beyond in beautifully crafted, lyrical prose. The artistry of this series of Edo essays, novels, and short stories would culminate in the 1937 work *Bokutō kidan* (A Strange Tale from East of the River), widely acknowledged to be the masterpiece of Kafū's later years. The change in focus to Edo themes after *Reishō,* occurring in the years 1911–1912, would thus define much of Kafū's later work, and it is for his lyrical depictions of the "flower and willow world" that he is best known. The sensual and erotic side of Kafū's use of Edo in these works has been well established by critics in both Japan and the West, and so this chapter focuses instead on Kafū's Edo thematic in terms of its critical nature. Kafū's turn to Edo has been seen as an abrupt escape from reality as he became increasingly withdrawn from society, but reading his work of 1909 through to 1912 in chronological order, a clear line of development becomes apparent. One's first reaction might be surprise at Kafū's seemingly sudden change in focus from stark opposition to Meiji to a more artistic concentration on Edo themes in a short space of time. But in pausing to consider this transition, one recalls the many hints and precursors to Kafū's thematic development, present in all the Returnee Stories—disappointment in the Meiji modernization enterprise, yearning and nostalgia for a disappearing Edo, and a passion for preserving what remained of that period in modern Tokyo. Kafū's turn to Edo in his later work may be seen as a natural development from the Returnee Stories, in which he urged a modernizing Japan to find its own sense of cultural identity and authenticity. This development is clear in the collection *Shinkō yawa,* acting as a bridge between the critical essays of *Kōcha no ato* and the later Edo fiction.

In examining *Shinkyō yawa,* I concentrate on the nine *shōsetsu,* or novellas, that formed the core of the original publication of 1912: *Kaketori* (The Bill Collector), *Iro-otoko* (The Gallant), *Kazagokochi* (Coming Down with a Cold), *Meika* (The Famous Flower), *Matsuba-domoe* (A Swirl of Pine Needles), *Satsuki-yami* (May Darkness), *Asase* (The Shallows), *Mijika-yo* (A Short Night), and *Hirusugi* (An Afternoon).[4] The two remaining pieces in this edition were the novel *Shōtaku* (The Kept Woman's House) and the play *Wakuraba* (Blighted Leaves). A pocket edition published by *Mita bungaku* came out in 1916, also entitled *Shinkyō yawa,* and was largely unchanged.[5] The third edition of 1920 appeared in Volume 4 of the *Kafū zenshū* published by Shun'yōdō. It kept the nine original stories, took out the novel and the play, and added *Botan no kyaku* (The Peony Garden), *Mihatenu yume* (An Unfinished Dream), and *Shukuhai* (The Toast), which Kafū had written much earlier (published in July 1909, January 1910, and May 1909, respectively). While a list of editions demonstrates Kafū's popularity during these years, the earlier works added to the third edition will not be included in this discussion. I wish to focus on the development of Kafū's ideas from *Reishō* to *Shinkyō yawa,* so the following analysis of *Shinkyō yawa* concentrates on the nine core *shōsetsu,* which are shared by the first and third editions.[6] As we shall see, some works in the collection read almost like parts of *Reishō* in their concentration on the ills of "modernity," whereas others have a more positive focus on the values and artistry of the vanishing Edo world.

The foreword of *Shinkyō yawa* shows Kafū's awareness that readers may be intrigued by his choice of subject:

> In the various short stories collected here I have written about the geisha. The intentions of an author who is writing about this kind of thing could, in the first place, perhaps be motivated by profit in selling books which follow vulgar fashions. On the one hand, it could resemble Daudet's portrayal of the frivolous and ostentatious lives of the city prostitutes, the *Histoires de Moeurs Parisiennes*, based on pure artistic interest; or it could be that I wanted to write something like Augier's play *L'Olympe*, or Margueritte's novel *La Prostituée* from around the same time, a severe investigation into questions of morality and society. And then again it could be just a tale of eternal, beautiful, poignant love, like Abbé Prévost's *Manon Lescaut*. All I can do is leave it up to the reader's judgement. (KZ 5.75)[7]

Kafū challenges the reader to discover what kind of work he has produced—frivolous, critical or romantic. Signaling his debt to both Paris and Edo, the references to French demimonde literature are balanced by the use of the traditional Japanese calendar. The foreword is dated "early autumn in the ninth calendar sign, Taishō year of the rat" (*Taishō mizunoe hatsu-aki*). This is a deliberate usage, since throughout *Saiyū-nisshishō, Amerika monogatari,* and *Shinkichōsha nikki* Kafū had distinguished himself from other writers by using the Western calendar. This preface bears out the argument put forward by Snyder, Iriye, and Seidensticker, that Kafū continued to be informed by French as well as Japanese demimonde fiction in this period, finding many parallels between the gay quarters of Edo and Paris.[8] Kafū's "return to the past" and choice of Edo themes did not necessitate turning his back on the French literary tradition, and his work would continue to show traces of Maupassant, Flaubert, and Balzac to the end of his career.[9] *Shinkyō yawa* moves fluidly between naturalistic depiction and ornate Edo-period language, while Paris and Edo emerge as linked symbolic spaces representing "genuine" culture, in Kafū's quest for *Nihon to iu Originalité.*

Although *Mijika-yo* (A Short Night)[10] is not the first in the collection, it was written earlier than the other stories, and is the most extreme in its illustration of Edo as a cultural ideal. The work takes the form of a dialogue between two lovers, the man asking the woman to tell him a story to while away the hours of a sleepless night. He asks specifically for a story of her hometown, because no matter how many times he hears her "dream-tales" they always carry his soul to "that distant, distant place" (p. 201). Repeating his request, he asks for "a tale of the ever more distant, ever more dreamlike, sorrowful reminiscences of your distant hometown" (p. 202). The emphasis on distance and the dreamlike state asks not for reality but an interpretation of it, situated in the past. The man says that the power of her tale to transport him far away is also held by the music of Schumann, while the shivers they cause resemble his physical reaction to reading Baudelaire's poetry. The striking juxtaposition of "tales of the distant hometown" with these Western artists sets the tone of contrast between old Japan and the modern West. Kafū next emphasizes the contrast between old Japan and modern Japan by having the man yearn for the mental stimulation and power of the new book *Shōnen* by "that young, up-and-coming writer" (undoubtedly Tanizaki Jun'ichirō's work of 1911), while he also asks the woman to talk to him as his mother would, to conjure up the image of Yonehachi and Tanjirō sleeping together with their child.[11] Two sets of polar opposites have been constructed in the opening pages, with Western art and Tanizaki's controversial new literature providing the modern contrasts against symbols of the past.

The woman's story is a vivid evocation of life in an old harbor town, set long ago in the north country, in a large well-established brothel on a summer evening before the Tanabata festival. The work takes on the theme of transience and change, as the woman describes the many relics in the storehouse—old clothes, utensils and picture books, vermilion-lacquer and raised-lacquer furniture, a chest adorned with family crests—a long list of forgotten items of great beauty and workmanship. She learns that the items belonged to a famous prostitute (*yūjo*) and muses on the ephemeral nature of human life, more transient even than the kimono being eaten by insects and the furniture slowly losing its lacquer (p. 204). The overwhelming image is that of fading glory and the passing of an age, emphasized by the man's response—whenever her thoughts are "pained and oppressed by the pressures of the ugly modern reality (*genjitsu*)," he urges, she should think of her hometown (*furusato*) and be comforted (p. 205). *Mijika-yo* was the first of these stories to be published after *Reishō*, overlapping with the last essays of *Kōcha no ato* in 1911. Considering this context, *Mijika-yo* may have been meant as a practical illustration of Kafū's "Theory of the Orient," preserving the cultural heritage of Japan through the writing of fiction. By opening with the juxtapositions of East and West, Edo and modernity, the theme of transience is related to Japan's situation in the transitions of the Meiji era, while Edo and the distant past are set up as a direct contrast to Meiji modernity.

Where *Mijika-yo* was the earliest of the *Shinkyō yawa* tales, the first story in the published collection was *Kaketori* (The Bill Collector), from February 1912. The plot is simple—a naïve young housemaid must travel all the way across Tokyo to Ōkubo in order to collect a bill for her mistress—but the work is interesting in its use of space. As the girl travels farther from the downtown, traditional area she has known since childhood, she becomes increasingly afraid of the clanging streetcars and multitudes of strangers in the vast city, and nearing the heights of Ōkubo she becomes convinced she will find foxes and badgers, traditional agents of mischief and danger. The story is reminiscent of *Fukagawa no uta* in the feelings of the main character, as the quiet, known value of the traditional place is found to be preferable to the confusion and noise of the new Tokyo. Contemporary readers would have found shades of Izumi Kyōka, whose works often featured an urban young man coming into contact with mystical forces in the mountains and rivers of the countryside.[12] Both writers used space as a means for negotiation between old and new, with physical displacement of the characters opening the way to new meaning and discovery. Where Kyōka's protagonist was usually male, however, Kafū's tales of this period are increasingly told from the point of view of a young woman, with a succession of maids, prostitutes and geisha acting as agents of a feminine, nonprogressive sensibility as well as "guardians of civilization."

The next story in the collection is *Iro-otoko* (The Gallant), from March 1912.[13] It begins with a comparison of modern Tokyo actors with the *iro-otoko* of Edo fiction, commenting that modern-day gallants treat women in an entirely different fashion from the days of Yonehachi and Tanjirō's romance in the late Edo period.[14] The hero Kyō-san is the son of a dealer in foreign imported goods on the Ginza, a *Ginza no tochikko* (child of the modern Ginza) as opposed to the traditional *Edokko* (child of Edo). The story's appeal lies in the plot, consisting of romantic and comedic twists involving a diamond ring. *Iro-otoko* and *Kaketori* share an awareness of modern versus traditional space. When the maid in *Kaketori* leaves the old *shitamachi* area, she becomes agitated and fearful. Similarly, Kyō-san ultimately cannot become part of the geisha's world because he is a modern man from the Ginza. The physical space of Ginza is thus delineated as purely "modern," while Shimbashi is equated with the Edo lifestyle and the floating world. If Kafū had sought pure escapism in these works they would have been set in the Edo period itself, but it seems he is making a statement, depicting what remained of Edo in the modern city as a rich and dynamic cultural heritage.

Kazagokochi (Coming Down with a Cold), published April 1912, begins with a man reading aloud from Tamenaga Shunsui's *Shunshoku umegoyomi*, but he is interrupted by the telephone, in an oblique observation on the intrusions of modernity into traditional Japanese life (p. 119). The story focuses on the independent geisha Masukichi, who has tuberculosis but is called out on a winter night to play the samisen. The man's abandonment of a Marunouchi office job in favor of living in the geisha quarter on Masukichi's earnings acts as a criticism of the Meiji values of success and worldly advancement (*risshin-shusse*), and he escapes both Meiji values and his fears for Masukichi's health by retreating into traditional Japanese literature. In the apartment there is electric light, the clock strikes to the tune of Gilbert and Sullivan's "*Miyasama, Miyasama*" from *The Mikado*, and Masukichi is picked up by an automobile outside the building. But this is the full extent of modernity's intrusion into their quiet lives. The appearance of Gilbert and Sullivan is so completely out of keeping with the rest of the apartment that it draws the reader's attention and reminds us of Kafū's previous criticisms of imitative Meiji fashions. The reference may be a comment on Meiji society's love of Western fads, even when those fads were something that caricatured or "Orientalized" Japan. The fact that the striking of the clock is accepted uncritically by the inhabitants of the room reflects Kafū's argument that people may be interested in Western fashions, but have no deeper understanding of the fundamental ideas of the West. The interior of the apartment is otherwise very traditional in appearance, filled with Masukichi's silk and padded kimono, Japanese lanterns, a *kotatsu*, a rake for good luck from the Otori Fair, and of course the *Shunshoku umegoyomi*. This makes a stark contrast to the building itself, an example of shoddy workmanship from the building boom in early Meiji. In the opening of Part Two of the story, Kafū criticizes the Meiji rush for modernization at the expense of quality with a lengthy passage on the building's structural and aesthetic failings (pp. 128–129). The clash between the external ugliness of the building and the tranquility of the more traditional atmosphere inside echoes the fundamental theme of the Returnee Stories—the conflict between superficial external appearances and what lies within, the essence of the Japanese Self. The contrast set up in *Kazagokochi* is not between Japan and the West, however, but between Meiji modernity and traditional Japan.

Asase (The Shallows) was published at the same time as *Kazagokochi*, in April 1912. It may be regarded as the exception in *Shinkyō yawa* in that it is the only work to use sustained, direct contrast with the Western Other. As the title suggests, its main theme is the shallow nature of modern Japanese society. A group of high-standing men meet to decide where to hold a welcome party for their friend recently returned from the West. Kafū focuses on the man of letters in the group, who had traveled to America and Europe in his youth but now gains satisfaction merely from listening to verses of the poet Okanishi Itchū (1637–1711). We find out the reason for his change of taste through his experience with a particular geisha. At first she had enchanted him, apparently the ideal geisha in possession of the Japanese essence. However, the girl became bent on improving herself, wanting to buy shares and to wear the badge of the Patriotic Wives' Association. In modernizing herself, the girl could no longer represent the perfect geisha, because: "All these things which are the *raison d"être* of the improper woman, she was determined to suppress in herself" (p. 195). The speaker complains that modern geisha no longer resemble the carefree, untidy women of Tokugawa literature—it is only the prostitutes in France who still embody this independent open spirit. The Japanese geisha is trying to make herself into something she is not, whereas the French prostitute remains unchanged. Kafū thus uses contrasting representations of the French and Japanese "improper woman" as a metaphor for genuine versus superficial civilization.

The narrator next laments the influence of Meiji modernization on the Japanese demimonde. If you become close to one particular geisha, the strict social rules of the modern "floating world" treat the relationship like a proper marriage, with everyone referring to you as "so-and-so's patron." If you boldly oppose such taboos, you invite slander. People do not appreciate the arts of *galanterie* and *flirtage* from the modern world—arts that come from France and are still alive there (p. 198). This complaint turns into a tirade against Japan, and the last pages of *Asase* read like *Reishō* or *Shinkichōsha nikki* in their diatribe on Japanese modernization: the land is too cramped for hunting and riding; there are too many fortified zones for the army and navy; factories have killed the fish in the rivers (p. 198). The narrator proposes that one could live in seclusion, living for song, music, incense, tea ceremony, Itchū and Utazawa, but outside, the unstoppable invasion of the new nation-building program makes the city a scene of destruction. The speaker wishes for neither the fashionable Meiji modernity nor the ancient Edo ways, but only for the aristocratic, graceful amusement of "civilization," as France has managed to sustain throughout its modernization process (p. 199). Once again, Kafū has found the middle ground between ancient and modern in France, where civilized society appreciates and nurtures its cultural identity.

Hirusugi (An Afternoon), published May 1912, takes the form of a dialogue between a host and his visitor. The two men discuss the changing weather and reminisce about drinking together three years ago, the year it flooded. "That was around the time of the fuss about Japan taking Korea" remarks the host, the historical moment serving to illuminate his own personal memories (p. 215). Kafū observes that the annexation of Korea in 1910 was a memorable national event, but also realizes that while political events stand out in the memory, so do things closer to home like the rebuilding of famous landmarks. The men look back on many events in Tokyo, including the fires in the Yoshiwara, the rebuilding of Nihonbashi, and the opening of the Imperial Theater. When the visitor suggests they go for a walk, however, the host replies that there is nowhere worth walking now that the narrow bridges and canals have been destroyed. Seven or eight years ago, before Japan was victorious in war, things were more promising, he grumbles, but now he gets more satisfaction from temple grounds and cemeteries. Parts of this dialogue could well be spoken by Nakatani from *Reishō* or Ryūsui from *Shinkichōsha nikki,* and the main theme emerges as the destructive nature of Meiji modernization, visible in the changing face of the capital. Much has been rebuilt, but the new is far from superior to that which it has displaced. The old men also reminisce about Tokugawa writers and famous works, but toward the end, the visitor quotes Maupassant and Catulle Mendès on love and passion (pp. 221–223). Just as in *Asase* above, the comparison of Edo and European writers illuminates the theme of "genuine civilization"—true expression in the literary form resides in both French and Edo literature because these cultures are genuine. In this way Edo becomes the contrastive Other to Meiji, as the repository of "*Nihon to iu Originalité.*"

Kafū continues his search for the essence of genuine Japanese culture in *Meika* (The Famous Flower), published in June 1912, by opening with a conference on Oriental civilization (*Tōyō no bunmei*). The program opens with "many abstracts addressing the nature of Oriental civilization" (p. 139), followed by a dance performance by a group of Shimbashi geisha, accompanied by a three-stringed ensemble playing traditional Japanese *nagauta* and Tokiwazu music. Many members of the audience leave, however, uninterested in the old-fashioned performance, and it is an old woman who sings the *nagauta,* suggesting the impending disappearance of such traditional talents. The feelings of the narrator on hearing the old woman sing are similar to those of Kōu in the *Tōyō shisō* passage of *Reishō,* focusing on the sorrowful nature of Oriental music (p. 140). The narrator also feels that the *nagauta* is particularly disappointing when performed in such a spacious, well-lit hall, reminding the reader of the question of how to reconcile traditional Japan with the electricity and other intrusions of the modern. Thus, in the opening few lines, Kafū has already signposted the work as one concerned with the presentation and discussion of the Japanese Self, in the disappearance of Japan's cultural heritage in favor of modern tastes.

After this introduction, the work turns out to be a harsh commentary on Meiji society, refracted through the character of the geisha Kokaji. The narrator knows her full past, having been involved with her himself until he heard rumors that she took Westerners and Chinese as customers and she was ostracized by other geisha as of the lowest order. He tells of her rise from tempura-shop waitress to a brothel prostitute to a low-class geisha under the name Hanachō, and finally to a geisha of the first rank in Meiji society. As "Kokaji," she practices calligraphy from the *Kokinshū* and socializes with members of high society. The irony of the title is that Kokaji is indeed famous, having pushed herself forward into Meiji society, but is shunned by the prostitutes and geisha who know her true character. Although the women of the brothels and teahouses will not accept the hypocrisy and ruthless ambition that characterize Kokaji's ascent, her uncritical acceptance by the upper class reveals "high society" to be as shallow and hypocritical as Kokaji herself. Her room is a chaotic jumble of Western and Japanese furniture and screens, gaudy objects with disparate styles from the fashions of all different periods. She shows no sign of discomfort at the display, sparking a tangent of criticism from Kafū on the evils of the nouveau riche. Meiji society is set on profit and exhibition, marrying into rich families, getting a peerage, and joining fancy clubs, even if one's origins were in the *shitamachi* (p. 153). Unlike *Shinkichōsha nikki,* which contrasted this superficial fashion-following with the "genuine civilization" of the West, criticism in *Meika* is directed at the characteristics of Meiji society itself. Japan's "modernity" comes under close scrutiny and is found wanting in all aspects, symbolized by Kokaji, "the absolute incarnation (*gonge*) of modernism" (p. 156). *Meika,* even in its title, is reminiscent of *Reishō* in its unvarnished look at Meiji society, criticising the taste, fashion, and superficiality of the modern age. In its destruction of true Japanese civilization and "*Nihon to iu Originalité,*" Meiji modernity has replaced the West as the contrasting Other to Kafū's essentialized Japanese past.

Kafū expands the theme of modern versus old Japan in *Matsubadomoe* (A Swirl of Pine Needles), July 1912, a sorrowful tale of lost love along the lines of Edo *giri-ninjō* novels and plays. The story is an explanation of the hero Yūkichi's obsession with traditional Utazawa music, beginning with a nostalgic look at his youth, a time when the telegraph, telephone, cars, and streetcars were making their presence felt, but the traffic and smoke of the modern city was still to come, and Tokyo was still criss-crossed with bridges over the Sumida (pp. 158–159). As in *Kaketori,* Kafū conjures up an image of Tokyo when it was still divided on the outskirts by rice fields and patches of countryside, and the different parts of Tokyo seemed far away from each other. Although Yūkichi is deeply in love with the geisha Kotama, his parents arrange for him to marry the daughter of an army general. Torn between passion and filial duty, Yūkichi gives in to duty and never sees Kotama again. His new wife exemplifies the modern Meiji woman, who is involved in every sort of club, practises tea ceremony and *naginata,* speaks English, is a member of the Red Cross, and reads Tennyson and Longfellow (pp. 167–168). The wife's fashionable interest in clubs and her intellectual association with the West are contrasted with Kotama's training in the Edo arts. Yūkichi escapes from his home life by taking up Utazawa lessons. The instructor's mode of dress, speech, and manner are all from a bygone era, and he finds happiness in a rediscovered past. Yūkichi finds that the romantic tragedies in Utazawa give expression to his own pain, and muses that the one thing that eases his suffering comes from the time of Ansei (1854–1860). "In other words, Yūkichi had found the ideal form of performance to which he could entrust his dreams of the past" (p. 171). *Matsuba-domoe* shows the value of the old arts and their relevance to the present, as the Utazawa ballad has become the only form of true emotional expression open to the Japanese man.

The contrast drawn between the values of old Japan and those of modern Meiji is even sharper in *Satsuki-yami* (May Darkness), published in September 1912, a drama that turns on the anxiety of a young geisha for her child who is dangerously ill. Much of the tension in the first half comes from the heroine Tsutayo trying to find an excuse to leave her patron to see the child, while the patron suspects that she is trying to leave to go to another, perhaps younger lover. Finally, Tsutayo finds an opportunity to escape, and she runs to Azabu to see her child, taking to the dark, narrow alleys. The wind picks up and it begins to rain, and many times she trips and almost falls. Her Shimada coiffure falls out of shape, her hair streams in the wind, and her kimono becomes disarrayed at the collar and skirts. Heedlessly she runs on, out of breath, until she runs headlong into a group of young delinquents and is surrounded. Her screams bring a plainclothes policeman to the scene, but her dishevelled appearance on such a dark night raises his suspicions and she is taken to the police station. Tsutayo repeats her story over and over in tears until the police are satisfied of the facts. However, the police take an unsympathetic view:

> If that is the case, then you should still walk in a modest fashion, so as not to attract people's attention. From now on you must restrain yourself from such behavior as having your hair and skirts in a mess, making an excessive display of wearing sensational red colors, and rushing around the night streets—no matter how serious the emergency. (p. 186)

The police repeatedly lecture her, and by the time they call her employer to pick her up it is nearly midnight. The coldness of rational society is set up against the passion of an anxious mother, and Tsutayo is helpless to avert disaster. The news spreads quickly, and the evening newspaper has a bold headline on the "Shimbashi Geisha's Distress." In describing Tsutayo's encounter with the young men the article uses the ambiguous word *hazukashime,* which could mean anything from shame and humiliation to violation and rape. Debt collectors gather around the lattice doors of Tsutayo's *machiai,* and by the next morning newspaper articles are flourishing, portraying the "rape" as fact. The youths are rounded up and Tsutayo is brought in again and again to see if she remembers anything more about that night. Tsutayo's circle of acquaintances narrows, and she can no longer show her face at the *machiai.* She puts the baby in hospital, and finds that to repay her debts she must now leave Japan entirely and go to Korea to raise the money. The reactions of Meiji society to Tsutayo's situation, from the police to the newspapers, Tsutayo's employers and her social circle, are indicative of a cold society which thrives on gossip and is uninterested in the truth. Where Yūkichi in *Matsuba-domoe* found refuge from Meiji society in the Japanese cultural tradition, Tsutayo is forced to leave Japan completely. The finality of such an ending is an indictment of a society that stifles the expression of true human emotion. *Satsuki-yami* is undoubtedly the harshest of these works in its depiction of Meiji society, as if Kafū despairs that there is no room in modern Japan for the genuine emotion and honest intentions of the naïve Tsutayo. As a geisha, Tsutayo is one of Ryūsui's "guardians of civilization," but the other geisha are oblivious to her problems and it seems that the old civilization has disappeared for good.

Taking the stories of *Shinkyō yawa* as a whole, we see that the essentialized space of Meiji modernity has progressively replaced that of the West as the primary defining contrast to Kafū's idea of "genuine Japan." The West appears briefly, in a literary reference to

Baudelaire's poetry or Maupassant's characters, or in the imitative Western fashions of Meiji high society, in order to illustrate certain points about Meiji Japan or the idea of a "genuine" civilization. But the West in *Shinkyō yawa* is not used as the only contrastive Other to modern Japan, and is balanced by a strong focus on Edo and a search for "Japanese" characteristics. The West takes a more substantial role in *Asase* to mourn the loss of a type of woman—the confident, reckless Japanese geisha—and to point out that French prostitutes retain these qualities in abundance because their civilization remains true to its past. "Edo" and "France" were thus linked in Kafū's imagination as loci of "genuine culture." Both spaces possessed a thriving demimonde and a literature to portray it, a significant urban culture, and the figure of the connoisseur as *flâneur* or *tsū*, but the difference was that France had been able to bring those elements into the present while Japan had relegated them to the past. Kafū saw it as his duty to collect data and knowledge about the old streets and customs of Edo, and then to preserve them in writing. Looking at his works of 1909 to 1915, we see him first constructing his critique in the Returnee Stories, then preserving knowledge in the nonfictional *Edo geijutsuron* and *Hiyorigeta*, and dramatizing Edo in his fictional works. In the stories of *Shinkyō yawa*, the beauty of Edo is allowed to live and breathe, and to speak for itself. In this way we may see *Shinkyō yawa* as the writing out in practice of Kafū's "Theory of the Orient," where he argued that modernity may be reconciled to "the genuine" in Japan through the preservation of Edo culture. By making Edo the main subject and theme of *Shinkyō yawa*, Kafū was carrying out his own mission to define and represent *"Nihon to iu Originalité."*

Kafū's "Edo" represents a number of interconnected ideas. It represents the culture and tradition that Japan inherited from its "Oriental" origins of China and the mainland, in the form of aesthetics governed by a sense of sorrow. This cultural heritage operates as the antithesis to both the Occident in the Returnee Stories and to Meiji modernity in *Shinkyō yawa*. "Edo" also signifies the physical remnants of that cultural heritage still to be found in the city of Tokyo, in suburbs and outskirts, the geisha districts, and monuments like the Shiba mausoleum. As Koizumi Kōichirō (1984) has argued, these parts of the city that retain their "Japanese" characteristics and resist Westernization are set up by Kafū as a counter-space to Meiji, and the world of the geisha is set up in opposition to the Meiji *kokka* (pp. 48–49). Personified in Tsutayo, the true Edo geisha is thrust out of the Meiji state, where only hypocrites like Kokaji can thrive and succeed. Kafū's use of Edo in these ways may be read as strikingly oppositional in nature. The fundamental opposition of Edo and Meiji underlies the entire collection of *Shinkyō yawa,* which portrays modern Japan as a shallow and insensitive civilization bent on imitation and social ambition with no regard for the traditions of the past. The two themes of preservation of Edo and critique of Meiji modernity are inseparable in the collection as Meiji civilization becomes the antithesis of "*Nihon to iu Originalité.*" At the same time, France continues to reign as the supreme example of a state that has managed to modernize while still retaining its integrity, symbolized by the freedom and decadence of the Quartier Latin. The function of Paris as a model for Japan in *Reishō* takes on added significance in *Shinkyō yawa,* as the geisha become not only the "guardians of civilization" but also the guardians of free expression and true human feeling. The decadence of Edo and Paris are set up in stark opposition to the frigid and unfeeling Meiji state, with its emphasis on regulations, social niceties, and law. The central ideas of *Shinkyō yawa* thus emerge as a natural progression when viewed in the light of Kafū's argument for finding the genuine in Japanese civilization, first set out in the Returnee Stories of 1909–1910 and developing through the period of 1911–1912.

An analysis of *Shinkyō yawa* thus demonstrates Kafū's depiction of "Edo" as inextricably bound up with his Meiji critique and intentions of preserving the national identity. However, the Edo thematic of *Shinkyō yawa* has been open to many interpretations, and Western scholars have not on the whole perceived its critical nature. Donald Keene (1984), for example, is dismissive of Kafū's critical stance in late Meiji:

> Kafū saw the pretensions and vulgarity of Meiji Japan and despised them, but the only solution that offered itself was withdrawal from society, rather in the manner of the *bunjin* (gentlemen scholars) of the past. . . . Kafū was in no sense a philosopher, and the hostility he displayed toward the world around him often seems mere crankiness, rather than a morally inspired criticism of society. (pp. 386–387)

This dismissal of Kafū's criticism as "mere crankiness" echoes Edward Seidensticker's (1965) influential portrayal of Kafū as an irritable "scribbler," as opposed to a serious writer:

> The longing for the past often seems ambivalent and contradictory, for it is not a reasoned position. How . . . can the young individualist rebelling against his father so admire the world of the blindly superstitious and submissive?

> The realm of the Edo courtesan is also the realm of the domineering Edo father, and resentment at paternal authority constantly seems to teeter on the edge of a longing to submit completely. (p. 35)

Seidensticker's argument rests on the assumption that Edo represented nothing more to Kafū than the world of superstition and paternal authority, governed by the domination and submission of the Confucian moral system. However, Kafū's position may be understood as a reasoned one if we view his construction of Edo and the Japanese past as part of a purposeful focus on what was genuinely Japanese as opposed to what was Western (or Westernized) in the Meiji state. Kafū's "Edo" signified freedom from domineering Confucian morals in a world dedicated to love and beauty, where individuals shunned by society lived as guardians of a disappearing culture. Any longing that Kafū had to "submit" was to submerge himself in this world, thus cutting himself off completely from family, Confucian morality, and the Meiji values of ambition and success. Kafū's longing for Edo is neither ambivalent nor contradictory, but an unequivocal statement that authentic Japanese culture, and a genuine Japanese life, lie only in the past, in a time before Meiji modernization produced the metamorphosis of Edo into Tokyo.

Ken Ito examines Kafū's longing for Edo in terms of René Girard's "triangular desire," which we examined in Chapter 3. Ito (1991) argues that Kafū treats Edo in the same way that he earlier treated the West in *Amerika monogatari,* as an exoticized representation of place filled with a mystery, color, and excitement lacking in Meiji Japan (pp. 34–46). In *Fukagawa no uta,* Ito argues, Edo becomes the new "topography of longing," and the light that shines on the Fudō Shrine is the same light that earlier illuminated the monuments of Washington:

> If the dramatic landscape of Washington showed us the "West" as the "Orient," this passage takes that vision and turns it upon a corner of the actual Orient. Kafū imbues with the imaginative hues of the "West" a Fukagawa that represents the vestiges of the lost world of Edo. . . . Kafū recovered his "other world" amidst the Tokyo landscape he found so disagreeable. (pp. 47–48)

Ito sees Kafū's turn to Edo as a rediscovery of the Other, once represented by America or Paris, at home in Japan. Edo was certainly an Other for Kafū in the search for Japanese identity. But where Kafū used contrast with the West as Other to narrow down elements of what were "Japanese," the function of the Edo Other was necessarily different, because Edo was also Japanese. Edo functioned not as Other to Japan to define what was "Japanese," but rather functioned as Other to the modern. Edo stood for all that was not Meiji, the pristine cultural condition that existed before Meiji modernization, Westernization and superficial imitation appeared in Japan. The Edo Other thus took on a significance not found in contrasts with the West, as Kafū now became engaged in finding the essence of Japanese "genuine" culture in the immediate past. Edo was indeed a "topography of longing," but that longing was directly tied to Kafū's critique of modernity.

Ito also describes Kafū's turn toward the Oriental past as a "reformulation of European Orientalism," which heavily depended on the Oriental past for theories of origin and self-definition (p. 55). A superficial reading of *Reishō* and *Shinkyō yawa* may give the impression that Kafū's search for uniquely Japanese elements of his culture equated to a "re-Orientalizing" of Japan, but a closer reading of the texts shows Kafū's *Tōyō shisō* as the end result of an argument developed to prevent Meiji Japan from losing its sense of identity in the rush toward modernity and Westernization. Rather than creating a new "Orient" out of Japan in the representation of Edo, Kafū claimed a cultural heritage of genuine civilization for Japan in its own immediate past, and thereby reasserted Japan's agency, or ability to find origins in its own culture. This kind of assertion is diametrically opposed to Orientalism, in which system Kafū would remain as voiceless object. A good illustration of Kafū's understanding of the "Orient" and the constructive methods of Orientalism is found in the fourth installment of *Kōcha no ato* (September 1910). Musing on summers past, the narrator recalls a midsummer noontime spent on the second floor of a Yanagibashi backstreet. Four or five geisha occupy the room, crammed with their makeup stands, novels, and books, while their yukata hanging outside on the drying platform contrast brilliantly with the blue sky. As the women variously sit, stand, lie on the floor, play the samisen, complain, quarrel, and play with a kitten, the narrator is spellbound:

> I merely stood silently, watching what everyone was doing. It was because the lines of those young women's bodies, under just one layer of yukata, looked so soft and ample in their various captivating postures, that for me it was just as if I were intoxicated by the kind of sweet, gentle sentiment that one can experience from an Orientalist oil

> painting depicting a group of Turkish beauties gathered on the tiled floor of a palace—or yet again, from an Utamaro *ukiyo-e* print. (*MB* 1.5: 127)

Kafū places the narrator as a silent observer of the scene, which gives a feeling akin to that given by an Orientalist painting or Utamaro print. It is significant that the "Orient" of the Orientalist depiction is named as Turkey, while the Edo-period artist depicts Japanese beauties. Kafū knows himself to be neither an Orientalist nor an Utamaro; the women before him are neither Turkish beauties nor Edo-period geisha. It is the feeling given by the scene that reminds him of both art forms, as he references the constructive power of each artistic process. The Western Orientalist rhetoric is placed on par with homegrown artistic tradition, both able to create a mood of sensuous languor and beauty. Both art methods are far removed from one another and from the present age, representing the two alternatives to the Meiji present found in Kafū's critique. The *tōyō* of the Turkish Orient and the *tōyō* of Edo cultural artifacts are here juxtaposed to highlight Kafū's awareness of the constructive process of art.

Rather than seeing Kafū as some kind of "Orientalist" himself, then, I believe that the definition and representation of "*Nihon to iu Originalité*" in the Returnee Stories and the Edo thematic in *Shinkyō yawa* should be understood as constructions of Occidentalism. In Xiaomei Chen's (1995) definition, Occidentalism has two main parts: the use of constructs or images of the West by intellectuals (or the government) for political policies or critique; and "self-appropriation": indigenous creation and participation in constructing the Self even after it has already been constructed by Others (pp. 4–5). My analysis of the Returnee Stories in the previous chapter demonstrated that Kafū's critique of Meiji to a large extent depended on contrast with the Western Other, and I argued that this may be seen as a form of Occidentalism, corresponding to the first part of Chen's definition. Similarly, Kafū's use of Edo in *Shinkyō yawa* may be read as an affirmation of the Japanese Self in response to rapid Westernization and to what Kafū saw as the superficial Meiji approach to modernization. Kafū's search for "*Nihon to iu Originalité*," and his focus on recovering Japan's cultural heritage, symbolized by Edo, may be read not only as part of his critical stance against Meiji but also as an act of "self-appropriation," corresponding to the second part of Chen's definition of Occidentalism. Taken together, Kafū's use of the West and his use of "Edo," both of which allowed him to come to a clearer definition of "Japan," form a constellation of Occidentalist construction.

Reading Kafū's use of Edo in this way challenges previous readings in Western criticism, which focus mainly on the idea of his "escape" into the Edo world. Rather than escaping into the past, Kafū tried to make traditional Japanese culture relevant to his present-day audience, before it was swept away by the "hideous apparition" that was Meiji modernization. Reading Kafū's "return to Edo" as a continuation of the Meiji critique, rather than as an abrupt thematic reversal or simple romantic escapism, is upheld by Kafū's consistent dedication to Edo themes in his work of 1911–1918, culminating in the apologia *Hanabi* (Fireworks), written in July 1919. *Hanabi* is an essay of eleven pages, most of which deals with Kafū's reaction to political events of the late Meiji and early Taishō periods. There is one much-debated passage, however, in which Kafū explains his reasons for taking up the Edo theme in his work after the Returnee Stories. The shift in theme is represented as a conscious decision, expressed in terms of Kafū's reaction to the High Treason Incident of 1910–1911:[15]

> In Meiji 44 [1911], around the time when I was working at Keiō University, I was passing through Ichigaya on my way to work as I did sometimes, when I saw five or six prisoner wagons go past in succession, going towards the Court House in Hibiya. In all the incidents I have experienced in this world up to now, I have not felt such an unspeakably ghastly feeling as I did at this moment. As a writer, I must not keep quiet on this question of principles. Did not the novelist Zola go into exile outside his own country because he cried out for justice in the Dreyfus affair? But I, along with all the other writers, said nothing. I somehow felt an unbearable agony of conscience. I felt exceedingly ashamed of myself as a writer. Since then, I considered that there was nothing for it but to reduce the quality of my own art to the level produced by the Edo writers of frivolous and vulgar fiction. Since that time I began to wear a tobacco pouch, to collect *ukiyo-e* prints and to play the samisen. The frivolous writers and masters of *ukiyo-e* art at the end of the Edo period saw such things as the coming of the Black Ships to Uraga and the assassination of the Senior Minister at the Sakurada Gate as things which had nothing to do with them, the common people—instead of denying this, I made up my mind that it was awe-inspiring, and that I should respect rather than deride their intentions in the moment of creating their erotic novels and prints. (KZ 15.12)

This passage has been called "Kafū's literary turning point" (Satō, 1995, p. 138). What stands out most in this confession is Kafū's sense of shame as a writer who stands by and says nothing about the oppression of intellectual currents in the Kōtoku Incident. Kafū's thoughts on the Incident and on the role of the writer are not to be taken lightly when trying to understand the nature of the change in his literature after *Reishō,* when he turned almost exclusively to Edo themes. Any discussion of Kafū's Edo thematic must refer to the critical debate surrounding *Hanabi.* There is an almost inexhaustible supply of essays on *Hanabi* in both Japan and the West, and most critics refer to it even if only in passing. It has been the subject not only of serious academic criticism, but also of more informal "roundtable discussions."[16] A large part of the question has been the fact that 1919 is at quite some remove from the events of 1910–1911 that the essay describes. The main points of discussion among critics in trying to comprehend Kafū's "literary turning point" have been Kafū's feelings of shame, his decision to live the rest of his life as a *gesakusha* (an Edo writer of frivolous or erotic fiction), and whether the time lapse between the High Treason Incident of 1910–1911 and the writing of *Hanabi* in 1919 is significant. The question of whether Kafū's "unbearable agony of conscience" (*ryōshin no kutsū ni taerarenu yō na ki*) was a true confession of his real feelings at the time of the High Treason Incident has also been much debated. It is not a trivial question, because Kafū puts this forward as the reason why he felt compelled to live out his life as a *gesakusha* away from the rest of society. If we cannot take Kafū's statement at face value, then there must be other reasons for his withdrawal.

Seidensticker (1965) is sceptical as to whether Kafū really suffered "unbearable agonies of conscience," and argues that *Hanabi* should not be taken seriously as a critical turning point in Kafū's outlook on literature and its role in society:

> There is no reason to doubt that Kafū was upset by the Kōtoku case—for Kōtoku and his fellow defendants were the prisoners in the "five or six police wagons." Yet it is hard to believe that he emerged from the encounter significantly changed. Whatever his own views on the matter, he never showed much sign of being a Zola. It is one thing to complain about the dirt and clutter of Meiji Japan, but quite another to fight for social justice. A liking for the things of Edo, on the other hand, including its more disreputable institutions, had been much in evidence before he left for

> the United States and France. It is important to remember, too, that Kafū did not get around to telling of the "crisis" until 1919, when he was in a slump and no doubt receptive to dramatic explanations for it. The common notion that the Kōtoku case was somehow crucial to Kafū's writing, then, has about it an ex-post-facto look. (pp. 46–47)

Seidensticker believes Kafū was using the Kōtoku Incident as a convenient excuse to indulge his interests in Edo and the Yoshiwara, and argues that Kafū, never a serious writer, was largely untouched by the Incident and the surrounding issues of intellectual oppression. To support his argument Seidensticker relies on the idea of the "ex-post-facto" circumstances of the writing of *Hanabi* eight years after the event, and maintains that the Kōtoku Incident had little effect on Kafū's work as it changed in neither subject nor tone: "The writings of 1910 and 1911, theoretically the years of the great crisis, show few signs of intensified suffering. Indeed things seem to go on much as always, the main themes being familiar enough, annoyance at Meiji and love for Edo" (p. 47). But Seidensticker, perhaps because he ignores the bulk of the Returnee Stories, has not realized that from *Reishō* onward there is indeed a change in tone and subject, to focus increasingly on Edo. *Kōcha no ato*, Seidensticker notes wryly, is full of repetitive references to the Tokugawa mortuary shrines in Shiba Park, because Kafū is "not ashamed of repeating himself" (p. 49). But this has more to do with the importance Kafū placed on the buildings as emblems of a decaying age than with simple repetition. The symbolic significance of the tombs is shown in their prominent placing in *Reishō*, exactly where the main character comes upon the realization that Japan possesses a valuable cultural heritage. Kafū's consistent publications of the years 1911–1918 demonstrate his commitment to working through these ideas in writing. *Hanabi* may be read not as a sudden reversal after a "slump," but as a moment of reflection following the completion of the twin novels *Udekurabe* (1916–1917) and *Okamezasa* (1918), hailed as masterpieces of Kafū's Edo-themed literature.

The more psychological question of whether Kafū really felt shame over betraying the intellectual establishment by keeping silent, and guilt over his inability to act as a Zola in the Kōtoku case, may be answered by the fact that this was not the first time that Kafū had thought about the Dreyfus affair and matters of intellectual suppression. The critical essay *Emiiru Zora to sono shōsetsu* (Émile Zola and his Novels) was published in September 1903, the first anniversary of Zola's death.[17] Setting out to explain Zola to the Japanese reading public, Kafū examined Zola's methods of research and his role in the Dreyfus affair of 1898. Clearly describing how *J'accuse* was written in the name of justice as a decisive stance against the French government in defence of Dreyfus (KZ 18.248), Kafū demonstrates keen awareness of Zola's political stance in writing this novel. Seidensticker and others cite the essay *Hanabi* as a late reaction to the Kōtoku Incident of 1911, and criticize Kafū for reading emotions of guilt back into the situation of 1911 where he must have felt no such guilt at the time. But *Emiiru Zora to sono shōsetsu* shows that Kafū was already thinking about the political relationship between writers and the state, in the example of Zola and Dreyfus, well before 1911 and sixteen years before the writing of *Hanabi*. Furthermore, Isoda Kōichi (1989) points out that in his introduction to the 1913 edition of *Sangoshū* (Coral Anthology), Kafū included photographic plates of Zola and discussed Zola's role in the Dreyfus case (p. 117). Kafū was thinking of the significance of the Dreyfus case and its implications for the role of a writer in an authoritarian state long before 1919.

Moreover, as Satō Shizuo observes, the passage in *Hanabi* dealing with the Kōtoku Incident was not the first time that Kafū had experienced the intellectual oppression of the Meiji government. When *Furansu monogatari* was banned in 1909, Kafū commented in a newspaper interview:

> I have already vented my resentment countless times on the actions of the authorities, so now that even my own work has been banned, it isn't a particularly rare event worth getting freshly surprised or angry about. In fact, I'm not as resentful now as I was last year when the translations of Molière and Zola were banned.[18]

Kafū had thus experienced governmental suppression of expression and publication well before the Kōtoku Incident. Nor was his reaction to the Kōtoku Incident the first time he had expressed feelings of shame at his own hesitation to fight against the authorities for intellectual freedom. Satō Shizuo (1995) states that Kafū's interview in 1909 and the later essay *Hanabi* are similar because both express shame over Kafū's hesitation and both blame Japanese society for creating a state with no artistic freedom (pp. 142–143). In the interview Kafū comments:

> My thoughts on the matter have nothing to do with it. My opponent is a strong government, while I am nothing but a

>weak poet. I recalled how hard the many poets had fought for those rights in the court trials surrounding Baudelaire's *Les Fleurs du Mal* and Flaubert's *Madame Bovary*, until the art of France came to be free and independent as it is today. The poets of Japan have not yet fought like them even once up until today, so of course it is unavoidable that artistic freedom is unseen in Japanese society. So although I think it proper to fight with all my heart in this case, when I come to consider whether I would win or not, I think of the general character of French society, and end up hesitating, with no self-respect. If it were the case that I wanted to win this fight for rights against the authorities, it would be absolutely necessary to have sympathy from the general drift of society. This broad sympathy, which loves the freedom of the ordinary Frenchman, and which respects art, is only built up by many examples—what strength it must have given to the movements of a single poet.[19]

Once again, France is held up as the shining example of intellectual freedom, but what stands out here is Kafū's construction of the power of the Meiji state vis-à-vis the intellectual. The words "opponent" (*aite*), "strong" (*tsuyoi*), "weak" (*yowai*), "fought" (*arasotta*), "fight with all my heart" (*hisshi ni natte arasou*), and "fight for rights against the authorities" (*tōkyokusha to kenri wo arasou*) can leave us in no doubt that Kafū understood the role of the marginalized writer in protest against authoritarian measures.

Jay Rubin references another 1909 interview in his argument that Kafū was a writer keenly aware of issues of intellectual oppression by the Meiji state. Rubin writes that the late Meiji period after the Russo–Japanese War was one of increasingly strict censorship as the government tightened its laws on public morality.[20] On the banning of Oguri Fūyō's *Ane no imōto* (Big Sister's Little Sister) in June 1909, Kafū lamented that "The authorities don't read our stories and novels as literature or art: They treat them strictly as "printed matter." Furthermore, he stated, "We who publish fiction and the authorities who suppress it live in different worlds."[21] In Rubin's view, Kafū purposefully took up this stance against society as a means to escape the oppressive system symbolized by the censorship laws:

>Kafū could only conclude that writers and policemen lived in two separate worlds, that art was an irrelevancy, a means of escape. He concluded this and concluded this and concluded this over and over and over again in fiction,

> poetry, essays, and interviews until he had fashioned for himself and the public a unique persona embodying his bitter rejection of all that was acceptable and thus respectable to the state. (p. 121)

Rubin has clearly demonstrated that a large part of Kafū's writing in 1909 was directed against the Meiji state, which he saw as authoritarian and oppressive. As we have seen, Kafū's oppositional stance emerged and strengthened through *Amerika* and *Furansu monogatari*, becoming more pronounced after the banning of *Kanraku* in September 1909. Through the essays of *Kōcha no ato* from 1911 to 1912, he had also signed himself "Yoshino Kōu" to remind readers of his experience with censorship and his view that art and the state were diametrically opposed. This stance was taken up more directly in a historical novel *Chiru yanagi mado no yūbae* (Willows Shedding their Leaves at an Evening Window), written from 1912 to 1913, wherein the hero is a writer experiencing the harsh Tempō reforms of 1842.[22]

There is thus a substantial amount of material to indicate that Kafū's turn towards Edo themes was part of his wider concern with matters of censorship, intellectual restriction, the search for a reconciliation of modernity and genuine culture, and a critical view of the Meiji authorities. It seems logical that most critics would therefore see Kafū's use of Edo as part of his critique against Meiji Japan. However, Shiozaki Fumio writes that Kafū's declaration that he would live out the rest of his life in the guise of an Edo *gesakusha*, a writer of frivolous or erotic fiction, has been one of the biggest stumbling blocks for academic research on Kafū's critique to date. Shiozaki (1992) sees Kafū's stance in the Taishō period as unequivocally critical, and places him on a par with Sōseki and Ōgai as a "representative critic of civilization" (*daihyōteki na bunmei hihyōka*), but he writes that critics and researchers have been slow to take up this position mainly because of Kafū's self-proclaimed *gesakusha* stance (p. 43). Even David Earhart (1994), whose work stresses the critical nature of Kafū's later wartime writing, considers the "literary alter ego" of the *gesakusha* stance to be "eccentric" and a mask of "self-indulgence" (p. 490). The difference between "yearning for the Edo past" in the Returnee Stories, and actually "returning to the Edo past" by living as a *gesaku* writer is a large one. The first part of Kafū's declaration for becoming a *gesakusha* in *Hanabi* has to do with the image or persona of the Edo writer:

> I considered that there was nothing for it but to reduce the quality of my own art to the level produced by the Edo writers of frivolous and vulgar fiction. Since that time

> I began to wear a tobacco pouch, to collect *ukiyo-e* prints and to play the samisen.

The "frivolous and vulgar" fiction here is the decadent literature of late Edo, which is rarely seen as serious. "Decadence" implies sex and eroticism, and indicates a culture at a point just past its apogee—not the height of a civilization's achievement but the proof of its downward turn. Many Japanese critics have accordingly linked Kafū's *gesakusha* stance to his own private hobbies and proclivities. Karatani Kōjin maintains that Kafū, a popular novelist, would not have thought deeply about matters of the Meiji state or about the Kōtoku Incident. Noguchi Takehiko agrees with Karatani that *Hanabi* does not represent a true confession of feelings of guilt. Noguchi's explanation of the above passage is that Kafū wanted to enjoy the lifestyle of a *gesakusha* and so wrote *Hanabi* to provide a splendid excuse.[23] An even simpler view is put forward by Matsumoto Hajime (1998), who says Kafū had always loved Edo and was merely returning to this passion, not making a political statement in writing *Hanabi* (pp. 108–109). At first glance, this seems a viable viewpoint: Kafū loved Edo and wanted to live as a *gesaku* writer. But to maintain that this was all there was to Kafū's actions and writings at the time is overly simplistic, and ignores the political tone of the rest of the essay *Hanabi*. It is unreasonable to overlook the political significance of Kafū's writing, especially when Kafū himself is pointing to that significance by placing his decision in the context of the High Treason Incident.

It is clear that the frivolous, erotic, rakish overtones of the word *gesakusha* have done much to lessen Kafū's status as a serious critic. But the more significant implications of Kafū's decision are held in the second part of his declaration:

> The frivolous writers and masters of *ukiyo-e* art at the end of the Edo period saw such things as the coming of the Black Ships to Uraga and the assassination of the Senior Minister at the Sakurada Gate as things which had nothing to do with them, the common people—instead of denying this, I made up my mind that it was awe-inspiring.

Kafū was interested not only in acquiring the physical and cultural accoutrements of the dandy—playing the samisen, wearing a tobacco pouch, and collecting *ukiyo-e* prints, although these were an important part of keeping in touch with a disappearing tradition. What inspires Kafū about the *gesakusha* is their spirit of indifference to matters of state. In taking up the position of the *gesakusha*, Kafū was declaring that matters of the nation were to have no interest for him from now on. It is the relationship of the *gesakusha* with society and the state which gives this declaration its critical stance.

Kafū's perception of the role of the *gesaku* writer in Edo society is inseparable from the idea of opposition to the state. We have seen that Kafū used Edo as a counter-space to modern Meiji, and that his defence of Edo underpinned his critique of Meiji civilization. Perhaps the most striking way in which Kafū uses Edo in opposition to Meiji, however, is in his association of Edo with the "town culture" or *chōnin bunmei* of the Tokugawa period. Kafū's "Edo" functioned as a symbol of the *shitamachi*, home of the "town culture" of the merchants and artisans that flourished in the Tokugawa period, represented most often in Kafū's essays by the *ukiyo-e* art form. Kafū saw this thriving artistic culture as something that developed in spite of suppression by an authoritarian state. Kafū saw town culture as imbued with the spirit of opposition and resistance, as the artist and the *gesaku* writer struggled with the state for freedom of expression. This function of Edo and the role of the *gesakusha* and artist may be seen in Kafū's essays of 1913–1914, collected under the title *Edo geijutsuron* in 1920. That Kafū perceived the possibilities of opposition and resistance in Edo town culture may be seen in a well-known passage from *Ukiyo-e no kanshō* (An Appreciation of *Ukiyo-e*), the first essay in the collection:

> For me, an appreciation of *ukiyo-e* does not stop at its mere value as art, as it does in the appreciation of foreigners, but truly, like a religion, it makes me feel a spiritual consolation. This unique art originated in the hands of the oppressed (*appaku seraretaru*) Edo commoners, and such a development was, moreover, a great accomplishment in their unceasing subjection to the persecution (*hakugai*) of the government. Under the patronage of the government of the day, the Kano line, that is to say the works of the eighteenth-century Japanese Academy of Art, undoubtedly failed to transmit the artistic glory of this period. That merit belongs to the despised town artist, virtually set adrift into exile and suffering in shackles. *Ukiyo-e* expresses the spirit of the commoners who would not submit to government persecution, and it plays their song of triumph. (KZ 14.5)

It is not the government-sponsored art of the Tokugawa period that moves Kafū to religious feeling, but the spirit of *hankō*: resistance to authority and oppression, where artists risked their careers for the sake of their work. Kafū's view of the *gesakusha* and the "town artists" as commoners who worked without patronage, in exile, and suffering the threat of persecution by a feudal government, portrays the relationship between the *gesakusha* and the state as fundamentally oppositional in nature.

This association of *gesaku* writing with an "oppositional" spirit of Edo town culture fits in well with the intellectual context of late Meiji. Carol Gluck (1998) argues that "Edo" (signifying the Edo period rather than the city) could mean different things in the Meiji period depending on the use to which it was put by those invoking it, as "the agents of Edo-memory returned, almost obsessively, to that past to find in it whatever they were missing in the present or hoping for the future" (p. 263). To official Meiji bureaucrats and conservatives, Edo at first represented a feudal, backward era that should be modernized through *bunmei-kaika*. Later, a "national" Edo was constructed as a linear continuity of national tradition, shoring up the polity and emperor system (pp. 265–269). For political progressives, Edo came to symbolize freedom and protest: "From peasant uprisings to the "ecological opposition" of Andō Shōeki, Edo-memories constituted a heritage of protest that animated the struggle to contest the power of the modern state" (p. 264). Those on the political left used the idea of an "oppositional Edo" to protest against what remained of feudal oppression in modern society. Complementing the growing number of cosmopolitan, disaffected intellectuals from the 1910s to the 1930s, another kind of oppositional Edo-as-tradition arose as "a cultural space, timeless and unchanging, where the spirit abraded by the masses, machines and modish modernism could 'return' to be refreshed and re-Japanned." Gluck includes Kafū as a writer who used Edo as a refuge.[24] However, I would argue that in this model of Edo constructions, Kafū belongs not only to the group of disaffected writers using Edo as a timeless space inspiring a return to tradition, but also to the counter-discursive group of thinkers who believed that Edo held the key to a tradition of protest and critique.

Gluck writes that Tokugawa commoner society and culture became elevated in the Meiji period by those who "saw modernity itself as the iron box and sought an escape hatch in an Edo where commoners enjoyed a freedom that had now been lost. . . . Despite—or more likely, because—everyone knew that the small samurai elite ruled during Tokugawa, one of the strongest images of Edo depicted commoner vitality" (p. 277). In celebrating and seeking to preserve in literature the Tokugawa flourishing of town culture, manifest in *ukiyo-e* prints and geisha society, Kafū may be seen as part of the Meiji intellectual discourse of opposition which used Edo as an emblem of freedom in the margins of society and as a symbol of the possibilities of counter-discourse in those margins. Masao Miyoshi (1991), in his re-reading of the Japanese literary tradition, states even more clearly that we can view the position of *gesaku* literature in the Tokugawa period as one of resistance, counter-discourse and critique:

> If the earlier Edo prose (such as Ihara Saikaku's) celebrated the Tokugawa order that had finally arrived after a centuries-long chaos of civil wars, the *gesaku* seems to sense the coming end to the order, and it exhibits growing irritations at its realization of the conflict between feudal restriction and bourgeois liberality. *Gesaku*, often taken to be a literature of decadence, is at the same time an expression of resistance and criticism, however modest its scale and impact. (p. 19)

Miyoshi sees the *gesaku* writing as a typical product of *chōnin* culture and an integral part of what was oppositional to the Tokugawa shogunate, regardless of its actual impact upon the state. Miyoshi describes *gesaku* as the prose literary form of the "Edo ur-capitalist feudalism" or the proto-capitalism of *chōnin* culture, the emergence of which, with its signs of a monetary economy and an emerging bourgeoisie, has been characterized by some historians as a "commercial revolution" in the face of the centralized feudal Tokugawa shogunate (p. 18). Historians have long argued that the rising *chōnin* culture of the Edo period may indeed be seen as "resistance" or challenge to the Tokugawa center.[25] Miyoshi draws on this argument to state that *gesaku* fiction and *chōnin* culture are both oppositional in nature, because they represent the rising economy that was a challenge to the status quo. Kafū's appropriation of the *gesaku* tradition thus implies opposition since Edo town culture opposed the order of the Tokugawa shogunate in its flourishing economy, arts and values. Other historians take a more moderate view in stating that *chōnin* culture represented not a political, but a social or cultural challenge to the Tokugawa center. W.G. Beasley (1990) describes the new town merchant culture as something opposed in its noise, color, and gaiety to samurai values of frugality, not to mention disdain for money. This was not a political opposition, as the gaiety of town life and its entertainment "constituted an escape from political thought, not a stimulus to it" (p. 19). But Beasley concedes: "This was hardly the material for a political revolution, but it provided the subject-matter for an art and literature that had the makings of a social one" (p. 20). Katō Shūichi (1979) also sees Edo town culture as escapist, and fundamentally disinterested in matters of state: "*Chōnin* culture took a down-to-earth interest in matters of immediate daily life unrelated to the wider issue of the state of the nation, and also attempted to escape from mundane reality" (p. 48).

The two main views of historians and critics, then, are that *chōnin* culture was escapist, apolitical, and not interested in the state; and that elements of *chōnin* culture may in fact be seen as opposed to the state. Kafū's position is confusing because he took up both of these elements in *Hanabi*. Isoda Kōichi (1989) comments that although we can see Kafū's criticism of the nation (*kokka hihan*) in *Hanabi* we can also see a retreat from the present reality (p. 202). Kafū's *gesakusha* stance thus combines the "awe-inspiring" life of the *gesakusha*, lived in total indifference to matters of state, with an implied opposition to that state. This stance is not only evident in the famous passage on the Kōtoku Incident that I have discussed here, but runs throughout the entire essay. As Rubin (1984) noted, *Hanabi* "is in fact a unified essay with a clearly stated theme": the fact that Kafū has become withdrawn from society and has little to do with festivals, celebrations or national events (p. 192–193). An analysis of the essay as a whole shows that Kafū's separation from society, referred to variously as "escape" or "withdrawal," may be seen rather as an extension of his critical stance against Meiji Japan.

The Kōtoku Incident is only one of many events listed in *Hanabi* from the late Meiji and early Taishō periods, including the end of World War I, the events of the Russo–Japanese War, the annexation of Korea and the rice riots in Tokyo. The string of events is held together by Kafū's sense of isolation from the Japanese state and society, visible from the opening paragraph:

> When I went to get my chopsticks for dinner there was the sound of fireworks popping somewhere. It was a cloudy day some time after the rainy season had ended. A cool breeze was ceaselessly moving the rattan blinds on the window. When I looked out, the national flag was out on the eaves of all the houses along the back of the narrow lane. The only one without a flag was the lattice door on my house. For the first time I remembered that today was the occasion of the celebration of Armistice Day in Tokyo. (KZ 15.7)

The key to the essay lies in Kafū's realization that the country has gone on without him—the celebration of a national holiday is forgotten until he hears the fireworks. The fact that Kafū's is the only house without a flag emphasizes that he is no longer a part of the Meiji state. The street outside his house is quiet as everyone else is in Hibiya or Ueno for the occasion. Kafū feels completely cut off from the world, to the extent that he declares: "Between the world and myself there was now not even one direct connection" (KZ 15.8). Satō Shizuo observes that in *Hanabi* and the *Danchōtei nichijō*, the diaries that Kafū kept from 1917 until his death, Kafū portrays himself as a hermit (*itsumin*), separated from the "society of the nation" (*kokka shakai*).[26] By the time *Hanabi* was written, Kafū had moved out of his Ōkubo house, divorced his second wife, seen his father die, stopped teaching at Keiō University and resigned as the editor of *Mita bungaku*. Kafū was living in actuality the life of a hermit portrayed in this essay.

Kafū's portrayal of himself as existing outside society has been called the "outsider consciousness" (*autosaidaa ishiki*) by Japanese critics, Satō Haruo going so far as to call his life a "hell of isolation" (*kodoku jigoku*).[27] On one level, as Rubin (1984) observes, many Meiji writers found themselves marginalized by the state, because: "The function of the individualistic writer . . . lay entirely outside the established system of values" in the moral *kokutai* laid down by the Meiji state (p. 6). Janet Walker (1979) argues that literature in the utilitarian Meiji period was seen as useless, with little commercial or moral value (pp. 26–28), while Irena Powell (1983) calls Kafū and the Meiji writers "exiles from society" (p. 30). It may also be argued that Kafū's "outsider consciousness" came partly from the dislocation felt on his return to a country that had little need of more critics. As Roger Goodman has shown, Japan has a long history of treating its returnees from abroad with varying degrees of ambivalence, admiration, or contempt depending on the political, social, or economic conditions prevailing within Japan at the time. The Meiji period swung from granting returnees a place in the government almost automatically in the early years to viewing returnee intellectuals as somewhat problematic individuals, no doubt due the extensive questioning they put to Japanese society in their works, often on the basis of their observations overseas.[28] Kafū's isolation came also from artistic differences, since his writing, along the lines of French naturalism and the Decadent School, was very different to the "Japanese naturalism" (*shizenshugi*) of 1906–1910. Kafū found himself popular among the hedonistic, aestheticist, and "anti-naturalist" writers at a time when the *bundan* was dominated by naturalism, and was thus positioned outside the central literary discourse. Moreover, where the *shizenshugi* writers lived in poverty or subsisted on newspaper salaries, Kafū lived in leisured circumstances. Nakamura Mitsuo (1978) writes that Kafū's alienation from the dominant literary group contributed greatly to his isolation in later life (pp. 291, 317–318). To a large extent, then, Kafū's "outsider consciousness" may be attributable to external marginalization.

However, in personal terms, it was Kafū who resigned from *Mita bungaku* and his position at Keiō and avoided his literary acquaintances after 1916. I agree with Asada Akira that the "outsider consciousness" was for the most part created and cultivated by Kafū himself. Asada argues that Kafū was very aware that once he had created the *gesakusha* position, he was then trapped into doing everything in the role of the persona he had constructed.[29] Isoda Kōichi also argues that Kafū's "outsider consciousness" was a deliberate, defiant construction.[30] Noguchi Takehiko, who argues against Kafū's status as a "serious critic," concedes that the fact Kafū had such a completely dispassionate stance toward his surroundings may be seen as critical (*hihyōteki*) in itself. Noguchi cites the *Danchōtei nichijō,* staunchly uninvolved in Japanese society, with not even one line about the outbreak of World War I, as an example of Kafū's stubborn critical attitude.[31] This alienation from society was thus also constructed by Kafū himself.

Even though Kafū had withdrawn from society, however, he was by no means completely dispassionate or indifferent to his surroundings. It is most significant that Kafū did not give up his critical stance against state authority and act "indifferent" to matters of state like the *gesakusha* he claimed to respect for that very indifference. In *Hanabi* and the *Danchōtei nichijō,* Kafū used his writing to broadcast his hermit-like existence to Japanese society, and to reiterate his reasons for refusing to participate in that society. Kafū may well have respected the Edo writer's indifference to matters of state, but he could not help commenting on these matters, including the Kōtoku Incident. Kafū's writing was not only not indifferent, but also actively critical of the state. Satō Shizuo (1995) argues that *Hanabi* was written in direct criticism of such national festivals as the celebration of Armistice Day, and that Kafū was writing against the authority of the nation-state (*kokka kenryoku*). Satō maintains that Kafū's hatred, opposition, scorn, and criticism of a state authority that put itself against the common people of the "*minshū*" or "*kokumin*" were entirely bound up in his stance as "hermit," and that we must think of Kafū's concealment as his determination to live as a critic of state society (pp. 138–141).

Through a close reading of the famous passage in *Hanabi* describing Kafū's "return to Edo" (*Edo kaiki*), and a consideration of the essay as a whole, we may conclude that *Hanabi* demonstrates a clear stance of critique and opposition against the Meiji state. Contrary to the "ex-post-facto" argument that Kafū used the Kōtoku Incident as a convenient excuse and did not think seriously about the role of the writer in upholding intellectual freedom, we have seen that Kafū's awareness of the role of the intellectual, as well as feelings of shame over hesitating to fight openly against the authorities as Zola had in the Dreyfus case, are evident in his writings from as early as 1903, continuing through the travel collections to his essays and interviews of 1909. Similarly, Kafū's idea of the *gesakusha* as representative of an Edo spirit of resistance may be seen in his writing of 1913–1914 in *Edo geijutsuron*. The guilt feelings and declaration of the *gesakusha* stance in *Hanabi* should therefore be seen as the expression of ideas that had been developing over a substantial period of time, rather than a sudden reversal or excuse. Reading the *gesakusha* stance in *Hanabi* as a decisive identification with critique and opposition does much to clarify the ambiguities that have been associated with the critical nature of the essay. Such a reading also leads to the conclusion that Kafū's "return to Edo" may be read as a continuation of his critique of Meiji.

A large part of Kafū's critique of modernity in the years after 1909 thus involved the concept of a return to the Japanese past in Edo themes. This concept of a return to the "true" or essential Japan, situated mainly in the idealized Japanese past, characterizes the work of many Meiji and Taishō intellectuals, including Tanizaki Jun'ichirō. Kafū's discussion on the nature of Oriental sorrow and music in *Reishō*'s "Theory of the Orient" is very similar in theme and content to Tanizaki's famous essay *In'ei raisan* (In Praise of Shadows, 1933–1934).[32] The similarity is not surprising, considering Kafū was Tanizaki's patron and model. Tanizaki's essay on the characteristic qualities of traditional Japan is considered a masterpiece for its definitions of what it means to be Japanese, and its success is itself a measure of the success of Kafū's work and his arguments toward preserving the culture of Edo.[33] An interesting point about the respective "returns to Japan" made by Kafū and Tanizaki is that although Tanizaki found it necessary to move to the Kansai area to write about the "real Japan," Kafū stayed in Tokyo, concentrating on finding a way to reconcile the modern capital with the essence of Japanese identity and culture from the past. This is part of what distinguishes Kafū—he discovered a way to be authentic while still holding onto his passion for the city of Tokyo, the modern incarnation of his beloved Edo.

This idea of a "return to the past," which Kafū shares with Tanizaki may be seen as part of a wide-ranging discourse from the turn of the century right through to the 1930s, based on the idea of a return to pure Japanese traditions after the Westernization of the Meiji period. Most critics refer to this discourse as *Nihon e no kaiki*, or "return to Japan." This discourse affected a wide range of intellectuals writing on quite disparate subjects, but all shared the search for those essential features that made Japan "Japanese." Kafū's role in shaping this discourse has been undervalued to date, even though his use of the Edo thematic in *Shinkyō yawa* and *Edo geijutsuron* arguably influenced two of the most famous works on Japan's cultural identity, Tanizaki's *In'ei raisan* and Kuki Shūzō's 1930 treatise on Edo aesthetics, *Iki no kōzō* (The Structure of Edo Aesthetic Style).[34] *Iki no kōzō* is regarded variously as an admirable reflection of Japanese cultural identity and a "pernicious example of *Nihonjinron,* that ubiquitous discourse on Japanese uniqueness" (Pincus, 1996, p. 3). *Iki no kōzō* shares the conviction of Kafū's *Edo geijutsuron* that Japan's true cultural identity may be found in an idealized "Edo." Leslie Pincus notes that Kuki "borrowed" many examples of Edo architecture and design directly from *Edo geijutsuron,* and included excerpts from it in *Iki no kōzō* (pp. 53, 113). Although the extent of literary influence is notoriously difficult to measure, it may be argued that in his impact on Tanizaki and Kuki Shūzō, Kafū played a significant part in shaping the discourse on Edo and the return to the Japanese past that characterized intellectual discourse through the Taishō and early Shōwa eras.

Kafū's turn to Edo themes also represents his search for an authentic way of reconciling Japanese traditional culture with "modernity" without losing the essence of the Japanese Self. In this search, Kafū was writing on matters that preoccupied many Japanese intellectuals of the early twentieth century—issues of national expression, cultural heritage, and how Japan could best reconcile its civilization with modernity without sacrificing its identity. Kafū's concern with these issues may thus be seen as an integral part of a wider discourse on national identity from late Meiji through the interwar years. Dale (1986), Gluck (1985) and Tanaka (1993) have demonstrated that Japan's search for a clearer definition of what it meant to be Japanese through the Meiji period involved issues of national "uniqueness," ideas of the *kokutai* or "national essence," and the definition of Japan's place in the world in relation to both the West and Asia. In his work on the intellectual trends of the interwar years, J. Thomas Rimer (1990) states:

> The perceived need among Japanese thinkers to determine what elements or qualities might be defined as truly Japanese in the context of the development of their general concept of culture, itself inspired by underlying categories familiar to Western thought but new to them, remained a matter of central concern. (pp. x–xi)

The intellectual milieu between the wars was thus one of seeking to define characteristics of culture, particularly Japanese culture, in contrast both to the Westernization of the modern period, and to the concept of "modernity" itself. And through the late 1920s and 1930s, Japan experienced a strong surge of nativism as an influential intellectual force.[35] As Ken Ito (1991) observes, "the whole phenomenon of *Nihon e no kaiki* is an enormously complicated one," and it is "a concept of questionable utility that obscures as much as it reveals" (pp. 102, 101). Not enough has been written on the links between fiction writers and the larger trend toward nativism in the approach to the 1930s, and it is risky to attempt to make generalizations in such a complex area of investigation. But the fact remains that Japanese writing in the first half of the twentieth century seems to have been dominated by a search for national identity, and Kafū should be understood as part of this wider discursive trend.

Hisaaki Yamanouchi (1978), examining the search for authenticity by writers in Meiji Japan, argues that the tension between the impact of the West and the native tradition "came to constitute one of the central themes of modern Japanese literature" (pp. 3–4). Yamanouchi expresses this dilemma of modernity in the question:

> How could Western culture and their native tradition be harmoniously reconciled to one another when often it persuaded them to hate whatever of their own culture and themselves they had been reared to respect? They felt compelled to imitate and thus be authentic, a contradiction that obviously gnawed at their consciousness. (p. 4)

Of Kafū's generation, Yamanouchi discusses Natsume Sōseki, Mori Ōgai, Shimazaki Tōson, and Shiga Naoya. Kafū, however, was also struggling with these very problems. The dilemma of "how to be authentic" constituted the main theme of all the Returnee Stories, on a grand scale: How can Japan be authentic? How can we make Tokyo an authentic city? When is Meiji going to develop a genuine character of its own? Kafū's focus on the idea of "the genuine" in his argument against Meiji Japan's superficial, imitative modernization has much in common with the ideas of Natsume Sōseki, who argued that Enlightenment in the West came from within, in a process of "self-awakening," while Japan's enlightenment (*kaika*) was produced under pressure from external forces. Sōseki used the terms *naihatsu-teki* and *gaihatsu-teki* to mean "inner-directed" and "outer-directed."[36] The influence of the West and Westernization on Japan's modernization process meant that Japanese modernity was being "outer-directed," and thus derivative and imitative in nature. Sōseki's solution was to attempt to be more honest in attaining a deeper understanding of the West and of "civilization" and "modernity," in order to become more "authentic." But Sōseki's conclusion was ultimately negative: he found this authenticity to be impossible for Meiji Japan in general, and concluded that only the individual self could try to be authentic by standing apart from the Meiji state. In contrast, Kafū's solution was positive, in turning to Edo to find and define what was genuine in Japanese civilization. Even though he lived as a hermit in his Dyspepsia House, Kafū would continue to encourage the Japanese to find their own "*Nihon to iu Originalité*." Kafū arrived at this solution through use of the West and the modern Meiji state as defining contrasts. Despite their differences, Sōseki and Kafū were seeking answers to the same fundamental questions, wrestling with the same issues of Westernization and modernity. Kafū searched in earnest to find his own "authentic" answer to the Meiji predicament. Kafū's adherence to Edo helped him to reconcile the history and culture of Western civilization with his native Japanese tradition without succumbing to Meiji modernity. By basing his arguments on the criteria of culture and the genuine, Kafū perhaps came closest to solving the modern dilemma.[37]

The difference between Sōseki and Kafū on this point may be seen in the direction taken by their novels. Sōseki's novels of later years illustrate the *gaihatsu-teki* nature of Meiji modernization and the impossibility of attaining true *naihatsu-teki* improvement, either on a social or individual scale. Sōseki's protagonists are tortured by their alienation and failure to engage with wider society, fated to die without ever finding the answers they so desperately seek. Kafū's fiction of the Taishō period, by contrast, may be seen as a working out of his *Tōyō shisō* in practice, promising a positive solution for his readers in reconciling "authentic" Japan with the modern age. Kafū has been criticized for moving with the times, as the geisha of his Meiji-period writing are replaced by café waitresses in Taishō and dancing girls in Shōwa. Read in the light of the argument put forward here, however, this adaptability speaks for Kafū's optimistic approach to his subject. The "guardians of civilization" would always be present, in the decadent margins of the counter-discursive space. Kafū's Edo-themed fiction was extremely popular and won him an even broader audience than his earlier travel collections. A brief discussion of the major fiction here should illustrate how Kafū was able to dramatize the *Tōyō shisō* in literary form. These novels complemented the essays of *Edo geijutsuron* and the observations of *Hiyori-geta,* to demonstrate how "Edo" still lived in the modern city of Tokyo.

The first major work, *Udekurabe* (Rivalry), began serialization in *Bunmei* from August 1916, just months after Kafū resigned from Keiō and *Mita bungaku*. As such, it best represents what Kafū wanted to accomplish with fiction at the time. The novel is set in Shimbashi, illustrating the beauty of the pleasure quarter as well as the precarious position of the women who live there. Stephen Snyder notes that Shimbashi was the "preferred entertainment district of the new political elite" and the site of much "patriotic support for the militarists" in the Sino–Japanese and Russo–Japanese Wars.[38] By choosing Shimbashi as his setting, a site that celebrates modern nationalism and also preserves the past in the atmosphere of the *machiai,* Kafū strengthens his argument for the geisha as "guardians of civilization" in modern Japan. The plot revolves around Komayo, a young geisha who has recently returned to the quarter after seven years in Akita, where she had gone to marry her patron. Now a widow, Komayo struggles to balance new patrons, love and financial considerations, and her world is plunged in turmoil when rivals Rikiji and Kikuchiyo finally take their revenge on her. Omniscient narration is interspersed with the thoughts of individual characters, and the reader, privy to everyone's motives, is torn between feeling sympathy for the geisha and marveling at their manipulative skills. The highly contrived nature of chance meetings and overheard conversations resembles an Edo *sharebon* novel, and the specialized jargon of the pleasure quarters combines with Kafū's customary ornate sentence structure to create multilayered impressions and images in the reader's mind. If Kafū set out to make Edo live on the page, then in *Udekurabe* he certainly succeeded, and many critics see it as his most masterful novel.

The idea of "Edo," and the "genuine" in Japanese culture, is brought to life in the novel in a number of ways. Seidensticker (1965) traces the linguistic style "back to such Meiji writers as Higuchi Ichiyō, Izumi Kyōka, and Kōda Rohan, and through them to the fiction of the Edo period" (pp. 89–90). This is joined by almost obsessive attention to detail in the clothing, ornaments, makeup, and hairstyles of the geisha and actors, all of which held special meaning to the wearer. The colors and textures of the fabric, the composition of a tobacco pouch, the placement of a pearl pin or a sword-shaped clasp, all function as shorthand for memories, social status and how the character is regarded by others.[39] This is the world of the *tsū,* the connoisseur, and it is this world to which Kuki Shūzō would refer in *Iki no kōzō* years later. Kafū also recreates Shimbashi through attention to architecture, gardens, and cobblestone streets, but the great triumph of *Udekurabe* is the evocation of mood. The old manager of Komayo's *machiai* is so enraptured by the scene around him one evening that he completely forgets to tend to his plants on the rooftop:

> . . . the elderly Gozan, watering can in hand, made his way up to tend the morning glories that grew on the platform beneath the drying rack. He stepped out onto the roof at just the moment when shamisen practice in the neighboring houses fell silent, giving way to the hour of the bath, when cotton robes hung out to dry flapped in the evening breeze carrying the smell of coal fires and telephones began to ring impatiently. Evening in the pleasure quarters. There on the platform, he stood admiring the beauty of the scalloped clouds that covered the sky. Forgetting to count the buds on his plants, he watched the crows as they flew home toward the woods that surrounded the Hama Palace. (p. 55)

"Edo" is also personified by Komayo, adept at dance and Sonohachi singing, and passionate like the heroine of a *jōruri* ballad. Refined and modest, she is careful in her dress and observes all custom and etiquette, functioning as the ideal Japanese woman. By contrast, her rival Kikuchiyo has no care for custom, manners, or taste. Immodest and slatternly, she engages in sexual acts that other geisha will not. The patron Yoshioka likens her to "occidental whores" in her brazen attitude and white skin (pp. 84–85). Kikuchiyo is all that Komayo is not, highlighting the "Japaneseness" of Komayo by contrast.

Kafū's critique of Taishō society is clear in the ambitious, scheming nature of the characters, who are all, "in their own ways, fakers, actors, or prostitutes" (Snyder, 2000, p. 101). While Kikuchiyo reminds one of Kokaji in *Meika*, the strongest criticism is directed against the male characters, whose treatment of women illustrates the gendered oppression inherent in Japanese society. Yoshioka is cruel and controlling, and both he and the client known as "the sea monster" enjoy sex with Komayo precisely because she finds it distasteful. While Yoshioka seems oblivious to the pain he causes Komayo, the other client forces himself on her purposefully to see her cringe. Together with the portrait of Tsutayo in *Satsuki-yami*, *Udekurabe* gives a sympathetic view of geisha's lives as well as critiquing the system that perpetuated female degradation—or as Snyder puts it, the "gender inequality and victimization of women in Taisho Japan" (Nagai, 2007, p. xii). In Komayo, Kafū created a truly realistic woman, a "three-dimensional" human being who could act as a desiring subject as well as an object for the desires of others.[40] The realistic portrayal of Komayo does much to forward Kafū's critique of Taishō society, effected organically through the story rather than through narrative intrusion. The reader comes away with a feeling of having learned something of the geisha's life without having been lectured, showing a more mature and balanced approach than that of earlier works.

Kafū reminds us of his own aims in the character of Kurayama Nansō, observer and chronicler of the Shimbashi quarter: "As one of his duties as a writer, he felt compelled to listen to the stories told by those who had lived in bygone days, no matter who they were, and to write them down for future generations" (p. 27). By this time, Kafū did not need to issue a preface as he did for *Sumidagawa,* nor a justification like *Reishō ni tsukite.* His intentions are clear in the aims of the fictional novelist, and the fact that they share initials is surely no coincidence.[41] Kurayama's garden and the villa next door are associated totally with geisha, poetry, samisen music, and song, making it one of the physical remnants of Edo that Kafū sought to preserve in novels and essays of the period.

The next major work, *Okamezasa* (Dwarf Bamboo, 1918), is often seen as a companion volume to *Udekurabe,* set in the seedier pleasure districts of the Yamanote.[42] The central character Uzaki Kyoseki is a passive hero, an unsuccessful painter whose mentor, the famous artist Kaiseki, has been passing off Kyoseki's work as his own. Kyoseki is a likeable character, who nonetheless seizes the opportunity to blackmail an important personage in order to set up his own business. Unlike the aestheticized view of geisha life in *Udekurabe,* the geisha in *Okamezasa* are clearly little more than prostitutes, with skin problems, dirty bedding and venereal disease. In fact, the book ends with the death of a respectable married woman after contracting such a disease from her husband. Kafū manages to treat the subject with humor and irony rather than heavy-handed criticism, but the novels both reveal social hypocrisy: *Udekurabe* shows relations between men and women to be dependent on money and status, while *Okamezasa* critiques the art world, where paintings are just commodities manufactured and sold for profit, with the price depending on the reputation of the artist rather than any intrinsic aesthetic value. The two books are effective in their critique of a superficial world, but the resulting picture of human life is quite dark. Most critics see *Okamezasa* as a return to French naturalism in both its language and approach to the subject of human weakness. The profligate ways of the artist Kaiseki are inherited by his son Kan, recalling Zola's focus on heredity and environment, but unlike Zola, Kafū does not judge his characters, merely depicting their personalities from all angles. In this his character sketches are more like Balzac's, and we are reminded that Kafū's understanding of "French naturalism" was much wider than most Japanese writers of the time.

Okamezasa is often disparaged by critics for its incompleteness, with events that appear to lead nowhere and narrative structure that at times seems back-to-front. Snyder (2000) argues that these flaws were intentional, as Kafū was drawing attention to the fictive "lie" created by an author for his audience. In *Udekurabe*, plot devices and stock characters played out according to reader expectation, but *Okamezasa* constantly defies expectation to problematize the reading process (pp. 98–102). Although this self-reflexivity may certainly be seen in some of the stories from *Amerika monogatari*, from this point onward it would take center stage in Kafū's fiction.[43] *Ameshōshō* (Quiet Rain, 1921), brings the writing process further into focus. Kimpū, a hermit-like *gesakusha* who has given up on writing fiction, spends his days among his pens, ink, and books, revising old manuscripts to satisfy his publishers. *Ameshōshō* itself is a layering of different kinds of texts—diary excerpts, letters between Kimpū and his friend, poems from China, Japan and France, a book by Henri du Régnier—all separated by time as part of different recollections and reminiscences. The one link between the texts is Kimpū himself, joining his memories and jottings in his head and then writing them down to while away the hours of solitude. *Ameshōshō* was produced at the same time as *Okamezasa*, when the writerly side of fiction was clearly in Kafū's mind. The difficulty of classifying the genre of the work—Seidensticker (1965) calls it "something halfway between essay and novel" (p. 101)—may also be seen as related to Kafū's self-reflexive performance.

Ameshōshō laments the disappearance of traditional culture: Frequent quotations from Chinese and Japanese poetry point to the sources of Japan's cultural heritage, while Kimpū and his friend Yō-san discuss samisen music as an "antique" and despair that the Sonohachi form may die out, as a quiet, sad style with few followers (Nagai, 1972, pp. 91–92). Yō-san attempts to set up a Sonohachi school to be run by the geisha O-han, but she turns out to be fickle and uninterested in the old cultural forms. Melancholy at the changing times is balanced by humorous touches, as when Yō-san throws O-han out of his house—not because she was having an affair, but because the object of her affection was a *benshi*, or narrator for the movie houses. Seidensticker (1965) reads the overall tone of the work as "resignation" (p. 102), but the playfulness of the text suggests that Kafū was enjoying the creative process. The pose of hermit/*gesakusha* here may also be read as reinforcing Kafū's dedication to the spirit of *hankō*. In the constant rains of autumn and the narrator's preoccupation with his garden, we see that the beauty of nature and the elements will always have the power to bring forth emotion. To a large extent, Kafū seems to be saying, we can create our own worlds to inhabit. Isoda Kōichi and others link Kafū's individualism to his "outsider consciousness" in a somewhat negative light, but this pose also can be taken as a strong statement of creative subjectivity.

The next major work did not appear until 1931, but *Tsuyu no atosaki* (During the Rains) is equally as powerful as *Udekurabe* in its strong depiction of women and naturalistic observation of Ginza café culture. Far from being stuck in the past, Kafū moves with the times to present the richly detailed world of the Ginza in all its spectacle and performance. Kafū's interest in the dispossessed, the women who work on the margins of society, crystallizes in the figure of Kimie, a café waitress who somehow keeps herself afloat in a dangerous life of violent patrons and scandalous liaisons. The 1930s café provided alcohol, snacks and unlicensed prostitution in an alternative to the more traditional pleasure district. One would expect that the contrast between café waitress and geisha would be clear in the novel, but the boundary is presented as shifting and malleable, to the extent that one character says: "These days, what with geishas becoming waitresses and waitresses turning into geishas, there's no difference anymore" (p. 72).[44] Kimie is amoral, shiftless and slovenly, but her geisha friend Kyoko is no better. Both girls are remarkably complaisant about their customers, going with any patron and engaging in a threesome with an old man—an event overheard in the house next door, leading to gossip and ugly rumours. Elements of traditional culture are used for contrast, as when a geisha's appearance in a back-alley lends elegance to the otherwise tawdry meeting of Kimie and her lover Yata (p. 33). Kimie likens a Japanese-style garden to a "stage set," while Yata underscores the contrast between past and present by saying "It's different from the café, isn't it. A touch of old Edo, one might say" (p. 34). This "touch of Edo" seems relegated to the *shitamachi*, however, and Kimie and Kyoko seem equally rooted in the modern world, disassociated from their own cultural heritage.

Remnants of Edo do exist in the family gardens of Kiyooka Susumu, a popular writer who looks "just like one of the movie stars that one sees in publicity photos" (p. 23). Kiyooka attained his fame by taking one of Bakin's stories about a kite and updating it into an airplane adventure, subsequently serialized in the newspaper, dramatized in the theater, and even made into a film (pp. 23–24). This bastardization of Edo literature is especially poignant since the Kiyooka lineage is both distinguished and learned, exemplifying Edo values and occupations. The grandfather Genzai, "a scholar of medicinal herbs who had been employed in the herb gardens of the Tokugawa shogunate," had refused to work for the new Meiji government and "held true to his principles," retiring to his country retreat (p. 62). Chapter 5 opens with a long, lyrical description of the residence, set among the tea fields and farmhouses of Setagaya. In a cinematic sequence we follow a young woman opening the gate, stepping through the blossoming garden, and opening the lattice door of the house. This is Tsuruko, Kiyooka's common-law wife of five years, who has regularly come to visit her father-in-law in a glowing example of filial piety. Sophisticated, beautifully dressed, observant of social duty and custom, Tsuruko provides the vision of the ideal Japanese woman so lacking in Kimie and Kyoko.[45] Tsuruko has been schooled in French language and etiquette, as well as Japanese classical literature and calligraphy (p. 67), making her the perfect product of two genuine cultures. The figure of Tsuruko seems at first to represent Kafū's message to his reading public—now the world has moved on, geisha are no longer the sole repository of Japanese culture, and it is up to educated women like Tsuruko to learn the best of both Japanese and Western culture and make it their own. However, this ideal vision is revealed as impossible in 1930s Japan, as Tsuruko leaves for France with no firm indication that she will return. In the real world, the future lies with Kimie, whose development through the book shows that the real hope for Japan will be found in strength of character and resilience, in the face of oppression and violence.

The plight of the café waitresses in Taishō society is shown through the cutthroat world they inhabit as well as their lack of power as "fallen" women. Cafés are revealed to be just as hierarchical as the Shimbashi *machiai*, with Ginza locations far more prestigious than Ueno Pond, and cafés on the main street better than those in back alleys. Unlike geisha, who are born into the profession or brought up in it from an early age, the waitresses have taken many varied routes to their present occupation. Among the girls at the Don Juan, where Kimie works, are an ex-dancer, an ex-hairdresser's assistant, and the ex-wife of a dentist now fallen on hard times (p. 22). Kafū explicitly links the figure of the waitress to her pitiable situation, as the spectacle of the changing city "provoked in the observer an astonishment, along with a certain sense of pathos. . . . this pathos was felt especially keenly when one thought of the circumstances of the waitresses who had to make their living in this district" (pp. 92–93). Kimie becomes a symbol of the new floating world, marginalized by society yet determined not to give in to masculine power. Kimie's relationship with her patron Kiyooka reads like a detective story in her suspicions that he is behind the many ominous happenings to her of late. It is gradually revealed that the slashing of Kimie's sleeves on the street, the stealing of her hair ornament and the leaving of a dead kitten in her closet were indeed all Kiyooka's doing, as well as a scandalous story that appeared in the newspapers. Ironically, Kimie also suspects that Kiyooka is behind the most violent incident in the book, where she is thrown from a moving taxicab by a disgruntled former lover. Although Kimie's lifestyle and occupation are what leave her open to this kind of attack, she blames Kiyooka. Her emotions at this point are powerfully evoked:

> Along with a sense of fear like a sudden cold gust against the nape of her neck, Kimie felt defiance surge up in her. Kiyooka might be Kiyooka, but Kimie was Kimie. She was not about to knuckle under to him. (p. 122)

This surge of defiance and show of confidence make Kimie one of Kafū's strongest characters, and speaks to the freedom and independent will that he saw in both the Edo-period plebeian culture and the life of the French demimonde. Taken together, *Udekurabe* and *Tsuyu no atosaki* provide a strong indictment of male-centered Taishō society, and may be read in terms of feminist critique.[46]

Kafū's critique is more politicized in the next novel, *Hikage no hana* (Flowers in the Shade, 1934), where the café waitresses are harassed by the police and frequently arrested. The power of the state is clear, its presence frequently announced through the shouts of newspaper boys on the streets. The main character O-chiyo is an aging unlicensed prostitute who, rejected by the top cafés, is taken on by an establishment that forces her to cruise the streets for customers. Newspapers are central to the plot, as O-chiyo finds her daughter Tamiko, long ago given up for adoption, through the published lists of police arrests. Kafū deftly shows the narrow scope of O-chiyo's world when, scouring the papers every day for news of her daughter, she is disappointed that they "had only war reports from Chin-Chou and Tienstin" (p. 204).[47] Later in the novel her lover Jukichi finds military songs and newsboy shouts to be merely annoying, although the news in question is of the important Shanghai Incident (p. 211). Distant wars are either ignored or seen as an intrusion into everyday life, emphasizing the marginal position of people without connections to "society" (*shakai*) or "country" (*kokka*).

Kafū has often been lauded for his "anti-war stance" and opposition to militarist policy, but his subtle portrayal of the oppressive state here is probably as far as a writer could go without censorship in 1934.[48] *Hikage no hana* illustrates Kafū's "indifference" to matters of state by focusing on more human themes through economic and natural disasters. The Great Kantō Earthquake of 1923 and the Depression affect everyone in the novel, as "In the spring of the second year of Showa, nearly every bank in Tokyo closed its doors" (p. 163). As Jukichi asks after the safety of O-chiyo's parents after the Earthquake and O-chiyo laments the disappearance of the Mitsukoshi department store, Kafū captures the personal impact of the events, and the novel emphasizes the human connections amongst the disaffected. O-chiyo's longing for her child is one of the most moving passages of Kafū's prose (pp. 204–205), and Tamiko's letter to her benefactor at the end of the novel transcends sentimentality to achieve true pathos (pp. 218–223). However, the reunion of Tamiko and her mother is no romantic vision of family harmony but a realistic assessment of what their future holds: Tamiko will come to work as a prostitute in her mother's business. *Hikage no hana* is a subtle yet detailed portrait of men and women in the back streets of a city that would rather be rid of them.

Widely acknowledged as Kafū's masterpiece, *Bokutō kidan* (A Strange Tale from East of the River) was serialized in the *Asahi* newspaper from April to June 1937. Most critics see the novella as the culmination of all Kafū's writing to that point, combining naturalistic descriptions of the city with a playful, self-referential narrative structure. The story follows the novelist Ōe Tadasu through the back streets of Tamanoi as he searches for a suitable setting for his current novel, only to run into the prostitute O-yuki in a rainstorm. The relationship between 57-year-old Ōe and 24-year-old O-yuki is surprisingly realistic, despite the contrived nature of their meeting, and their emotions are subtly drawn through sparse dialogue and provocative descriptions of the season. Many themes and motifs present in earlier works appear in exaggerated form. Ōe personifies the *bunjin* ideal, while his connoisseurship of fine materials lands him in trouble with the police when a lady's singlet is found in his possession. The arrogant, interrogative nature of the policeman here is later offset by the reaction of another, who becomes kindness itself upon finding a large amount of money in Ōe's wallet. Police treatment depends on the objects one happens to have in one's possession, revealing the arbitrary, meaningless nature of police surveillance as well as the constructed nature of the "self" that one's appearance can present to the world. The freedom that can be gained from constructing one's own idea of "self" appears a few times in the work—Ōe enjoys dressing shabbily as he can then act however he likes, while O-yuki prefers the independent life of a prostitute to the indentured slavery of a geisha. *Bokutō kidan* thus brings together many ideas and themes that had been present in Kafū's writing since *Amerika monogatari*, including a return to the structures of embedded narrative.

Where stories in *Amerika monogatari* tended to bracket oral narratives of an event, *Bokutō kidan* brackets written texts as well, with the outermost text being *Bokutō kidan* by Nagai Kafū, the central text being the narrative of novelist Ōe Tadasu, and the innermost text being the book Ōe is writing, titled *Whereabouts Unknown*.[49] Unlike the earlier stories, however, *Bokutō kidan* shifts fluidly between Ōe's narrative and his book, and the reader is always conscious of the presence of both. The most highly self-conscious of all Kafū's fictions, *Bokutō kidan* reprises ideas from *Okamezasa* and *Ameshōshō* to draw our attention to the writing process. Apart from the "novel within a novel" conceit, Kafū unsettles the reader by making both major characters untrustworthy—O-yuki may be lying about once being a geisha in Ustunomiya, while Ōe dresses in disguise to visit Tamanoi and never reveals to her that he is a novelist. This kind of lying in the main narrative reflects the wider fiction being created by Kafū. Meanwhile we are constantly reminded that Ōe is narrating the story to us, as he begs our forgiveness for using trite expressions or contrived situations that one would find in Edo literature. Most critics commenting on *Bokutō kidan* focus on this self-referentiality, with Snyder (2000) describing it as a truly Modernist work, a "powerful critique" of the I-novel genre and its underlying assumptions of realistic, representative fiction (pp. 137–138). Snyder outlines the layered metafictions of Kafū's text by showing how Ōe's narrative and his story about Taneda intersect, with the characters bleeding into one another and Taneda mysteriously becoming aware of his status as a created character (pp. 139–142). Reading this self-reflexivity in light of Kafū's argument for the Japanese Self, it also becomes clear that Kafū himself intrudes into the work, with his own agenda most startlingly visible in Chapter 6.

This chapter opens with a detailed history of the Tamanoi pleasure quarter, explaining how shifting street patterns and train lines have affected the prominence of its various buildings (pp. 129–130). This history is followed by an emphasis on O-yuki's old-fashioned hairstyle and dress, with Ōe describing her as a "skilful yet inarticulate artist with power to summon the past" (p. 131), reminding us of Kafū's mission to record the changes in the city and to "summon the past" through the writing of literature. The challenges inherent in the act of writing are next emphasized by Ōe complaining about the difficulty of negotiating the written versus the spoken word (pp. 132–133), followed by a chatty example of writing from a geisha of the traditional Yanagibashi pleasure quarter, a true representative of the old ways (p. 133). Ōe concludes his musings (and Kafū concludes his chapter) with a rhetorical question: "The Takeya Ferry is gone, and so is the Makurabashi Ferry. Where am I to search for relics over which to lament my youth?" (p. 133). The chapter thus begins with a record of "relics" and ends with a cry worthy of *Shinkichōsha nikki*, making an explicit link between *Bokutō kidan* and the Returnee Stories. That the act of writing is emphasized throughout the work makes us even more aware of Kafū in his role of chronicler and preserver of the Japanese Self. O-yuki is "inarticulate" in her power to summon the past because the figure of the woman is constructed as object to the writer's gaze, not a speaking subject like Kimie or Komayo but reduced to a symbol in order to cast a brighter light on Kafū's writerly process. It is to Kafū's great credit that the central human relationship between Ōe and O-yuki is not lost in the labyrinth of narrativity, and the work remains an atmospheric and cinematic expression of the powerful impact of fleeting love. It lends itself well to the medium of film, and has been adapted more than once.[50] It is entirely possible that Kafū may have foreseen such adaptation, making the famous opening line "I almost never go to see a moving picture" (p. 278) yet another example of his own intrusion into the text of the work.

In 1952, Kafū was awarded the *Bunka kunshō*, the Imperial Cultural Decoration, for breaking new ground in research on Edo literature, for his efforts in translating foreign works, and for his literary achievement in producing works that managed to be poetic and critical at the same time. In 1953 he was made a member of the Japanese Academy of the Arts (the *Geijutsuin*). These perhaps represent the recognition given to Kafū for his efforts in portraying what he felt to be "genuinely Japanese," defining the cultural heritage as something to be treasured, rather than running headlong after Western imitation. Perhaps the reason why Kafū's later novels are considered to be his best is because he had finally found a suitable technique through which to express his ideas—he had worked his way through other forms of critique and appropriation, had been censored and banned, had written severe criticism and invective, and had found that it was more constructive to offer a positive, affirming vision of the Japanese Self and a "genuinely Japanese" form of civilization.

In reviewing Kafū's "return to Edo," I hope to have shown that it was neither an abrupt thematic reversal nor simply an escapist withdrawal from society, but a development and continuation of the critical stance put forward in the Returnee Stories of 1909–1910. Kafū's "Edo" functioned on many interlinking levels, symbolizing not only the cultural heritage of Japan's "Oriental" past but also the possibilities of resistance and critique inherent in the *gesaku* tradition. Kafū's use of Edo was the basis for his critique of Meiji on the one hand and his argument for a genuine Japanese modernity on the other. His construction of Edo thus combined political critique, or counter-discourse against Meiji, with affirmation of the Japanese Self in an act of self-construction. I believe that Kafū's constructions of the West and of Edo may be read as constructions of Occidentalism, because Kafū ultimately used them to oppose Meiji policies of modernization and to affirm his vision of the Japanese Self. Furthermore, because Kafū constructed his vision of the Japanese Self in response to, and in opposition to, the superficial Westernizing policies of Meiji modernization, these works may be read as what Chen calls "anti-official" Occidentalism—constructions of the Western Other used within the domestic political sphere to posit a counter-discourse to the government in power. Throughout this chapter, and the previous chapter, we have seen that Kafū's constructions of the West and of Edo allowed him to criticize Meiji Japan and find an alternative, counter-space to Meiji in Edo. The spirit of opposition that Kafū so admired in the Edo *chōnin* culture comes through in his appropriation of the *gesakusha* stance, marginalizing himself from Japanese society. If we read Kafū as Occidentalist then he is undoubtedly the "anti-official" Occidentalist, fundamentally opposed to the political status quo of the modern Japanese state.

Conclusions

In this book I have argued that Nagai Kafū's writing of 1903–1912 may be read as a concerted critique against Meiji Japan, that this critique, based on contrasts with the Western Other, may be read as Occidentalism, and furthermore, that in its fundamental stance of opposition against the Meiji government's policies of modernization, this critique may be read as "anti-official" Occidentalism, in a counter-discourse against the Meiji state. Nagai Kafū's Occidentalism may be understood in terms of how he used the West in his attempt to define the Japanese Self. Kafū constructed his "West" in different ways depending on how he intended to use that construct. In the early parts of *Amerika monogatari*, Kafū created a complex array of traditional and immigrant Japanese culture, American racial discrimination, and the Americans' status as "outsiders" in the immigrant communities, in order to portray the harsh realities of immigrant life as opposed to the Meiji dream of America as the "sacred land of liberty." Later in the collection, however, Kafū constructed the West as a homogeneous, monolithic entity, and America as the ideal country of freedom, in order to provide a contrast against which he could criticize Meiji Japan as feudal, backward, and restrictive. Kafū demonstrates time and again that categories are not fixed—the West is not a monolithic homogeneous ideal except when he chooses it to be, in order to make "the West" stand for something in contrast to "Japan." At other times, "the West" is revealed as a complex mix of modern America, the aesthetic civilization of Europe, the literary history of Paris, and structures of racial and sexual power. Kafū is a complex writer in that his essentialized spaces of Paris, America, Japan, the "West," and the "Orient" stand out of time in a symbolic, unchanging, almost stereotypical fashion in order to represent a particular ideal or to make a point of contrast or definition—but at the same time Kafū does not allow these spaces to restrict his writing, or his positioning of himself in respect to them. Kafū's work shows that binary opposition, while a strong literary tool of construction, does not necessarily imply a static, restrictive system of "binarism." Kafū's use of a dynamic array of positions both within and between opposing binary constructs does not limit him to operating strictly along the axes defined by the polar opposites.[1] Rather, Kafū uses these constructs and moves between them, playing with a flexible sense of Otherness and location to suit his own purposes.

If his primary use of the West was as a contrastive Other, Kafū also used the West by appropriating the rhetorical strategies of Orientalist discourse. Through *Furansu monogatari* in particular, Kafū used the binary system of Orientalist literature to explore the significance of the "West," the "Orient," and "Japan" in terms of colonial power and representation. This appropriation of Orientalist discourse may also be described in terms of Occidentalism, as Kafū's writing depended on using the Western discourse as its referential authority. Kafū's "Occidentalism" in this appropriation, however, should not be seen as a kind of "reverse Orientalism," because Kafū never opposed the Orientalist discourse. Instead he modeled himself on the Orientalist writers and took their position vis-à-vis the Oriental object. Kafū's flexible positioning in regard to the West, the Orient, and Japan may be read in terms of the writer's agency within a discourse, demonstrating that Said's idea of the closed binary system cannot be upheld. Binary systems within Kafū's works are used flexibly for specific purposes, while Kafū's positioning outside the binary system of Orientalist–Orient as observer/narrator further disrupts the closed nature of such totalizing systems.

Kafū's third use of the Western Other is seen in his critique of Meiji modernization. Kafū's critique of Meiji Japan in the Returnee Stories of 1909–1910 was based on contrast with the "genuine" nature of Western civilization, which prized its history and culture, as opposed to the superficial, external Westernization of Meiji Tokyo. Kafū's use of the West as contrasting, defining Other to Japan may be read as Occidentalism not only in its construction and use of the West, but also in its fundamental stance of opposition and critique against Meiji government policy. In considering counter-discourse as constituting an important part of Occidentalism, I have followed Foucault's insistence on the possibilities of counter-discourse from the margins. In Kafū's argument for "genuine" Japanese civilization, from the Returnee Stories through to *Shinkyō yawa,* Edo became a counter-discursive space to Meiji as the locus of Japan's true cultural heritage. Kafū's use of Edo may be read as a construction of the Japanese Self in opposition to

Meiji modernity, and this use of Edo in turn may be read as the "self-appropriation" that forms part of Chen's definition of Occidentalism. Kafū's so-called "withdrawal" into Edo themes after 1912 may be read as a continuation of his critical stance against Meiji Japan, and in its oppositional outlook may best be described as "anti-official" Occidentalism in a counter-discourse to the authoritarian state.

Kafū's critique of Meiji in the works of 1903–1912 may thus be read as an example of Occidentalism in four main ways: in the construction of the West as contrasting, defining Other; in the appropriation of Western rhetorical discourse; in the use of the Western Other as a contrast for critique of government policies at home; and in the use of this contrast as the basis for self-appropriation of a "genuine" Japanese culture. An Occidentalist framework is certainly not the first thing that comes to mind when reading Kafū's works, so is such a reading sustainable? Does reading Kafū as a critic, and reading his critique as Occidentalism, provide a good model of understanding Kafū and his works? A good model should provide a way of looking at the subject that not only adds to existing methods and readings, but also furthers them by resolving outstanding problems or ambiguities that other readings may have failed to address. If this model of understanding Kafū's texts is sustainable, then it should be applicable not only to the texts discussed in this book, but to all of Kafū's works. It is at this point which Seidensticker's model fails, because his explanation is not applicable to the criticism of Meiji in the Returnee Stories, which had to be omitted from his argument. I have not examined all of Kafū's works in this book, and a lengthy examination would be out of place here, but a short examination of some other works should test this point briefly.

Kafū's Zola period, and his wide reading of foreign literature before he left for America in 1903, may be seen as the foundation on which Kafū's high expectations of France were based, and also as the source of referential authority in *Furansu monogatari*. The beginnings of Kafū's Meiji critique may be seen in the work *Yashin* (Ambition, 1902), which takes for its subject the ideals of ambition and advancement inherent in the concept of *risshin shusse*. Although Kafū meant for the work to take after Zola's naturalistic and critical style, *Yashin* has been criticized for its immaturity and superficial approach to naturalism.[2] However, Kafū's focus on Meiji values in *Yashin* prefigures his argument in the Returnee Stories that the failure of Meiji modernization lies in its dependence on outer form rather than inner substance. From *Amerika monogatari*, we can see the importance of inner feeling to Kafū's argument, as much of Kafū's critique of Meiji Japan in the collection focuses on the contrast between American and Japanese values, the internal part of "civilization." The contrasting system of values regarding race, courtship, family relations, and democracy constructed in *Amerika monogatari* would become the foundation of his later critique. Kafū's journey to the West and his writing there would develop the method of contrasting Japan against the Western Other, providing a depth and breadth to his critical perspective not found in *Yashin*. A common thread may be seen running through Kafū's work from *Yashin* onward, however, and that is a focus on inner values as opposed to external, material aspects of civilization. Reading Kafū's work as the development of a critique of Meiji civilization thus seems sustainable in relation to his earlier Zola period.

At the other end of the chronological spectrum, reading Kafū's works in terms of critique and dissent is also borne out in a consideration of his later writing, particularly during World War II. David Earhart has analyzed Kafū's "wartime diary" as a protest against an authoritarian state. Earhart argues that Kafū writes about Japan's cultural decay from the point of view that "Japanese modernization tended to equate human progress to the progress of the state and was thus culturally and morally debilitating." That is, Kafū recognized that cultural development needs "intellectual and creative freedom," not militarism and authoritarian control. Earhart (1994) interprets the nature of Kafū's critique as anti-statist, and considers *Bokutō kidan* as "anti-military" (pp. 488, 491). Earhart focuses on Kafū's mocking, disdainful, yet shocked attitude to the war effort and the decay of culture, expressed through sarcasm, detachment, and cynicism, and then fear and panic during the air raids on Tokyo. Regardless of the many omissions and additions that the wartime diary undoubtedly went through in the editing process, it still stands as a document purposefully constructed for publication, written in the self-proclaimed *gesakusha* persona, and thus acts as further testament to Kafū's critical stance against the state and its atmosphere of intellectual suppression and censorship.

In terms of the Edo-themed fiction from 1918 onward, I have read Kafū's "return to Edo" (*Edo kaiki*) as an affirmation of the genuine in the Japanese Self, but Kafū's nostalgia for the past has proved problematic in other readings. Seidensticker and Keene argue that once Kafū retired into seclusion, determined to live in the past, it was already the Taishō period, and the immediate past was no longer Edo but Meiji. In his later writings of the Shōwa period, Kafū would look back with fond nostalgia on the Meiji period he found so abhorrent only twenty years or so before (Keene, 1984, p. 420; Seidensticker, 1965, pp. 138–139). If he really had been writing in a "counter-discourse" to

Meiji and the oppression of an authoritarian government, then how are we to explain such nostalgia for the Meiji period? First, we may recall Kafū's enthusiasm for the ever-changing appearance of the Ginza.[3] It was not change itself which Kafū opposed, nor even the rapidity of that change, but the fact that change seemed to be happening with little thought given to what development and progress really meant for Japan. In the last installment of *Kōcha no ato*, Kafū looks back on early Meiji in wonder, thinking just how much power must have been held by the words *bunmei-kaika* at the time. Although many aspects of the movement now seem childish or even foolish, he argues, "how dynamic was the general atmosphere of the period!" (*MB* 2.9: 141–2). People were able to push boldly forward with their ideas and take advantage of the opportunity for enterprise, without letting fears hold them back. "Compared to contemporary times forty-four years later, considering how the world of ideas is withering under the forcible repression of militarism, it seems more and more like a dream" (p. 142). Early Meiji thus had much to recommend it, and we can only imagine how the increasing strictures of Taishō censorship must have made Kafū long for the comparative freedom of even late Meiji.

Second, we may consider that even though the chronological settings of Kafū's works necessarily shifted from Meiji to Taishō and Shōwa as he grew older, the essential aims of his work remained constant. Kafū's works after 1912, whether set in Shimbashi, Yanagibashi, or Ōkubo, or later, in Tamanoi or "east of the river," revolve around the world of the geisha and their patrons. Set in the various red-light districts, the works tend to focus on the problem of how to preserve a disappearing culture that represents the "genuine" Japan. In *Bokutō kidan*, the narrator finds in the margins of the city an antidote to the noisy radios, moving pictures and traffic chaos of the center. Even though the time frame has shifted, and geisha in some stories are replaced by prostitutes, dancing girls, or café waitresses, the Taishō and Shōwa counterparts to the Edo and early Meiji geisha are seen as fulfilling the same function—in their "shameful" occupations these women are looked down upon by society, yet represent the only solace, human kindness, and reasonable conversation that the narrator can experience in a world of war and interfering police.[4] The counter-discourse of Ryūsui's "guardians of civilization" is still evident in Kafū's later works, as life on the margins provides an alternative to the state. Reading Kafū as a critic of civilization thus seems sustainable in regard to his later fiction.

Kafū's Edo-themed fiction may also benefit from Edward Said's "methodology of the text," locating texts within larger bodies of work in terms of referential authority. A common construct in Kafū's later work, particularly in *Ameshōshō* and *Bokutō kidan,* is the juxtaposition of Chinese or Tokugawa poetry with modern-day reality. Tomi Suzuki (1996) illustrates with the example of *Bokutō kidan*:

> In reading Yoda Gakkai's *Twenty-Four Views of Sumida* while he crosses the Sumida River, the "I" enjoys not so much the vision of the evoked past itself as the interaction between the literary vision and the present raw reality. . . . It is the gap between the literary vision of the lost past and the present site of squalid alleys that defamiliarizes and enlivens both. (p. 148)

As we saw in *Furansu monogatari,* Kafū is strategic in his use of reference and juxtaposition, evoking Loti in relation to distance and romance, and Kipling and Delibes in consideration of the British Empire. Kafū's strategic positioning vis-à-vis other texts, and his use of referential authority in joining the formation of a body of texts, is repeated in *Bokutō kidan* and *Ameshōshō* with the formation of Chinese and Edo works. The use of China indicates that Kafū's argument after the Returnee Stories rests on the "Theory of the Orient," while references to Henri du Régnier indicate the "genuine" nature of French civilization that Japan should take as a model. Said's methodology of the text seems applicable to these later works, providing a useful model that can take into account a greater number of works than some previous readings.

One of my aims in demonstrating the coherence of Kafū's works was to resolve some of the ambiguities of his literary classification. The short overview of works above suggests that Kafū's Zola period and his later turn to Chinese and Tokugawa literature may be read as part of a coherent development of Kafū's argument, both in the focus on social attitudes and values, and in the method of strategic textual reference. Reading Kafū's works as a sustained critique resolves some of the ambiguities inherent in a purely "literary" reading, in which the disjointed combination of Kafū's Zola period, hedonism, and despair in New York, sudden withdrawal from society in 1916, and later turn to Edo themes and eroticism, represents Kafū as an overly complex character with contradictory tendencies. By reading these phases as part of a developing critique, Kafū's works of late Meiji and early Taishō emerge as parts of a sustained way of looking at things and questioning how Japan should look at itself in relation to the rest of the world. Reading Kafū as a critic can help us see reasons behind seemingly eccentric behavior, such as resigning from Keiō and withdrawing from society, while reading him as an Occidentalist can help explain his great affinity for French art *and* his turn to Japanese culture in a quest for the genuine. It is possible to read Kafū without becoming caught up in contradictions.

Reading Kafū in this way does raise questions about the oppositional stance as "political" critique. If Kafū was writing about "genuine Japan," the Japanese sense of self or identity, and the status of modernity in the Meiji state, as well as commenting as he did on the *kokka, kokumin,* and the margins of society, then is this not part of a political discourse? Why is Kafū not generally seen as a political author, a writer of dissent? Quite apart from the studies that represent Kafū as a simple pleasure-seeking hedonist, there is also another reason to do with approach and methodology. In part, this is due to traditional definitions of "political criticism," as overt or direct involvement in affairs of the government or state. Over the past thirty years, however, the concept of what constitutes the "political" has gained a much broader application. Foucault's work on discourse and discursive systems have led to all sorts of utterances, acts, and texts being deconstructed and read both in their political context and as political themselves, as all utterances are ultimately seen as structures of knowledge/power by the subject/agent. However, even without such a broad application of the "political," Kafū's works can still be read in terms of traditional politics and the role of the state.

First we may consider Kafū's commentary on American democracy and racial inequality; the treatment of immigrants as U.S.–Japan tensions rose in 1906; and the restrictions on artistic expression in a supposedly open society. Next, we have the observations on the strength of the French state as a patron of the arts, as opposed to Meiji Japan where literature is treated merely as "printed matter." Third, there is an extended commentary on Meiji censorship, given both directly in interviews, and indirectly through his fiction. Yoshino Kōu's publication *Kōkotsu* was banned in exactly the same manner as Kafū's *Kanraku* in 1909; Yoshino Kōu becomes Kafū's new pen name in 1911; and many of Kafū's essays refer to the authoritarian repression of the Meiji state. His comments on the impossibility of artistic expression in such a regime are as heartfelt as they are repetitive, and we see a great deal of anguish over the Dreyfus/Zola example in relation to the Kōtoku Incident. Political commentary is certainly direct in the essay *Hanabi,* in which Kafū declares his willful and public withdrawal from state participation, serving as a commentary on citizenship in the Taishō period. With such sustained focus on the idea of the state and its role with respect to artists and the arts, I would conclude that

Kafū is indeed a "political" critic, or in the words of Satō Shizuo, a "critic of the state" (*kokka no hihyōsha*) (1995, p. 141).

In this book I have grouped Kafū's works according to their shared focus and themes, beginning from 1903 to 1908 with the travel works, then 1909 to 1910 with the Returnee Stories, 1911 to 1912 with *Shinkyō yawa*, and the Edo-themed works that followed *Edo geijutsuron* from 1913 to 1914. The dates correspond with major events in Kafū's life: leaving and returning to Japan, the end of the Meiji period, and his decision to withdraw from society and live as a *gesakusha*. I have concentrated on the Meiji period because Kafū himself wrote primarily about "*Meiji bunmei*," and "*Meiji no kindai*" throughout these works, but it is necessary to remain aware that the "Meiji period" is itself a construct (Karatani, 1993a). A more significant problem with my approach is that I have constructed a narrative by representing Kafū's argument as a development over time. Although my reading has brought out the critical aspects of Kafū's argument and has demonstrated his coherence by using this "development over time" model, it raises problems because narrative assumes the telling of a "whole" story. There is much to Kafū that has not been discussed in this book, however, and it is by no means a whole representation of Kafū and his works. One of my aims has been to avoid essentialization and the totalizing systems of generalization and binarism, and I do not wish this study to "totalize" Kafū. I have followed the example of the Japanese studies by Suzuki Fumitaka and others, who argue that to understand Kafū's reasons for writing, we must take into account his early works and the development of his ideas. By showing the development of Kafū's critique, from contrast against an idealized West to his "Theory of the Orient" and critical stance against the Meiji state, I hope to have demonstrated that Kafū's criticism is not a piecemeal complaint about modernization, but a well-reasoned argument for the preservation of Japanese culture.

In attempting to provide another angle from which to approach Kafū and his works I have been most critical of Edward Seidensticker's argument. *Kafū the Scribbler* and the included translations of Kafū's shorter novels have been very influential, and Seidensticker's translations of *Sumidagawa* and *Botan no kyaku* are so well known that I have used them as references in this book. My objections to Seidensticker lie in his misrepresentation of Kafū's Returnee Stories as nonliterary works full of complaints, minimizing the critical aspect in favor of an image of Kafū as an eccentric, grumbling "scribbler." It is precisely because Seidensticker's work has been so influential that I have focused on overturning this image and re-presenting Kafū as a serious critic. However, as Edward Fowler has shown, Seidensticker's work was conditioned by the postwar climate of publishing and translation that needed to present a "re-Orientalized," or exotic and unthreatening, image of Japan. There is, therefore, a reason for Seidensticker's misrepresentation. On this point, it must be said that Kafū has always been read for his aesthetic appeal and the beauty of his depictions of the "flower and willow world," and the artistry of his prose is one of the lasting appeals of Kafū for the reader. Reading Kafū only in this way, however, is to reproduce and reinforce the discourse of "exotic Japan" created by early travelers to the country. The readings of Japanese art forms as quaint, exotic, beautiful, and charming; as representative of an alien or unique tradition; or as an artifact soon to be lost to modernization, can all be found in nineteenth-century British writing on Japan. Continuing to read Kafū merely as an example of quaint, unthreatening, "teahouse" Japan reinforces the Orientalist discourse that underlies these and postwar constructions. To broaden the view of Kafū to include his critical works, then, is not only to understand the reasons for his search for an "authentic" Japanese culture, but to overturn the idea of Kafū's "authentic Japan" as standing for some Orientalist comprehension of Japanese culture.

If we are not to read Kafū as some kind of "self-Orientalist," then what of reading his works as Occidentalist critique? Suzuki Fumitaka, Kanno Akimasa, and indeed many Japanese critics have attributed Kafū's critique of Meiji thought and values to his experiences in the West, which prompted him to contrast American democracy and independence with the restrictive atmosphere back home. Kafū's time in the West is thus seen as a sort of ideological crucible in which Kafū's critique of Meiji was formed. My reading agrees with this view but focuses more attention on the actual technique of contrast as a method of construction and representation, and extends the reading of that technique to describe it as Occidentalism. Is this a good model for understanding Kafū's works? Does it add something we cannot obtain from other readings? In the introduction to this book I acknowledged a problem raised by calling Kafū "an Occidentalist," an individual exponent of a discourse. It is impossible to have a discourse of Occidentalism completely encapsulated in one writer's texts, as the term *Occidentalism* implies a whole system of ontological and epistemological understanding, as well as issues of domination and power in imperialistic acts. It is necessary, therefore, to view the writer as one part of a wider discourse, in light of the intellectual and cultural context, in relation to other writers and thinkers of the time. I have endeavored to situate Kafū in his historical and political context by considering the climate of American–Japanese relations from 1903 to 1907, by sketching the major transformations in Tokyo created by reforms to the transport system, and by considering Kafū's reactions to Meiji censorship and the Kōtoku Incident. I have also attempted to situate Kafū in his intellectual context, by considering his argument for genuine modernization in comparison to Natsume Sōseki, who is widely recognized as a critic on this subject; by indicating Kafū's influence on later writers such as Tanizaki Jun'ichirō and Kuki Shūzō; and by situating Kafū in relation to discourses on Edo in the Meiji period as well as in relation to the discourse of *Nihon e no kaiki* prevailing in the Taishō period. However, a sustained comparative analysis of Kafū and the writers of Meiji and Taishō would have been out of place in a book that aimed to analyze the constructions and arguments of one writer. How then to reconcile the idea of Kafū as an Occidentalist and as part of a system of thought, with a book structured as a case study of one individual? One of my aims was to avoid generalizations and the totalization of such binary constructions as East–West, Orientalism–Occidentalism, and so on by focusing on a particular set of texts in a particular historical moment. Although this aim has been met in carrying out a case-study analysis of one writer, it still remains that the idea of Occidentalism as a discourse and discursive practice in Meiji Japan needs more reflection and further research.

Although Chen (1995) warns against using Occidentalism as a "new orthodoxy," easily applicable to all historical periods and nations, she has drawn a "historical parallel" between Chinese Occidentalism and North Korean Occidentalism (pp. 13–16). Drawing a similar parallel with Japanese Occidentalism may shed light on how different parts of Asia have constructed different (or similar) Wests for different (or similar) purposes, in both "official" and "anti-official" modes of discourse. Many images of the West were constructed in Meiji Japan and used for different ideological and political purposes, in a climate of anxiety over unequal treaties with the West and the nature of Japanese modernization. This was also the time when many Western theories of civilization, politics, and modernization were first introduced to Japan, and the Japanese began to use, or appropriate, Western theories for their own domestic political agendas. The combination of construction, appropriation, and the threat of Western power in the Meiji period makes it an ideal case study for applying ideas of Occidentalism and discursive practice to Japan. However, Meiji Occidentalism would not have been used to dominate the West but to advance the Japanese cause for attaining equality with the Western powers. Research on Meiji Occidentalism would have to focus on the constructions of the West used by the Meiji government at home in Japan rather than trying to argue that Occidentalism in Japan was an imperialistic act of discursive practice. In this way, I agree with Chen and others who have argued that Said overemphasizes the connections between discursive practice and imperialistic acts of aggression (Chen, 1995, p. 48). Even so, the issue of colonialism in regard to Japan has been an important one, and theories of Orientalism and Occidentalism should prove useful in providing a framework for further discussion.

One of the reasons why the relationship between imperialism/colonialism and Japan is problematic is that it involves both the Western colonial presence in Asia and Japan on the one hand, and the Japanese colonial presence in Asia on the other.[5] The "semi-colonial" status of both China and Japan has raised many questions on the applicability of theories of Orientalism to the area.[6] In 1999, Harootunian and Sakai despaired that critical theory had made little substantial impact on Japanese Studies in America, and suggested that part of the reason may lie in the colonialist nature of "area studies" in America, bound up in the military strategies for "knowing the enemy" in World War II and the Occupation.[7] Taking up Orientalist theory, they argued, would make explicit the ontological assumptions of domination and power operating between America and Japan, resulting in an uncomfortable situation that academics therefore seek to avoid (Harootunian & Sakai, 1999). However, Japanese Studies also exists outside America, and we cannot generalize about the discipline as a whole in this way. A simpler reason could be that postcolonial theory has not been popular in Japanese Studies because Japan's status as a colony is open to debate. On one hand, critics like Ning Wang (1997) argue that Japan experienced a "double coloniality," experiencing first the cultural "colonization" by China from the eighth century, and then the "colonization" from America in the twentieth century, in particular in the Allied Occupation (1945–1952). On the other hand, P. L. Pham investigates Japan as a semi-colonized state, asking how theories of Orientalism might be applied to Japan "in the absence of political domination" by the West. Pham (1999) analyzes English representations of Japan as "Orient" and concludes that, even without actual colonialism, the discourse in which the English described and positioned Japan was underpinned by a logic of political domination (pp. 163–164, 180).

Both these arguments take as their starting point the idea of Japan as a colonized "Orient." Turning this approach on its head, the question now seems to focus more on Japan's role as "Orientalist" or colonizer. Eiji Oguma (2002, pp. 352–353n12) has criticized Japanese academics for their naïve acceptance and application of Said's model of Orientalism in describing Japanese representations of Chinese and Koreans. Nishihara's analysis of Tanizaki's *Shina shumi* in particular has been criticized by Pinnington on this point (2006, pp. 89–90). Despite such criticism, however, such treatments of Tanizaki's "Orient" have created an increasingly popular view of Japan as "Orientalist"—either in literary representations of the Asian Other, or in self-representations of Japan as some kind of exotic space. I hope to have already demonstrated some of the problems inherent in this approach over the course of this book, but what is the significance of the debate? What does it matter if we view Japan as a "reverse Orientalist" when depicting itself, or as a "colonizing Orientalist" when representing Asia? Put bluntly, it is significant because continuing academic usage of the "Orientalist" model to understand power structures operating in Asia perpetuates a hierarchical power dynamic that remains unacceptable to non-Japanese nations in the region. As Tessa Morris-Suzuki (1998) has noted, the Japanese self-image in regard to its historical relationship with Asia continues to affect relations between Japan, China, Korea, and Taiwan today (pp. 87, 106). The issues of historical memory, textbook representations of the war, and Japanese actions during the colonial era are so sensitive as to be potentially explosive in political terms. If the region is to move forward, the question of power relations inherent in the Japanese idea of *tōyō* must be clarified.

Morris-Suzuki argues that the question of whether Japan was or was not part of Asia was crucial to foreign policy as it governed the treatment of the colonies:

> Was Japan's right to rule the colonies based on the innate racial superiority of the Japanese rulers vis-à-vis their colonial subjects? Or was it based, on the contrary, on racial or cultural *commonalities* between rulers and ruled? Or did it derive from the fact that Japanese society embodied a more advanced form of a single modern "civilization"? Each of these claims had its own implications for colonial policy and for Japan's relationship with the established colonial powers. (pp. 86–87, emphasis in original)

These were huge questions, especially during the late Meiji period as the Japanese empire expanded. Eiji Oguma demonstrates that the annexation of Korea on August 29, 1910 sparked a flurry of articles on Japan's status as a "mixed nation," made up of heterogeneous elements either issuing from or shared with the Asian mainland.[8]

Kafū's interest in the question of *tōyō* thus places him squarely in the contemporary discourse debating the relationship between Japan and Asia. If Kafū is to be criticized for anything during this period it is perhaps his comparative silence on Japanese imperialism before and during the Fifteen Years' War (1931–1945). The colonies provide a safe escape for his fictional characters needing exile from Japan (notably Tsutayo in *Satsuki-yami*), but Kafū remains silent on the issue of Japanese aggression in Asia. Is Kafū guilty of the same offence as Natsume Sōseki, who "wrote out Asia" in his novels of late Meiji?

James A. Fujii's concern over this kind of silence centres on the idea that fixed conceptions of "the modern" and "the individual" in Sōseki's *Kokoro* have, in Western and Japanese criticism, concealed the reality of the historical context in which the work was actually written. The historical context and reality of imperialist power structures in Asia in the early twentieth century have been forgotten, overlooked, in the construction of a "canon" based on concepts of modernity and the individual. Fujii (1993) writes that what is interesting about *Kokoro* and *Man-Kan tokorodokoro* (Here and There in Manchuria and Korea), is how a writer managed to "experience firsthand the Japanese occupational presence in Asia, without letting it touch her/his literary production" (p. 196). Fujii argues for a historicized reading of Sōseki and other texts, which would take into account the Japanese colonial experience in Asia. "*Kokoro* continues to be read in ways that ignore the specific conditions of Japanese modernity and nation-ness that give rise to this text. What must be endeavored is to bring into focus the oft-neglected relationship between Japan and its Asian neighbors as a way of thinking about Japanese modernity and 'modern Japanese literature' . . ." (p. 197). This book has provided a study of Kafū's use of the West to counter-write the Meiji state. Along the way, we have seen glimpses of Kafū in Asia, representing British colonialism in Singapore and separating the *tōyō* of China and Japan from the Middle Eastern "Orient" of Western Orientalist discourse. What are the implications of Kafū's "Asia" for Orientalism, colonialism, and Japan?

Kafū's awareness of colonial issues in Asia is clear in his depiction of the "Westerners with sinister features" supervising the Chinese and Malay coolies in *Shingapōru no sūjikan*. On the other hand, the Japanese colonial presence in Asia is not represented. The annexation of Korea is mentioned in passing in *Hirusugi,* and newspaper headlines of the war in China provide an auditory backdrop to *Hikage no hana,* but otherwise Japanese imperialism and the events of the China Incident and the Pacific War are striking in their absence from Kafū's later work. This silence on Japan's escalating militarism may be interpreted as part of the *gesakusha* stance—perhaps Kafū chose to see the Japanese colonization of Asia as a matter of state, part of the machinations and workings of the authoritarian "*kokka*" he had come to despise. Or perhaps Kafū was merely waiting for an end to the harsh wartime censorship, which threatened torture or death for writers of dissent, before publicly airing his feelings on these matters. In 1947, Kafū ended his own silence by publishing his diary of 1941–1945 as *Risai nichiroku* (A Daily Account of the Calamity), which clearly expresses antimilitarist feeling as well as sympathy for Chinese and Southeast Asian victims of Japanese aggression. Kafū also censures the Japanese "family nation" for its thievery of Southeast Asian resources in the colonial period.[9] Of course, this diary was an edited, constructed publication like any other, and the antiwar sentiment may have been strengthened or even added anew in the editing process (Seidensticker, 2002, p. 143). But Kafū's sympathy in the diary for the Asian victims of Japanese wartime action is consistent with the strong sense of shared culture and history expressed in his *Tōyō shisō*. While the *gesakusha* stance entailed deliberate silence on matters of national polity, Kafū nonetheless remained dedicated to the search for Japan's national identity and a resolution of Japan's relationship with Asia. If his *gesakusha* stance and turn to Edo themes show Kafū's positive affirmation of the Japanese Self, his willingness to question the idea of *tōyō* makes him a significant contributor to twentieth-century Japanese discourse on Asia.

In defining Japan against its Western and Oriental Others, Kafū focused on Japan as a nation of the world, trying to make sense of how Japan should fit into and relate to that world. Kafū's ideas, couched in a literary formation, would not generally be seen as contributing to "foreign policy" discourse. Kafū is so widely acknowledged to be a superb craftsman in his lyrical prose that the political content of his works is easily overlooked. But there is value in reading literature not just for its literary merits, but in order to examine the purposes of the writer in producing the text, and to place the literature as text in its historical context and in relation to wider discourses of power in the state. According to James Fujii, such an enterprise is not only useful but necessary, if we are to uncover the processes of canon formation in creating what we call "modern Japanese literature." Kafū's work has undoubtedly been read as a fine example of "modern Japanese literature," but the interesting thing about this statement is that Kafū himself contested its constituent parts. He constantly questioned the meaning of "modern" and the relevance of "*kindai*" to Japan, as well as how to reconcile the idea of *kindai* with an ancient cultural tradition. He questioned the nature of "Japan" and its boundaries, seeking a definition of *tōyō* in the sense of both "Orient" and "Asia." And finally he questioned and interrogated the nature of literature, drawing new connections between the literary "demimonde" of Edo and France, writing dozens of essays on French poetry and prose, experimenting with new writing styles from symbolism to bracketed narration, and protesting the repression of literary expression in an authoritarian state. This questioning, challenging spirit, reflecting the essence of *hankō*, is what Kafū brought to modern Japanese literature and how he shaped its future.

Notes

Notes to Introduction

1. On the invention of "Edo" and "Meiji" as loci of cultural identity see Gluck (1985, 1998) and Morris-Suzuki (1998).

2. Irena Powell (1983) argues that Kafū's treatment of the erotic goes beyond a purely sensual approach, whereas Itō Sei believed that his work "belongs to the order of logic and criticism" (pp. 95–96). Nakamura Mitsuo (1978) and Stephen Snyder (2000) argue that Kafū's theoretical and intellectual criteria for writing, and his grasp of the self-consciousness of narrative, derive largely from French naturalism and European aesthetics.

3. This phrase was first used by the poet and critic Sōma Gyōfu (see Yoshida Seiichi, 1971b, p. 43).

4. Tomi Suzuki (1996) has examined Kafū's later work *Bokutō kidan* (A Strange Tale from East of the River, 1937) as an example of the "I–novel" or *shishōsetsu* form, a confessional genre closely associated with Japanese *shizenshugi* (pp. 135–150).

5. Nakamura Mitsuo (1978, pp. 291–292). Itō Sei (1978–1979) also examines Kafū's naturalism and "anti-naturalism": see *Nihon bundanshi,* 6.219, 16.179–80, 18.10–13. Henshall (1982) disputes the idea that European naturalism was "purer" than *shizenshugi.* Sibley (1968) observes that usual definitions of the "main line of *shizenshugi*" follow Shimazaki Tōson's *Hakai* (The Broken Commandment, 1906) and Tayama Katai's *Futon* (The Quilt, 1907) through to Masamune Hakuchō and Tokuda Shūsei. Earlier Japanese works of naturalism, which more closely imitated French naturalism and Zola in particular, written by Kosugi Tengai, Oguri Fūyō, and Nagai Kafū, are thus differentiated from the main line by classifying them as "pre-" or "*zenki*" (early) *shizenshugi* (pp. 159–160).

6. Nakamura Mitsuo (1978, p. 292); Itō Sei, *Nihon bundanshi,* 13.25. Ueda Bin and Mori Ōgai were involved in Kafū's later employment at Keiō University: see Itō Sei, 16.15–20. On the close relationship between Ōgai and Kafū see Snyder (2000, pp. 8–33).

7. Fowler (1992, p. 42). Harootunian and Sakai (1999) liken Japan Studies in America to a colonial structure, as "area studies" was organized in terms

of the war and Allied Occupation. On earlier Orientalist approaches to Japan see Minear (1980, pp. 507–517) and Miyoshi (1991, pp. 9–13).

8. For example, see Dower (1986, p. 92); Goodman, White, and Kwon (1998, pp. 5–8).

9. Loti's *Madame Chrysanthème* (1887) inspired works from Giacomo Puccini's opera *Madame Butterfly*, which premiered in Milan in 1904, through to the film *Teahouse of the August Moon* (dir. Jack Cummings, 1956) and the musical *Miss Saigon* (Claude-Michel Schönberg, Alain Boublil, and Richard Maltby), which premiered in London in 1989.

10. See for example, Lowe (1991), MacKenzie (1995), Porter (1991), Moore-Gilbert (1986), Pratt (1992), and Melman (1992).

11. These two points have formed the basis of many thorough critiques of Said, notably Behdad (1994) and Young (1990). MacKenzie (1995) gives a detailed overview of Said's argument and subsequent criticisms of it: see pp. 8–15 (theoretical criticism), pp. 20–39 (historical criticism).

12. See Matsuzawa (1984) and Sakamoto (1997).

13. I will refer to "Orientalist discourse" to mean both the writings of the Orientalists as a body and the power structures underlying that discourse which made it possible; to Kafū's "discourse" as the body of texts which make up his constructed version of the "Orient," the "West" and "Japan"; and to Kafū's "counter-discourse" to mean a body of writing as a speech act against the prevailing discursive practices of Meiji society.

14. For further discussion of these artists see Doug Slaymaker's forthcoming book *Paris, mon amour: Japanese representations of France.*

15. I will use the capitalized W in "West" and "Western" rather than the neutral "w." The term *seiyō* (West, Occident) usually appears in the work of Kafū and other Meiji writers as part of a binary contrast, a construct set up against Japan or "the Orient"/*tōyō*. Binary systems and their subversion are an important consideration in this book and postcolonial studies as a whole, and so the capital W is used as a reminder of this constructive act.

16. See Ito (1991) and Snyder (2000) on desire in the fiction of Tanizaki Jun'ichirō and Nagai Kafū; see Silver (2008) on desire for the Western Other in Taishō detective fiction.

17. Foucault's binary structures are respectively seen in *Discipline and Punish* (1977), *The History of Sexuality: Volume One* (1979), and *Madness and Civilization* (1967).

18. For a more thorough exploration of these problems see Hutchinson and Williams (2006, pp. 3–4).

19. See W.G. Beasley (1990), Wray and Conroy (1983), Storry (1960), G.B. Sansom (1950), Seidensticker (1983, 1990), Waley (1984), and Tayama Katai (1987).

Notes to Chapter 1

1. See Mitsuko Iriye (1969) for a fuller exploration of Kyūichirō's motives here (pp. 53–54).

2. Translated by Mitsuko Iriye as *American Stories* (Nagai, 2000). There is also a partial translation by Stephen W. Kohl (1979, pp. 58–68). All translations in this book are my own unless otherwise specified.

3. On Kafū's naturalism, see Kanno (1996); on Western literary influences see Akase (1976, 1995) and Iriye (1969). On narrative structure see Snyder (2000, esp. pp. 34–53) and Matsuda (1994).

4. The first two approaches form the basis of Isoda Kōichi's *Nagai Kafū* (1989), whereas dilettantism is discussed in Sasabuchi (1976).

5. Many critics have written on music as a significant motif of difference in the collection, especially on Kafū's use of Wagner, so I do not focus on this theme. See Shindō (1997), Nakamura (1987), and also Shiozaki (1994).

6. See, for example, *Saiyū-nisshishō* (Leaves from a Journal of a Western Voyage), entry for January 5, 1904. *Saiyū-nisshishō* is in Nagai Kafū, *Kafū zenshū* (1962–1974), 19.5–54. *Kafū zenshū* is hereafter abbreviated as KZ, and page references will appear in brackets in the main text. Where unspecified in this chapter, the volume is vol. 3.

7. *Shōsetsu sakuhō* (How to Write a Novel, 1920), KZ 14.395-408; see also Ueda (1976, pp. 27–30).

8. The constructive act is also foregrounded by the choice of hiragana script for the "*amerika*" and "*furansu*" in the titles of the travel collections (Hutchinson, 2007, p. 326).

9. Some of the following material on the immigrant stories of *Amerika monogatari* appeared in a somewhat different form in *Monumenta Nipponica* 62: 3 (Autumn 2007, pp. 323–345).

10. Kafū was known to append fictional dates to his writings, to match dates in the published diary or to create an image of faster or slower travel from place to place. I follow the dates of writing given in *Saiyū–nisshishō,* which although unreliable are the most generally accepted dates for these works. If dates of writing are indeterminable I give the date of publication.

11. Iriye (1969) goes beyond author-narrator conflation here by conflating Kafū with Yanagida and Kishimoto, as two aspects of his own personality (p. 67).

12. On the immigration experience see Suenobu (1997); also Ito Kazuo (1973).

13. Real name Shiba Shirō (1852–1922). See Sansom (1950, pp. 435–439) and Sakaki (2000).

14. This story has an alternate title, *Noji no kaeri,* translated as "A Return Through the Meadow" by Iriye (Nagai, 2000, pp. 9–17).

15. See Akase (1976, pp. 42–44). The similarities are clear, but Kafū does not mention *Sur L'eau* in the diary until August 3, 1905. He may have chosen to emphasize his reading of Maupassant at the later date to strengthen his image as a growing connoisseur of French literature.

16. Written in kanji as *Nihonjin,* with furigana *jappu.*

17. Akira Iriye (1975, pp. 74–76). See also Suenobu (1997, pp. 39–40).

18. For a closer examination of this story in terms of Levinas's "face-to-face" meeting with the Other, see Hutchinson (2007).

19. See the diary entry in *Saiyū-nisshishō* for December 14, 1903.

20. On Kafū's "Zola period" see Yoshida (1971b, pp. 31–44), Akiba (1977, pp. 65–68), Homma (1983, pp. 8–11) and Kanno (1996, pp. 56–78). Some argue that French naturalism is so different to *shizenshugi* that the two movements should be seen in terms of opposing interests: see Henshall (1982, pp. 401–421) and Sibley (1968, pp. 159–160) on this debate. While the styles have their differences, I see many of the same motivations at the base of *shizenshugi*, naturalism and *shasei* (sketching from life) and think it both limiting and problematic to classify Kafū's work as either "early *shizenshugi*" or "European naturalism." I will therefore refer to Kafū's style simply as naturalism.

21. For a detailed analysis of this work see Furuya (1999, pp. 90–105).

22. Conversation with the author in Kalamazoo, January 22, 2007.

23. Strauss (1985) and Angles (2006) describe the high level of interest in Japan held by the citizens of Kalamazoo. Kafū and his compatriot Katō Katsuji gave several talks on Japanese culture at the Kalamazoo Ladies' Library, and performed in an evening of Japanese theater and music for the Century Forum Club on May 5, 1905.

24. This character is probably inspired by Katō Katsuji, the only other Japanese student at Kalamazoo College in the years 1904–1905 (see Angles, 2006; Strauss, 1985).

25. Kafū's landlady was Stella A. Hart, while a schoolmate was named Stella Cornelia Fisher (the daughter of Reverend Fisher from Yokohama). Stella Fisher kindly gave Kafū the address of a friend in Chicago who could show him around on his Spring break (Angles, 2006, pp. 42, 54). Given the Chicago setting, it is likely that Stella Fisher provided Kafū's inspiration in this instance.

26. Kafū's use of the word *Yume* probably refers to Schumann's Opus 15, no.7, *Träumerei*.

27. The setting is undoubtedly based on Kafū's experience of Kalamazoo College, where he studied French language and philosophy from 1904 to 1905.

28. See *Saiyū-nisshishō*, April 12 and 16, 1906; *Amerika no omoide*, KZ 17.205; also Sakagami (1997, p. 98).

29. For such a reading see Hutchinson (2006).

30. *Saiyū-nisshishō*, July 19, 1905.

31. See Itō Sei (8.171). The essay was published in 1909 and may be found in KZ 18.277–304. As Akase Masako notes, Kafū may have read *Sur L'eau* much earlier (1976, pp. 42–44). Kafū would later write in *Danchōtei nichijō* (April 8, 1939), as well as various essays, that *Sur L'eau* was the first French work he read in the French language, so the date of that reading is a topic of some discussion. See for example, Minami (2007, pp. 60, 358n17).

32. *Saiyū-nisshishō*, September 13, 1905.

33. Iriye (1969, p. 62) and others doubt that the relationship was serious, arguing that it functioned more as an exercise in promoting Kafū as romantic hero in the published diary. For a detailed examination see the chapter "Idesu monogatari" in Komon (1972).

34. Kafū's transcript from Kalamazoo College shows his name as Sokichi Nagai, from Tokio, Japan. His three semesters of first-year French resulted in

grades of 87, 80, and 84. No other grades are recorded, perhaps because Kafū enrolled as an "auditor" and may have just attended classes that suited his tastes without having to take final examinations.

35. A more detailed analysis of power relations in *Ichigatsu ichijitsu, Rinkan,* and *Chōhatsu* is found in Hutchinson (2006).

36. This story was published in May 1907, one year after Kafū's own visit to Coney Island, dated in *Saiyū-nisshishō* as May 13, 1906. As noted earlier, Kafū's dates are not entirely reliable, and he may have manipulated the date in the diary (published in 1917) in order to create this anniversary. In either case, the scenery and setting of the story are consistent with weather in mid-May.

37. See for example, Noguchi Takehiko's comments in the roundtable discussion edited by Karatani Kōjin (1992, p. 199).

38. For example, he reads Saitō Ryokū's obituary and the news of Japan's success in Port Arthur: see *Saiyū-nisshishō*, June 27, 1904, January 2, 1905.

39. See Iriye (1969, p. 83) and Snyder (2000, pp. 34–53).

40. *Saiyū-nisshishō*, June 20, 1906.

41. *Saiyū-nisshishō*, June 29, 1906.

42. *Saiyū-nisshishō*, July 8, 1906.

43. See diary entry for August 26, 1906. On September 17 he also mentions reading Maupassant's *Yvette* on his sickbed.

44. On the impact of *Les Soeurs Rondoli* on *Amerika monogatari* see Snyder (2000, pp. 41–53).

45. See entry for January 20, 1906.

46. See Minami (2007, pp. 82–88) on the significance of the "iconographic *jibun*" in *Rinkan, Ochiba,* and *Rokugatsu no yoru no yume.*

47. Keene (1984, p. 405), Seidensticker (1965, p. 23), Ito (1991, p. 36). Komon Katsuji's (1972) chapter on Kafū and Baudelaire was sparked by seeing a photograph of Baudelaire and realizing how closely Kafū managed to resemble the French author in his choice of fashion and hairstyle (pp. 253–282).

48. Yoshida Seiichi (1971b) also argues that we can clearly see the literary influence moving from Zola to Maupassant, reflected in what Kafū was reading in *Saiyū-nisshishō* (p. 57). Akase (1976) traces the influence of Zola, Maupassant, and Baudelaire in chapters 4 and 5 of her book; Iriye (1969) performs a similar genealogy.

49. On *Yoru no onna* and *La Maison Tellier* see Akase (1976, pp. 51–53), Snyder (2000, pp. 38–41); on *Chōhatsu* and *La Moustache* see Akase (1976, pp. 50–51); on *Natsu no umi* and *Sur L'eau* see Minami (2007, pp. 70–71); on *Suibijin* and *Les Souers Rondoli* see Akase (1976, pp. 45–47); on *Nezame* and *Allouma* see Snyder (2000, pp. 51–52).

50. Iriye compares entries in the published and unpublished diaries to show the gap between Kafū's persona, as someone who reads French easily, and the painful reality (1969, pp. 54–55n2).

51. "Orient" is placed in quotation marks and written as *higashi no kuni* in kanji, with a furigana gloss of "*orian*" in katakana, emphasizing the foreign origin of the word (p. 296).

Notes to Chapter 2

1. "*Furansu monogatari* no hatsubai kinshi," *Yomiuri Shimbun* April 11, 1909: see also KZ 26: 87–90; Rubin (1984, p. 120).

2. This story first appeared in the appendix to the 1908 collected volume of *Amerika monogatari,* together with *Rōngawa no hotori* (The Banks of the Rhône) and *Aki no chimata* (Autumn Scenes). They were moved to *Furansu monogatari* for the first *Kafū zenshū* (Shun'yōdō) in 1919. Page numbers in this chapter refer to KZ vol. 3 unless otherwise indicated.

3. This essay was part of the appendix of essays on various European and American art forms, included in the original *Furansu monogatari* that was banned on publication. The essay was not included in any collections until the 1948 Chūō Kōron *Kafū zenshū.*

4. See, for example, Azuma Hideki (1998, p. 16). Kafū noted in his original diary that he visited Maupassant's statue in the Parc Monceau on March 30, 1908, two days after arriving back in the capital after his eight-month stay in Lyon. This part of the diary was not published in the 1917 edition of *Saiyū-nisshishō,* perhaps contributing to confusion over the timing of the visit. Kafū's original "Agenda pour 1908" is contained in KZ 19.56–66.

5. See Hutchinson (2007) on power and observation in the immigrant stories of *Amerika monogatari.* On the importance of vision in *Rinkan* see also Hutchinson (2006, pp. 69–70).

6. Kafū's growing scholarly interest in French poetry and its translation would result in the publication of *Sangoshū* (The Coral Anthology, 1913), still a popular and well-known work.

7. The six stories set in Lyon include the two from the 1908 edition of *Amerika monogatari* (*Rōngawa no hotori* and *Aki no chimata*), plus the first four stories of *Furansu nikki,* first published as follows: *Hebitsukai* (The Snake Charmer), *Waseda bungaku* 36 (November 1908); *Bansan* (The Dinner), *Shumi* 4.1 (January 1909); *Matsuri no yoru gatari* (Tales of a Festival Night), *Shinchō* 10.1 (January 1909); and *Kiri no yoru* (Misty Night), *Warai* 3.1 (January 1909).

8. Stendhal is the pen name of Marie-Henri Beyle (1783–1842). His mix of clear analytic realism with romantic emotion was unappreciated during his lifetime, but by the early twentieth century he had acquired a new, enthusiastic audience.

9. Kafū's translation points to his own understanding of Stendhal's method: "*Ware wa sono mama ni mono no keishō wo utsusan to wa sezu, keishō ni yorite kanjitaru kokoro no sama wo kakan to suru mono nari*" (I do not attempt to reflect the shape of things as they are, but to portray the state of my heart as it responds to them with feeling) (p. 384).

10. Kafū uses the katakana ヴオーグ for this word, presumably referencing the German *volk,* a term that would not have been out of place in Meiji discussion of German social theory. The French word for "gypsy," *tzigane* or *gitan,* is not used in the story, making it probable that this conversation stemmed from Kafū's imagination rather than reality.

11. First published as *Bansan no yoru* (Evening of the Dinner), retitled for the March 1909 *tankōbon* edition of *Furansu monogatari.*

12. The original diary of 1908, kept in a notebook marked "Agenda pour 1908," is found in KZ 19.55–66; for the published version of the 1908 diary see KZ 19.48–54.

13. Kabuto (2005, p. 7).There is quite some difference between the original "Agenda" and what was later published as *Saiyū-nisshishō* in 1917. Kabuto compares the draft diary against the Lyon stories in exhaustive detail, literally walking in Kafū's footsteps to provide new insight into this understudied set of works.

14. Originally titled *Joya* (New Year's Eve), retitled for the first *Kafū zenshū* (Shun'yōdō) in 1919.

15. The "Agenda" version reads: *kono hi, kōzen to jihyō wo ginkō ni dashite* (KZ 19.61), whereas *Saiyū-nisshishō* reads: *kono hi ginkō yori iyoiyo kaiko no mei wo uketari* (KZ 19.51). It is the published version to which Seidensticker refers (1965, p. 26).

16. For a critique of this approach see Hutchinson (2006, pp. 57–59).

17. On Fujita see Doug Slaymaker's *Paris, mon amour: Japanese representations of France* (forthcoming); on Endō's religious pluralism see Mark Williams (2011).

18. On the intertextual references here see Minami (2007, pp. 126–127). *Omokage* was first published as *Karuchiē Ratan no ichiya* in Taiyō 15.1 (January 1909).

19. Tsukuhara is based on the well-known artist Kuroda Seiki (real name Kiyoteru, 1866–1924), and the work is his famous *Morning Toilette* of 1893. Painted in Paris, the nude portrait of a woman doing her hair in a mirror caused great controversy when exhibited in Japan.

20. Minami emphasizes the gap between author and narrator here: Kafū would not have written such an essay on the painting himself, being only fifteen at the time of the exhibition (2007, p. 130).

21. By contrast, the gloom of Kafū's London in *Pari no wakare* (Farewell to Paris) is comparable to Natsume Sōseki's description in *The Tower of London* (1992b).

22. First published in *Shinshōsetsu* 13.12 (December 1908), retitled as *Saikai* for the *tankōbon* edition.

23. See Mori (2005); on the relationship between Ōgai and Kafū, see Snyder (2000, pp. 8–12). *Hitoritabi* was first published in *Chūgaku sekai* 11.11 (September 1908).

24. Readers familiar with *Bokutō kidan* (A Strange Tale from East of the River) will notice that the umbrella is instrumental in more than one Kafū relationship; see also *Pari no wakare.*

25. See Noguchi Takehiko (1991, p. 88).

26. *ADIEU (wakare)* appeared in *Shinchō* 9.4 (October 1908), retitled for the *tankōbon* edition.

27. On reactions to this ban see Rubin (1984, pp. 96, 106–107, 128–129).

Notes to Chapter 3

1. KZ 3.296. Where unspecified in this chapter, the volume is vol. 3 (it includes both *Amerika* and *Furansu monogatari*).

2. Minami (2007, pp. 50–51). Emphasizing American imperialism, Minami cites the annexation of Hawai'i in 1898 and the transferral of the Philippines to American control in the outcome of the Spanish–American War. Whether Kafū knew this history is impossible to ascertain.

3. The terrible fate of Mantellaut is one that many of Kafū's young readers would have liked to succumb to themselves. The carnal body expiring in pleasure makes a stark contrast to the military body extinguished by war, a contrast that would come to be very significant in the *nikutai bungaku*, or "carnal literature" of the immediate postwar period (see Slaymaker, 2004).

4. Tanaka (1993, p. 4). See also Tsuda Sōkichi's essay "Tōyō bunka wa nanka?" (1984).

5. Seidensticker does not identify the story by title (1965, p. 22).

6. See chapter one of this book, also KZ 3.238–44, 541–57.

7. See René Girard (1965, pp. 5–7, 10).

8. Elsewhere I have criticized this approach as "gap theory," a model that emphasizes the gap between East and West and focuses on cultural differences rather than on the writer's representations and critical analyses (2006, pp. 57–59). A more balanced model is found in Yamanouchi (1978), who examines the contradictions felt by Meiji writers between imported Western culture and Japanese tradition, in their search for cultural and individual authenticity.

9. One of the few instances of Kafū reading history as opposed to fiction may be seen in *Saiyū–nisshishō*, January 23, 1906, but this work too is actually a history of French literature.

10. For a thoughtful consideration of connections between colonial power dynamics and literature, see Said (1993).

11. KZ 27.30–31. A translation of the passage may be found in Keene (1984, p. 394).

12. In *Shinkichōsha nikki*, written 1908: KZ 4.196.

13. See *Saiyū–nisshishō*, entries for July 26, 1906 and January 2, 1907.

14. *Kaerimichi* is comprised of four stories, first published as follows: *ADIEU (wakare)*, *Shinchō* 9.4 (October 1908), retitled *Pari no wakare* (Farewell to Paris) for the *tankōbon* edition; *Tasogare no Chichūkai* (Twilight on the Mediterranean), *Shinchō* 9.5 (November 1908); *Pōto Setto* (Port Said), originally titled *Sabaku* (The Desert), first published in the *tankōbon* edition; and *Akkan* (Revulsion), *Shūsai bundan* 9.1 (January 1909), retitled as *Shingapōru no sūjikan* (A Few Hours in Singapore) for the Chūō Kōron collected works of 1948. *Tasogare no Chichūkai* recently appeared in translation: see Nagai (2005).

15. It is unclear why Kafū chose to transliterate the name of the town as "Pōto Setto" rather than "Pōto Saiido." No reason is given in either the Iwanami Shoten or the Shinchō bunko edition of *Furansu monogatari*. Most Japanese critics avoid the problem by using the original title of *Sabaku* (The Desert).

16. See entry for February 9, 1906.

17. Suzuki (1995, p. 179). On Orientalism as an artistic genre see MacKenzie (1995).

18. On Flaubert as Orientalist see Said (1995, pp. 184–190); on Chateaubriand see pp. 170–175.

19. *Saiyū–nisshishō*, February 14, 1907.

20. Leconte De Lisle's nineteenth-century assumption that Greece was the fount of European civilization may be taken as evidence for the shift away from regarding Egypt and the Biblical lands in this way, which took place during the eighteenth century. See Bernal (1987).

21. See *Saiyū-nisshishō*, January 7, 1907, where he reads "the sorrowful poetry of Musset" for the first time.

22. KZ 3.578. The bracketed English represents Kafū's Japanese translation.

23. It is worthwhile to note the danger of merely replacing a China–Japan dialectic with a West–Japan dialectic as soon as the Meiji period begins. As James Fujii (1993) argues, the division of premodern and modern Japanese literature into discourses respectively shaped by China–Japan and West–Japan oppositions "reflects the unquestioned assumption of Western humanist–realist conventions as the basis for reading modern Japanese texts" (pp. 196–197).

24. Said (1995, p. 24). Although Robert Young (1990) points out the fundamental incompatibility of the agency of the individual in this statement and Said's insistence on the totality of a closed system (pp. 134–137), I believe it can be useful because I do not depend on closure, and thus can admit the agency of the individual writer as well as the authority of the textual formation he relies upon.

25. Edwin McClellan (1969) notes that Sōseki's English verse was "unsuccessful" (p. 7), while Aiko Ito and Graeme Wilson term it "appalling" (see Natsume, 2002, p. xiii).

26. Arishima Takeo's travel diary, kept partly in English, is a good example: see *Arishima Takeo zenshū* vol.12. He may also have been trying to retain his written ability in the language, after completing his Master's degree at Haverford College in 1904 and taking several postgraduate courses at Harvard University (Morton, 1988, pp. 58, 63). English was also useful for keeping private thoughts secret from servants and family, and held special significance as the medium by which he experienced Christianity (Morton: e-mail correspondence, June 9, 2010). A notable exception for the period is Yone Noguchi, whose remarkable facility in English allowed him to publish several volumes of poetry, critical essays, travelogues, and a novel, with publishing houses from London to New York, San Francisco, and Boston. His poetry influenced Ezra Pound, Willa Cather, and William Yeats, while his essays on Noh and *ukiyo-e* were popular both at home and abroad. See the edited collections of Noguchi's work (1990–1992, 2007).

27. A one-act opera by Pietro Mascagni (1863–1945).

28. *Tristan und Isolde*, a three-act opera by Richard Wagner (1813–1883).

29. The term *jōruri* denotes a variety of dramatic performance using musical accompaniment (usually samisen) to the recitation of the plot.

30. Takemoto Gidayū (1651–1714 or possibly 1724) established *jōruri* as an independent art form. His name *gidayū* is now a common noun denoting both recitation and reciter.

31. Miyakōji (later Tokiwazu) Mojidayū (1709–1781) created an important form of *jōruri* considered a narrative style particularly used in kabuki drama.

32. Utazawabushi denotes a type of romantic ballad in a style developed by Sasamoto Hikotarō (Utazawa Yamato-no-Daijō) in the Edo period.

33. See entry for March 21, 1907 (written in English): *Arishima Takeo zenshū* 12.1060–1063.

34. The narrator in Sōseki's travelogue is presented as Sōseki himself, but as Brodey argues, he is still a deliberately constructed figure (Natsume, 2000, pp. 22–30). Arishima's observations are presented in diary format, but we may assume that he edited and mediated his diary entries for publication, much as Kafū did with *Saiyū-nisshishō*.

35. The word "subaltern" carries with it an enormous array of meaning and signification, but usually implies an opposing voice to the overwhelming Western Orientalist tradition, or a reclaiming of subject/agent status. See O'Hanlon (1988).

36. Said is criticized more on the point of closure and agency than any other point, as it ultimately involves enormous questions of human agency, including the question of humanism versus determinism. It is by now well established that the monolithic, determinist binary systems that inform Said's work are untenable as a theoretical framework. For a thorough examination of closure and determinism in *Orientalism*, see Young (1990, esp. ch.7: "Disorienting Orientalism").

37. Cited in Minami (2007, p. 147).

38. For details on the ban and its enforcement see Rubin (1984, pp. 117–120).

Notes to Chapter 4

1. These works were first published as follows: *Fukagawa no uta, Shumi,* February 1909; *Botan no kyaku, Chūō kōron,* July 1909; *Kanraku, Shinshōsetsu,* July 1909; *Donten, Teikoku bungaku,* March 1909; *Kitsune, Chūgaku sekai,* January 1909; *Kangokusho no ura, Waseda bungaku,* March 1909; *Sumidagawa, Shinshōsetsu,* December 1909; *Shinkichōsha nikki* (original title *Kichōsha no nikki*), *Chūō kōron,* October 1909; *Reishō, Tokyo Asahi Shimbun,* December 1909–February 1910.

2. See Karatani (1993b, p. 76). Karatani analyzes the expression of both "self" and interiority in relation to a wider confessional system in modern Japanese literature.

3. All page numbers in this chapter refer to KZ vol. 4 unless otherwise stated.

4. Natsume Sōseki (1977, p. 17; 1997, pp. 256–257).

5. See Seidensticker (1983, pp. 44–47) on the confusion caused by the streetcar system, also Maeda Ai's comments on Tayama Katai's journal (2004, pp. 332–333).

6. See Dodd (2004) on the idea of "home" in the writings of Kunikida Doppō, Shimazaki Tōson, Satō Haruo, and Shiga Naoya. This discourse reached a high point with Kobayashi Hideo's essay of May 1933, "Literature of the Lost Home," lamenting the loss or lack of "home" in the modern metropolis of Tokyo (Kobayashi 1995, pp. 46–54).

7. Translated by Lane Dunlop (Nagai 1994b, pp. 11–30).

8. Maeda (2004, p. 105), translated by William F. Sibley.

9. Fukuzawa Yukichi's (1835–1901) books were bestsellers, particularly *Seiyō jijō* (Conditions in the West, 1866), *Gakumon no susume* (An Encouragement of Learning, 1872–1876), and *Bunmeiron no gaimyaku* (An Outline of a Theory of Civilization, 1875). Katō Hiroyuki (1836–1916) was well known for the essay "Bunmei kaika," in which he called for Japanese to "all embrace civilization and expose for what they are such notions as those that hold that foxes change themselves into human form" (see Maeda 2004, p. 102). Both men were part of the Meirokusha society and published in the journal *Meiroku zasshi*, from 1874.

10. Keene 1984, p. 416; the translated phrase from *Donten* is also Keene's (1984, p. 415).

11. KZ 4.55–56; quoted in Rubin (1984, p. 123). Rubin's translation.

12. Page numbers for *Botan no kyaku* refer to Seidensticker's translation in Nagai (1972, pp. 47–53).

13. Yoshida Seiichi and Horiguchi Daigaku both commented on the similarity of *Fukagawa no uta* and Henri du Régnier's *Les Rencontres de Monsieur de Bréot*, set in Venice (Akase, 1995, p. 48). Akase discusses Kafū's essay of February 1909 "Renie no shi to shōsetsu" (Akase, 1995, p. 45) and also compares the two novels (1976, pp. 155–156).

14. Rubin (1984, pp. 115–117). On the Shimbunshi Hō (Press Laws) of 1909 see Kasza (1988, pp. 14–20) and Mitchell (1983, pp. 141–144).

15. The Shinkankaku-ha, or New Perception School, experimented with literature to directly express the action through the sense experience of the narrator. Yokomitsu Riichi's novel *Shanghai*, published 1928–1931, is a good example. Dennis Washburn explains the New Perception manifesto in his afterword to *Shanghai* (Yokomitsu 2001, pp. 221–225).

16. Translation by Matsumoto Ryōzō (Nagai 1961, p. 31). The story *Kanraku* is found in KZ 4.3–47; for the collection of the same name see KZ 4.1–173.

17. Page numbers for *Sumidagawa* refer to Seidensticker's translation in Nagai (1972, pp. 9–46).

18. On the advent of *shimpa* theater see Powell (2002, pp. 11–23), also Ortolani (1990, pp. 219–228).

19. Tamenaga Shunsui's (1790–1843) *Shunshoku umegoyomi*, 1832–1833, is regarded as the foremost example of late Tokugawa *ninjōbon* literature. See Keene (1976, pp. 417–423).

20. The following discussion of Kafū's constructions of the West in *Shinkichōsha nikki* and *Reishō* is indebted to an earlier article (Hutchinson, 2001). *Shinkichōsha nikki* is found in KZ 4.175–248.

21. For a detailed analysis of the Edo/Tokyo theme here see Schulz (1997). On the importance of Tokyo to Kafū's literature see Kawamoto (1996), Seidensticker (1983), and Waley (1984, 1991).

22. Construction on the Basilique du Sacré–Coeur began in 1875, and was completed in 1914.

23. Snyder (2000) argues that the figure of the geisha in Kafū's fiction derives as much from European as from Edo literature, and that the link between Kafū's geisha and "Edo" has been overemphasized (pp. 54–57), but this passage specifically pairs the geisha with Edo to emphasize their protective cultural role.

24. Koizumi Kōichirō (1984) expresses this counter-discourse in terms of the difference between the cultural *minshū*, headed by the geisha, and the Meiji state or *kokka* (p. 49). Evelyn Schulz (1997) describes the idea of Edo in *Shinkichōsha nikki* as an "aesthetic counterworld" by which he may criticize modernization. On the subversion of social norms through the figure of the geisha or prostitute in the demimonde fiction of Japan and France, see Snyder (2000, p. 61).

25. On the shifting meanings of *bunmei* see Morris–Suzuki (1998, pp. 140–160).

26. Maeda (2004, pp. 336–337). Maeda cites Barthes' article as "Semiotics and a Theory of the City," translated into Japanese by Shinoda Kōichirō as "Kigōgaku to toshi no riron" in *Gendai shisō* (October 1975) (Maeda, 2004, p. 349n16). The English translation quoted here is titled "Semiology and the Urban," a lecture originally given on May 16, 1967 at the University of Naples (Barthes, 1997).

27. Walter Benjamin's idea of the *flâneur* is applied to Kafū's work by Snyder (2000).

28. *Hiyorigeta* may be found in KZ 13.293–391.

29. For example, see Minami Asuka (1992, p. 155). *Reishō* is found in KZ 4.249–465.

30. Yokomitsu Riichi, "On Pure Fiction" (*Junsui shōsetsu ron*): see Bourdaghs (2002, p. xxiiin21).

31. See *Reishō ni tsukite*, KZ 13.44.

32. On *aware* see Tsunoda, de Bary, and Keene (1958, pp. 176–178, 283–284).

33. Pinnington (2006, pp. 89–90n3) makes a strong argument against Nishihara (2003) and what we might call the "reverse Orientalism" school, which does not take the power dynamics of Orientalism into account and casts Japan only in the role of colonizer, not colonized.

34. The essay is also in *Kōcha no ato* part 5 (*Mita bungaku* 1.6, October 1910): see pp. 243–244.

35. In the original Japanese, "*koto wo mo niowashita tsumori de aru.*"

36. See Tanizaki 1977, pp. 7–8. The essay was first published in *Keizai orai* (December 1933 and January 1934).

Notes to Chapter 5

1. Good examples are Isao Hata's poem in vol. 1.2 (June 1910) and the previously mentioned essays by Yone Noguchi. *Mita bungaku* will hereafter be abbreviated in the notes as *MB*.

2. *MB* 2.8 (August 1911, p. 144).

3. All the *Shinkyō yawa* tales were published in *MB* except for *Kazagokochi,* which appeared in *Chūō kōron*. *Edo geijutsuron* was published as one volume in 1920.

4. Publication details are as follows: *Kaketori, MB,* February 1912; *Iro–otoko, MB,* March 1912; *Kazagokochi, Chūō kōron,* April 1912; *Meika, MB,* June 1912; *Matsuba–domoe, MB,* July 1912; *Satsuki–yami, MB,* September 1912; *Asase, MB,* April 1912; *Mijika–yo, MB,* August 1911; *Hirusugi, MB,* May 1912. All were published in one volume by Momiyama Shoten, November 1912.

5. The enduring popularity of this format for the collection may be seen in the fact that my own paperback version, released on 14th printing by Iwanami Shoten in pocket edition in 1996, keeps the same configuration of stories.

6. Jay Rubin discusses the content and censorship of *Shukuhai* (1984, pp. 124–125); on *Shōtaku* see Keene (1984, pp. 419–420).

7. Page numbers in this chapter refer to KZ vol. 5 unless stated otherwise.

8. Seidensticker emphasizes the lure of the "lower reaches of society" in both Paris and Edo (1965, p. 25). Snyder argues that French and Edo literature had "equivalent importance" for Kafū's narrative and themes (2000, p. 62), with the demimonde fiction of both Paris and Edo providing models for his female characters (2000, p. 56). Iriye also emphasizes the equivalence of the Edo gay quarters and the French salon in Kafū's thinking (1969, pp. 192, 211).

9. Tanizaki Jun'ichirō found the influence of both Flaubert and Maupassant to be strong in *Tsuyu no atosaki* (During the Rains, 1931): see Seidensticker (1965, p. 131).

10. Originally titled *Nemurarenu yoru no taiwa* (Dialogue on a Sleepless Night).

11. Yonehachi and Tanjirō are major characters from Tamenaga Shunsui's *Shunshoku umegoyomi.*

12. See for example *Kōya hijiri* (The Holy Man of Mount Kōya, 1900) as well as *Shunchū* and *Shunchū gokoku* (One Day in Spring, Parts One and Two, 1906), translated by Charles Shirō Inouye. On Kyōka's urban–rural counterpoint see Inouye's introduction (Izumi, 1996, pp. 1–10).

13. Originally titled *Wakadanna* (The Young Master).

14. On Tanjirō's complex relationships see Kazuya Jinbō (1964, esp. ch.2, "*Shunshoku umegoyomi* wo megutte," pp. 83–131).

15. The High Treason (or Kōtoku) Incident, a plot uncovered to assassinate the Meiji emperor resulting in the execution of twelve socialists including Kōtoku Shūsui, is thoroughly examined in Notehelfer (1971, pp. 152–200), Banno (1989, pp. 306–308), and Keene (2002, pp. 680–692). For the

reaction among other Meiji intellectuals and writers see Rubin (1984, pp. 145–194).

16. A good example is the discussion between Asada Akira, Noguchi Takehiko, Hasumi Shigehiko, Karatani Kōjin, and Miura Masashi, "Taishō hihyō no shomondai" (Karatani, 1992, pp. 199–203).

17. The essay can be found in KZ 18.231–53.

18. The interview appeared in the *Yomiuri Shimbun*, April 12, 1909, in a piece entitled "*Furansu Monogatari* no hatsubai kinshi." See Satō Shizuo (1995, p. 142).

19. *Yomiuri* interview, April 12, 1909, quoted in Satō Shizuo (1995, pp. 142–143).

20. Rubin (1984, pp. 7–8). For details on the Meiji Press Laws see pp. 115–117.

21. From an interview in *Chūō kōron*, July 1909, quoted in Rubin (1984, p. 120).

22. See Rubin (1984, pp. 117–125; 190–191).

23. See the discussion in Karatani Kōjin (1992, pp. 200–201).

24. (1998, p. 271). Other writers Gluck includes in this group are Tokutomi Sohō, Kuki Shūzō, Yanagita Kunio, and Watsuji Testurō.

25. See Spencer (1958, p. 197), Sheldon (1958), and Ike (1950), also Smith (1962, pp. 215–219).

26. Satō Shizuo (1995, pp. 138–139). Kafū named the "Danchōtei" (Dyspepsia House) after his illness. Although some, like Earhart (1994), take the diary more or less at face value, others point out its edited, constructed nature (Seidensticker 2002, p. 143). The point here is how Kafū chose to portray himself in the persona of a "hermit," the deliberate construction of which is supported by the idea of an overly edited diary. Seidensticker's comments on the 1917 diary are also applicable here (1965, p. 94).

27. Satō (1947, p. 9); see also Isoda Kōichi's comments in "Nagai Kafū no sekai" (Isoda Kōichi, Maeda Ai, and Nakajima Kunihiko, 1984, p. 22).

28. Goodman (1990, ch. 7: "*Kikokushijo* in Historical Perspective," esp. pp. 196–197). Also see Bennett, Passin, and McKnight (1958, pp. 28–42).

29. See Asada's comments in Karatani Kōjin (1992, p. 200).

30. See Isoda Kōichi's comments in the discussion with Maeda Ai and Nakajima Kunihiko, "Nagai Kafū no sekai" (1984, p. 22).

31. See comments in Karatani Kōjin (1992, p. 199).

32. Tanizaki (1977); see also *Tanizaki Jun'ichirō zenshū* (1966–1970), 20.515–557.

33. A further measure of Kafū's influence on Tanizaki is that Ken Ito's book *Visions of Desire* (1991) deals substantially with Kafū's work in order to illuminate aspects of Tanizaki's. On Kafū's relationship with Tanizaki see Seidensticker (2002, p. 143).

34. The work appears in *Kuki Shūzō zenshū* (1981), 1.1–83. Translated by Hiroshi Nara (2004).

35. A good historical overview is found in Najita and Harootunian (1988).

36. On Sōseki's speeches, *Gendai Nihon no kaika* (The Enlightenment of Modern Japan, Aug. 1911), and *Watakushi no kojinshugi* (My Individualism,

November 1914), see Yamanouchi (1978, pp. 76–79). The latter speech has been translated twice: compare Rubin's translation (Natsume, 1992a, pp. 285–322) with Tsunematsu's (Natsume, 2005, pp. 25–57).

37. Washburn (1995) expresses the "dilemma of the modern" as an attempt to resolve the discontinuities between past and present through narrative, which reasserts continuity by virtue of its conventional literary form. Washburn shows how Kafū, Sōseki and Ōgai were engaged in similar projects of formal experimentation in addressing this deep sense of discontinuity.

38. (Nagai, 2007, p. viii). Snyder's 2007 translation of the 1956 unexpurgated version of *Udekurabe* reinstates many sections that do not appear in Meissner and Friedrich's 1963 translation. Kafū had privately published a complete version of the novel in late 1917, but the commercial edition of 1918 was heavily edited to avoid censorship. Meissner and Friedrich's translation, based on the 1918 text, omits scenes of a sexual nature that do much to explain the tensions between Komayo and her patron Yoshioka. Page numbers in the text refer to Snyder's translation.

39. On the importance of the gaze in *Udekurabe,* see Snyder (2000, pp. 78–84).

40. On Komayo as desiring subject see Snyder (2000, pp. 72–78, 90). Yoshida Seiichi described Komayo as "three-dimensional" (1971, p. 129), and *Udekurabe* is generally received as a "realistic" novel. Komayo may have been based on Kafū's wife of 1914–1915, the geisha Yaeji (see Nagai, 2007, pp. viii–ix). On their tumultuous relationship see Seidensticker (1965, pp. 54–58).

41. In March 1916 Kafū returned to his family home in leafy Ōkubo to build the Danchōtei studio in the grounds. Critics tend to use the similarity between the Nagai residence and Kurayama's to suggest Kurayama is a fictionalized Kafū (see Snyder, 2000, p. 87).

42. Serialized in *Chūō kōron* and the journal *Kagetsu* from January to December 1918. On the complex publication details of this work see Snyder (2000, p. 92).

43. On self-reflexivity in *Amerika monogatari* see Hutchinson (2007, p. 325).

44. References in the text are to Lane Dunlop's translation (Nagai, 1994a, pp. 1–133).

45. Mitsuko Iriye sees Tsuruko as the Japanese version of Rosalyn, Kafū's ideal Western woman from the end of *Amerika monogatari* (1969, p. 79).

46. Mochida Nobuko (2005) presents a "feminine Kafū," a writer whose love of nature and restaurants, independent strength and hatred of war resonate well with contemporary female readers. Reading Kafū's works more thoroughly in terms of feminist theory would seem to be the next logical step in analyzing his social critique.

47. References in the text are to Lane Dunlop's translation (Nagai, 1994a, pp. 137–223).

48. Earhart (1994) presents Kafū as a "staunch individualist long opposed to authoritarianism and militarism" (p. 488), while Seidensticker (1965) describes Kafū's silence as a viable alternative to being "swept up in the hysteria" of the war (p. 156). Keene (1984) notes that although Kafū "in no way opposed the war in China or in the Pacific," he also "wrote absolutely

nothing in support of the war" and expressed "contempt for the militarists" in his diary (pp. 434–435).

49. This is Seidensticker's translation of the title *Shissō*. Page numbers for *Bokutō kidan* refer to Seidensticker's translation in Nagai (1972, pp. 106–156).

50. Compare the classic style of Toyoda Shirō (1960) with the more recent version by Shindō Kaneto: *The Strange Tale of Oyuki* (1992) emphasizes Kafū's anti-war stance as well as dramatically eroticizing the central relationship.

Notes to Conclusion

1. On the axes of class, race and sanity in *Amerika monogatari* see Hutchinson (2007).

2. For example see Keene (1984, p. 396). *Yashin* appears in KZ 1.431–514.

3. See *Kōcha no ato*, part 10 (*MB* 2.8, August 1911, p. 144).

4. Compare *Bokutō kidan* with *Kunshō* (The Decoration, 1946), both in Nagai (1972).

5. Comaroff (1989) emphasizes that "colonialism" is not itself a homogeneous, "monolithic," easily definable experience, but a highly varied and contextualized one (pp. 661–685).

6. See Tang (1993), Hershatter (1993), also Hockx and Smits (2002).

7. Seidensticker's own experience with the Pacific War and Occupation is detailed in his memoir, *Tokyo Central* (2002).

8. Oguma (2002, pp. 3–92; esp. 81–92). Oguma posits the "mixed nation" theory as far more popular and influential than the competing "national polity" discourse that argued for Japan as a homogeneous and singular unit.

9. See quotations from the diary in Earhart (1994, pp. 492–496, 501).

Bibliography

Where unspecified the place of publication is Tokyo.

Akase Masako. (1976). *Nagai Kafū to Furansu bungaku*. Aratake.

———. (1995). *Hikaku bungaku / hikaku bunka: Furansu bungaku / Furansu bunka no eikyō*. Momoyama Gakuin Daigaku Sōgō Kenkyūjo.

Akiba Tarō. (1977). *Nagai Kafū den*. Shun'yōdō.

———. (1983). *Shinkō Nagai Kafū*. Shun'yōdō.

Akiyama, Masayuki. (1981). The American Image in Kafū Nagai and Henry James. *Comparative Literature Studies, 18*, 95–103.

Amino Yoshihiro. (1992). Nagai Kafū: Edo bunka e mukerareta me. *Kokubungaku Kaishaku to Kanshō, 57*(5), 64–71.

———. (1993). *Kafū bungaku to sono shūhen*. Kanrin Shobō.

Angles, Jeffrey. (2006). Nagai Kafū to Karamazū to sono jidai. *Mita bungaku 84*(Winter), 38–57.

Arishima Takeo. (1924–1925). *Arishima Takeo zenshū* (12 vols.). Sōbunkaku.

Azuma Hideki. (1998). *Kafū to Ru Gorubyujie no Pari*. Shinchōsha.

Banno Junji. (1989). *Taikei Nihon no rekishi vol. 13: Kindai Nihon no shuppatsu*, Shogakukan.

Barthes, Roland. (1997). Semiology and the urban. In Neil Leach (Ed.), *Rethinking architecture: A reader in cultural theory* (pp.166–172). London & New York: Routledge.

Beasley, W.G. (1990). *The rise of modern Japan*. Tuttle.

Behdad, Ali. (1994). *Belated travelers: Orientalism in the age of colonial dissolution*. Durham, NC & London: Duke University Press.

Bennett, John W., Passin, Herbert, & McKnight, Robert K. (1958). *In search of identity: The Japanese overseas scholar in America and Japan*. Minneapolis: University of Minnesota Press.

Bernal, Martin. (1987). *Black Athena: The Afroasiatic roots of classical civilization, Vol. I: The fabrication of Ancient Greece 1785–1985*. New Brunswick, NJ: Rutgers University Press.

Bourdaghs, Michael. (Ed. & Trans.). (2002). *Transformations of sensibility: The phenomenology of Meiji literature, by Kamei Hideo*. Ann Arbor: Center for Japanese Studies, University of Michigan Press.

———. (2003). *The dawn that never comes: Shimazaki Tōson and Japanese nationalism*. New York: Columbia University Press.

Burke, Kenneth. (1969). *A grammar of motives*. Berkeley: University of California Press.

Buruma, Ian, & Margalit, Avishai. (2004). *Occidentalism: The West in the eyes of its enemies*. New York, Toronto, & London: Penguin.

Carrier, James G. (1992). Occidentalism: the world turned upside-down. *American Ethnologist, 19*(2), 195–212.

———. (Ed.). (1995). *Occidentalism: Images of the West*. Oxford: Clarendon Press.

Carter, Steven D. (1988). What's so strange about *A Strange Tale*? Kafu's narrative persona in *Bokutō kidan*. *Journal of the Association of Teachers of Japanese, 22*(2), 151–168.

Chen, Xiaomei. (1995). *Occidentalism: A theory of counter-discourse in Post-Mao China*. Oxford & New York: Oxford University Press.

Comaroff, John L. (1989). Images of empire, contests of conscience: Models of colonial domination in South Africa. *American Ethnologist, 16*(4), 661–685.

Dale, Peter. (1986). *The myth of Japanese uniquenes*. London & Sydney: Croom Helm.

Dodd, Stephen. (2004). *Writing home: Representations of the native place in modern Japanese literature*. New York & London: Harvard University Press.

Dower, John W. (1986). *War without mercy: Race and power in the Pacific War*. New York: Pantheon Books.

Earhart, David C. (1994). Nagai Kafū's wartime diary: The enormity of nothing. *Japan Quarterly, 41*(4), 488–503.

Foucault, Michel. (1967). *Madness and civilization: A history of insanity in the age of reason*. London: Tavistock.

———. (1977). *Discipline and punish: The birth of the prison*. London: Allen Lane.

———. (1979). *The history of sexuality* (Vol. 1). London: Allen Lane.

Fowler, Edward. (1992). Rendering words, traversing cultures: On the art and politics of translating modern Japanese fiction. *Journal of Japanese Studies, 18*(1), 1–44.

Fujii, James A. (1993). Writing out Asia: Modernity, canon, and Natsume Sōseki's *Kokoro*. *positions, 1*(1), 194–223.

———. (2004). Introduction. In James A. Fujii (Ed.), *Text and the city: Essays on Japanese modernity, by Maeda Ai* (pp. 1–17). Durham, NC & London: Duke University Press.

Furuya Kenzō. (1999). *Nagai Kafū: fuyu to no deai*. Asahi Shimbunsha.

Girard, René. (1965). *Deceit, desire and the novel: Self and other in literary structure* (Yvonne Freccero, Trans.). Baltimore & London: Johns Hopkins University Press.

Gluck, Carol. (1985). *Japan's modern myths: Ideology in the late Meiji period*. Princeton, NJ: Princeton University Press.

———. (1998). The Invention of Edo. In Stephen Vlastos (Ed.), *Mirror of modernity: Invented traditions of modern Japan* (pp. 262–284). Berkeley, Los Angeles, & London: University of California Press.

Goodheart, Eugene. (1991). *Desire and its discontents.* New York: Columbia University Press.

Goodman, Roger. (1990). *Japan's "International Youth": The emergence of a new class of schoolchildren.* Oxford: Clarendon Press.

———, White, Gordon, & Kwon, Huck-ju. (1998). *The East Asian welfare model: Welfare Orientalism and the state.* London & New York: Routledge.

Groemer, Gerald. (2001). The guild of the blind in Tokugawa Japan. *Monumenta Nipponica 56*(3), 349–380.

Harootunian, Harry, & Sakai, Naoki. (1999). Japan studies and cultural studies. *positions, 7*(2), 593–641.

Henshall, Kenneth G. (1982). A call for the reconsideration of the Japanese concept of naturalism. In A.R. Davis & A.D. Stefanowska (Eds.), *Austrina: Essays in commemoration of the 25th anniversary of the founding of the Oriental Society of Australia.* Sydney: Wentworth Press, pp. 401–421.

Hershatter, Gail. (1993). The subaltern talks back: Reflections on subaltern theory and Chinese history. *positions, 1*(1), 103–130.

Hibi Yoshitaka. (1998). Kikoku chokugo no Nagai Kafū: "Geijutsuka" zō no keisei. *Nihongo to Nihonbungaku, 26,* 21–33.

Hockx, Michel, & Smits, Ivo. (Eds.). (2002). *Reading East Asian writing: The limits of literary theory.* London: RoutledgeCurzon.

Homma, Kenshiro. (1983). *The literature of naturalism: An east–west comparative study.* Kyoto: Yamaguchi.

Hutchinson, Rachael. (2001). Occidentalism and critique of Meiji: The west in the Returnee Stories of Nagai Kafū. *Japan Forum, 13*(2), 195–213.

———. (2006). Who holds the whip? Power and critique in Nagai Kafū's *Tales of America.* In Rachael Hutchinson & Mark Williams (Eds.), *Representing the other in modern Japanese literature: A critical approach* (pp. 57–74). London & New York: Routledge.

———. (2007). Positioning the observer: Interrogations of alterity in Nagai Kafū's *Amerika monogatari. Monumenta Nipponica. 62*(3), 323–345.

———, & Williams, Mark. (2006). Introduction. In Rachael Hutchinson & Mark Williams (Eds.), *Representing the other in modern Japanese literature: A critical approach* (pp. 1–18). London & New York: Routledge.

Ike, Nobutaka. (1950). *The beginnings of a political democracy in Japan.* Baltimore: Johns Hopkins University Press.

Iriye, Akira. (1975). Japan as competitor, 1895–1917. In Akira Iriye (Ed.), *Mutual images: Essays in American–Japanese relations* (pp. 73–99). Cambridge, MA & London: Harvard University Press.

Iriye, Mitsuko. (1969). *Quest for literary resonance: Young Nagai Kafū and French literature.* Unpublished doctoral dissertation, Harvard University, Cambridge, MA.

Isoda Kōichi. (1989). *Nagai Kafū,* Kōdansha.

———. (1990). *Shisō to shite no Tōkyō—kindai bungaku shiron nōto.* Kōronsha.

———, Maeda, Ai, & Nakajima Kunihiko. (1984). Nagai Kafū no sekai. *Kokubungaku Kaishaku to Kanshō, 49*(4), 18–36.

Ito Kazuo. (1973). *Issei: A history of Issei immigration in North America*. Seattle, WA: Japanese Community Service.

Ito Ken. (1991). *Visions of desire: Tanizaki's fictional worlds*. Stanford, CA: Stanford University Press.

Itō, Sei. (1978–1979). *Nihon bundanshi* (24 vols.). Kōdansha.

Izumi Kyōka. (1996). *Japanese gothic tales* (Charles Shirō Inouye, Trans.). Honolulu: University of Hawai'i Press.

Kabuto Hirokuni. (2005). *Kafū no Riyon: "Furansu monogatari" wo aruku*, Hakusuisha.

Kamei, Shunsuke. (1975). The sacred land of liberty: Images of America in nineteenth-century Japan. In Akira Iriye (Ed.), *Mutual images: Essays in American–Japanese relations* (pp. 55–72). Cambridge, MA & London: Harvard University Press.

Kanno Akimasa. (1996). *Nagai Kafū junreki*, Iwanami Shoten.

Karatani Kōjin. (Ed.). (1992). *Kindai Nihon no hihyō: Meiji-Taishō hen*. Fukutake Shoten.

———. (1993a). The discursive space of modern Japan. In Masao Miyoshi & H.D. Harootunian (Eds.), *Japan in the world* (pp. 288–315). Durham, NC & London: Duke University Press.

———. (1993b). *Origins of modern Japanese literature* (Brett de Bary, Trans. & Ed.). Durham, NC & London: Duke University Press.

Kasza, Gregory James. (1988). *The state and mass media in Japan, 1918–1945*. Berkeley & London: University of California Press.

Katō, Shūichi. (1979). *A history of modern Japanese literature, Vol. 3: The modern years* (Donald Sanderson, Trans. & Ed.). Tokyo, New York, & London: Kodansha International.

Kawamoto Saburō. (1996). *Kafū to Tōkyō*. Toshi Shuppan.

Kazuya Jinbō. (1964). *Tamenaga Shunsui no kenkyū*. Shirohisha.

Keene, Donald. (1976). *World within walls: Japanese literature of the pre-modern Era, 1600–1867*. London: Secker & Warburg.

———. (1984). *Dawn to the west: Japanese literature in the modern era*. New York: Holt.

———. (1993). Japanese literature in the world. *Southern Humanities Review, 27*, 305–319.

———. (2002). *Emperor of Japan: Meiji and his world, 1852–1912*. New York: Columbia University Press.

Kobayashi Hideo. (1995). Literature of the lost home. In Paul Anderer (Trans., & Ed.), *Literature of the lost home: Kobayashi Hideo—Literary criticism 1924–1939* (pp. 46–54). Stanford: Stanford University Press.

Kohl, Stephen W. (1979). An early account of Japanese life in the Pacific Northwest: Writings of Nagai Kafū. *Pacific Northwest Quarterly, 70*, 58–68.

Koike Masatane. (1984). Nagai Kafū to Edo: *Edo geijutsuron* no kiban. *Kokubungaku Kaishaku to Kanshō, 49*(4), 112–117.

Koizumi Kōichirō. (1984). *Shinkichōsha Nikki* no isō. *Kokubungaku Kaishaku to Kanshō, 49*(4), 44–50.

Komon Katsuji. (1972). *Nagai Kafū no shōgai*. Tōjusha.

Komori Yōichi. (1997). Rekishi.chisei-teki sakka Nagai Kafū: *Furansu monogatari* kara *Bokutō kidan* e. *Eureka, 29*(3), 124–135.

Kōno Kensuke. (1997). Sei, tairiku, koroniarizumu—*Amerika monogatari, Furansu monogatari* ni okeru "intercourse." *Eureka, 29*(3), 170–175.

Kuki Shūzō. (1980–1982). *Kuki Shūzō zenshū* (12 vols.). Iwanami Shoten.

Lamarre, Thomas. (2005). *Shadows on the screen: Tanizaki Jun'ichirō on cinema and "Oriental" aesthetics* (Michigan Monograph Series in Japanese Studies, no. 53). Ann Arbor: Center for Japanese Studies, University of Michigan Press.

Levinas, Emmanuel. (1999). *Alterity and transcendence* (Michael B. Smith, Trans.). New York: Columbia University Press.

Lowe, Lisa. (1991). *Critical terrains: French and British Orientalisms*. Ithaca, NY: Cornell University Press.

MacKenzie, John M. (1995). *Orientalism: History, theory and the arts*. Manchester: Manchester University Press.

Maeda Ai. (1982). *Toshi kūkan no naka no bungaku*. Chikuma Shobō.

———. (2004). *Text and the city: Essays on Japanese modernity* (James A. Fujii, Ed.). Durham, NC & London: Duke University Press.

Matsuda Ryōichi. (1994). Sakkyoku suru <watashi>: Nagai Kafū *Furansu monogatari* no katari. *Kokubungaku Kaishaku to Kanshō, 59*(4), 102–107.

Matsumoto Hajime. (1998). *Kafū gokuraku*. Sanshōdō.

Matsuzawa, Hiroaki. (1984). Varieties of *Bunmei Ron* (Theories of Civilization). In Hilary Conroy, Sandra T.W. Davis, & Wayne Patterson (Eds.), *Japan in transition: Thought and action in the Meiji era, 1868–1912* (pp. 209–223). London & Toronto: Associated University Presses.

McClellan, Edward. (1969). *Two Japanese novelists: Sōseki and Tōson*. Chicago & London: University of Chicago Press.

Melman, Billie. (1992). *Women's Orients, English women and the Middle East, 1718–1918: Sexuality, religion and work*. Ann Arbor: University of Michigan Press.

Minami Asuka. (1992). Nagai Kafū *Reishō*. *Kokubungaku Kaishaku to Kanshō, 57*(4), 153–158.

———. (2007). *Nagai Kafū no Nyū Yōku, Pari, Tōkyō: zōkei no kotoba*, Kanrin Shobō.

Minear, Richard H. (1980). Orientalism and the study of Japan. *Journal of Asian Studies, 30*(3), 507–517.

Mitchell, Richard H. (1983). *Censorship in imperial Japan*. Princeton, NJ: Princeton University Press.

Miyoshi, Masao. (1991). *Off center: Power and culture relations between Japan and the United States*. Cambridge, MA & London: Harvard University Press.

Mochida Nobuko. (2005). *Asane no Kafū*. Jimbun Shoin.

Moore-Gilbert, B.J. (1986). *Kipling and "Orientalism."* London & Sydney: Croom Helm.

Mori Ōgai. (1962). Under reconstruction (Ivan Morris, Trans.) In Ivan Morris (Ed.), *Modern Japanese stories: An anthology* (pp. 37–43). Tokyo & Rutland, VT: Tuttle.

———. (2005). The dancing girl (Richard Bowring, Trans.). In J. Thomas Rimer & Van C. Gessel (Eds.), *The Columbia anthology of modern Japanese literature, Vol.1: From restoration to occupation, 1968–1945* (pp. 10–25). New York: Columbia University Press.

Morris-Suzuki, Tessa. (1998). *Re–inventing Japan: Time, space, nation.* Armonk NY & London: M.E. Sharpe.

Morton, Leith. (1988). *Divided self: A biography of Arishima Takeo.* Sydney, Wellington, London & Boston: Allen & Unwin.

Myers, Ramon H., & Peattie, Mark R. (Eds.). (1984). *The Japanese colonial empire, 1895–1945.* Princeton, NJ: Princeton University Press.

Nagai Kafū. (1961). Pleasure (Kanraku). In Matsumoto Ryōzō (Trans.), *Japanese literature new and old* (pp. 31–74). Hokuseido Press.

———. (1962–1974). *Kafū zenshū* (28 vols.). Iwanami Shoten.

———. (1963). *Geisha in rivalry* (Kurt Meissner & Ralph Friedrich, Trans.). Rutland, VT & Tokyo: Tuttle.

———. (1972). *A strange tale from east of the river and other stories* (Edward Seidensticker, Trans.). Rutland, VT & Tokyo: Tuttle.

———. (1994a). *During the rains and flowers in the shade: Two Novellas by Nagai Kafu* (Lane Dunlop, Trans.). Stanford, CA: Stanford University Press.

———. (1994b). The Fox. In Lane Dunlop (Trans.), *Autumn Wind and Other Stories* (pp. 11–30). Tokyo, Singapore, & Rutland, VT: Tuttle.

———. (1996). *Sumidagawa. Shinkyō yawa.* Iwanami Shoten.

———. (2000). *American stories* (Mitsuko Iriye, Trans.). New York: Columbia University Press.

———. (2005). The Mediterranean in twilight (Mitsuko Iriye, Trans.). In J. Thomas Rimer & Van C. Gessel (Eds.), *The Columbia anthology of modern Japanese literature, Vol.1: From restoration to occupation, 1968–1945* (pp. 213–217). New York: Columbia University Press.

———. (2007). *Rivalry: A geisha's tale* (Stephen Snyder, Trans.). New York: Columbia University Press.

Najita, Tetsuo, & Harootunian, H.D. (1988). Japanese revolt against the West: Political and cultural criticism in the twentieth century. In Peter Duus (Ed.), *The Cambridge history of Japan, Vol. 6: The twentieth century* (pp. 711-774). Cambridge: Cambridge University Press.

Nakajima Kunihiko. (1992). Kodōgu to shite no Seiō geijutsu: kichō chokugo no Kafū to Takuboku no setten. *Bungaku, 3*(3), 23–35.

———. (1994). Nagai Kafū *Kichōsha no nikki*: Sōseki sakuhin wo hojosen to shita shōmei. *Kokubungaku Kaishaku to Kyōzai no Kenkyū, 39*(7), 59–65.

Nakamura Kyōsuke. (1987). *Seiyō no oto, Nihon no mimi: kindai Nihon bungaku to Seiyō ongaku.* Shunjūsha.

Nakamura Mitsuo. (1951). Kaisetsu. In Nagai Kafū, *Furansu monogatari.* Shinchōsha, pp. 263–267.

———. (1978). *Kindai no bungaku to bungakusha.* Asahi Shimbunsha.

Nakamura Shin'ichirō. (1970). *Kindai bungaku e no gimon.* Keisō Shobō.

Nakazawa Chimao. (1996). *Kafū to odoru,* San'ichi Shobō.

Nara, Hiroshi. (2004). *The structure of detachment: The aesthetic vision of Kuki Shūzō: with a translation of Iki no kōzō*. Honolulu: University of Hawai'i Press.

Natsume Sōseki. (1977). *Sanshiro* (Jay Rubin, Trans.). Seattle & London: University of Washington Press.

———. (1992a). My individualism. In Jay Rubin (Trans.), *Kokoro: A novel and selected essays* (pp. 285–322) Lanham, MD: Madison Books.

———. (1992b). *The Tower of London* (Peter Milward & Kii Nakano, Trans. & Ed.). Brighton: In Print.

———. (1997). *And then: Natsume Sōseki's Novel Sore Kara* (Norma Field, Trans.). Ann Arbor: Center for Japanese Studies, University of Michigan Press.

———. (2000). *Travels in Manchuria and Korea*. In Inger Sigrun Brodey & Sammy I. Tsunematsu (Eds. & Trans.). *Rediscovering Natsume Sōseki* (pp. 33–146). Folkestone, Kent: Global Oriental.

———. (2002). *I am a cat: Three volumes in one* (Aiko Ito & Graeme Wilson, Trans.). Tokyo & Boston: Tuttle.

———. (2005). My individualism. In Sammy I. Tsunematsu (Trans.), *My individualism and the philosophical foundations of literature* (pp. 25–57). Tokyo & North Clarendon, VT: Tuttle.

Nishihara Daisuke. (2003). *Tanizaki Jun'ichirō no Orientarizumu: Taishō Nihon no Chūgoku gensō*. Chūō Kōron Shinsha.

Noguchi Takehiko. (1991). *Kindai bungaku no kesshōtai: Sōkan Nihon no bungaku* (Vol. 21). Shintensha.

———. (1992). Mizu to Hōtō. *Bungaku, 3*(3), 36–47.

Noguchi, Yone. (1910). Whistler. *Mita bungaku, 1*(8), 159–162.

———. (1911). Cherry blossom. *Mita bungaku,* 2(5), 99–102.

———. (1990–1992). *Selected English writings of Yone Noguchi: An east–west literary assimilation* (2 vols., Yoshinobu Hakutani, Ed.). London & Toronto: Associated University Presses.

———. (2007). *Collected English works of Yone Noguchi: Poems, novels and literary essays* (6 vols., Kamei Shunsuke, Ed.). Edition Synapse.

Notehelfer, Fred G. (1971). *Kōtoku Shūsui: Portrait of a Japanese radical*. Cambridge: Cambridge University Press.

O'Hanlon, Rosalind. (1988). Recovering the subject: *Subaltern studies* and histories of resistance in colonial south Asia. *Modern Asian Studies,* 22(1),189–224.

Oguma Eiji. (2002). *A genealogy of "Japanese" self-images* (David Askew, Trans.). Melbourne: Trans Pacific Press.

Okuno Takeo. (1970). *Nihon bungakushi: kindai kara gendai e*. Chūō Kōronsha.

Ortolani, Benito. (1990). *The Japanese theatre: From shamanistic ritual to contemporary pluralism*. Leiden: Brill.

Pham, P.L. (1999). On the edge of the Orient: English representations of Japan, circa 1895–1910. *Japanese Studies, 19*(2), 163–181.

Pincus, Leslie. (1996). *Authenticating culture in Imperial Japan: Kuki Shūzō and the rise of national aesthetics*. Berkeley, Los Angeles, & London: University of California Press.

Pinnington, Adam. (2006). Foreign bodies: "Race," gender and Orientalism in Tanizaki Jun'ichirō's *The Mermaid's Lament*. In Rachael Hutchinson & Mark Williams (Eds.), *Representing the other in modern Japanese literature: A critical approach* (pp. 75–95). London & New York: Routledge.

Pollack, David. (1986). *The fracture of meaning: Japan's synthesis of China from the eighth through the eighteenth centuries*. Princeton, NJ: Princeton University Press.

———. (1992). *Reading against culture: Ideology and narrative in the Japanese novel*. Ithaca, NY & London: Cornell University Press.

Porter, Dennis. (1991). *Haunted journeys: Desire and transgression in European travel writing*. Princeton, NJ: Princeton University Press.

Powell, Brian. (2002). *Japan's modern theatre: A century of continuity and change*. London: Japan Library.

Powell, Irena. (1983). *Writers and society in modern Japan*. Tokyo & New York: Kodansha International.

Pratt, Mary Louise. (1992). *Imperial eyes: Travel writing and transculturation*. New York: Routledge.

Rabson, Steve. (1982). Nagai Kafū: The River Sumida. In Thomas E. Swann & Kinya Tsuruta (Eds.), *Approaches to the modern Japanese short story* (pp. 225–232). Waseda University Press.

Rimer, J. Thomas. (1988). *Pilgrimages: Aspects of Japanese literature and culture*. Honolulu: University of Hawai'i Press.

———. (Ed.). (1990). *Culture and identity: Japanese intellectuals during the interwar years*. Princeton, NJ: Princeton University Press.

Rubin, Jay. (1984). *Injurious to public morals: Writers and the Meiji state*. Seattle & London: University of Washington Press.

Said, Edward W. (1993). *Culture and imperialism*. New York: Vintage.

———. (1995). *Orientalism: Western conceptions of the Orient*. London & New York: Penguin.

Saitō Ichirō. (1992). Kafū sensei to Gonkūru sensei. *Bungaku, 3*(3), 16–19.

Sakagami Hiroichi. (1997). Nagai Kafū *Amerika monogatari*: ikoku fūdo no hakken. *Kokubungaku Kaishaku to Kanshō, 62*(12), 93–98.

Sakaki, Atsuko. (2000). *Kajin no kigū*: The Meiji political novel and the boundaries of literature. *Monumenta Nipponica, 55*(1), 83–108.

Sakamoto, Rumi. (1997). *Imagining Japan: National identity and the representation of the other in early Meiji discourse*. Unpublished doctoral dissertation, University of Essex, Colchester, England.

Sansom, George B. (1950). *The western world and Japan*. London: Cresset Press.

Sasabuchi Tomoichi. (1976). *Nagai Kafū: daraku no bigakusha*. Meiji Shoin.

Satō Haruo. (1947). *Kafū zakkan*. Kokuritsu shoin.

Satō Shizuo. (1995). Kindai bungaku tanbō 20: Nagai Kafū *Hanabi*. *Minshu bungaku, 360*, 138–143.

Schulz, Evelyn. (1997). *Nagai Kafū: "Tagebuch eines Heimgekehrten": der Entwurf ästhetischer Gegenwelten als Kritik an der Modernisierung Japans* ["Diary of one who returned to Japan" by Nagai Kafū: The conception of aesthetic counterworlds as a means of criticizing Japan's modernization]. Münster: Lit–Verlag.

Seidensticker, Edward. (1965). *Kafū the scribbler: The life and writings of Nagai Kafū, 1879–1959*. Stanford, CA: Stanford University Press.

———. (1983). *Low city, high city: Tokyo from Edo to the earthquake*. London: Allen Lane.

———. (1990). *Tokyo rising: The city since the great earthquake*. New York: Knopf.

———. (2002). *Tokyo central: A memoir*. Seattle: University of Washington Press.

Sheldon, Charles David. (1958). *The rise of the merchant class in Tokugawa Japan*. Locust Valley, NY: Augustin.

Shindō Kaneto. (Dir.). (1992). *The strange tale of Oyuki (Bokutō kidan)*. Kindai Eiga Kyōkai.

Shindō Masahiro. (1997). *Nagai Kafū: Ongaku no nagareru kūkan*. Sekai Shisōsha.

Shiozaki Fumio. (1991). Nagai Kafū no Tōkyō: mizube no saihakken. *Kokubungaku Kaishaku to Kyōzai no Kenkyū, 36*(15), 180–181.

———. (1992). Kafū no Taishū. *Nihon bungaku, 41*(4), 43–56.

———. (1994). Kafū bungaku ni okeru yōgaku to hōgaku: *Fukagawa no uta* no kaiwai. *Kokubungaku Kaishaku to Kyōzai no Kenkyū, 39*(7), 101–103.

Sibley, William F. (1968). Naturalism in Japanese literature. *Harvard Journal of Asiatic Studies, 28*, 157–169.

Silver, Mark. (2008). *Purloined letters: Cultural borrowing and Japanese crime literature, 1868–1937*. Honolulu: University of Hawai'i Press.

Slaymaker, Douglas. (Ed.). (2002). *Confluences: Postwar Japan and France*. Ann Arbor: University of Michigan Press.

———. (2004). *The body in postwar Japanese fiction*. London & New York: Routledge.

———. (2006). Yokomitsu Riichi's others: Paris and Shanghai. In Rachael Hutchinson & Mark Williams (Eds.), *Representing the other in modern Japanese literature: A critical approach* (pp. 109–124). London & New York: Routledge.

———. (forthcoming). *Paris, mon amour: Japanese representations of France*.

Smith, Thomas C. (1962). The discontented. *Journal of Asian Studies, 21*(2), 215–219.

Snyder, Stephen. (2000). *Fictions of desire: Narrative form in the novels of Nagai Kafū*. Honolulu: University of Hawai'i Press.

Spencer, Daniel Lloyd. (1958). Japan's pre-Perry preparation for economic growth. *American Journal of Economics and Sociology, 17*(2), 195–216.

Storry, Richard. (1960). *A history of modern Japan*. Harmondsworth: Penguin.

Strauss, David. (1985). Kalamazoo's Japanese connection, 1900–1910. *Kalamazoo College Quarterly*, (Fall), 25–29.

Suenobu Yoshiharu. (1997). *Nagai Kafū no mita Amerika*. Chūō Kōronsha.

Sugawara Katsuya. (2001). The pilgrimage of Nagai Kafū to the US and France and his life of exile in Japan. In Yōichi Nagashima (Ed.), *Return to Japan from "pilgrimage" to the west* (pp. 109–124). Copenhagen: Aarhus University Press.

Suzuki Fumitaka. (1995). *Wakaki Kafū no bungaku to shisō*. Ibunsha.

Suzuki, Tomi. (1996). *Narrating the self: Fictions of Japanese modernity*. Stanford, CA: Stanford University Press.

Takada Mizuho. (1984). Kafū no tambishugi. *Kokubungaku Kaishaku to Kanshō, 49*(4), 9–12.

Takahashi Toshio. (1983). *Nagai Kafū to Edo bunen*. Meiji Shoin.

Takemori Ten'yū. (1992). Anakuronizumu wo kamen to shite—hōhō, shūji, taido. *Bungaku, 3*(3), 20–22.

Taketomo, Torao. (Trans. & Ed.). (1918). *Paulownia: Seven stories from contemporary Japanese writers*. New York: Duffield.

Tanaka, Stefan. (1993). *Japan's Orient: Rendering pasts into history*. Berkeley, Los Angeles, & London: University of California Press.

Tang, Xiaobing. (1993). Orientalism and the question of universality: The language of contemporary Chinese literary theory. *positions, 1*(2), 389–413.

Tanizaki Jun'ichirō. (1966–1970). *Tanizaki Jun'ichirō zenshū* (26 vols.). Chūō Kōronsha.

———. (1977). *In praise of shadows* (Thomas J. Harper & Edward G. Seidensticker, Trans.). Rutland, VT & Tokyo: Tuttle.

Tayama Katai. (1987). *Literary life in Tokyo, 1885–1915: Tayama Katai's memoirs (Thirty Years in Tokyo)* (Kenneth G. Henshall, Trans. & Ed.). Leiden: Brill.

Toyoda Shirō. (Dir.). (1960). *Bokutō kidan*, Tōhō.

Tsuda Sōkichi. (1984). Tōyō bunka wa nanka? in *Shina shisō to Nihon*, Iwanami Shoten, pp.103–200, first published as "Bunka shijō ni okeru tōyō no tokushokusei." *Tōyō shichō*, Iwanami Shoten, 1936.

Tsunoda, Ryūsaku, de Bary, William Theodore & Keene, Donald. (1958). *Sources of Japanese tradition*. New York: Columbia University Press.

Tsuruta, Kinya. (1998). Japanese perceptions of Westerners in modern fiction. In Keizo Nagatani & David W. Edgington (Eds.), *Japan and the West: The perception gap* (pp. 49–79). Aldershot: Ashgate.

Ueda, Makoto. (1976). *Modern Japanese writers and the nature of literature*. Stanford, CA: Stanford University Press.

Venn, Couze. (1993). *Occidentalism and its discontents*. London: New Ethnicities Unit, University of East London.

———. (2000). *Occidentalism: Modernity and subjectivity*. London, Thousand Oaks, CA, & Delhi: Sage.

Waley, Paul. (1984). *Tokyo now and then: An explorer's guide*. New York & Tokyo: Weatherhill.

———. (1991). *Tokyo: City of stories*. New York & Tokyo: Weatherhill.

Walker, Janet. (1979). *The Japanese novel of the Meiji period and the ideal of individualism*. Princeton, NJ: Princeton University Press.

Wang, Ning. (1997). Orientalism versus Occidentalism? *New Literary History, 28*(1), 57–67.

Washburn, Dennis. (1995). *The dilemma of the modern in Japanese fiction*. New Haven, CT & London: Yale University Press.

Williams, Mark. (2006). Free to write: Confronting the present, and the past, in Shiina Rinzō's *The Beautiful Woman*. In Rachael Hutchinson & Mark

Williams (Eds.), *Representing the other in modern Japanese literature: A critical approach* (pp. 230–252). London & New York: Routledge.
———. (2011). Crossing the deep river: Endō Shūsaku and the problem of religious pluralism. In Kevin Doak (Ed.), *Xavier's legacies: Catholicism in modern Japanese culture* (pp. 115–133). Vancouver: University of British Columbia Press.
Wray, Harry, & Conroy, Hilary. (1983). *Japan examined: Perspectives in modern Japanese history*. Honolulu: University of Hawai'i Press.
Yamada Tomoichi. (1985). *Kafū shoshi*. Shuppan Nyūsusha.
Yamanouchi, Hisaaki. (1978). *The search for authenticity in modern Japanese literature*. Cambridge: Cambridge University Press.
Yamazaki Masakazu. (1986). *Fukigen no jidai*. Kōdansha.
Yokomitsu Riichi. (2001). *Shanghai: A novel by Yokomitsu Riichi* (Dennis Washburn, Trans.). Ann Arbor: Center for Japanese Studies, University of Michigan Press.
Yoshida Seiichi. (Ed.). (1971a). *Gendai Nihon bungaku nenpyō* (Rev. suppl. ed.). Chikuma Shobō.
———. (1971b). *Nagai Kafū*. Shinchōsha.
Young, Robert. (1990). *White mythologies: Writing history and the West*. London & New York: Routledge & Kegan Paul.

Index